THE READING LESSON

THE
READING
LESSON

The Threat of Mass Literacy in
Nineteenth-Century British Fiction

PATRICK
BRANTLINGER

Indiana
University
Press

BLOOMINGTON AND INDIANAPOLIS

This book is a publication of

Indiana University Press
601 North Morton Street
Bloomington, Indiana 47404-3797 USA

www.indiana.edu/~iupress

Telephone orders 800-842-6796
Fax orders 812-855-7931
Orders by e-mail iuporder@indiana.edu

The paper used in this publication meets the minimum
requirements of American National Standard for Information
Sciences—Permanence of Paper for Printed Library
Materials, ANSI Z39.48-1984.

Manufactured in the United States of America

Library of Congress Cataloging-in-Publication Data

Brantlinger, Patrick, date
The reading lesson : the threat of mass literacy
in nineteenth century British fiction / Patrick Brantlinger.
        p.   cm.
Includes bibliographical references and index.
ISBN 0-253-33454-3 (cloth : alk. paper). —
ISBN 0-253-21249-9 (pbk. : alk. paper)
1. English fiction—19th century—History and criticism.
2. Popular literature—Appreciation—Great Britain—History—
19th century. 3. Working class—Great Britain—Books and reading—
History—19th century. 4. Books and reading—Great Britain—History—
19th century. 5. Literacy—Great Britain—History—19th century.
6. Fiction—Appreciation—Great Britain—History. 7. Books and
reading in literature. 8. Popular culture in literature. 9. Social
conflict in literature. 10. Literacy in literature.   I. Title.
        PR868.P68B73   1998
        823'.809—dc21   98-19906

1   2   3   4   5   03   02   01   00   99   98

CONTENTS

ACKNOWLEDGMENTS

The Reading Lesson incorporates substantially revised and updated portions of several articles, and I am grateful to the editors of the journals and anthologies in which they appeared for permission to do so. These include *Cultural Critique*, *Nineteenth-Century Literature*, *Studies in the English Literary Imagination*, *Victorian Review*, and *Victorian Studies*, and two anthologies, William Veeder and Gordon Hirsch, eds., *Dr Jekyll and Mr Hyde after 100 Years*, and Pauline Fletcher and Patrick Scott, eds., *Culture and Education in Victorian England*. Two of the articles that I have reworked for this study were co-authored by Rick Boyle ("The Education of Edward Hyde" in Veeder and Hirsch) and Don Ulin ("Policing Nomads," *Cultural Critique*, Fall 1993); I am grateful to both of them for their assistance.

I also wish to thank all of the graduate students and colleagues who have worked with me over the years on *Victorian Studies* and in the Victorian Studies Program at Indiana University, including James Eli Adams, Bill and Mary Burgan, Don Gray, Andrew Miller, Lee Sterrenburg, Martha Vicinus, and Paul Zietlow. Purnima Bose, Eva Cherniavsky, Jonathan Elmer, Chris Lohmann, Jim Naremore, and Steve Watt have also, in different ways, been supportive. Among the many graduate students whose conversation, seminar papers, and dissertations have helped to educate me, besides Rick and Don, I'm especially grateful to Todd Avery, Joe Bizup, John Glendening, Josephine Ho, Beth Kalikoff, Jean Kowaleski, Andrew Libby, Cynthia Patton, Steve Pulsford, Rob Richardson, Lewis Roberts, Elizabeth Rosdeitcher, Cannon Schmitt, Sherri Smith, and Gary Willingham-McLain. Among the many people at other colleges and universities whom I should especially thank are John Reed (Wayne State), Florence Boos (Iowa), William Veeder (Chicago), and William Thesing (South Carolina). I have also been much helped by the able and willing staff of the IU Library, including William Cagle, Tony Shipps, and Perry Willett. Thanks, too, to Bob Sloan of the IU Press and to Garrett Stewart for providing such a prompt, helpful evaluation of the manuscript. Some of my work has been supported by NEH and IU Summer Faculty Fellowships, for which I am also thankful. And Ellen Brantlinger, as always, assisted in more ways than I can recount or repay.

THE READING LESSON

1

Introduction

THE CASE OF THE POISONOUS BOOK

> If it is true, that the present age is more corrupt than the preceding, the great multiplication of Novels probably contributes to its degeneracy. Fifty years ago there was scarcely a Novel in the kingdom.
> —Vicessimus Knox, "On Novel Reading" (1779)

In Sheridan's *The Rivals* (1775), Mrs. Malaprop orders her niece "to illiterate" her lover from her memory. Lydia replies that "our memories are independent of our wills," which causes Sir Anthony Absolute to declare that Lydia's willfulness "comes of her reading" (Sheridan 49). He means, of course, Lydia's novel-reading, but her behavior provokes him to suggest that it would have been better if she had remained incapable of reading anything. Indeed, he would like "to illiterate" young women in general; he tells Mrs. Malaprop that "all this is the natural consequence of teaching girls to read. Had I a thousand daughters, by heaven! I'd as soon have them taught the black art as their alphabet!" (50).

Sir Anthony goes on to say that "a circulating library in a town," from which young women such as Lydia obtain novels, "is as an ever-green tree of diabolical knowledge! It blossoms through the year! And depend on it, Mrs. Malaprop, that they who are so fond of handling the leaves, will long for the fruit at last" (50). Sheridan, no doubt, viewed Sir Anthony's opinions about novel-reading, circulating libraries, and female education as both silly and extreme. But, as John Tinnon Taylor long ago demonstrated, between about 1750 and the 1830s many people objected to novel-reading as an abuse of literacy likely to do moral damage to readers and, indeed, to the national culture.[1] "Where the reading of novels prevails as a habit," opined no less an expert reader of novels than Coleridge, "it occasions in time the entire destruction of the powers of the mind." Novel-reading, Coleridge continues, "is such an utter loss to the reader, that it is not so much to be called pass-time as kill-time":

It . . . produces no improvement of the intellect, but fills the mind with a mawk-
ish and morbid sensibility, which is directly hostile to the cultivation, invigora-
tion, and enlargement of the nobler powers of the understanding. (*Seven Lectures* 3)

This negative opinion of novel-reading did not prevent Coleridge from reading
novels and writing reviews and articles about them; nor does his intellect seem to
have been adversely affected by exercising his literacy in this manner.

Objections to novels were often religious—the Society of Friends, for example, proscribed novel-reading—but this is not so with either Sheridan or
Coleridge. Whether secular or religious, however, such objections continued to
be expressed throughout the nineteenth century, though by the 1840s novels and
novel-reading were growing respectable.[2] With Jane Austen and Sir Walter Scott,
and through the emergence of new publishing and circulating-library practices
and institutions such as Mudie's, the novel gained widespread cultural acceptance, though not exactly aesthetic legitimacy.[3] Nevertheless, throughout the 1800s,
both specific novels and particular subgenres—Gothic romances, penny dreadfuls,
Newgate crime stories, sensation novels, Zolaesque naturalism, and so on—came
under attack for rotting the minds of their readers, promoting vice, and subverting
cultural standards. The often vehement opposition to novels and novel-reading, a
widespread reaction to one of the earliest forms of modern, commodified mass
culture, is familiar, well-charted territory. Less familiar is how that opposition
affected novels—how, indeed, criticisms of novels and novel-reading were inscribed in novels themselves in many ironic, contradictory ways. As Terry Lovell
puts it for the late eighteenth and early nineteenth centuries, "so universally were
the novel and novel-reading condemned that novelists themselves joined in the
chorus" (28). But the condemnation of novels by novelists characterizes the genre
throughout its history. The inscription of anti-novel attitudes within novels is so
common that it can be understood as a defining feature of the genre; accordingly,
any fictional narrative which does not somehow criticize, parody, belittle, or otherwise deconstruct itself is probably not a novel.

From this perspective, novels are always anti-novels, the *contre roman* coming of age before the age of Alain Robbe-Grillet, Samuel Beckett, and Kathy
Acker. In *The Dialogic Imagination*, Mikhail Bakhtin contends that the novel is
the one literary genre that by definition transgresses generic boundaries, even its
own: the "ability of the novel to criticize itself is a remarkable feature of this
ever-developing genre" (6). At least from *Don Quixote* forward, novels and novelists thrive on satirizing and parodying each other: *Shamela*, *Northanger Abbey*,
Crotchet Castle, *Pickwick Papers*, *Catherine*, *Erewhon*, *To the Light House*—the
list of parodic works into the twentieth century is long, and perhaps every interesting novel, at least, contains parodic features (cf. Shepperson, *The Novel in
Motley*). For the outright opponents of novels, however, it hardly matters that
many works of fiction parody other works and are often critical of novel-reading.
The general threat posed by novels is a moral and social one: the spectre of dis-

tracted or deluded masses of readers, or, in other words, of mass literacy producing the opposite of enlightenment. But the opponents of novels must, like Coleridge, know something about them in order to condemn them. From this angle, they join the masses of at least potential novel-readers that confronted writers as, in Coleridge's words, "the misgrowth of our luxuriant activity . . . a READING PUBLIC" (*Lay Sermons* 36). While novelists often express opinions common to anti-novel discourse—novel-reading is addictive or seductive, it is a frivolous waste of time, novels are mere commodities to be bought and consumed like any other perishable goods, and so forth—a major factor underlying the inscription of anti-novel attitudes within novels is the radical uncertainty all novelists share about how the reading public will interpret or misinterpret, use or abuse, the products of their imaginations. The focus of *The Reading Lesson* is consequently upon the ways anxiety about mass literacy and the huge, largely anonymous, ever-increasing readership for fiction affected a range of novels from the 1790s to the 1890s.[4]

I

As a genre, the modern novel was born with an inferiority complex: it wasn't classical, it wasn't poetry, and it wasn't history. When Henry Fielding calls *Joseph Andrews* a "history" and a "comic epic in prose," his attempts to identify it with more legitimate forms of discourse suggest the generic instability of the novel at least in the 1740s. Moreover, even when they seem to be defending novels against the opposition, novelists sometimes do the reverse. In chapter 5 of *Northanger Abbey*, Jane Austen takes time out from her story to defend the genre from its detractors:

> . . . we [novelists] are an injured body. Although our productions have afforded more extensive and unaffected pleasure than those of any other literary corporation in the world, no species of composition has been so much decried. From pride, ignorance, or fashion, our foes are almost as many as our readers. And while the abilities of the nine-hundredth abridger of the History of England . . . are eulogised by a thousand pens, there seems almost a general wish of decrying the capacity and undervaluing the labour of the novelist, and of slighting the performances which have only genius, wit and taste to recommend them. (58)

Although it is often taken at face value, Austen's defense of novels of course occurs in a story that satirizes novels and novel-reading. The irony is perhaps mitigated by the romance-novel distinction, which has allowed many readers to assume that, like Cervantes in *Don Quixote*, Austen is attacking romances, while defending her own more realistic novel. But Austen does not explicitly distinguish between romances and novels. In defending novels, she has partly in mind the works of Ann Radcliffe and the other Gothic romances that Catherine Morland and Isabella Thorpe have been reading. At most, she merely hints that novels by Maria Edgeworth, Fanny Burney, and other presumably more realistic writers are superior to those that Catherine and Isabella consume. *Northanger Abbey* both presents itself as a serious work of literature and participates in the general depreciation of novels and novel-reading. In doing so, it offers a striking instance of the way many novels published between 1700 and 1900 express ambivalence about—sometimes, outright contempt for—novels and novel-reading.

Similarly, half a century after Austen, in "Petition to the Novel-Writers," Wilkie Collins imagines belonging to a book club dominated by "dull people" whose insistence on "respectability" has led them to refuse to read novels. He abandons the book club, gets himself "a box-full of novels," loses "caste with our respectable friends in consequence," and founds the alternative "Disreputable Society" for reading fiction. But not only does he thereby, albeit ironically, surrender the field to the "respectable" people by apparently granting their premise that novels are "disreputable," he imagines himself immediately embroiled in a scandal:

> If the dull people of our district were told to-morrow that my wife, daughters, and nieces had all eloped in different directions, leaving just one point of the compass open as a runaway outlet for me and the cook, I feel firmly persuaded that not one of them would be inclined to discredit the report.

On the contrary, they would simply conclude that "this is what comes of novel-reading" (*My Miscellanies* 110). So Collins both insists that novel-reading is a pleasurable activity that he and other sensible people should engage in and agrees that it is disreputable—that scandal may very well be "what comes" of it.

Scandal hovered around the novel partly because it dealt with the private lives, including sexual behaviors and entanglements, of characters; partly because it seemed to many, novelists and critics alike, to represent the ultimate commercialization of literature; and partly because it was reading produced mainly for pleasure or amusement rather than self-improvement. For Collins as for his friend Dickens, if novel-reading was not clearly edifying, it could at least be defended as entertainment; in the words of Mr. Sleary in *Hard Times*, "People mutht be amuthed." But merely to say that novel-reading gives people pleasure was not an adequate defense against the evangelical and utilitarian moralists like Mr. Gradgrind, who opposed novel-reading altogether as frivolous, misleading, addictive, or seductive.

Like plays within plays, novel-reading within a given novel can reinforce the illusion that the main text is real, or just a shade removed from reality. In *Don Quixote* and *Northanger Abbey*, the novels within the main narratives are treated as both untrue and misleading, in contrast to the supposedly true stories in which they appear. But by suggesting the illusory nature of all novels, *Don Quixote*, *Northanger Abbey*, and similar fictions are self-indicting. The modern novel originates partly as epistemological contrast to the older romance form, and yet any claim that a particular work of fiction is truer or more realistic than previous works opens the way to similar claims by future stories in an endlessly relativizing process. According to Michael McKeon:

The empiricism of "true history" opposes the discredited idealism of romance, but it thereby generates a countervailing, extreme skepticism, which in turn discredits true history as a species of naive empiricism or "new romance." Once in motion . . . the sequence of action and reaction becomes a cycle: the existence of each opposed stance becomes essential for the ongoing, negative definition of its antithesis. (88)

By denying its own basis in imagination or fantasy, fictive realism becomes, in a sense, self-cancelling or at least contradictory. An extreme version of the self-cancellation of the novel is Zola's claim that, with naturalism, "the imagination no longer has a function" (207).

Frequently also self-indicting is the familiar trope of "the book of the world" (Stewart 275–300). Reworked in various ironic ways by Victorian realists from Thackeray and Dickens down to George Moore and Thomas Hardy, the trope points to a novel's failure to be "the book of the world" it nonetheless mimes. Reality may prove to be a "Book of the Insolvent Fates" like those invoked in Dickens's final novel; nevertheless, the world-book equation discloses the insufficiency of all language to represent the nontextual, nonverbal real, and therefore also the failure of book-learning or literacy to read the great book of the world. In this regard, Joe Gargery's illiteracy in *Great Expectations* or Boffin's in *Our Mutual Friend* signals an honesty, generosity, and innocence standing outside the necessarily failed, fallen contaminations of language.[5] Moreover, the examples of Joe and Boffin suggest that, at least for Dickens, illiteracy is not so problematic as certain uses or abuses of literacy: Pip's rejection of Joe and home, Silas Wegg's machinations as reader to Boffin, and schoolmaster Bradley Headstone's murderous jealousy.

Even more pointedly than the book-of-the-world trope, the rhetoric of toxicity undermines those novels that adopt it. In the context of the American and French revolutions, to some observers "the press" in general seemed both poisoned and poisonous. For anti-Jacobins such as Edmund Burke, the writings of the philosophes and Tom Paine were especially toxic, a major threat to the health of the body politic. In the supposedly antipoisonous, puritanical fiction of Mrs. Hannah More—the "Old Bishop in Petticoats," as William Cobbett called her (qtd. in Murphy 64)—the links among revolution, crime stories (always a staple of popular fiction), and the threat posed by mass literacy are especially vivid. More's general project, like that of other evangelical and utilitarian literary reformers, was to provide wholesome reading in place of the textual poisons she saw everywhere in her culture. Another evangelical writer, Jane West, gives a clear statement of the evangelical project in the introduction to her *The Infidel Father: A Novel* (1802):

The rage for novels does not decrease; and, though I by no means think them the best vehicles for "the words of sound doctrine," yet, while the enemies of our church and state continue to pour their poison into unwary ears through this channel, it behoves the friends of our establishments to convey an antidote by the same course; especially as those who are most likely to be infected by false principles, will not search for a refutation of them in profound and scientific compositions. (West ii)

Like West's anti-novel novel, More's "Cheap Repository Tracts" and her improving novel, *Coelebs in Search of a Wife* (1809), are also intended as "antidotes" to the "poison" of novels and other dangerous reading material.[6] The spread of literacy was itself dangerous, although now that it was happening, More believed, it needed to be directed into safe channels. "Of all the foolish inventions, and new-fangled devices to ruin the country, that of teaching the poor to read is the very worst," says Farmer Hoskins to Mrs. Jones, who is raising money for a new Sunday school. The exchange takes place in one of More's exemplary evangelical tracts, "The Sunday School," published in 1797. Mrs. Jones responds: "I . . . think that to teach good principles to the lower classes, is the most likely way to save the country. Now, in order to [do] this, we must teach them to read."

> "Not with my consent, nor my money," said the farmer; "for I know it always does more harm than good." "So it may," said Mrs. Jones, "if you only teach them to read, and then turn them adrift, to find out books for themselves." (376)

More's story is exemplary because she meant it "to teach good principles" to readers of whatever class. Everything she wrote is exemplary in the same didactic way: against the flood of poisonous literature that she believed threatened Britain with moral and political ruin, she and her evangelical allies created an alternative, improving literature. The moral effects of mass literacy, and the moral qualities of reading matter, are therefore major themes and structural elements in all of her stories or "tracts."

But "The Sunday School" is exemplary in a second manner: insofar as it expresses anxiety about mass literacy, it unintentionally implicates itself—pronounces a guilty verdict upon itself, so to speak—in a way that characterizes many fictional narratives and, indeed, the entire genre of modern prose fiction. This is so partly because "The Sunday School" promotes mass literacy even as it represents such literacy as a threat to national security. Just as Plato in *Phaedrus* employs writing to express the dangers of writing, so Hannah More, Jane West, and many later authors produce texts that preach to the new mass reading public about the perils of mass literacy. An even clearer illustration of this contradictory pattern is provided by More's "The History of Mr. Fantom, the New-Fashioned Philosopher, and His Man William." The protagonist, a self-taught, shallow, and vain "retail trader," falls victim to the wrong sort of reading:

> About this time he got hold of a famous little book written by the NEW PHILOSOPHER [Tom Paine], whose pestilent doctrines have gone about seeking whom they may destroy: these doctrines found a ready entrance into Mr. Fantom's mind. . . . (3)

All of More's tracts were intended as "antidotes" to Tom Paine's "poison" in particular, but to other "infidel" and criminal writers as well. Having imbibed

Paine's "pestilent" ideas, Mr. Fantom poisons the mind of his servant William. Learning from his master that there is no God and that "private vices are public benefits" (45), William robs the Fantom larder, absconding with its best spoons and bottles of wine. When Fantom and his friend Mr. Trueman catch up with him, William is already in jail not just for theft, but for murder: "Yes, sir," he tells Fantom, "you made me a drunkard, a thief, and a murderer."

William meets his end on the gallows, but not before writing, with Mr. Trueman's help, his "Last Words, Confession, and Dying Speech," which Trueman distributes to the crowd that shows up to watch the execution. William's "Dying Speech" is also reproduced in its entirety within More's story: "The crime for which I die is the natural consequence of the principles I learnt from my master . . ." (63–66). Besides repeating the sharp distinction that More makes in most of her stories between wholesome and poisonous reading, the remarkable feature of "The History of Mr. Fantom" is its inclusion within itself, in a frame-story structure, of a type of reading that More and many other observers, whether evangelical or not, often treated as toxic: namely, the confessions of condemned criminals, as in *The Newgate Calendar*. William's last words are of course not defiant, but contrite; not intended as an incitement to public disorder, but doctored to remove any possibility of poisoning the minds of More's readers by wicked example. More (or rather, More through William) provides no details about the murder for which William is hanged, but only reiterates the role Mr. Fantom (and pestilent Tom Paine through Fantom) has played in inducing William to commit robbery and murder. In this manner, perhaps, she detoxifies the criminal text that she inscribes within her anticriminal text.

"The History of Mr. Fantom" both declaims against poisonous literature and includes within itself the very thing it declaims against: it is both cure and poison. This isn't accidental on More's part but is instead a key feature of the design of *all* her stories. "With the wisdom of the serpent," as one of her biographers puts it (Jones 141), More produced her tracts "in the guise of the genuine chapman's pennyworth" of chapbooks or street literature "and sent [them] out, like sheep in wolves' clothing, to be sold by hawkers in competition with their 'old trash'" (Spinney 295). In other words, More sugared the pill of her didacticism (medicinal, she believed, not poisonous) with the conventions of the otherwise poisonous popular narratives that, along with Tom Paine's writings, she sought to combat. This is the principle of "inoculation," as Roland Barthes calls it in *Mythologies*, or of one version of the *pharmakon*, as Derrida finds it in Plato's *Phaedrus*: the poison that, in small doses, will hopefully serve as its own antidote.[7]

From an antithetical ideological perspective, the same pattern appears in William Godwin's *Caleb Williams* (1794), which is at once the criminal biography of Falkland, Caleb's master, and of its author-narrator, Caleb himself. The son of a peasant, Caleb acquires literacy and uses his reading and writing skills to become Falkland's secretary, from which vantage point he detects his master's deepest secrets. Caleb uses his literacy ultimately to indict, as well as indite, his master, bringing him to trial and punishment. Godwin implies, moreover, that the novel itself, as Caleb's story and written indictment, performs the final execution upon Falkland just as surely as the gallows would have done—an instance of fiction representing itself as lethal. The ideological contrast between Godwin's democratic, anarchist novel and More's evangelical, anti-Jacobin tract illustrates the extremes involved in the late-eighteenth-century conflict over the spread of literacy. Nevertheless, in both narratives, fictional form works to undo itself. Just as "Mr. Fantom" is both antidote and poison, so *Caleb Williams* is both an indictment (through Falkland) of aristocratic misgovernment and, insofar as it also can be read as criminal biography *and* acts, metaphorically at least, as lethal weapon, a self-indicting novel.

Within the history of the novel, moreover, the motif of poisonous or otherwise dangerous reading, a pattern that inevitably implicates any text in which it appears, runs straight through the nineteenth century and the now-canonical works of fiction that F. R. Leavis called the "Great Tradition." An especially striking example of the motif of poisonous reading in relation to mass literacy occurs in Dickens's *Oliver Twist*, where Fagin tries to poison Oliver's mind on the night before Bill Sikes takes him to burgle the Maylies' house. In this episode, Fagin's method of conversion entails forcing Oliver to read "a history of the lives and trials of great criminals" (shades of both "Mr. Fantom" and *Caleb Williams*). Of course Oliver is not converted to the paths of evil, but one of the surprises in Dickens's novel is that a workhouse orphan like Oliver can read, and another is that all of the thieves, including ogre-like Bill Sikes, can read, among other texts, the biographies of "great criminals."

Dickens protested mightily against the charge that readers of his novel might be led into lives of crime. As a primitive detective novel like *Caleb Williams*, however, *Oliver Twist* expresses the moral ambiguity of *all* crime stories (and all criminal reading) just as More's "Mr. Fantom" mimics the criminal literature it seeks to counteract. Even when moral or righteous in aim, representations of crime can always be accused of encouraging criminal behavior. No more than the romance/novel distinction prevents the recognition that all fiction is fiction (or in other words that the novel that one is reading, however realistic its form and style, is just as illusory as the silly romances the author contrasts to it), so in detective fiction there is no way to prevent the contamination of the (so to speak) law-abiding side of the story by the criminal side. In later, formulaic versions of detective fiction such as the Sherlock Holmes stories, the structure is always a double one, both poison and medicine, and therefore an exact analogue of Socrates' *pharmakon*. This is so because the story of detection in the law-abiding narrative present always consists of the reconstruction and retelling of the criminal past. Here again *Caleb Williams* is paradigmatic, in part because, for most of the narrative, its innocent detective-protagonist is treated like a criminal, and in part because Caleb declares that he has slain Falkland by writing the novel.

The novel that Caleb Williams pens doesn't poison Falkland—the metaphor Godwin has in mind is rather the dagger—but from the eighteenth century forward, it is as if many novelists agreed with the charge that, as one reviewer put it in the *Gentleman's Magazine* for 1805, novel-reading "poison[s] our leisure hours without improving them" ("Review" 1136).[8] When novel-reading is depicted as

something done by the characters within novels, moreover, it is often in poisonous terms. The Quixote pattern usually means that the ambiguity of the Socratic
pharmakon, both medicine and poison, is treated as unambiguous. Realistic novels like *Northanger Abbey* often seem to say: "Beware, reader, of illusory, poisonous stories like Gothic romances," and in the same stroke declare themselves
to be the truth-telling medicine that can cure the disease of romantic illusion. But,
as with Austen's novel, not always, or at least not exactly. In *Caleb Williams*, both
Caleb and his adversary have been influenced by their reading of romances; according to Caleb, Falkland has imbibed "the poison of chivalry" from his "earliest youth," and this "poison" has helped "hurry [him] into madness" (326). But to
what extent has Caleb also been poisoned? Further, is it entirely clear that Godwin's
novel is not just some new form of toxic illusion? Scott's Waverley, too, is a
Quixote figure, while the "historical romance" in which he figures partakes to
some indeterminable extent in the very sort of fantasy life that has absorbed and
misled him. There are, of course, many Quixote figures in later fiction, including
in their different ways Dickens's David Copperfield, Thackeray's Arthur Pendennis,
Meredith's Richard Feverel, Wilde's Dorian Gray, Hardy's Jude Fawley, and Conrad's Lord Jim. After the publication of Charlotte Lennox's *The Female Quixote*
in 1752, however, an increasing number of the Quixote figures in fiction are women:
Radcliffe's Emily St. Aubert, Austen's Catherine Morland, Thackeray's Amelia
Sedley, George Eliot's Maggie Tulliver and Dorothea Brooke, Mary Elizabeth
Braddon's Lady Audley, Trollope's Lizzie Eustace, and Hardy's Eustacia Vye, to
name a few.[9] Also, the old distinction between romances and novels seems gradually to blur and fade. Thus, in some nineteenth-century novels that adopt the
Quixote pattern, there is a deliberate, ironic identification of the main story with
the romantic, illusory stories that the characters read. A key example of the blur-
ring of the distinction between novel and romance is *Madame Bovary*, in which
the heroine's romantic illusions are fed by the intoxicating love stories she reads,
while Flaubert makes no claim to be writing anything other than a quite similar
story of illicit, adulterous love or lust. That his heroine kills herself by swallow-
ing rat poison seems only fitting: one way that Flaubert marks his masterpiece of
fictional realism as also poisonous.

"Bovaryism" means narcissistic egoism and eroticism, but also *caveat lector*: you become what you read, and what you are reading may not be good for
your mental health.[10] It was left to Oscar Wilde at the start of the 1890s, however,
both to praise others' poisonous books and explicitly to write one of his own, *The
Picture of Dorian Gray*. Wilde recognized what was especially illogical and hypocritical about the moralizers like Hannah More in the mass literacy debate. The
evangelizing or utilitarian do-gooders wanted the masses to read, but they wanted
the masses to read only purified literature: some impossibly nontoxic stuff that
would do no moral damage. They wanted the *pharmakon* of writing minus the
pharmakon's ambiguity. In his essay/dialogue "The Decay of Lying," Wilde contended that life imitates fiction, rather than the other way around. The examples
Wilde's character Vivian offers to illustrate this thesis come in part from controversies about working-class literacy and about the provision of wholesome, non-

toxic reading matter to the masses that run straight back to Hannah More and the evangelical revival of the late 1700s. "Life imitates art far more than Art imitates Life," Vivian declares:

> The most obvious and the vulgarest form in which this is shown is in the case of the silly boys who, after reading the adventures of Jack Sheppard or Dick Turpin, pillage the stalls of unfortunate apple-women, break into sweet-shops at night, and alarm old gentlemen who are returning home from the city by leaping out on them in suburban lanes, with black masks and unloaded revolvers. . . . The boy-burglar is simply the inevitable result of life's imitative instinct. He is Fact, occupied as Fact usually is, with trying to reproduce Fiction, and what we see in him is repeated on an extended scale throughout the whole of life. (56)

Here Wilde mocks the controversy that arose over the moral effects of reading supposedly poisonous Newgate novels like *Jack Sheppard*, plus the dozens of popular crime stories that were published throughout the century as "penny dreadfuls," "bloods," and "shilling shockers."[11]

In his criminal fantasy *The Picture of Dorian Gray*, Wilde describes the strange "yellow book" that Lord Henry sends to Dorian as "a poisonous book. The heavy odour of incense seemed to cling about its pages and to trouble the brain" (98). Dorian is fascinated by this dangerously intoxicating and ultimately toxic volume. He buys multiple copies of it in multicolored bindings. He reads it over and over, and as a result his conscience gradually gives way to a narcissistic search for mere pleasure. "Dorian Gray," we are told, "had been poisoned by a book. There were moments when he looked on evil simply as a mode through which he could realize his conception of the beautiful" (114–15). Dorian descends into a life of crime and ultimately murder, with the poisonous "yellow book" as his inspiration. On trial in 1895, Wilde was asked by the prosecutor to identify Dorian's "yellow book," and he responded that he had had in mind Joris-Karl Huysmans's 1884 novel *A Rebours*, about the decadent aristocrat Des Esseintes, who himself indulges in various forms of "poisonous" reading. Des Esseintes is especially fond of the "moral poison" (Huysmans's phrase) offered by the Marquis de Sade, Baudelaire, Flaubert, and Poe. These selected "flowers of evil" are obvious choices, but Des Esseintes also delights, in his morbid fashion, in reading the apparently innocuous novels of Charles Dickens.

While Huysmans's novel provided Wilde with a model for Dorian's "yellow book," a more interesting although more incriminating way to answer the prosecutor's question would have been to name *The Picture of Dorian Gray* itself. In both "yellow books," culture is identified with corruption, with loss of innocence, and ultimately with evil. Perhaps for similar reasons, George Eliot had earlier condemned that other "breviary" of the Decadent Movement, Walter Pater's *The Renaissance*, as a "poisonous book" (Eliot in Seiler, 92).[12] In any event, in his 1889 essay on Thomas Wainewright, painter, critic, and master poisoner, Wilde explored the seeming paradox that a highly educated practitioner of one of the fine arts could also be a murderer, and reached a conclusion deliberately at odds with Arnold's in *Culture and Anarchy*: "There is no essential incongruity," Wilde declared, "between crime and culture" ("Pen, Pencil and Poison" 98). That statement can serve as a precise summary of the oxymoronic idea of the poisonous book, and more specifically as a summary of one of the main themes of Wilde's own self-consciously poisonous crime novel.

The British novel in general, between the 1790s and 1900, is pervaded by the question of the moral and political effects of mass literacy, of reading, and above all of reading novels. A central, defining theme of the novel (whether implicitly or explicitly, unconsciously or consciously) is always some variant of Wilde's thesis in "The Decay of Lying": if life imitates art, what are the consequences to you, *hypocrite lecteur*, of consuming novels—indeed, of consuming the novel you are reading right now? Almost always the answer, in novels from *Caleb Williams* to *Jude the Obscure*, is either ambivalent or unambiguously negative. This is just how Socrates treats the *pharmakon* of writing: at its best, it is simultaneously both wholesome and poisonous; at its worst, it is poisonous. Reader, beware.

II

Even if they don't declare their novels to be poisonous, novelists often wittingly or unwittingly echo the eighteenth-century critic who likened novels to "intellectual gingerbread" (qtd. in Taylor 46). Trollope declared that the public consumed novels "as men eat pastry after dinner,—not without some inward conviction that the taste is vain if not vicious" ("Novel Reading" 126). Likewise Thackeray called "delightful . . . well-remembered" novels "sweet and delicious as the raspberry open-tarts of budding boyhood" ("On a Peal of Bells" 333). And in his study of Thackeray, Trollope says of his fellow novelist's early successes that he "had opened his oyster,—with his pen" (30). In the same essay, Trollope writes: "So it is with the novel" in general:

> It is taken because of its jam and honey. But, unlike the honest simple jam and honey of the household cupboard, it is never unmixed with physic. There will be the dose within it, either curative or poisonous. (202)

Trollope would, perhaps, prefer the novel to be just "honest simple jam and honey"; even when "curative" instead of "poisonous," any moral that it conveys must, he implies, be somehow less than "honest."

In relation to aesthetic taste, even metaphors of healthy eating and drinking place novel-reading in the emergent category of mass consumption, rather than in that of high or elite culture. In his study of "the making" of the reading public or, better, publics between 1790 and 1832, Jon Klancher notes:

> High-cultural production invites the language of "reception," the symbolic giving and receiving of texts between great writers and singular, sensitive readers. Mass-cultural production yields up the harsher vocabulary of "consumption," supply and demand among innumerable writers and vast, faceless audiences. (13)

Klancher points out that "this analytic double standard" found its philosophical "defense" in Kant's *Critique of Judgement*, "where the 'pure taste' of aesthetic judgment spirals away from the crude material 'interests' of less exalted tastes" (13). No doubt Thackeray and Trollope felt more comfortable situating their novels in terms of eating and drinking instead of any more rarefied, intellectual, or aesthetic version of taste, but doing so made it difficult to think of the best prose fiction as on the same cultural level with great poetry or drama.[13]

The apparent comfortableness of Thackeray and Trollope with their craft and careers arose partly from the growing respectability of novels and novel-reading. Novels were once justly reprobated, Trollope thinks, but Austen, Edgeworth, and Scott helped to sanitize them, and by the 1870s "novels . . . have in great measure taken the place of sermons" ("Novel-Reading" 114). Trollope is not sure that this is a good thing, however; after all, novels deal mainly with love, and reading them "can hardly strengthen the intelligence" (113). Further, though he is "anxious . . . to vindicate that public taste in literature which has created and nourished the novelist's work," Trollope is certain that by "the consent of all mankind who read, poetry takes the highest place in literature" (125). And he thinks that, in his own time, novels "feed the imagination too often in lieu of poetry" (114).

In terms of content, mainstream fiction certainly grew tamer—more respectable or, what amounts to the same thing, more bourgeois—from about 1800 to 1840. The change has less to do with new readers or the sheer increase of literacy than with, on the one hand, evangelical and utilitarian stress on reforming public morality and, on the other, the industrial and commercial restructuring of the "literary field," including printers, publishers, reviewers, booksellers, readers, and of course authors.[14] Like other sorts of cultural transformation, changes within the literary field seem often to evoke anxieties that are displaced or misrecognized. Thus, from the 1790s into the 1820s, as Ina Ferris notes, "the trope of female reading" articulated "a whole cluster of literary anxieties about technology, the market, sexuality, the body—in short, about that which was defined as outside the literary sphere yet obscurely threatened to erupt from within" (36–37). New techniques for the mass production and distribution of literature, whether viewed as progress or the reverse, were often personified, attributed to readerly demand or the corrupt "taste" of the "reading public."

From the 1820s and 1830s forward, there was a new, marked division of publishing labor, reflecting the social-class hierarchy, with the expensive, "three-decker" novel going upscale and the simultaneous emergence of a "cheap literature" industry, catering mainly to the burgeoning working-class readership in the major urban centers, giving new cause for alarm to upper-class observers. The three-decker format, popularized by Scott, became standard for respectable fiction through the long reign of Mudie's. Not until 1894 would Mudie's, in collaboration with its chief rival, W. H. Smith Booksellers, cause publishers to turn away from the three-volume design to cheaper formats.[15] In the 1830s and 1840s, both the radical press and the "penny fiction" directed toward working-class readers, much of it Gothic, criminally sensational, and salacious, gave rise to heated debate in the middle-class press and in Parliament. Nevertheless, respectable novels, clearly distinguished by price, format, and means of circulation from the more ephemeral and imitative or even plagiarized penny fiction, gained increasing legitimacy, and by the 1840s and 1850s, successful middle-class novelists were enjoying enormous popularity and profits.[16] Starting with *Pickwick Papers* in the 1830s, Dickens emerged as the superstar of the Victorian novel-reading public. "By dying a rich man (unlike Scott) and leaving an estate of £93,000," writes John Sutherland, "Dickens had helped make fiction writing as professionally respectable as the law, medicine or the civil service" (22–23). And, though second-fiddle to Dickens, by 1873 Anthony Trollope was able to say in his *Autobiography* that he had earned £70,000 through his novel-writing career, though he considered this a merely "comfortable" rather than "splendid" result (314).

The familiar, albeit double, assumption about Victorian novelists' relations with their readers claims both intimacy and mass-cultural success. This assumption has helped to explain the sense of respectable comfortableness expressed by Thackeray, Trollope, and Dickens, among others. The apparent intimacy between authors and readers stemmed partly from the practice of serial publication, partly from the moral "selectness" of Mudie's, partly from the pattern of reading aloud within family circles, and partly from the rhetoric of direct address adopted by novelists themselves—the rhetoric of "dear reader," "gentle reader," and "as the intelligent reader will observe." Of all the major Victorian novelists, the one who established the greatest rapport with his readers was undoubtedly Dickens. The instances in which Dickens altered his novels in the middle of their serial publication because of sales figures or, even more dramatically, because of fan mail or direct reader response are evidence that, at least for himself and several other successful novelists, the relations between reader and writer could be dialogical, almost conversationally familiar. As Sue Lonoff notes in her study of Wilkie Collins's readerly relations, "Dickens published his first book under the family nickname of Boz, and from the start of his career he identified his interests with those of his readers. Their tastes were his tastes, their problems his problems, and he came among them as an intimate" (5). However, according to George Ford in *Dickens and His Readers*, even "the extraordinary relationship between Dickens and his public was a more tempestuous affair than is always recognized" (42), a fact evident, for instance, in the embroilment of *Oliver Twist* in the controversy over so-called Newgate crime fiction. Though never on such intimate terms with his "dear readers" as Dickens, in his preface to *Pendennis*, Thackeray writes:

> . . . in his constant communication with the reader the writer is forced into a frankness of expression, and to speak out his own mind and feelings as they urge him. . . . It is a sort of confidential talk between writer and reader. (33)[17]

The assumption of intimacy between writer and reader conflicts with the very different thesis of increasing alienation caused by the capitalization and industrialization of publishing and the advent of mass literacy. The rhetoric of intimacy expresses nostalgia for face-to-face storytelling that print culture had long ago rendered unnecessary, though hardly extinct, as the practice of reading novels aloud in family or in public settings attests. As Klancher notes, the rise of the mass reading public and the romantic reaction to it were related to class conflict, which is in turn inscribed in the widening split between "high culture and mass culture, bourgeoisie and working class" characteristic of modernity (Klancher 13). One of the difficulties for the novel has been that, as a genre, it cannot easily or automatically be situated on one side or the other of the high versus mass culture division. Bestselling novels often seem both quintessentially bourgeois and mass cultural. Yet novelists often express various forms and degrees of alienation from readers, including criticizing novel-reading as an activity. The familiar image of the isolated romantic writer—Blake's "I am hid," Shelley's "unacknowledged legislator"—achieves a sort of ironic apotheosis at the end of the nineteenth century in the failed, suicidal novelists of Gissing's *New Grub Street*.[18]

Dickens's apparent intimacy with his readers is one extreme on a spectrum, at the other end of which lies Gissing's belief in the unredeemable vulgarity of the mass reading public. The Dickens phenomenon may also be evidence that, while for two or three decades—1836 into the 1860s—it was possible for novelist and reader to enter into a kind of intimacy, both before and after the Dickens era relations between writers and readers were not so (seemingly) harmonious. Whatever the case, the very rapport that Dickens and Thackeray established with their readers posed a problem for them, one which Thackeray worried more about than did the inimitable Boz. Throughout Thackeray's novels, novel-reading is treated with ironic suspicion, as the sort of activity that only foolish, self-indulgent, or otherwise not exactly praiseworthy characters engage in. As Kate Flint demonstrates, when Thackeray's rhetoric of direct address genders his reader female, it usually implies that some sort of misreading is likely to occur if he (the narrator) does not intervene with his sage advice. And in *Pendennis*, when Pen follows his friend Warrington's advice and takes up novel-writing as a career, he views it as merely a commercial activity, at odds with writing genuine literature or poetry.

That there are degrees of intimacy and distance between writers and readers is obvious. There is much correspondence between Victorian novelists and their friends and relations that verges on collaboration or even coauthorship. The best-known instance of such intimacy and collaboration is that between George Eliot and George Henry Lewes, but there are others. At the opposite extreme lies the anonymous, mass readership, who borrowed and purchased Dickens's or Thackeray's novels, but who otherwise did not communicate with the authors. And between these extremes were various mediating types of readers, some of them professional: the reviewers for journals and newspapers, the readers for publishers, the publishers themselves.[19] Collins suggests a related but more general sort of mediation when he looks to the "intelligent readers of the civilized world" to influence the "outlying mass" of readers. The "intelligent readers," he says, are of "all nations and all ranks."

Whether they praise or . . . blame, their opinions are equally worth having. They
not only understand us [novelists], they help us. Many a good work of fiction
has profited by their letters . . . to the author. . . . In places of private assembly
and . . . of public amusement, their opinions flow, in ever-widening circles, over
the outlying mass of average readers, and send them on their way to the work
of art, *when they might stray to the false pretence.* ("Reminiscences" 192; my
italics)

The last phrase registers Collins's anxiety about what "the outlying mass of average readers" might do, if not guided by the helpful "intelligent readers." This
category is a sort of informal version of Coleridge's "clerisy," or of the educated
minority necessary to educate or at least lead the majority.[20] Collins expresses the
same anxiety in his essay on the mass readership for penny fiction, "The Unknown Public." If not the novelist himself, then someone must act as a guide for
the mass of anonymous, "average" readers, otherwise they will not recognize
"art," but will instead be led astray by "the false pretence."

In his magisterial *Dear Reader: The Conscripted Audience in Nineteenth-
Century British Fiction*, Garrett Stewart analyzes the evolution and significance
of the rhetoric of direct address. But Stewart's rhetorical and phenomenological
approach leads him to underestimate the social anxiety implicit in that rhetoric,
which after all is *not* direct except in imagination. Because "the reader" addressed
in nineteenth-century novels is so insistently singular—the isolated individual to
whom the equally isolated narrator speaks in a simulacrum of face-to-face dialogue—it is easy to interpret the relationship between novelist and reader as one
of intimacy rather than of varying degrees of alienation and distance. As Stewart
notes, however, the singular "you" or "dear reader" involves the rhetorical reduction of the mass reading public to manageable size, providing the illusion, at
least, of individual proximity and cooperation. The reduction of mass to individual, readers plural to reader singular, itself manifests anxiety about controlling
reader response and perhaps also expresses more general concerns about the uses
of literacy, leisure, and pleasure. "What Dickens in private correspondence called
the 'many-headed,'" writes Stewart, "represents the potential multifariousness of
the public as mob. Yet it is an unruly body politic only manifested, as no one
knew better than Dickens, under the singularized plurality of the invested second
person." Stewart adds that "the novel gets written with and in you alone" (7), and
so he concentrates on the individual reader.

Acknowledging the difficulty of reconstructing the actual reading public in
the early nineteenth century, Klancher points out that the "English Romantics
were the first to become radically uncertain of their readers" (3). Though it may
never have been as cohesive as Jürgen Habermas contends, the literate, proto-
democratic "public sphere" of the eighteenth century gave way during the revolutionary crisis of the 1790s to clashing discourses and groups, including, Klancher
argues, "four strategically crucial audiences: a newly self-conscious middle-class
public, a nascent mass audience, a polemical radical readership, and the special

institutional audience—what Coleridge called the clerisy—that assumed its first shape in this contentious time" (4). Klancher finds these categories inscribed mainly in the periodicals of the time in their rhetoric of "audience making" or readerly invocation. But what is the status of this rhetoric as evidence? While it indicates the audiences that various periodicals and writers thought they were addressing, it may not reveal much about actual readers. Thus, Klancher's treatment of the "mass audience" through the evidence of such journals as Charles Knight's *Penny Magazine* tames the threat of "the crowd" considerably, keeping it at a remove from the "polemical radical readership" with which it may have overlapped.[21]

The various representations of "the crowd" in romantic writing, Klancher believes, both reflect and helped to shape the emergent mass reading public. But from 1780 through the 1840s, "the crowd" is almost always seen in negative terms; if it isn't "the mob" or "the swinish multitude" of Burke's *Reflections on the Revolution in France*, then it is "the public" of Wordsworth's 1815 "Essay, Supplementary to the Preface." Wordsworth distinguishes between "the public" as a category of unwholesome sophistication and the wholesome, innocent "people." As earlier in the "Preface to *Lyrical Ballads*," where Wordsworth had declared his intention of writing about "common life" in the "language really used by men" (71), so in the 1815 essay he associates poetry with the voice of the people, "that Vox Populi which the Deity inspires" (214). The people, identified with nature and with orality or "voice," articulates or, perhaps, *is* the truth; the public, identified with city life and literacy or print culture, veers away from the truth (cf. Hudson 144–48). In the Waverley novels, Scott similarly valorizes the oral culture of the Highlands as more genuine than the literate culture of the Lowlands and of England, while also valorizing the Union of 1707, the progress of civilization, and the spread of the language of literacy and civilization, English, to the Highlands. But just as George Eliot would later view the progress of civilization paradoxically as entailing the decline of individual heroism and the chances for sainthood, so Scott views the spread of English, of literacy, and even the popularity of his own novels as evidence of the death of chivalry and the advent of a kind of universal mediocrity. That incarnation of modern ambivalence and compromise, Edward Waverley, a tepid Quixote who acquires his romantic tendencies partly from novel-reading, learns to relegate both romance and Highland culture to the past. Novel-reading might train the reader to think in more subtle and refined ways, but not to act in more heroic and perhaps more innocent ways.

Jonathan Rose has recently pointed out that there now exists a good deal of evidence for reconstructing the actual "common reader" at least in the nineteenth century. Richard Altick, Louis James, Martha Vicinus, David Vincent, and others have assembled and interpreted much of this evidence. Nevertheless, the gap between the sociology of the common reader and the rhetorical analysis of readerly conscription is one that both Klancher and Stewart would like to bridge, because no sociology of readers can fathom exactly how actual readers responded to texts. Neither, however, can a strictly rhetorical approach get at real readers reading: the two approaches must complement each other, and even then can only approximate readerly experience. As Rose neatly puts it, the actual reader is always "outside the text" (70). It is partly this obvious fact, with its correlative uncertainty about how actual readers would react to their novels, that leads novelists so insistently to try to conscript, interpellate, or guide their imaginary "dear readers" in the directions they wish them to go. Even when a given novel is hugely popular and widely reviewed, it is not possible to be sure that actual readers are understanding it in the ways the author intended. Indeed, popularity magnifies the indeterminacy, dispersing the bestselling novel into the mysterious, anonymous reaches of what Collins called the "unknown public." Thus, the difficulties of historical reconstruction themselves reflect one major source of anxiety for novelists—indeed, for all modern authors: the ultimate unknowability of the common reader, and especially in the aggregate—the mass readership that arose with capitalism, urbanization, industrialization, and the progress of education.

In "The Unknown Public" (1859), Collins records his discovery of a vast, anonymous readership for "penny fiction." The essay reads like one of Collins's "sensation novels": it is a mystery story, with Collins as literary detective, trying, through the evidence provided him by five "penny-novel journals," to fathom the nature and composition of the "*monster* audience of at least three millions" he purports to have detected (262; my italics). "An immense public has been discovered," he declares in good sensation novel fashion; "the next thing to be done is, in a literary sense, to teach that public how to read" (263). But of course the Unknown Public can already read: the mystery has precisely to do with mass literacy rather than illiteracy. Collins's discovery causes him to be both optimistic ("a great, unparalleled prospect awaits . . . the coming generation of English novelists") and anxious about the unpredictability of reading and its effects—an anxiety, in short, about mass literacy: "what do we know of the enormous outlawed majority—of the lost literary tribes—of the prodigious, the overwhelming three millions? Absolutely nothing" (352). Collins's sampling of penny fiction is reassuring to him because the stories seem harmlessly formulaic and platitudinous. But their dullness leads him to infer, patronizingly, that the "Unknown Public is, in a literary sense, hardly beginning, as yet, to learn to read":

> The members of it are evidently, in the mass, from no fault of theirs, still ignorant of almost everything which is generally known and understood among readers whom circumstances have placed, socially and intellectually, in the rank above them. (263)

That Collins finds nothing morally reprehensible about penny fiction distinguishes "The Unknown Public" from the many attacks on novels and the mass readership for them published between 1700 and 1900. Such attacks frequently single out specific subgenres of fiction as especially dangerous to the moral and mental health of readers. Ironically, the outcry in the 1860s against sensation novels was partly aimed at Collins, whose *The Woman in White* (1860) was and continues to be regarded as setting the pattern for the "sensation mania" (see chapter 7). In any event, as Collins poses it, the problem, if not exactly crime, involved in penny fiction calls for disciplining the "enormous *outlawed* majority" to appreciate and demand superior forms of fiction (252; my italics). In this way, too, Collins operates as literary policeman, after the Foucauldian paradigm that D. A. Miller applies to sensation fiction. Perhaps all novelists express a policeman's—or, at least, schoolteacher's—desire to control readerly response. But when does that desire cease to be mere wishful thinking and go into effect? Like the rhetorical analysis of readerly conscription, a Foucauldian approach to fiction tempts the critic to deduce effects from intentions. If one agrees with Miller that the novel was a primary instrument in the construction, gendering, and policing of bourgeois subjectivity, then it becomes difficult to explain why novels and novel-reading were so often viewed as dangerous, even subversive to bourgeois respectability and morality. The penny fictions read by the Unknown Public may have seemed harmless to Collins, but not to many of his contemporaries; and Collins's own presumably superior literary productions did not seem harmless to many of the first critics of sensation novels.[22]

III

As the controversy over Newgate novels in the 1830s and early 1840s suggests, a novel like *Oliver Twist* already exhibits something of the "pathology" of reading and information that Alexander Welsh, in *George Eliot and Blackmail*, sees as becoming general in the 1860s. Welsh contends that the exponential increases in forms of knowledge and communications—book and journal publishing, rail transport, newspapers, the telegraph, the post office—produced pathological side-effects, at least, which show up symptomatically in novels as various as Mary Elizabeth Braddon's *Lady Audley's Secret* and George Eliot's *Felix Holt* (Welsh 33–59). But many commentators attributed pathological results to mass literacy long before the 1860s and 1870s. In *England and the English* (1833), for example, Edward Bulwer-Lytton, though a proponent of state-funded, universal education and thus of mass literacy, argues that diffusing knowledge inevitably dilutes it. Noting "the profusion of amusing, familiar, and superficial writings" in the early thirties, Bulwer-Lytton adds: "People complain of it, as if it were a proof of degeneracy in the knowledge of authors—it is a proof of the increased number of readers" (294). While the growth of the reading public is a sure sign of "the progress to perfection" (223), that growth nevertheless causes a decline in the general profundity and literary greatness of the culture of any nation in which it occurs. "Thus, if we look abroad, in France, where the reading public is less numerous than in England, a more elevated and refining tone is more fashionable in literature; and in America, where it is infinitely larger, the tone of literature is infinitely more superficial" (294). The nation fortunate enough to achieve mass literacy on its route to social perfection will simultaneously witness the decline and perhaps extinction of cultural excellence and creativity. In his chapter surveying "the state of education" in England, Bulwer-Lytton admonishes: "As you diffuse the stream, guard well the fountains" (165).

Who could predict, moreover, what the actual impact of even the most serious, most moral work of fiction might be on the ever-increasing millions of readers who, by the 1850s, had made novels the most popular form of secular reading that has ever existed? An author might try to guide or control the interpretation and effect of a work of fiction through authorial commentary, in a preface, or in the summing-up of the final chapter. But from Henry Fielding to Henry James, the practice of authorial commentary perhaps does little more than register the nervousness of authors about how their stories may be *mis*interpreted by readers whom they have no way of knowing, much less controlling. According to Walter J. Ong, "Nervousness regarding the role of the reader registers everywhere in the 'dear reader' regularly invoked in fiction well through the nineteenth century" (17). That nervousness has less to do with the individual reader than with readers, plural—that is, with the anonymous, phantasmal, ever-growing reading public.

Militant opposition to novels and novel-reading waned during the nineteenth century, but some of the older, moralizing antipathy to fiction continued, as in John Ruskin's diatribe against most modern novels in *Fiction, Fair and Foul* and in Matthew Arnold's "Copyright," both published in 1880. With a few exceptions for novels by Scott, Dickens, and one or two other authors, Ruskin condemns the fiction of his age—"tales of the prison-house"—as the diseased expression of "the thwarted habits of body and mind, which are the punishment of reckless crowding in cities . . ." (276). Arnold more temperately complains about "the system of lending-libraries," which keeps the cost of new books at an "exorbitant" level. This "system" both multiplies and protects "bad literature," while "keeping good books dear." The high-quality "three-shilling book is our great want . . . [not] a cheap literature, hideous and ignoble of aspect, like the tawdry novels which flare in the book-shelves of our railway-stations, and which seem designed, as so much else that is produced for the use of our middle-class seems designed, for people with a low standard of life" ("Copyright" 327–328). Rather than to novels in general, Arnold is referring only to the "tawdry" subspecies that, from the late 1840s, had come to be known as "railway fiction"—the cheap "yellowbacks" sold at W. H. Smith bookstalls. Nevertheless, the greatest literary critic of his generation has almost nothing good to say about novels anywhere in his criticism. Arnold treats novels as a subliterary, commercial form of amusement, in contrast to serious literature—poetry, drama, history.[23] In taking this deflationary view of fiction, however, Arnold echoes many novelists, including Dickens, Thackeray, Trollope, and Hardy. As an educator and inspector of schools, Arnold was a major promoter of mass literacy. Yet, like Bulwer-Lytton, he looked upon that goal with some trepidation, and he hoped for a better result than universal novel-reading.

The fiction question—that is, the questionable nature of novels and novel-reading—arises everywhere in nineteenth-century discourse about education and the uses and abuses of literacy. Thus, in the debates about establishing and operating public libraries, it echoes from the hearings conducted by the Ewart Committee in 1849 to Thomas Greenwood's *Public Libraries: A History of the Move-*

ment. . . . (1891).[24] During the 1849 parliamentary discussion, "the fear" was expressed that public libraries "would be filled with novels and the worst description of literature." But, said Henry Labouchère, this fear was groundless, because the respectable members of the town councils who would establish and manage the libraries would ensure that only serious books were acquired (Greenwood 63). Fiction, nevertheless, became a staple in the collections of many public libraries, and proved to be the most popular form of reading they offered.

As late as the 1890s, Greenwood shows, novels remained controversial. "The great fiction question is . . . the chief stumbling block in the minds of many" who might otherwise approve of public libraries. But the libraries continued to be opposed "on the ground of being the storehouses or vast reservoirs of fiction, and a class of fiction which is not at all times as wholesome as could be desired" (Greenwood 32–33). Greenwood himself supports the inclusion of "wholesome" fiction in the collections of public libraries, arguing that a taste for reading such novels will lead to better, more serious kinds of reading: "The testimony of very many librarians is that the tendency in the taste of readers is upwards rather than downwards, and that people who begin by being inveterate novel-readers usually drift into reading more profitable and instructive books" (Greenwood 33). Besides, he adds, the very best fiction can itself be "profitable and instructive" (33).

Greenwood wishes to defend all forms of literacy and reading—all are beneficial, and hence libraries in general are beneficial:

> [public] libraries are centres of light, and not only feed, but create a taste for reading, and, unquestionably, whatever does this is a benefit to the whole community, and aids materially in the repressing and taming of the rougher and baser parts of human nature. (35)

Against those who continued, as late as the 1890s, to oppose the inclusion of fiction in public libraries, Greenwood argues: "There are too many institutions of the strictly 'improving' kind, which inculcate a sort of priggish propriety, and leave no room for the healthy development of the universal desire for entertainment." Public libraries should provide their users "with newspapers, novels and other light reading." Yet to this affirmation, Greenwood appends the caveat that "the light readers ought not to stand in the way of the solid ones. . . . A man or woman who is merely skipping through a novel should give way for the reader who wants to read some works of solid literature" (36).

Though disagreeing with their stance, Greenwood also cites a number of arguments from the opponents of public libraries, who object that they encourage "loafing" and have a "demoralizing effect" on the public. In 1849, the Ewart Committee heard much testimony that libraries would reduce crime and wean working-class readers from pubs and alcohol. But in the 1890s, the opponents of tax-supported libraries sometimes turned the equation around. One self-proclaimed "Victim of Free Libraries" describes "a young man at Brighton, who could not be got to work. He was usually to be found at the Public Library, perusing light literature, and he asserts that the library ruined him. 'I mentioned this to a gentleman at the library (a visitor), and he said he had long seen it, and that no greater curse existed than these libraries, and he had rather see a young man hanging about a public-house than spending his time in these places'" (Greenwood 82).

Greenwood quotes another critic of libraries, who connects his objections specifically to novels and novel-reading (presumably, this is what the first critic means by "light literature"). According to the second person,

> whenever I have entered any of our Public Libraries, I have found, as a rule, every chair occupied—and by whom? In nine cases out of ten by loafing office boys or clerks, who were using their masters' time for devouring all the most trivial literary trash they could get. It is often stated that it is better to read trashy novels than not to read at all. One might just as well argue that it is better to eat poison than not to eat at all. . . . Light literature is, and has been, quite enough of a curse in our country without having our loafers and idlers deluged with it in the form of Public Libraries. Many are the crimes brought about by the disordered imagination of a reader of sensational, and often immoral, rubbish, whilst many a home is neglected and uncared for owing to the all-absorbed novel-reading wife. (Quoted in Greenwood 82)

Greenwood's examples demonstrate that, though it was on the wane, opposition to novels and novel-reading continued to be voiced through the end of the nineteenth century. Today consensually acclaimed great novels are canonized— that is, both memorialized as important in literary histories and regularly taught in literature classes—as major examples of high culture. Like some other forms of originally popular culture—Shakespeare's plays, for instance—the works of Jane Austen, Charles Dickens, George Eliot, even (perhaps) Wilkie Collins—are now accorded an uncontroversial reverence, except when viewed by demystifying critics as instruments of discursive or ideological surveillance, normalization, and subject-formation. Perhaps, however, neither those canonizers who treat great novels with almost the same reverence they accord to, say, Shakespeare, nor the demystifying critics who treat them as versions either of Foucault's panopticism or of Althusser's Ideological State Apparatuses, are as close to the mark as those earlier critics and moralizers—frequently including novelists themselves—who worried about the destabilizing, perhaps demoralizing, tendencies of fiction.

Given the widespread cultural anxiety aroused by novels and novel-reading, no easy case can be made for the novel as *merely* an ideological or discursive tool for the forging and policing of bourgeois subjectivity. A key problem for critics of all persuasions—the opponents of novels and novel-reading, the modern canonizers of supposedly great novels, the Marxist and Foucauldian demystifiers—was and remains pleasure, *le plaisir de texte*: what attitude should one adopt toward a form of reading that was and is also a main form of entertainment for the *literate* masses? The novel, especially the domestic fiction that Nancy Armstrong identifies with Jane Austen, Fanny Burney, Maria Edgeworth, and other turn-of-the-century women writers, often has much in common with the conduct manuals that Armstrong also surveys. The novel often is, both thematically and structurally, a site on which bourgeois subjectivity and respectability are constructed and valorized. But not always, and not exactly; while one can reasonably make such claims about, say, *Evelina*, one cannot make them about *The Monk*. Moreover, even with a safely domestic and domesticating novel like *Evelina*, there is something in excess that resists the straightforward interpellation of the bourgeois subject. That excess stems partly from the novel's status as fiction rather than reality and partly from pleasure—that is, from the entertainment value of reading about imaginary lives.[25]

As all those critics and opponents of the form who have considered the novel seductive have understood, the pleasure of fiction is at least partly erotic. Though the possible abuses of literacy seemed to be numerous, ranging from the "mechanic" teachings of the philosophes abhorred by Edmund Burke and Hannah More to mere time-wasting, novels often figured in debates about women's education and were readily seen, as in *The Rivals*, to promote sexual promiscuity. Certainly between 1760 and 1830, as Lovell points out, "the moral attack on the novel focused on women as readers" and also as writers (9–10).[26] Most of the objections to novels and novel-reading during that period, "when the literary credentials of the novel were at their lowest point" (Lovell 8), have little or nothing to do with explicit politics and a lot to do with frivolous entertainment on the one hand, and with gender and sexuality on the other.[27] The allegedly mindless publications of the Minerva Press, which partly occasioned Jane Austen's satire on Gothic romances in *Northanger Abbey*, were one major focus of alarm (see Blakey). That novel-reading could be sexy or could "enflame the passions" may have been the discovery of Renaissance writers and critics of so-called romances, but it was certainly also familiar to Samuel Richardson, John Cleland, and Charlotte Lennox in the eighteenth century—a possibility that the Marquis de Sade would pursue to its extremes.

But sex, though a powerful ingredient in many of the moral critiques of novels and novel-reading, is only one source of anxiety and opposition. With great regularity, novel-reading is represented, both by its critics and by novelists, as a form of leisure activity done instead of something else—a something that is almost always, as the 1890s opponents of libraries suggest, categorizable as mental improvement and therefore as a sort of work, albeit cultural or spiritual work. For Arnold and many others, the long struggle for public education and universal literacy seemed nugatory if the main reading of the masses consisted of novels.

By the 1880s, moreover, other pathologies of novel-writing and reading seemed to have emerged, even for—perhaps, especially for—novelists. Besides expressing his own alienation from the vulgar, semi-literate masses, Gissing was also morbidly worried about what he saw as the overproduction of books and reading matter. It is as if Gissing and many other writers of his generation were witnessing the tragic fulfillment of Bulwer-Lytton's prediction about the downside of mass literacy, a cultural entropy caused by overcultivation, or in other words a case of too much of a good thing—reading—subverting itself. In the 1880s, Alfred Austin and others worried about the "disease" or "vice" of too much reading.

Their concern was not just novel-reading, but reading in general which, as Kelly Mays shows, could even be seen as a threat to national and racial "integrity" (Mays 175). According to Austin, "Reading . . . has become a downright vice,— a vulgar, detrimental habit, like dram-drinking . . . a softening, demoralising, re-laxing practice, which, if persisted in, will end by enfeebling the minds of men and women, making flabby the fibre of their bodies, and undermining the vigour of nations" (qtd. in Mays 170).

In considering the so-called cheap literature movement of the late 1820s and early 1830s, Bulwer-Lytton, despite his optimism about progress through univer-sal education, had come close to Gissing's bleak vision of a society inundated with books, the suicide of literacy and culture:

> The rage for cheap publications is not limited to Penny Periodicals; family li-braries of all sorts have been instituted, with the captivating profession of teach-ing all things useful. . . . Excellent inventions, which, after showing us the il-limitable ingenuity of compilation, have at length fallen the prey of their own numbers, and buried themselves amongst the corpses of the native quartos which they so successfully invaded. (292)

Here is a Gothic scenario to match anything in Gissing or, for that matter, Alfred Austin: if the morally safe albeit "superficial" volumes produced for "family li-braries" threaten the cultural violence suggested by Bulwer-Lytton's metaphors, what about the great diversity of books that, by Gissing's time, the spread of education and the industrialization of printing had spawned? Books both safe and unsafe?

The advance of literacy to near universality by 1900 was often cited as indis-putable evidence of social progress. But mass literacy continued to seem threat-ening to many observers, as in debates about what Arnold in 1887 labeled the "new journalism" and condemned as "feather brained" ("Up to Easter" 347). A new age of mass journalism had certainly arrived by 1896, when on May 4 the first issue of Alfred Harmsworth's *Daily Mail* sold 397,215 copies. During the Boer War, its circulation sometimes exceeded a million copies. With that war as context, in *The Psychology of Jingoism* (1901), J. A. Hobson declared that "a biased, enslaved, and poisoned press has been the chief engine for manufactur-ing" the "war spirit" (11). Similarly, G. M. Trevelyan was only echoing Arnold, Hobson, and other critics of mass journalism when, with the 1900 Boxer Rebel-lion in China in mind, he declared that the "yellow peril" was not nearly so dan-gerous to Western civilization as the "white peril" made up of "uniform modern man," the masses of the "great cities" who were also the readers of papers like the *Daily Mail*. According to Trevelyan:

> Journals, magazines, and the continued spawn of bad novels, constitute our na-tional culture, for it is on these that the vast majority of all classes employ their power of reading. How does it concern our culture that Shakespeare, Milton, Ruskin, in times gone by wrote in our language, if for all the countless weary

ages to come the hordes that we breed and send out to swamp the world shall browse with ever-increasing appetite on the thin swollen stuff that commerce has now learnt to supply for England's spiritual and mental food? (1049–1050)

Trevelyan deplored the "uprooting of taste and reason by the printing press" (1050) and saw the "white peril" as a new barbarian onslaught on civilization, only this time the invasion was coming from within and the barbarians could read.

If the mass consumption of newsprint was threatening to Hobson, Trevelyan, and other late-Victorian cultural critics, so was the mass consumption of novels, even to novelists. Though a moderately successful novelist himself, Gissing's cultural pessimism is based partly upon the paradox that Bulwer-Lytton stresses: the more any good thing is widely shared or disseminated, the more degraded and perhaps degrading it becomes. Popularity equals vulgarity, and mass culture equals barbarism. The period that witnessed the achievement of near-universal literacy was also the age of "crowd psychology," with its diagnoses of the mindless vandalism of the masses, and of the literary and artistic "decadence," with its modish echoes of the decline and fall of Rome.[28]

Bulwer-Lytton's and Gissing's nightmare of books cannibalizing books suggests that in some sense all books may be unsafe. And, even if that thought is nonsensical, who could be sure that readers, especially those whom Arnold characterized as the "raw, unkindled masses," would not misinterpret even the safest books and put them to culture-subverting uses? The school of thought that viewed all novels as unsafe, moreover, has lasted well into our own century, though nowadays much of its censorious attention is focused upon film and television. One even hears that illiteracy is on the rise because of the mind-rotting effects of the visual mass media. But that is another, later, albeit related, story. The one I am concerned with here has as its central plot the many ways in which, from the 1790s to the 1890s, novels and novel-reading were viewed, especially by novelists themselves, as both causes and symptoms of the rotting of minds and the decay of culture and society.

CHAPTER

2

Gothic Toxins

THE CASTLE OF OTRANTO, THE MONK, AND
CALEB WILLIAMS

> The horrible and the preternatural have usually seized on the
> popular taste, at the rise and decline of literature. Most power-
> ful stimulants, they can never be required except by the torpor
> of an unawakened, or the languor of an exhausted, appetite.
> —Coleridge, review of *The Monk*, 1797

The accerelating production of fiction from the 1750s to the early 1800s, according to Ian Watt, consisted largely of inferior works of "sentiment and
romance," in contrast to the more serious, realistic novels of Richardson and Fielding. While "occasionally of some interest as evidence of the life of the time or of
various fugitive literary tendencies such as sentimentalism or Gothic terror," Watt
thinks that most fiction after midcentury has "little intrinsic merit." Instead, it
reveals a "literary degradation" caused by publishers and circulating libraries
pandering to the reading public's "uncritical demand for easy vicarious indulgence" (Watt 290).

Watt echoes eighteenth- and early-nineteenth-century critics, many of whom
saw the novel as an inferior literary form, though they often also saw various
subgenres—the sentimental novel, the Gothic romance—as even more inferior,
and more dangerous to public morality, than the main genre.[1] But simply to relegate "sentiment and romance" to the basement of "intrinsic" literary merit does
not explain why these subgenres were and often still are regarded as inferior and
perhaps dangerous to their readers' mental and moral health. Such "literary tendencies," moreover, were hardly "fugitive": between 1764 and the 1820s, some
three hundred Gothic romances were published (Haggerty, "Gothic" 223), and
Gothic's popularity continues, as shown by the bestselling and cinematic status
of the vampire novels of Anne Rice and the horror stories of Stephen King, as
well as by the many film versions of *Frankenstein*, *Dr. Jekyll and Mr. Hyde*, and
Dracula.

Watt's anxiety about "uncritical" standards and "easy vicarious indulgence" blames the reading public more clearly than writers for the "literary degradation" he identifies partly with Gothic romances. But besides increased size, the reading public of the 1780s and 1790s was probably not much different in social class, gender make-up, or education from that of the 1730s or 1740s. The American and French revolutions, however, made writers and politicians acutely aware of such collective categories as "the people," "the crowd," and "the mob," and also of "the reading public." According to Ina Ferris:

> The period is filled with signs of an urgent, widespread sense that large numbers of new and diverse readers had appeared on the scene. Whatever the empirical data on literacy (and these are notoriously problematic), the *perception* in the reviews was of a huge, recent increase in readers. (22)

The fluidity of collective categories—the potential interchangeability of "the mob" and "the reading public"—is registered, moreover, not just in reviews or journals but also in novels, and perhaps especially in Gothic romances. But not only was the actual reading public at the end of the 1700s probably not much different in its class and gender composition than in the middle, neither of the "fugitive literary tendencies" named by Watt—sentimental novels and Gothic romances—was entirely new.[2] Nevertheless, circulating libraries and the increased capitalization and mechanization of book production were factors generally encouraging to sentimental and Gothic fiction after the 1750s, as also to a lot of hasty, sloppy writing (Blakey; Taylor 40–48). These factors, however, did not determine the specific features of such fiction. This is not to say that the anxieties aroused either by Gothic romances or by a large, expanding, and anonymous reading public were entirely unreasonable. Both the sentimental novel and the Gothic romance deal with the effects of potentially "degrading" desires and of liberating individuals from emotional and moral restraints. In these general terms, both subgenres reflect, as in a glass darkly, the dual revolutions of industrialization and democratization.

Echoing the long line of anxious critics of Gothic romances, Watt signifies by "easy vicarious indulgence" the enjoyment of pleasures that are, if not exactly forbidden, at least criticized, mocked, or partly repressed in more realistic, supposedly superior or at any rate more serious fiction. But that Gothic fiction is somehow about liberating or indulging what more realistic fiction represses does not automatically align the former with progressive, democratic values and the latter with political oppression. Individual Gothic romances often express a range of conflicting social, political, and ideological values. *The Monk*, *Frankenstein*, and *Dracula* send such complex ideological signals as to be virtually indecipherable in standard political or even moral terms (Baldick 1–9; Miles 3–4). While such complexity and ambiguity contribute to the mythic quality of these stories, they have not seemed any less meretricious to realistically inclined critics who prefer the clear light of day to nightmares.

The "easy vicarious" pleasures of Gothic range from the irrational but apparently harmless wonder aroused by the marvellous, the horrific, and the sublime, to the presumably harmful passions stimulated by tales of lust and sexual transgression bordering on pornography. The general formula for the troubling *jouissance* of Gothic is fantasies of violent sexuality partially masked or distanced by medieval superstition. For many early critics, mixing pseudo-religion with sexuality only made Gothic romances all the more poisonous to their readers. But what did the fictional resurrection of superstition in a rational age signify? If the sexual content of Gothic romances was worrisome, so was the supernatural content. The scandal of Gothic arises partly because, in relation to both religion and sexuality, it demonstrates that rationality is either impotent or itself profoundly irrational. "The dream of reason produces monsters," as Francisco de Goya declared.[3] Moreover, although the portents and apparitions in Gothic fictions seem, as often as not, ironically authored, they can sometimes be read as at least approximating blasphemy, just as their sexual content, whether manifest or only latent, can be read as approximating pornography. And the blasphemy is, in a sense, double, as is just about every other feature of this Manichaean genre: against religious orthodoxy (or, anyway, against "superstition," "priestcraft," and Roman Catholicism), *but also* against Enlightenment rationality.

I

Well before the advent of the Gothic romance as a non-fugitive literary tendency, Samuel Johnson, in the fourth number of *The Rambler* (31 March 1750), expressed his anxiety about novels and novel-reading:

> These books are written chiefly to the young, the ignorant, and the idle, to whom they serve as lectures of conduct, and introductions into life. They are the entertainment of minds unfurnished with ideas, and therefore easily susceptible of impressions . . . not informed by experience, and consequently open to every false suggestion. . . . (21)[4]

Johnson distinguishes between "the heroic romance," filled with "incredibilities," and "familiar histories," based on "accurate observation of the familiar world" (19–20). Of the two, the former poses "very little danger" to the reader, because "every transaction and sentiment" in romances is "remote from all that passes among men" (21). However, the latter, more realistic kind of narrative is much more apt, Johnson thinks, to serve as a pattern for readers' behavior. "Familiar histories" (or realistic novels), if wisely written so as to give virtue the advantage over vice, might therefore be of "greater use than the solemnities of professed morality." But Johnson warns that realistic novels can captivate the minds of unwary readers and, in effect, brainwash them:

> . . . if the power of example is so great, as to *take possession* of the memory by a kind of *violence*, and produce effects *almost without the intervention of the will*, care ought to be taken that . . . the best examples only should be exhibited; and that which is likely to operate so strongly, should not be mischievous or uncertain in its effects. (22; my italics)

Though Johnson worries more about realistic novels than about romances, his comments seem prophetic of Gothic fiction, with its central motif of villains who "take possession," or threaten to do so, of innocent heroines "by a kind of violence," and its apparent aim of mesmerizing rational judgment in the reader (gendered female) so that she, too, will be possessed by the story "almost without the intervention of [her] will," as Catherine Morland, in *Northanger Abbey*, becomes temporarily possessed by the illusions of Gothic reading.

Documenting attacks on novel-reading as an especially feminine, dangerous activity, Taylor cites a number of examples in which novels are held to seduce their female consumers and thus lead to their real-life seductions—violations by the book, so to speak. Thus, Rousseau declared that "no chaste woman has ever read novels," while John Bennett, in his *Letters to a Young Woman*, asserted: "The most profligate villain . . . could not wish a symptom, more favourable to his purpose, than an imagination, inflamed with the rhapsodies of novels." And a writer in the *Lady's Magazine* for 1780 opined that novels "are the powerful engines with which the seducer attacks the female heart. . . . Never was there an apter weapon for so black a purpose" (qtd. in Taylor 77). From this perspective, all novels are pornographic, because they all—no matter what their specific contents—violate the chaste, inexperienced imaginations of their readers.[5]

Like Don Quixote, moreover, Johnson's idle, ignorant, young novel-readers are in danger of becoming—or of trying to become—what they read. According to this logic, there is a doubling of the novel's mimetic operations: the novel imitates life; the reader imitates the novel. Perhaps it is even the case that, as Oscar Wilde puts it in "The Decay of Lying," "Life imitates art far more than Art imitates life" (74), but in any event the process is reciprocal. At the same time, Johnson's argument that realistic novels pose a major threat to their readers' mental health, while "heroic romances" pose little or no threat, reverses the Quixote pattern. The dominant view, emergent in Johnson's time, was that realistic novels such as those by Cervantes and Defoe were both aesthetically and morally superior to unrealistic romances. As in Watt's *Rise of the Novel*, this division of fictional labor—rational, morally acceptable, realistic novels versus irrational, seductive, unrealistic romances—has been the standard one down to the present. In her analysis of the "poetics of Gothic," Anne Williams remarks that "twentieth-century keepers of the House of Fiction [assume] that great fiction is Realistic fiction" (1). In contrast, the Gothic has been "the black sheep of the [fiction] family, an illegitimate cousin who haunts the margins of 'literature,' pandering cheap and distressingly profitable thrills. . . . [D]isreputable Gothic appears shocking and subversive, delighting in the forbidden and trafficking in the unspeakable" (Williams 1, 4).

Critics from the 1700s onward have often held that the "disease" or "poison" of romance could be cured by the realistic novel. "Between uncritical surrender to novel reading and a wholesale rejection of novels in favor of 'serious' reading," notes William Warner, "Richardson and Fielding traced a third pathway for the novel. In [Clara] Reeve's words, the strategy was to 'write an antidote to the bad effects' of novels 'under the disguise' of being novels. This requires a cunning pharmacology" (Warner 5).[6] This rhetorical and generic tactic was also, of course, Hannah More's antidote to poisonous fiction, which she served up in her "Cheap Repository Tracts." For Richardson and Fielding, as for Cervantes and Jane Austen, the medicine consisted in reworking romance materials, partly through parody or satire. That the realistic novel always involves the Quixote pattern—is always in some sense a disillusioning critique of the illusions fostered by romance—has often been noted. In general, "to serve as an antidotal substitute for the poison of novels, the elevated novels of Richardson and Fielding had to be founded in an antagonistic critique and overwriting of the earlier novels of Behn, Manley, and Haywood" (Warner 7).

For many later novelists, however, the distinction between realism and romance is far from clear. In *Ghosts of the Gothic*, Judith Wilt notes that, just as "Scott, Dickens, and [Charlotte] Brontë each create a personal shape for the artistic expression of Gothic intensities and possibilities," so do more realistic (or less romantic) novelists including Jane Austen and George Eliot. Rather than rejecting Gothic conventions, these writers all make use of them. Viewed in this way, *Northanger Abbey* is less a parody than a revision of *The Mysteries of Udolpho* in a more realistic register: "Not quite a parodist, almost an imitator, Austen is in fact an heiress of Radcliffe" (Wilt 130–131). At least it is true that Austen, like any good parodist, has it both ways at once by simultaneously invoking and mocking "Gothic intensities and possibilities." Furthermore, in *The Secular Scripture*, Northrop Frye contends that the romance is the most fundamental type of narrative, underlying all others.[7] If that is so, then realistic novels are always palimpsests inscribed on subtexts whose "intensities and possibilities," haunting the cellars or attics of imagined reality, in some sense always return, as in the Freudian "return of the repressed." So realistic novels are perforce reformed, often parodic romances, or else contain repressed romances within their common-sensical, moralizing, and normalizing confines, just as More's "Mr. Fantom" contains the supposedly toxic reading of Tom Paine and crime stories.

As in Freud's treatment of the uncanny, the repressed that returns in Gothic romances, far more vividly than in most realistic novels, is simultaneously supernatural and sexual (for Freud, of course, the supernatural is a manifestation of the sexual). The Gothic is a fantasy form whose conventions demand that, on some level or in some way, the religious and the sexual be fused or, better, confused, as they are, say, in *Hamlet*; the authors of such fiction, therefore, cannot avoid a sort of inexorable flirtation, at least, with both pornography and blasphemy. In analyzing Hoffmann's story "The Sandman," Freud emphasizes the connections among infantile desires, repressed sexual urges, and religious sensititivity or, better, credulity: "An uncanny experience occurs either when repressed infantile complexes have been revived by some impression, or when the primitive beliefs [superstitions] we have surmounted seem once more to be confirmed" (157). Freud also claims that the uncanny motif of the *Doppelgänger*, so prevalent in Gothic, involves "a harking-back to particular phases in the evolution of the self-regarding feeling, a regression to a time when the ego was not yet sharply differentiated from the external world and from other persons." In Lacanian terms, the spectral narcissism of the double evokes the uncanny terror of a sudden regression backward through the looking-glass, the mirror stage in reverse.[8]

The pattern of psychological regression involved in Gothic, seemingly threatening to (and thrilling *because* threatening to) the stability and unity of the adult, rational ego, is doubled or mirrored by historical regression. Readers in an enlightened age could dismiss Gothic superstition as just that—superstition. Why resurrect the fraudulent beliefs of the past, albeit in the guise of mere entertainment? The idea that "romance" is inferior to "novel" of course derives partly from the tradition, exemplified by *Don Quixote*, that identifies the former with the superstitious Middle Ages and the latter with an enlightened modernity. And the question of the marvellous is often treated, by romance writers as well as their critics, under the dismissive rubric of superstition. But even in the enlightened present, the reading of Gothic romances might take violent possession of at least credulous readers through the fictional resurrections of magic and "priestcraft." In the preface to *Roderick Random*, Tobias Smollett suggests this danger:

> Romance . . . owes its origin to ignorance, vanity and superstition. In the dark ages of the world . . . when the minds of men were de-bauched by the imposition of priestcraft to the utmost pitch of credulity; the authors of romance arose, and losing sight of probability, filled their performances with the most monstrous hyperboles. (xliii–xliv)

De-bauched is a key term here, hinting not just at the danger of resurrecting superstition through romance-writing and reading, but at something obscene about "the imposition of priestcraft," just as Freud would later stress the connection between superstition and sexuality in the uncanny.

The figure of the terrifying, sexually threatening or transgressive priest in such Gothic romances as Ann Radcliffe's *The Italian* and Matthew Gregory Lewis's *The Monk* has many precedents, back to the anti-clerical and anti-Catholic propaganda of the Reformation and beyond.[9] J. M. S. Tompkins notes that, well before Radcliffe and Lewis, the "nunnery tale" had been a staple of such propaganda, spilling over into pornography. In more legitimate, mainstream literature, from Joseph Addison's "Theodosius and Constantia" (*The Spectator* 164; 7 September 1711) to Edward Jerningham's *The Funeral of Arabert, Monk of La Trappe* (1771), "the conflict of love and [religious] vows was a recognized source of pathos" (Tompkins 275).[10] Besides the "thrill of that warm complacency which always stole through a British bosom when meditating Continental tyrannies" (Tompkins 276), there was another sort of thrill involved in British retellings and retailings of nunnery tales. Long before Radcliffe, "the lasciviousness of priests, monks and nuns [had] added an ugly ingredient to the hellish brew of the sensational writer" (Tompkins 277). At least in Radcliffe's practice, the Gothic romance involves a taming of the "scandalously indecent" (Tompkins 277) materials in such tales.

All stories of monastic superstition and sadistic, priestly tyranny illustrate the same proto-Freudian moral: excessive sexual repression conjures up its obscene opposite. The lack that is the Name of the Father is also the opening through which the "obscene father," with all of his terroristic, incestuous energy, invades the haunted "family romance" of modern, supposedly enlightened reality. Gothic monsters are usually images of this undead, unholy figure of *jouissance* and abjection, embodiment of everyone's worst nightmares, the demon-father whose own demon-father is, according to Gothic convention, the Devil. Thus, as Slavoj Žižek argues, "one has to go beyond the standard 'Lacanian' reduction of the motif of a double to imaginary mirror relationship: at its most fundamental, the double embodies the phantom-like Thing in me; that is to say, the dissymmetry between me and my double is ultimately that between the (ordinary) object and the (sublime) Thing"—*das Ding*, endlessly personified in Gothic and later horror fiction as "Father Enjoyment," the obscene opposite, shadow-twin, of the law-giving fathers of the Symbolic Order (Žižek, *Enjoy* 124–125). Enjoying himself at the expense of others, the anti-father, whether diabolical priest, monster, or mad scientist, brings devastation and terror with him.

Smollett's negative opinion of superstitious romances did not prevent him from helping to stimulate interest in Gothic themes and motifs. His *Ferdinand Count Fathom* (1753) in particular, as David Punter says, is "the first important eighteenth-century work to propose terror as a subject for novelistic writing," and is therefore a forerunner of such Gothic works as *The Castle of Otranto* and *The Mysteries of Udolpho* (Punter 45). Smollett's novel evokes terror especially through Fathom's imprisoning and abuse of the victim-heroine, Monimia, extending Richardson's exploitation of "the threat of rape and violence" toward "a kind of sadistic pornography" (Punter 47). Nevertheless, *Fathom* does not depend on supernatural machinery; and anyway, in an enlightened age, who could be so credulous as to believe in phantoms and necromancy? In terms similar to Smollett's, though less anxious about the effects of romance, the narrator of *Tom Jones* declares that, while authors in the superstitious past resorted to the supernatural, modern writers who do so are likely to arouse in their readers merely "a horse-laugh." Says the narrator: "The only supernatural agents which can . . . be allowed to us moderns are ghosts; but of these I would advise an author to be extremely sparing. These are indeed like arsenic, and other dangerous drugs in physic, to be used with the utmost caution" (399). Here again is the arsenical motif, though this time suggesting, rather than the poisoning of the reader, the poisoning of the text against any serious reception by the reader.

Identified with medieval superstition and priestcraft, romances evoked the question of why, even if their only raison d'être was the feeble one of mere amusement, recycling defunct beliefs could be entertaining? Does it take a superstitious reader to experience the uncanny frissons conjured up by Gothic "marvels"? The thought that many readers might not be enlightened—might in fact be irrational enough to credit Gothic romances just as Don Quixote credits *Amadeus of Gaul*—appears in many early criticisms of Gothic. This idea again often points to the gendering of the readership for romances as female. The "female Quixotes" who crop up in eighteenth-century fiction and criticism, from Charlotte Lennox's heroine Arabella, who takes French romances for her model of the world, to Jane Austen's Catherine Morland, are not just readers of any and all novels: they are young, idle, ignorant, and above all highly impressionable readers of romances. Quite apart from whether women did or did not constitute the majority of the novel-reading public, both in critical discourse and in Gothic romances, women readers were often depicted as being "possessed" and "violated" by what they read, just as Johnson suggests that novels can "take possession . . . by a kind of violence." For many critics, the novel-reading public in general seemed to be made up mainly of "female Quixotes." The only sure way to keep women readers from being violated by improper reading was to keep them illiterate, as Sir Anthony Absolute recommends in *The Rivals*, something clearly impossible in an enlightened age when even female servants such as Moll Flanders and Pamela Andrews could read and also write the stories of their masters' assaults upon their virtue.[11]

Laurie Langbauer remarks that Lennox's *The Female Quixote; or, The Adventures of Arabella* (1752) both critiques and enacts the identification of women readers and writers with the romance form. Lennox's novel, in other words, repeats in a realistic register the romantic improprieties it seeks to transcend by way of "ridicule" or satire. *The Female Quixote* is ostensibly about the taming of Arabella's romantic "madness," but neither she nor Lennox escapes from the romance paradigm. Indeed, one "way to read the mad Arabella is as the novelist's . . . wish-fulfillment" of "the ideal reader, completely given over to the sway of the text, attesting to the power of romance, a power the novelist desires for her form too" (Langbauer 65). In any event, just as thoroughly as do male critics such as Johnson, Smollett, and Fielding, Lennox identifies "romance's faults—lack of restraint, irrationality, and silliness" as also "women's faults" (78). Yet these "faults" are the result of women's subordination under patriarchy, including the insistent reduction of women's stories to sexual ones. Lennox's novel "affirms that the only history or adventures a woman can have are sexual": "The construction of romance as a realm of freedom is associated particularly with women's freedom, the freedom of her sexuality, a freedom so extreme it becomes licentious" (79–80). How can a virtuous young woman have any "adventures" at all before marriage and still remain virtuous? The eighteenth-century answer is, she cannot; even reading about the exploits of the heroines of romance is dangerous, involving the imaginary violation of the innocent reader by the knowing text, a prompting of licentious behavior, if only in fantasy.

Negotiating novelistic reality through the values and illusions of romances, Arabella the female Quixote expresses Lennox's central dilemma as a female novelist. The "novelistic world" that *The Female Quixote* "strives to establish through a critique of the emptiness of romance has no real place for woman except in repeating her association with romance" (Langbauer 62). Lennox's novel does not reject romance through satire so much as reinscribe the romance paradigm in seemingly more realistic terms as the only available set of conventions for the writing and reading of women's stories. By showing how Arabella is trapped within the romance paradigm—how she has, in a sense, been possessed and violated by her reading of romances—Lennox's novel also shows "women's dispossession," revealing "the lack of stable ground on which women might situate their own stories" (Langbauer 62–63).

That Gothic romances always convey some at least implicit threat of sexual violation or transgression, excess or *jouissance*, makes the boundary between them and pornography shifting, indeterminate. The boundary becomes especially unclear when, as in Matthew Gregory Lewis's *The Monk*, the threat of violation is realized. Besides nunnery tales, a more obviously secular subgenre of pornographic fiction emerged in the second half of the eighteenth century, from John Cleland's *Memoirs of a Woman of Pleasure (Fanny Hill)* (1748–1749) to the Marquis de Sade's *Justine* and *Juliette*. In comparison, the Gothic romance is the soft porn of the late Enlightenment. Though more realistically portrayed than in most Gothic romances, the prolonged threat of violation and then actual rape of Clarissa Harlowe in Richardson's novel both echoes seventeenth-century libertine writing and looks forward to that cultural division of emotive labor whereby the same threat of sexual possession/imprisonment/rape becomes a preoccupation of Gothic, while the increasingly purified realistic novel distances or dismisses that threat as an aspect of romance. In other words, even as de Sade was foregrounding them, sexual license and pornography go partially underground at least in British fiction, adopting the suspect but murky, supposedly inferior form of the Gothic romance.

In *Northanger Abbey*, the threat of sexual violence and wife-murder that Catherine Morland conjures up from her reading especially of *Udolpho* proves to be merely fantastic. But Austen's fictional rendering of the standard critical anxieties about the effects of romance-reading is as much a satire upon those anxieties as a straightforward expression of them. Her defense of novels in chapter 5, while citing what she apparently considered improvingly realistic fictions like her own (*Cecilia* and *Camilla* by Fanny Burney and *Belinda* by Maria Edgeworth, rather than *Udolpho* or the other Gothic titles rattled off by Isabella Thorpe) is also a defense of the course of reading undertaken by Catherine and Isabella.[12] Catherine's enthusiastic response to *Udolpho* misleads her, much to her embarrassment, but the damage is only temporary: she is basically an intelligent young woman who simply has not seen much of the world or, for that matter, read much about it. Far from driving her to "madness" as romance-reading does Lennox's female Quixote, Catherine's reading experience ultimately benefits her.

Aided by Henry Tilney's "astonishing generosity and nobleness of conduct," Catherine learns not to mistake "the alarms of romance" for "the anxieties of common life" (202–203). At the same time, she also learns that the readership for romances consists not just of credulous young women such as herself and Isabella, but of young men of the world such as Henry and Isabella's brother, John. According to *Northanger Abbey*, moreover, there are at least two types of male readers of novels: stupid and intelligent. After declaring, "I never read novels; I have something else to do," John Thorpe contradicts himself by declaring that he does read them: "Novels are all so full of nonsense and stuff; there has not been a tolerably decent one come out since Tom Jones, except the Monk; I read that t'other day; but as for all the others, they are the stupidest things in creation" (69). For Austen, part of the joke seems to be that John is so lacking in critical discrimination as to lump Fielding's realistic novel with Lewis's Gothic romance. Austen may also be hinting that his phrase "tolerably decent" is especially inapplicable to *The Monk*, a work of fiction excoriated by many of its early critics for being intolerably indecent. In any event, John as a stupid reader of fiction presents a clear contrast to Henry as an intelligent one. When Catherine reinforces the gender stereotype of the readership for novels by telling Henry that "they are not clever enough for you—gentlemen read better books" (121), she is suprised by his response, which reinforces Austen's earlier defense of novels and novel-reading:

> "The person, *be it gentleman or lady*," [says Henry,] "who has not pleasure in a good novel, must be intolerably stupid. I have read all Mrs. Radcliffe's works, and most of them with great pleasure. The Mysteries of Udolpho, when I had once begun it, I could not lay down again;—I remember finishing it in two days—my hair standing on end the whole time." (121; my italics)

Of course Henry's last phrase—"my hair standing on end the whole time"—ironizes his experience of reading *Udolpho* as at once amusingly thrilling and nonserious. A well-educated, discriminating novel-reader, he is able to exercise just enough willing suspension of disbelief and no more—a lesson in how to read fiction that Catherine learns in the course of Austen's pro- rather than anti-romance novel. Austen simultaneously contests the stereotyped gendering of novel readers as female and the simplistic idea that novels, including Gothic romances, have uniform, always deleterious effects on their readers. Nevertheless, she does at least hint that there are major differences between individual novels such as her own and *Udolpho*, and perhaps also between types or subgenres of fiction: realistic novels (her own again, *Tom Jones*, *Belinda*) and Gothic romances (*Udolpho*, *The Monk*, *The Orphan of the Rhine*), though Henry's comments render the romance versus novel distinction unclear.

II

"If the emergence of the novel itself celebrates the codification of middle-class values," writes George Haggerty, "the Gothic novel records the terror implicit in the increasingly dictatorial reign of those values" (Haggerty 221). Perhaps more obviously, the Gothic challenges the limits of Enlightenment faith in reason, while offering variations of transgression against family and sexual norms. Often associated with the French Revolution and the Reign of Terror, the "tale of terror" as written by a Gothic "terrorist" seemed to threaten cultural havoc in several directions. In his genealogy of madness and sexuality, Foucault points out that both the Gothic romance and Sadean pornography flourished in the 1790s and early 1800s in part because, while the experts had freed insanity from medieval notions of demonic possession, they had not yet fully medicalized it or rendered it scientifically comprehensible, and in part because sexuality was also being subjected to increasingly modern forms of surveillance through the rationalizing techniques of "pedagogy, medicine, and economics," among other expert discourses (Foucault, *History* 116). In the nightmare confessionals of Gothic, the meanings of both insanity and sexuality are at stake, contested between medieval superstition and Enlightenment rationality, with the final victory often going to superstition, or at least left in doubt.[13]

As in *The Castle of Otranto* and *The Monk*, the Gothic often cloaks its transgressive themes in medieval superstition and the "marvellous." The supernatural in Gothic tends to function like an aspect of dreamwork, partially—but only partially—displacing or disguising the sexual energies that lie at the heart of its nightmarish fantasies. Horace Walpole's *jeu d'ésprit* of 1764, moreover, adds to (obviously incredible) medieval superstition the modern disguise or displacement of ironic self-denigration through a decadent campiness that expresses a sophisticated amusement while insisting upon the irrationality of that amusement. Often cited as the first Gothic romance, Walpole's *Otranto* helped to establish several of the defining traits of the subgenre (cf. Miles 30). Walpole's preface to the first edition, describing the discovery of the supposedly Italian, late medieval manuscript "in the library of an ancient catholic family in the north of England" (3), establishes or at least emphasizes one tendency of both the romantic and the realistic fiction that followed it. This is the masochistic tendency of the text to undermine its moral and epistemological status by stressing its spurious and perhaps dangerously misleading qualities (including its fictiveness) while asserting its authenticity.

Besides its medieval, Italian origin and the virtues of its style, the "editor" makes two main claims about *Otranto*. One is that it is a moral, even religious story, in contrast to modern, fictive romances: "The piety that reigns throughout, the lessons of virtue that are inculcated, and the rigid purity of the sentiments, exempt this work from the censure to which romances are but too liable" (5). Whether or not this claim to piety and virtue is credible, Walpole's tale is itself a romance, so that the claim is self-cancelling. But before claiming virtue for the romance it introduces, the preface makes a very different assertion. In the period when it was supposedly written, the editor says, "letters were then in their most flourishing state in Italy, and contributed to dispel the empire of superstition" (3). At the same time, that empire was being ruthlessly defended by—as Smollett, the French philosophes, and Tom Paine all called it—the "priestcraft" of Roman Catholicism. It is probable, the editor suggests, that *Otranto* was written by "an artful priest" attempting to "confirm the populace in their ancient errors and superstitions" (3). The preface continues:

> If this was his [the artful priest's] view, he has certainly acted with signal address. Such a work as the following would enslave a hundred vulgar minds

> beyond half the books of controversy that have been written from the days of
> Luther to the present hour. (3–4)

As a stand-in for both the author and the obscene father, the "artful priest" seeks
to "enslave"—possess, violate—all readers of *Otranto*. Walpole thus registers
anxiety—mixed with a self-ironizing hopefulness—about the possible effects of
his Gothic romance on present-day "vulgar minds," like Johnson's ignorant, idle,
young novel-readers, or perhaps even like "the mob" (19) that shows up to reinforce the terror and superstition of Manfred after the gigantic helmet crushes his
sickly (unmanly and un-Manfred-like) son Conrad just as the story begins.

The editor declares, however, that the only reason anyone in an enlightened
age would want to read such a superstitious, retrograde tale is for mere "entertainment" (4). For the enlightened reader, the text poses no danger at all: it will be
merely amusing. A "vulgar mind" may be possessed, violated, book-raped by this
tale by an "artful priest"; a rational reader will not take it seriously. Even so, the
editor thinks that "some apology for" offering it to the public "is necessary.
Miracles, visions, necromancy, dreams, and other preternatural events, are exploded now *even from romances*" (4; my italics). So what Walpole offers the
reading public is an anti-Enlightenment fantasy more freighted by the credulous
fantasies or superstitions he calls "Gothic" than appear in other, presumably more
sane and sensible, modern romances.

This opinion was shared by Clara Reeve, who, while taking *Otranto* as a
model for *The Old English Baron* (1778), objected to Walpole's excessive reli-
ance on supernatural machinery. Echoing Fielding, Reeve declares that "the appearance of a ghost" might be permissible, and "we can even dispense with an
enchanted sword and helmet; but then they must keep within certain limits of
credibility." She then proceeds to list several of the "marvels" of *Otranto* that she
considers outré:

> A sword so large as to require an hundred men to lift it; a helmet that by its own
> weight forces a passage through a court-yard into an arched vault, big enough
> for a man to go through; a picture that walks out of its frame; a skeleton ghost
> in a hermit's cowl:—When your expectation is wound up to the highest pitch,
> these circumstances . . . destroy the work of imagination, and . . . excite laugh-
> ter. (Sabor 77)

Reeve's list does not include all of the "marvels" with which Walpole lards his
romance. She omits the ominously semaphoric black plumes on the gigantic helmet, the statue-cum-nosebleed, and the conclusive (and concussive) vision that
follows the death of Matilda. Walpole's description of this vision offers a clear
indication of his ironic stance toward the supernatural, an irony only slightly more
exaggerated than that in many later Gothic romances:

> A clap of thunder . . . shook the castle. . . . The moment Theodore appeared, the
> walls of the castle behind Manfred were thrown down with a mighty force, and
> the form of Alfonso [from whom Manfred's grandfather Ricardo had usurped

the princedom], dilated to an immense magnitude, appeared in the centre of the ruins. Behold in Theodore, the true heir of Alfonso! said the vision: and . . . accompanied by a clap of thunder, it ascended solemnly towards heaven, where the clouds parting asunder, the form of saint Nicholas was seen; and receiving Alfonso's shade, they were soon wrapt from mortal eyes in a blaze of glory.

The beholders fell prostrate on their faces, acknowledging the divine will. (108)

What besides mere "entertainment" was Walpole's excuse for including such "incredibilities" (as Johnson called them) in his story? By his own admission, such "miracles . . . are exploded now even from romances," so that *Otranto* begins to sound like a parody romance. The answer seems to be that Walpole wanted to write what Freud would call a "family romance," not so much in the guise of a medieval fantasy as in that of a Shakespearean tragedy with a strongly oedipal dimension—*Hamlet* once more, but in the lighter, sprightlier mode of enlightened, modern entertainment.[14] Walpole claims that the story follows the Aristotelian "rules of the drama," and particularly the rules of tragedy involving "pity" and "terror" (4). Whether or not *Otranto* imitates Shakespeare via Aristotle, the repeated insistence of the first preface that the romance it introduces is something other than a romance—medieval Italian manuscript, classical or Shakespearean tragedy—again underscores Walpole's sense of the *il*legitimacy of the fantasy that he is offering to the reading public. It is a romance (and therefore an inferior form of literature—it is not even a novel); but, doubling as medieval document or perhaps as narrativized tragedy, it may not be entirely ridiculous, albeit the counterfeit of some other, legitimate form.

Walpole said that the inspiration for *Otranto* came to him in a dream, "of which all I could recover was, that I had thought myself in an ancient castle . . . and that on the uppermost bannister of a great staircase I saw a gigantic hand in armour" (in Sabor 65). The other phallic marvels in *Otranto* follow metonymically from this colossal steel hand: colossal helmet; colossal black feathers; colossal sword; and so forth. These prodigies all seem to be Freudian-Brobdingnagian jokes or tall tales, forming a camp, fetishistic mélange expressing the wrath of the Law by way of the dismembered body parts of an invisible Law-giver or Father (whether God or the ghost of Alfonso hardly matters) against the living, obscene, tyrant-father and incestuous wife-abuser, Manfred. The false prince of Otranto, though apparently desperate to beget a male heir, recovers quickly from his dismay at the squashing of his unmanly son by the gigantic helmet. Manfred schemes to divorce Conrad's saintly mother, Hippolita, so that he can marry Conrad's quondam fiancée, Isabella; he imprisons and threatens to torture and execute the manly hero, Theodore; and he accidentally stabs his daughter, Matilda, to death. While Manfred blusters and blunders his way toward perdition, ranting against the women in his life, the not especially *unheimlich* portents and ghostly marvels accumulate. Though *Otranto* can hardly be called autobiographical, it isn't difficult to see, behind the camp machinery of Walpole's fantasy, the actual family romance that he is partially exposing and, perhaps, hoping to exorcize through a sort of

surrealistic mockery. The hints of incest seem to be little more than markers pointing toward a generalized but secret family guilt (whether Walpole knew about the
rumors of his own possible illegitimacy is uncertain). And the incredible, dreamlike "marvels" in the story allow him both to express and to distance himself from
the unhappiness of his relationship with his famous, powerful, law-making and
executing father, Sir Robert Walpole.

Horace Walpole's chief oedipal revenge (and pleasure from that revenge)
may have derived, however, not from the analogy between the tyrant Manfred
and his father, but simply from his having written and published such a romance,
especially one so full of "Gothic" "incredibilities." To the serious world of politics that his father thrust upon him, Horace preferred what he saw as the nonserious
world of art, theater, fantasy, and dilettantism. How Sir Robert, who died in 1745,
might have reacted to *Otranto* is moot, but that a Gothic romance is not a government document or a piece of legislation is self-evident; so, too, Strawberry Hill
was not a real Gothic castle, only an architectural toy. *Otranto*'s emphasis upon
fantasy—the built-in incredibility or, better, decadent playfulness—helped to preserve it from the censure visited upon some later Gothic romances (especially
The Monk) and even made it possible for Eleanor Fenn, alias "Mrs. Teachwell,"
to recommend to "young ladies" the reading of certain "beautiful passages which
are interspersed through the whole work." "The whole volume is replete with
refined morality," Fenn believed, although "I dare not place [the whole of] *Otranto*
in Mrs. *Teachwell*'s library (it is not suited to the perusal of early youth)" (in
Sabor 82).

Fenn's anxiety about how *Otranto* might be misunderstood—or understood
—by "early youth" does not seem to reflect its not particularly graphic sexual
content, but perhaps instead its ironic tone and status as a *non*believable fantasy
dealing with religious matters. Perhaps "Mrs. Teachwell," like many of her contemporaries, found problematic *any* work of fiction written merely to entertain
—in the case of *Otranto*, merely to stimulate emotions such as terror in its readers
for the ironic sake of pleasure. The castle in Walpole's fantasy isn't Xanadu, and
at the end of the story it lies in ruins. Nevertheless, it is a thoroughly modern
example of literary architecture: a pleasure palace intended not for "vulgar minds,"
but for sophisticated, ironizing readers able to appreciate its Gothic humor.

Perhaps because Walpole's main purpose in writing *Otranto* was his own
pleasure, it is a Gothic romance that repeatedly and in a variety of ways insists
upon its cultural and, in some sense, political illegitimacy. In the main story, despite Walpole's vehement anti-Catholicism throughout his political career, the
priest—Father Jerome—doesn't appear to be "artful"; he is clearly more pious
than Manfred. Yet the first preface suggests that *Otranto* may be the product of
"an artful priest" aiming to delude the masses. Walpole doesn't expect modern,
enlightened readers to "fall prostrate on their faces" before the concussive final
vision of the ghost of Alfonso. On the contrary, via its ironic incredibility, *Otranto*
at least approximates blasphemy, a charge that would later be registered against

Lewis's *The Monk*. As the first preface states, "letters" or literacy helped "to dispel the empire of superstition" (3), causing the Dark Ages to give way to the Reformation and Enlightenment. But in these terms, a Gothic romance is inevitably a self-contradictory form: in "letters" or print, for a literate, enlightened audience, it feigns the presence of "miracles, visions, necromancy, dreams" (4)—that is, of nonpresences. For any sufficiently enlightened reader, the medium in which it does so dispels the asserted primacy of incredible, visionary presence.

Immediately after the grand "blaze of glory" that climaxes the various nonbelievable ("superstitious") occurrences in the story, the inheritance problem that decides who is the legitimate heir to the princedom of Otranto is clarified by Manfred's confession that a "fictitious will" had made his grandfather, poisoner of Alfonso, the prince. The lawful prince proves to be the peasant hero, Theodore. So a fraudulent document has bamboozled all concerned into the belief that Manfred and his lineage are the true rulers of Otranto. Moreover, when Father Jerome, who has himself been revealed to be the Count of Falconara and father of Theodore, declares that he has "an authentic writing" that will corroborate Manfred's confession, it is rejected by Manfred as unnecessary, because "the horrors of these days, the vision we have but now seen, all corroborate thy evidence *beyond a thousand parchments*" (122; my italics). Writing and documentary evidence ("parchments") are thus discredited in a text that also discredits the other sort of evidence—visions, dreams, apparitions—that Manfred and the rest of the characters regard as convincing. As Walpole conceived it, the Gothic romance is a form of self-discrediting "entertainment" that undermines its possible status as serious literature, much less as historical document, by describing "visions" and presences that are blatantly fantastic, in a medium—writing or printed text—that is obviously not "authentic," immediate presence. The formula of *Otranto*, in other words, is that of a fraudulently historical text describing fraudulent ("superstitious") miracles and apparitions. Between amusing counterfeit and wild superstition, both quasi-blasphemous, the "artful priest"—the author's double and self-image as the obscene father of *Otranto*—can just be glimpsed slipping uncannily back out of sight, behind his fantastic mirror, having *not* written his autobiographical confessions, his authentic family romance.

In many later Gothic romances—*Frankenstein, Dr. Jekyll and Mr. Hyde, Dracula*—editorial frames, stories-within-stories, documents and fragments of documents multiply, circling around and around missing or unrepresentable centers. The record for this sort of textual doubling and redoubling probably belongs to Charles Maturin's *Melmoth the Wanderer*. The multiplication of stories and texts within one main story, as if enacting Freud's repetition compulsion, gestures obsessively toward the "traumatic kernel" of "the Real" (Žižek 123) and therefore also toward their insistent failure to reach that impossible center. In doing so, the Gothic romance calls into question the authenticity of all stories and texts, shadowing forth the ultimate anti-Enlightenment scandal: the thought that representation as such may be only a form of superstition. The Gothic romance is thus related not only to pornography but to the documentary hoax, an aspect of its history that Edgar Allan Poe especially would exploit in, for example, *The Narrative of A. Gordon Pym*.[15]

III

Though it would be "too easy to say that female readers are attracted to the thrill of illicit sexuality or the masochistic enjoyment of their victimization that the Gothic everywhere represents," that is part of the fascination of the form (Haggerty 226). Rather than the Middle Ages, the Gothic often seems to be resurrecting the cavalier and Restoration tradition of libertinism that is also at work in *Pamela* and *Clarissa*. A central ingredient in this patriarchal, apparently heterosexual, but misogynistic tradition is the threat to the heroine-victim posed by the aristocratic villain—"virtue in distress"—a motif also basic to much stage melodrama from the 1790s forward.[16]

The motif of the lascivious, decadent aristocrat pursuing the virtuous heroine reaches its nineteenth-century Gothic climax in *Dracula*. But there is another motif or tendency in Gothic, also evident in *Dracula*, that Eve Sedgwick calls "paranoid" and identifies as homosexual. "The Gothic was the first novelistic form in England to have close, relatively visible links to male homosexuality, at a time when styles of homosexuality, and even its visibility and distinctness, were markers of division and tension between classes as much as between genders" (Sedgwick, *Between Men* 91). At the same time, both homosexuality and homophobia seem to be at work in those romances that are most clearly paranoid, again as in *Dracula*. Rather than hinging upon the villain's pursuit or persecution of an innocent heroine, paranoid Gothic involves the pursuit or persecution of one male character by another. In *Caleb Williams*, *Frankenstein*, and James Hogg's *Confessions of a Justified Sinner*, the fundamental transgression is valenced homosexuality, with one (or both) of the twinned male protagonists playing the role of sadistic villain, and the other (or both) playing the role of masochistic victim.[17] If justice, virtue, and heterosexism are to emerge victorious in these narratives, then the *Doppelgänger* roles of submissive victim versus dominating villain must be reversed, at least in the minds of readers. The thrill of transgression can be maintained even through the ending, however, if both victim and villain perish together, in a sort of *Liebestod* for doublegoers, like the arctic swansongs of Frankenstein and his male, apparently heterosexual, monstrous alter ego.

In contrast to paranoid Gothic with its male doublegoing pattern, the works of Horace Walpole, William Beckford, and "Monk" Lewis—"our first homosexual novelists," as George Haggerty calls them ("Literature and Homosexuality" 176)—feature the apparently heterosexual virtue-in-distress paradigm, but do so in ways that emphasize the inability of either the novel-form or legal and moral constraints to contain the "sexual frenzy" and "unresolved passion" of the protagonists. Heterosexuality in their romances "is harrowing in its 'aberrant' nature and in its association with the perversion of power" (169). Haggerty continues:

Our first homosexual novelists, then, offer . . . a gruesome picture of . . . human experience: corrupt authority, forced confinement, isolation and torture, secret sins, contorted familial relations, incest, rape, necromancy, murder—every possible "aberration," it seems, but that which would be most appropriate here. (176)

Walpole's *Otranto*, Beckford's *Vathek*, and Lewis's *The Monk*, through the very excesses and improbabilities that are, perhaps, the most fundamental features of Gothic, manage to speak the unspeakable, expressing the anxiety and terror of their authors' "private obsessions" that could not otherwise be publicly expressed, much less legitimized.

Apart from heterosexual prurience bordering on the pornographic, *The Monk* fulfills all of the conditions that Sedgwick identifies with paranoid Gothic. On one level, it is possible to read *The Monk*, like *Otranto* and *Vathek*, as a camp, decadent *jeu d'ésprit*, a semi-parody, at least, of other Gothics or *Schauerromane*, similar to Lewis's obviously stagey play, *Castle Spectre*. But *The Monk* is also both closer to pornography and more explicitly homosexual than *Otranto* or most other Gothic romances. Straightforward lust rather than homophobic enmity and persecution is the first form of (seemingly) male-male bonding in Lewis's romance. Ambrosio first becomes excessively fond of the attractive young novice Rosario, who soon turns out to be the cross-dressing, passionate Matilda, and then still later a sorceress and amanuensis of Satan. So the equation is clear: Ambrosio grows overly attached to Rosario while still believing her to be a boy; though sexual union between the two is consummated only heterosexually, both Ambrosio's initial desire and the gender-switching of Satan's emissary can be read as homosexual fantasy.

The pattern is reinforced by the first appearance of Satan. Ambrosio "beheld a figure more beautiful than fancy's pencil ever drew. It was a youth seemingly scarce eighteen, the perfection of whose form and face was unrivalled. He was perfectly naked . . ." and so forth (273). When Rosario/Matilda encourages Ambrosio in his lust for the youthful Antonia, moreover, *youthful* is the key word. She is so young and innocent as to be almost genderless; yet she is beautiful, desirable, and Ambrosio eventually gets his way with her, murdering her interfering mother, Elvira, and raping and murdering Antonia in the catacombs beneath the convent of St. Clare. Except for a mention of Antonia's "swelling breasts," the description of her body and her reactions during the rape could also be one of a homosexual rather than heterosexual violation.

Once Ambrosio has fallen, seduced by Rosario/Matilda, he becomes obsessed by lust and the sadistic pleasures involved in the abuse of his power and authority. Given the boyishness of the main, apparently female objects of his lust, his sexual frenzy seems indiscriminate—bisexual, perhaps, but in any event only ambiguously heterosexual. The most obvious feature of *The Monk*, however, is misogynistic sexual excess leading to rape, homicide, and worse—to incest, sororicide, and matricide—because Antonia turns out to have been Ambrosio's sister, and

Elvira, his mother. As in *Otranto*, incest appears to be a signifier for any and all sexual excess, but also for the intensely private, secretive nature of such excess, a mystery buried alive, as it were, in the vaults of a dysfunctional family romance, yet sure to spring back to life along with the other specters of sexual, textual, and political transgression in the course of a Gothic nightmare.

The first critics' main objections to *The Monk* had to do with its pornographic quality; its sexual "indecency" was, however, not clearly identified as homosexual or as anything more specific than "lust." But there were two other objections, which point to what made and continues to make *The Monk* fascinating (the scandal and censorship it aroused, of course, only increased its allure; see Peck 28–29). The first concerned Lewis's borrowings from other romance-writers. His reputation as "a shameless plagiarist" sprang up almost immediately and remains an issue at least for scholarly source hunters (Peck 20–21). The point worth stressing is that charges of plagiarism contributed to rather than undermined interest in a text which, like *Otranto*, insists upon a certain literary and cultural *illegitimacy*. The charge of literary theft, whether fair or not, adds to the list of crimes that the main story records. The text itself becomes a sort of criminal object, quite apart from the details of its plot, style, and so forth. But Lewis seems not to have realized that he was doing more literary borrowing than authors legitimately do all the time. Lewis's "Advertisement" to the first edition, after all, lists a number of his sources.

Within the story, however, Lewis underscores its literary illegitimacy in another, very striking way. Besides sexual indecency and plagiarism, a third, even more troubling factor for several of the early critics of *The Monk* is what they identify as its "blasphemy." In his 1797 review of *The Monk*, Coleridge begins by noting its borrowings; however, he stresses that "the manufacturers" of such stories generally expend "little . . . thought or imagination" upon them. "But, cheaply as we estimate romances in general, we acknowledge, in the work before us, the offspring of no common genius" (370). Plagiarism is thus for Coleridge not a major issue; he goes on to praise *The Monk* for its several literary excellencies. But he nevertheless considers Lewis's romance "poisonous," a word he repeats several times in the review, for two other reasons. The first is, as for its other early critics, its sexual indecency:

> The shameless harlotry of Matilda, and the trembling innocence of Antonia, are seized with equal avidity, as vehicles of the most voluptuous images; and . . . the most painful impression which the work left . . . was that of great acquirements and splendid genius employed to furnish a *mormo* for children, a poison for youth, and a provocative for the debauchee. (374)

As if its indecency were not enough, Coleridge continues, *The Monk* is also a work of "blasphemy." He quotes at length the offending passage, wherein Ambrosio, plotting to seduce Antonia, comes upon her while she is reading the Bible. Ambrosio pauses to wonder how she can read the Bible and yet remain so innocent (his phrase is: "so ignorant")? He recalls, however, that Antonia's mother, Elvira, has asked a similar question.

> That prudent mother, while she admired the beauties of the sacred writings, was convinced that, unrestricted, no reading more improper could be permitted a young woman. Many of the narratives can only tend to excite ideas the worst calculated for a female breast: every thing is called plainly and roundly by its name; and the annals of a brothel would scarcely furnish a greater choice of indecent expressions.

How shocking, Ambrosio reflects, that the Bible forms the chief reading of young women, despite the fact that it "but too frequently inculcates the first rudiments of vice, and gives the first alarm to the still sleeping passions" (258). In the case of the text Antonia is reading, however, Elvira has taken care to expurgate it, so that "all improper passages" have been "either altered or omitted" (258).

In this astonishing scene of reading, the text inside the main one is not a supposedly poisonous romance, criminal biography, or work of political radicalism, but, at least for Hannah More and her evangelical ilk, the one and only, absolute antidote for all forms of secular literature, the Bible. Lewis turns More's pattern inside out: within his own semi-pornographic romance, he represents the Bible as a potentially pornographic work. Of course the Bible, as Lewis clearly understands, has been put to countless worldly uses, many of them nefarious.[18] William Blake has something close to this thought in mind in "The Marriage of Heaven and Hell." After the poet's visit to the "printing house in Hell," he announces that the angel who guided him there has turned into a devil and that "we often read the Bible together in its infernal or diabolical sense, which the world shall have if they behave well" (Blake 134). Further, there seem to be *two* distinct, conflicting Scriptures, because the poet immediately declares that "I have also the Bible of Hell, which the world shall have whether they will or no" (134). Similarly, in his powerful version of paranoid Gothic, *Confessions of a Justified Sinner*, James Hogg portrays his homicidal maniac, Robert Wringham, as justifying his actions in biblical and theological terms. Given his fanatical version of Calvinism, Wringham is an expert reader and interpreter of Holy Writ. And in *I, Pierre Rivière*, Foucault presents the case of a remarkably literate young French peasant, who in the 1830s murdered his family and used the Bible to justify his actions in court. But, except for Blake's, these appropriations of the Bible for diabolical purposes can be easily dismissed as the rationalizing of criminally insane behaviors. No such rationalizing is going on when Ambrosio observes Antonia reading the Bible. And the suggestion that the Bible is sexually too explicit or indecent for young women to read seems all the more provocative coming from a character who, though fallen from holiness, knows his Bible well.

Just what Lewis had in mind when he penned the Bible-reading scene is unclear; he seems to have been genuinely surprised when the critics identified him with the bad priest or obscene father of his novel, and especially dismayed by the charge of blasphemy (for Lewis's "apologia," see Peck 36). Yet he must have known he was courting censure even more severe than that provoked by his steamy descriptions of lust and sexual violation. He might have defended himself on the grounds that the blasphemy was Ambrosio's, not his—in other words, that it is in keeping with Ambrosio's downfall for him to think such impious thoughts about the Bible. But having Elvira agree with Ambrosio that the unexpurgated Bible is not fit reading for her daughter undercuts such a defense. It seems unlikely, moreover, that Lewis meant to suggest that even the best-intentioned or most tightly policed text can produce unpredictable effects and meanings in readers, an idea consonant with James Hogg's romance (and also with modern reader-response theory). Ambrosio—and Elvira—clearly believe that texts have specific, determinable effects on their readers, and that blasphemous and indecent texts, whether the Bible or *The Monk*, will corrupt innocent readers like Antonia. But what is the difference in morality or immorality between the Bible and *The Monk*? Lewis implies that there is none, at least where sexual indecency is concerned.

Perhaps Lewis is also suggesting that too much reading of any kind is corrupting, a version of the old equation between sin and knowledge. This interpretation seems likely given the other allusions to the Bible in *The Monk*, together with the thought that the only book *all* of the literate characters in Lewis's romance can be certain to have read is the Bible. It is the Bible, of course, that forms the principal text in Ambrosio's education—and look at the result![19] It is the Bible that, no matter in how distorted a fashion, authorizes the Inquisition and also that monastic life that *The Monk* reveals to be a thin crust of hypocritical, superstitious repression over a volcano of lust, murder, tyranny, horror, and proto-revolutionary violence. In many Gothic romances, the theme of superstition is linked to a virulent anti-Catholicism that keeps them from seeming overtly blasphemous. And yet the implication is the same as in *The Monk*: if the Bible was the main reading and source of education in unenlightened ages of superstition and priestcraft, then how can it be a pure, morally edifying text in the present?

Whether Lewis was thinking along these lines cannot be known, but in *The Monk* other references to the Bible connect it to the theme of superstition. It is "superstition" rather than "true devotion" that "reigns with . . . despotic sway . . . in Madrid," reads the first paragraph. It must therefore also be superstition rather than genuine religion that informs the powerful sermon Ambrosio delivers in the opening scene, a sermon in which he "explained some abstruse parts of the sacred writings in a style that carried with it universal conviction" (45). Moreover, "a large bible" together with a crucifix forms a prominent part of the hocus-pocus with which the Wandering Jew exorcises the Bleeding Nun (180). And the Nun herself, of course also Bible-educated, utters a schizophrenic mixture of blasphemies and prayers: "Sometimes the castle rung with oaths and execrations: a moment after she repeated her paternoster: now she howled out the most horrible blasphemies, and then chaunted De profundis as orderly as if still in the choir" (153)—a mixture of the "impious" and the "devout," in other words, like that in many Gothic romances including both *Otranto* and *The Monk*, which of course resurrect, at least for the sake of entertainment, the very "superstitions" they seem to condemn.

At the end of *The Monk*, a book very different from the Bible provides the reading that, Ambrosio hopes, will save him from the Inquisition if not from hell. Imprisoned along with Matilda for the crimes that she has prompted him to commit, Ambrosio is astonished when she appears in his dungeon, apparently a free woman, and presents him with "a small book" (407). By reading the first four lines of the seventh page of this book backward, she tells him, he can once again bring Satan to his aid and, if he chooses, can liberate himself as she has done. She then vanishes in a "cloud of blue fire" (410). Ambrosio reads this necromantic text, though it is "in a language whose import was totally unknown to him" (412). Satan then appears, "parchment" and "iron pen" in hand, and after several attempts persuades Ambrosio to sign his soul away in his own blood. These final, fearful, hesitantly repetitious acts of reading and writing in *The Monk* underscore the link between Satan and forbidden knowledge and therefore also the possibility that reading and writing—literacy in general—may be blasphemous, diabolical. After all, Matilda's "small book" of sorcery, which Ambrosio reads without understanding, is like *The Monk* itself—like any novel, any book of secular reading—in being an alternative Bible or, rather, anti-Bible. Within *The Monk*, Satan's book doubles the Bible. But *The Monk* also doubles or redoubles the Bible, emerging in the course of its reception as a "blasphemous" anti-Bible.

In Freud's analysis of demonic possession, the Devil appears to hapless Christoph Haitzmann in a "'loathsome shape bearing in his hand a Booke the which is full of naught but wizardrie and blacke magicke'" (Freud 271). This text not only doubles and thereby blasphemes the Bible, just as Satan both doubles God and serves as the obscene substitute for Haitzmann's deceased father, it is also a part of a textual maze, an elaborate series of documentary, fragmentary mirrors (which among other effects, make Freud's historical reconstruction of this case read like a Gothic romance: compare Cixous on Freud's essay on "the uncanny"). It turns out that, among all this textual doubling and counterfeiting, Haitzmann himself claimed to have signed not just one but *two* pacts with the Devil, one in ink and one in blood, a feature of the case that Freud has most difficulty in explaining. But what are all instances of textual doubling and counterfeiting in the Gothic except disclosures of that "delirious discourse" through which neurosis speaks (Cixous 530)? The Gothic romance, written in plain English, is also written in a second, incomprehensible, or as-if necromantic language. Alongside rational, waking discourse, there is always this "delirious discourse," doubling the former just as the obscene father doubles the sane, virtuous lawgiver, just as the *Unheimliche* doubles the *Heimliche*, and just as the Gothic romance doubles the realistic novel. In the realm of uncanny mirrors that is the Gothic, there will invariably be *at least* two texts—reality and nightmare, sermon and blasphemy, Bible and anti-Bible (which in Lewis's case, can be *The Monk* as readily as Satan's necromantic book). In this manner, "blasphemous" both against religious orthodoxy and against Enlightenment reason, the "delirious discourse" of Gothic threatens to engulf all discourse, just as the madness of its mad heroes and villains threatens to bring down the world in some final, revolutionary catastrophe of apocalyptic terror.

Lewis had the impudence or the naivete to sign himself, on the title page of the second edition of *The Monk*, as if signing his own pact with the Devil, "Matthew Gregory Lewis, M.P." For Coleridge, the identification of the author as a Member of Parliament increased the scandal: "Yes! the author of the Monk signs himself a legislator! We stare and tremble." In *The Pursuits of Literature* (1799), echoing Coleridge, Thomas Mathias declared:

> ... there is one publication of the time too peculiar, and too important to be passed over in a general reprehension. . . . A legislator in our own parliament . . . an elected guardian and defender of the laws, the religion, and the good manners of the country, has neither scrupled nor blushed to depict . . . the arts of lewd and systematick seduction, and to thrust upon the nation the most open and unqualified blasphemy against the very code and volume of our religion. (239)

In a footnote, Mathias adds that he believes the main "blasphemous" passage, in which Ambrosio treats the Bible as an indecent book, is "indictable at Common Law." It is unclear whether Lewis was in fact taken to court, but Attorney General Sir John Scott was pressured by the Society for the Suppression of Vice to indict him for blasphemy (Peck 34; Parreaux 109–119; Thomas 179–184). With at least the threat of legal action hanging over him, Lewis carefully expurgated the fourth edition (1798). The passage about the Bible disappeared, and Lewis also meekly "expunged every remotely offensive word in his three volumes, with meticulous attention to *lust*" (Peck 35; Parreaux 120–121). All subsequent editions of *The Monk* down to 1950 remained safely detoxified. If nothing else, Lewis had discovered just how terroristic critics of novels and novel-reading could be. Writing in *The British Critic* for 7 June 1796, one of these critical terrorists declared of *The Monk*: "We are sorry to observe that good talents have been applied in the production of this monster" (677).[20]

IV

A quite different version of paranoid Gothic is evident in Godwin's *Caleb Williams*, involving an antithetical reaction to the question of mass literacy. Whether Godwin's Jacobin novel falls within the boundaries of Gothic is debatable, but several of its structural features make it reasonable to compare it to *Otranto*, *The Monk*, and other Gothics by both male and female writers.[21] Godwin's *St. Leon*, with its attention to alchemy and the supernatural, is perhaps more definitely Gothic than is *Caleb Williams*, but the latter is at once a tale of terror, a narrative featuring the paranoid pattern of male doublegoers locked in deadly struggle, and a sensational crime story involving, as does *The Monk*, a fall from ideal innocence to the diabolical opposite.

It is as a story of class conflict, however, that *Caleb Williams* most obviously reflects the related conflict over mass literacy. Despite his peasant origins, Caleb gains an education, and as a young man is so skilled at reading and writing that Falkland hires him as his secretary. Both through observation of his master's erratic behavior and through reading letters and other clues, Caleb as detective pieces together the story of Falkland's murder of Tyrrell. Through a Bluebeard-like reversal, however, Falkland detects Caleb's detection, and for much of the novel their roles are reversed: Falkland pursues Caleb as if Caleb were the criminal. Caleb is arrested, tried, imprisoned, harrassed, imprisoned again, and so forth. It is only through his ability to read and write that Caleb is finally able to rectify the situation, demonstrate his innocence, and bring Falkland to justice.

Caleb's literacy proves to be more than a match for Falkland's. After fleeing his master's service, Caleb goes on to become a writer of poems, essays, and ultimately of his own history, the criminal biography, as it were, of Caleb Williams and his doublegoing persecutor, Falkland. Of course it is Falkland, not Caleb, who is the criminal; but Falkland manages almost to write Caleb into a guilty corner, so to speak, before Caleb writes his way out of that corner. Toward the end of the novel, Caleb discovers that he has achieved a sort of literary fame as the subject of a criminal biography, the sort of poisonous text that Hannah More included in "Mr. Fantom" and also that Godwin declares he read in researching his male-male version of "the tale of Bluebeard" (340). Hiding in London, Caleb hears a hawker of street literature advertising his wares, including "the most wonderful and surprising history, and miraculous adventures of Caleb Williams," in which, for a halfpenny, the reader can learn all about Caleb's alleged crimes, robberies, prison escapes, and disguises down almost to the last minute (268–269). This criminal biography is a sort of counterfeit or simulacrum of Godwin's novel, the supposedly true story we are reading and that Caleb has presumably written. The novel—Caleb's writing, that is—undoes the falsehoods of "The Most Wonderful and Surprising History," but only by becoming the criminal biography of Falkland. The true narrative, Caleb's, incorporates and partially reproduces the false one, just as More's antidote to such poison texts as criminal biographies includes the last words and confession of thieving, murdering William.

One of the lessons that Caleb learns from his master, if not from his earlier education, is that knowledge is power, and vice versa. Illustrating the thesis that "the pen is mightier than the sword," Caleb's empowerment through literacy— his ability to write and publish the true account of Falkland's crimes—ultimately liberates him and kills his former master. "No, I will use no daggers! I will unfold a tale—!" says Caleb; and he treats his final literary act, the penning of the inside-out criminal biography *Caleb Williams*, as itself an act of murder (though also of justice): "With this engine, this little pen I defeat all his machinations; I stab him in the very point [Falkland's honor] he was most solicitous to defend!" (314–315). Narrating his compelling story both in court (orally) and in the novel (through writing), Caleb believes that he has caused Falkland's death. Falkland survives this double telling "but three days. I have been his murderer" (325), writes Caleb, thus also suggesting that the novel itself has struck the final blow—the novel not as poison, but nevertheless as dagger or perhaps as guillotine, helping to end the centuries-long tyranny of aristocracy and the *ancien régime*.

From at least the 1750s forward, literacy was held to be a cure for many social evils, just as Caleb uses it to free himself from Falkland's persecution and to render justice. Especially during and after the French Revolution, however, the spread of literacy was also held to be a source of potential danger and social disruption. No modern reader is likely to interpret Caleb's main act of literacy, his novel-writing, as one of homicide rather than justice, though how Hannah More and other anti-Jacobin writers viewed it is a different matter. That Caleb, with his lowly peasant background, can read and write in so effective a manner as to become Falkland's secretary, then the detective of his crimes, then a professional author, and finally the author of Falkland's execution, by a novel that behaves like a dagger or a guillotine, expresses Godwin's belief in the revolutionary power of democratic literacy and enlightenment to correct the Gothic abuses and injustices of the past.

CHAPTER

3

The Reading Monster

Books are in every hovel.
—Coleridge

Many critics have observed that Gothic "tales of terror," from 1789 onward, reflect the terrors of the French Revolution. Stories of priestcraft, sexual violation, and imprisonment in medieval castles or convents can be read as at least indirect attacks on the *ancien régime*. But if sublime or murky enough in their social and political references, they can just as easily be read as attacks on the events in France: the *ancien régime*, whether perceived as tyrannical or not, threatened or overthrown by the modern, Robespierrian terror and tyranny. In his 1800 essay on the novel, the Marquis de Sade declared that Gothic fiction like *The Monk* was "the inevitable result of the revolutionary shocks which all of Europe had suffered." The Revolution familiarized people "with the full range of misfortunes wherewith evildoers can beset mankind," and therefore the average novel was no longer interesting. Every novelist and novel-reader had "experienced in the short span of four or five years more misfortunes than the most celebrated novelist could portray in a century. Thus, to compose works of interest, one had to call upon the aid of hell itself" (109). By this logic, rather than being mere fantasy, *The Monk* comes closer to describing revolutionary reality than do more realistic novels.

Gothic fiction served at least "as a metaphor with which some contemporaries in England tried to understand what was happening across the channel in the 1790s," writes Ronald Paulson; "The first Revolutionary emblem was the castle-prison, the Bastille and its destruction by an angry mob, which was fitted by the English into the model of the Gordon Riots" of 1780 (217–218). The crowd is a central actor in all accounts of the Revolution; the crowd is central as well in many Gothic romances, where it sometimes figures as a metaphor or, at least, specular image for the reading public. In *Northanger Abbey*, when Catherine

Morland announces that "something very shocking . . . will soon come out in London . . . more horrible than any thing we have met with yet," Miss Tilney supposes that she means mob violence on the order of the Gordon Riots or the French Revolution, and her brother elaborates: "a mob of three thousand" attacking the Bank and the Tower, and "the streets of London flowing with blood," though he realizes that Catherine means only another Gothic romance (Austen 126–127). The crowd that gathers around the gigantic helmet in *Castle of Otranto* plays merely the role of nonviolent, credulous witness or chorus to the supernatural violence that Manfred's crimes precipitate. In contrast, the crowd in *The Monk* and in other Gothic romances from the 1790s forward is a dynamic, irrational, destructive agent of history.[1]

With both the French Revolution and the Gordon Riots as context, portrayals of collective action, even in fantasies seemingly far removed from present-day politics, often turn hellish. *The Monk* was for its author mainly an apolitical exercise in aesthetic sublimity, but Lewis nonetheless describes the catastrophic results of oppression (and repression) in ways that reflect the Revolution. Those results are seen on two levels: the misogynistic violence of Ambrosio, but also the equally misogynistic violence of the "incensed populace" that, after it learns of the imprisonment and supposed murder of Agnes by the wicked prioress, destroys the Convent of St. Clare and murders every nun it lays its hands on. The description of the sacking of St. Clare might well be one of the storming of the Bastille or of the sacking of the Tuileries by the Parisian "mob." The rioters in their vindictive "frenzy" torch the convent, and soon "the conflagration" engulfs them, too: "the columns gave way: the roofs came tumbling down upon the rioters, and crushed many of them beneath their weight. Nothing was to be heard but shrieks and groans; the convent was wrapped in flames, and the whole presented a scene of devastation and horror" (Lewis 345).

This is indeed a hellish account evocative of the French Revolution, the sort of imagery to be found in Burke's *Reflections on the Revolution in France* and numerous other horrifying accounts by anti-Jacobin writers: violence begetting violence, the cannibal Revolution devouring its children. Lewis's attitude toward the rioters is, however, ambivalent: acting on impulse, they are both avengers and victims. As Paulson puts it, "The convent of St. Clare represents corruption, superstition, and repression" and deserves its fate, though most of the nuns who perish are at least as innocent as Agnes. Its destroyers, moreover, are "no more admirable than the tyrants" who have ruled it (Paulson 219). With a few exceptions such as Godwin's *Caleb Williams*, most Gothic romances are ideologically ambivalent or only very abstractly political. Godwin's novel belongs to the strain of Jacobin fiction, whereas *The Monk*, *The Mysteries of Udolpho*, and the majority of Gothic romances are fuzzily anti-Jacobin in their implicit politics. But no matter what political messages their authors thought they were conveying, depictions of crowds, riots, and collective action in all sorts of literature from 1789 forward reflect the revolutionary experience, and in doing so inevitably express anxieties about democracy, enlightenment, and literacy, as well as the role of "the populace," "the mob," or "the public"—including "the reading public"—in history.

I

If from 1789 onward, Gothic terror often reflects revolutionary terror, nonfictional accounts of the events in France often read like Gothic romances. Certainly Burke's anti-Enlightenment rhetoric in *Reflections* and elsewhere shares much with that of Lewis and other Gothic romancers. Thus, Burke often utilizes the language of demonism and the supernatural. For Burke, the Revolution is "a drunken delirium from the hot spirit drawn out of the alembick of hell" (187). France is like "a madman, who has escaped from the protecting restraint and wholesome darkness of his cell" (90) to wreak havoc on the world. In an extended analogy combining black magic with the cannibal Revolution, Burke offers a horrific family romance: revolutionaries eager to tear down the past and establish society on an entirely new basis are "children of their country . . . prompt rashly to hack that aged parent in pieces, and put him into the kettle of magicians, in hopes that by their poisonous weeds, and wild incantations, they may regenerate the paternal constitution, and renovate their father's life" (194).

Burke declares that history is "a great volume . . . unrolled for our instruction"; but readers of it will learn that "history consists, for the greater part, of the miseries brought upon the world by pride, ambition, avarice, revenge, lust, sedition, hypocrisy, ungoverned zeal, and all the train of disorderly appetites" (247). Burke then waxes Gothic by declaring that "these vices [which] are the *causes* of [the] storms of history" (248) are constantly shape-shifting, always "assum[ing] a new body":

> The spirit [of evil] transmigrates; and, far from losing its principle of life by the change of its appearance, it is renovated in its new organs with the fresh vigour of a juvenile activity. It walks abroad; it continues its ravages; whilst you are gibbeting the carcass, or demolishing the tomb. You are terrifying yourself with ghosts and apparitions, whilst your house is the haunt of robbers. (248)

This spirit of evil, transmigrating from body to body and generation to generation, appears to Burke to have reached a monstrous culmination in the "orgies" of destruction, massacre, and "rapine" in France. In the first of Burke's *Letters on a Regicide Peace* (1796), history becomes especially monstrous and phantasmagoric:

> . . . out of the tomb of the murdered monarchy in France has arisen a vast, tremendous, unformed spectre, in a far more terrific guise than any which ever yet have overpowered the imagination and subdued the fortitude of man. Going straight forward to its end, unappalled by peril, unchecked by remorse, despising all common maxims and all common means, that hideous phantasm overpowered those who could not believe it was possible she could at all exist. . . . (*Works* 5:237)

Citing this passage in his introduction to *Reflections*, Connor Cruise O'Brien notes that "the spectre haunting Europe in *The Communist Manifesto* (1848) . . . walks for the first time in the pages of Burke" (9).

The various terrifying phantoms that haunt the rhetoric of anti-Jacobin writers—and later, by ironic appropriation, of Marx—are not, like the marvels in *Otranto*, the emanations of medieval superstition. They are instead the emanations of modern Enlightenment. That is to say, anti-Jacobin rhetoric itself operates by ironic appropriation and reversal, applying the language of superstition, alchemy, and Gothic "hauntology" to the "false lights" of the Enlightenment and its revolutionary results.[2] The bloodthirsty "band of cruel ruffians and assassins" who invade the Queen's bedchamber in Burke's account are acting under the inspiration of "the furies of hell" (164–165), but these "furies" include Rousseau and the other advocates of "the rights of man." The "mob" does not succeed in murdering the King or in raping and murdering the Queen, but Burke says that their attempt leaves the palace "swimming in blood, polluted by massacre, and strewed with scattered limbs and mutilated carcases" (164). These horrors lead Burke to the famous peroration: "the age of chivalry is gone.—That of sophisters, oeconomists, and calculators, has succeeded; and the glory of Europe is extinguished for ever" (170). However, just what part have the "sophisters, oeconomists, and calculators"—that is, as Burke later calls them, "the political Men of Letters" (211)—played in the attack on the Tuileries or in any of the other instances of mass violence during the Revolution? The answer is, of course, that "the mob" does not act merely by reflex or mindless impulse. It instead acts on the basis of a system of ideas—an ideology—that it has learned from the "sophisters, oeconomists, and calculators." The Revolution is the outcome not so much of ignorance as of education gone awry, or rather of the wrong sort of education, an indoctrination of the people of France in the "barbarous" and "mechanic philosophy" of treasonous intellectuals: "In the groves of *their* academy, at end of every visto [sic], you see nothing but the gallows" (171–172).

Burke does not go so far as some anti-Jacobins in elaborating a conspiracy theory of the Revolution—Abbé Barruel's claim, for instance, that its ultimate cause was a conspiracy of the Illuminati and Freemasons.[3] Nevertheless, "the monied interest" in France, combined with those "Men of Letters" who, "fond of distinguishing themselves, are rarely averse to innovation" (211), having dispensed with loyalty to the monarchy, to religion, and to the past, are indoctrinating the people with their treasonous ideas through "the medium of opinion" (212). To its detriment, France has become "a nation of philosophers" (239), led by "the mechanics of Paris," who have "dismembered their country" (142). The chief means of indoctrination, moreover, have been "literature" and the printing press:

> Writers, especially when they act in a body, and with one direction, have great influence on the publick mind; the allegiance therefore of these writers with the monied interest had no small effect in removing the popular odium and envy which attended that species of wealth. These writers, like the propagators of all

novelties, pretended to a great zeal for the poor, and the lower orders, whilst in their satires they rendered hateful, by every exaggeration, the faults of courts, of nobility, and of priesthood. They became a sort of demagogues. They served as a link to unite, in favour of one object, obnoxious wealth to restless and desperate poverty. (213–214)

The power of radical propaganda, disseminating the diabolical "spirit" of democratic and "atheistical fanaticism" to the masses, is one of the major themes of *Reflections*, and Burke at times makes that propaganda itself sound like the stuff of Gothic tales of terror: "These writings . . . have filled the populace with a black and savage atrocity of mind, which supersedes in them the common feelings of nature" (262) and so forth.

Throughout *Reflections*, Burke pays as much or more attention to what he considers to be the treason of the intellectuals than he does to any other causal factor, in part because the revolutionary teachings of the *philosophes* threaten to replace religion altogether with secular ideas: "These atheistical fathers have a bigotry of their own; and they have learnt to talk against monks with the spirit of a monk" (212). The "mechanic philosophy" of the intellectuals purports to be scientific, enlightened; but it is just as superstitious in its way as the religion of the priests. Here and elsewhere, however, Burke's Gothic rhetoric of extremes threatens to leave no middle ground: if the past belonged to the darkness, fanaticism, and superstition of the old priests, and the present belongs to the darkness, fanaticism, and superstition of the new priests (that is, the *philosophes* and Jacobins), then where does one locate genuine enlightenment? Burke's answer, of course, is that the truth lies in the patient moderation and the respect for the "learning" of "antiquity," for religion, and for tradition that he identifies with the "liberal descent" (121) of British laws, institutions, and culture. But this answer also involves him in a paradoxical defense of "prejudice" and, indeed, ignorance:

> You see, Sir, that in this enlightened age I am bold enough to confess . . . we are generally men of untaught feelings; . . . instead of casting away all our old prejudices, we cherish them to a very considerable degree, and, to take more shame to ourselves, we cherish them because they are prejudices. . . . We are afraid to put men to live and trade each on his own private stock of reason; because we suspect that this stock in each man is small. . . . (183)

Of course Burke identifies prejudice with wisdom instead of with ignorance, but here and elsewhere he comes close to expressing a preference for the superstitions of the past to those of the present. The two rival sorts of superstition, however, are also rival forms of "learning" or culture, as in the famous passage about the "swinish multitude." In the past, writes Burke, European "civilization" was based on "two principles . . . the spirit of a gentleman, and the spirit of religion"— that is, on "the nobility and the clergy." These principles both defended and promoted learning against barbarism and chaos throughout the centuries, the one by "patronage" and the other by "profession."

Learning paid back what it received to nobility and to priesthood; and paid it with usury, by enlarging their ideas, and by furnishing their minds. Happy if they had all continued to know their indissoluble union, and their proper place! Happy if learning, not debauched by ambition, had been satisified to continue the instructor, and not aspired to be the master! Along with its natural protectors and guardians, learning will be cast into the mire, and trodden down under the hooves of a swinish multitude. (173)

Here Burke offers both a history and a theory of culture or learning, and of the role of the clergy and other intellectuals in either promoting or subverting culture. The passage can also be read as an early, negative forecast about the results of modern attempts to diffuse learning to the "multitude" or the masses, and therefore about mass education and literacy. On this model, learning is the special preserve or "profession" of the clergy, who disseminate morality and wisdom through religion to both the populace and "the nobility." But this dissemination does not involve turning either learning or religion over wholesale to the people, nor even necessarily teaching the people how to read and write. Learning is essential to civilization, but it must be carefully protected from careless dissemination and other possible forms of degradation by the ignorant (that is, by the people, the "swinish multitude").

Burke's commentary on learning versus the "swinish multitude" drew much counterfire from the radical press. The lengthy list of periodicals, pamphlets, and poems ironically echoing Burke's phrase include James Parkinson's *An Address to the Hon. Edmund Burke from the Swinish Multitude* (1793); Daniel Isaac Eaton's *Hog's Wash* (later renamed *Politics for the People, or a Salmagundy for Swine*, 1794); Thomas Spence's *Pig's Meat, or Lessons for the Swinish Multitude* (1793) as well as his satirical poem, *Burke's Address to the Swinish Multitude*; "Citizen Lee's" *The Rights of Swine* (1794); and the anonymous *A New Catechism for the Use of the Swinish Multitude, Necessary to be Had in All Sties*, possibly by Richard Porson (1792). Burke tried to defend himself by claiming that he was "thinking not of the innocent English pig, but of the 'wild boar of the Gallic forest'"; however, the satiric clamor continued well into the nineteenth century. In 1816, William Cobbett told the readers of his *Political Register* that they were not, contrary to the opinion of their oppressors, a "swinish multitude"; in the following year, William Hazlitt accused Coleridge and Southey of using the insulting phrase (Coleridge had done so in one of his letters to the *Courier*).[4] And in 1820 Percy Bysshe Shelley produced *Swellfoot the Tyrant, or Oedipus Tyrannus*, in which the main characters are swine, including the "chorus of the Swinish Multitude"—a forerunner, though with different political significance, of George Orwell's *Animal Farm*.

Burke's bestial image of the "swinish multitude" is also one of monstrosity, and therefore again—at least in one ancient meaning of *monstrosity*—of the masses, the populace, the "many-headed monster" of Shakespeare's *Coriolanus* and Hobbes's *Leviathan*. For Hobbes, society itself appears to be monstrous or at any rate gigantic, though nonetheless human: the "body politic" is "but an artificial man; though of greater stature and strength than the natural" (Hobbes 19). Metaphorical diseases of the social body that endanger the life of this "artificial man" or that render him insane include, for all conservative thinkers such as Hobbes and Burke, rebellion and revolution, often figured as dismembering that body. Moreover, in *Reflections*, Burke treats the idea of creating an entirely new "artificial man" as thoroughly monstrous. O'Brien quotes Burke's letter of 10 October 1789 to his son regarding "the portentous state of France—where the Elements which compose Human Society seem all to be dissolved, and a world of Monsters to be produc'd in the place of it" (14). In *Reflections*, Burke calls the Revolution a "monstrous tragi-comic scene" (92). The "licentious and giddy coffee-houses" and "clubs" that dictate to the King and the National Assembly are "composed of a monstrous medley of all conditions, tongues, and nations," whereby "publick measures are deformed into monsters" (160). "The spirit of money-jobbing," converting land into "paper" (the assignats, the national debt), has also assumed "an unnatural and monstrous activity" (308). And the writing of the revolutionary "constitution" has produced a "monster," whose continuation will bring disaster to the French economy (313).

As Lee Sterrenburg, Chris Baldick, and others have noted, for anti-Jacobin writers the rhetoric of monstrosity was standard. To take just one example besides Burke, Joseph de Maistre, in his *Considerations on France* (1797), attacks "all the monsters who are overrunning France" (14). The revolutionary government is a "monstrous power, drunk with blood and success" (16). But "all the monsters born of the Revolution" will only serve, as the ultimate climax of the bloody mayhem and terror, to restore the monarchy (16). Thanks to the revolutionary monsters, "the king will reascend his throne with all his pomp and power, perhaps even with an increase of power" (16). Thus will the "black magic" (17) that has created those monsters finally destroy itself, working its own damnation.

The rhetoric of monstrosity, moreover, crops up in Jacobin as well as anti-Jacobin accounts of the Revolution. For Tom Paine and William Godwin, the monsters to blame for the Revolution are the aristocracy and the clergy, or "force" and "fraud" (Paine 81). Paine hopes that the Revolution will "exterminate the monster, aristocracy, root and branch" (92), while Godwin writes: "The feudal system was a ferocious monster, devouring, wherever it came, all that the friend of humanity regards with attachment and love" (*Political Justice* 476). If the revolutionary movement itself has grown monstrous, that is because of the prior monstrosity that has misruled France and the rest of Europe through the ages. More ambiguously, in her *Historical and Moral View of the ... French Revolution* (1794), Mary Wollstonecraft distinguishes sharply between "the people," who conduct themselves rationally and heroically, and "the mob" of "ruffians" and "vagabonds," who, among other dastardly acts, invaded the Tuileries and tried to murder the king and queen. This event was, she writes, "one of the blackest of the machinations that have since the revolution disgraced the dignity of man":

> ... these wretches beheaded two of the guards, who fell into their hands; and hurried away towards the metropolis, with the *insignia* of their atrocity on the

points of the barbarous instruments of vengeance [pikes]—showing . . . by the difference of their conduct, that they were a set of monsters, distinct from the people. (206)

Part of what Burke identifies as monstrous about the Revolution is "the very idea of the fabrication of a new government," which "is enough to fill us with disgust and horror" (117). Burke insists that "the science of constructing a commonwealth . . . is . . . not to be taught *a priori*" (152). Hobbes may have called society an "artificial man," but for Burke the artifice pertains more to nature than to human powers, and is in any case not repeatable. The attempt by the National Assembly to write a new constitution will produce a textual "monster," which if it remains in force will bring ruin to the French economy (313). In contrast to this recent attempt at legislative counterfeiting, the British constitution is the largely unwritten, slow growth of the ages, based on the generous principle of "inheritance" rather than on the selfish and short-sighted "spirit of innovation" (119). This is not to say that the "liberal descent" of the British constitution is independent of writing and documentation: "It has a pedigree and illustrating ancestors. It has its bearings and its ensigns armorial. It has its gallery of portraits; its monumental inscriptions; its records, evidences, and titles" (121). It is just such old documents and "inscriptions" that the Jacobins have scrapped in order to write the new constitution by their "false lights" (124). Nevertheless, Burke registers his suspicion about the legitimacy or authenticity of *any* sort of writing: from his perspective, *any* act involving the inscription of a new authority in place of the old begins to seem monstrous, while antiquity—the only sure gauge of authority, according to Burke—merges into a prehistory, an origin in nature or an authenticity prior to literacy, a Logos before language.

In much the same way, de Maistre rejects the idea of "a written constitution, such as that which rules the French today" (de Maistre 57). The new, written constitution of 1793 "is only an automaton possessing merely the exterior appearance of life"—a sort of monster, in short.[5] According to de Maistre, "Although written laws are merely declarations of anterior rights, it is far from true that everything can be written down; in fact there are always some things in every [national] constitution that cannot be written and that must be allowed to remain in dark and reverent obscurity on pain of upsetting the state" (50). This version of legislation and legitimacy suggests government on the basis of Burke's theory of the sublime, one key to Gothic romanticism; if so, however, its focus would be on terror, the main emotion evoked by sublimity, as much as on reverence. De Maistre, after all, makes the executioner, along with the Pope, one of the two essential functionaries of the absolutism he defends. In any event, in regard to writing, de Maistre adds, "The more that is written, the weaker the institution becomes" (50).

The suspicions about writing expressed by both Burke and de Maistre were partly extensions of their profound distrust of mass literacy, of empowering the wrong people to read and write, and therefore to begin questioning and attempting to rewrite the forms of traditional authority. But anti-Enlightenment thinkers were caught in a dilemma: they had to use what, at least on some subliminal level, they considered to be the monster-producing instruments of terror—reason, representation, writing, literacy—to oppose those very instruments. The only way to combat the false publications of the *philosophes* and Jacobins was through more publication, also appealing to that rapidly growing monstrosity, the reading public. It was not the case that the "swinish multitude" was trampling all "learning" into "the mire." Instead, a new, alternative learning (or superstition, or ideology), produced (indeed, mass-produced) by treasonous "Men of Letters," was supplanting the old.[6] Burke, de Maistre, and other opponents of the Revolution had no recourse but to oppose this new learning or superstition with a textual production of their own, also appealing to the reading monster, the new, mass public and its wraith-like "opinion." Anti-Enlightenment texts are thus always, like Hannah More's "Mr. Fantom," versions of writing as *pharmakon*, both poison and antidote.

II

Burke's "swinish multitude" phrase stirred up so much hostile commentary partly because numerous members of that "multitude" could read and many of them could write back. E. P. Thompson states that "no other words have ever made the 'free-born Englishman' so angry—nor so ponderous in reply" (90). The wrath aroused in the radical press by Burke's figure of the "swinish multitude" also forms part of the context of Coleridge's remarks about the monstrosity of the "reading public" in *The Statesman's Manual*, remarks underscored by the Burkean images of "the learned pig" and "the reading fly." Coleridge says that he would have preferred to address his "lay sermon" to "men of *clerkly* acquirements, of whatever profession," rather than to a "promiscuous audience" (36). But this is not a possibility, due to that "misgrowth of our luxuriant activity . . . [the] READING PUBLIC" (36). Coleridge adds that this is "as strange a phrase . . . as ever forced a splenetic smile on the staid countenance of Meditation" (37). Yet the "reading public" is a major modern reality, because "Readers have, in good truth, multiplied exceedingly, and have waxed proud" (37–38). This "vast company"— the new mass readership of Britain and the rest of the industrializing, democratizing world—is unfortunately "dieted at the two public *ordinaries* of Literature, the circulating libraries and the periodical press" (38). Coleridge does not exactly say that literary consumption of this sort is poisonous, but it is unsound, unhealthy ("From a popular philosophy and a philosophic populace, Good Sense deliver us!" [38]). Yet there is no turning back. Once started, the process of educating the entire populace, the nation, must continue, for "the inconveniences that have arisen" from making literacy "too general, are best removed by making it universal" (40).

However, Coleridge declares, it is also not the case that "a national education will have been realized whenever the People at large have been taught to read and write" (40). A sound system of education cannot come from a "vast moral steam engine" such as either of the competing educational programs of Joseph Lancaster and Dr. Andrew Bell. If their goal is the merely mechanistic one of teaching literacy, these mechanistic programs will result in "poisoning the children of the poor" (40). Education, says Coleridge, must consist in "*educing* the faculties, and forming the habits" in wise, loyal, and religious ways. But the enlightenment of the masses has already proceeded along revolutionary lines in France, in the United States, and is threatening to do so in Britain and the rest of Europe.

> Reflection and stirrings of mind, with all their restlessness, and all the errors that result from their imperfection, from the *Too much*, because *Too little*, are come into the world. The Powers, that awaken and foster the spirit of curiosity, are to be found in every village: Books are in every hovel. The Infant's cries are hushed with *picture*-books: and the Cottager's child sheds his first bitter tears over pages, which render it impossible for the man to be treated or governed as a child. (39–40)

In addition to these remarks, Coleridge provides an extended footnote about the reading public in which he quotes at length from a text similar to Tom Paine's *Common Sense*. This passage, one that Coleridge himself may have composed as a parody of Paine and other radical intellectuals, champions "the READING PUBLIC in this ENLIGHTENED AGE, and THINKING NATION," against the "prejudices" and "superstitious awe" of the "*Dark Age*" in which "scholastic jargon" helped to "deform our Church-establishment" after the image of "the grostesque figures in the nitches of our old gothic cathedrals" (36–37). Coleridge continues with what he regards as further examples of the absurdity of Enlightenment ideas about the liberating, progressive effects of mass literacy. He claims that he has recently heard "a thinking and independent smuggler," a member of "the READING PUBLIC," arguing vociferously against the 1816 attempt by the Royal Navy to stop piracy along the Barbary Coast by forcing its rulers, including the Dey of Algiers, to comply. According to the smuggler, however, "As to Algiers, any man that has half an IDEA in his skull, must know, that it has been long ago dey-monstered, I should say, dey-monstrified, &c"—the smuggler means "demonstrated" (37). These monstrous malapropisms by a smuggling member of the reading public leads Coleridge to the presumably parallel example of the Dutch traveller who, having witnessed the feats of "THE LEARNED PIG" in a showman's caravan, "met another caravan of a similar shape, with THE READING FLY on it. . . ." The Dutchman exclaims, "Why, dis is voonders above voonders!" and he keeps on wondering until his error is corrected by the announcement that this particular "fly" is bound for Reading. Coleridge offers the moral that "a Reading Public is (to my mind) more marvellous still" than the idea of "the reading fly" (37–38).[7]

If images of bestial readers such as the Learned Pig and the Reading Fly are expressions of anxiety about mass literacy, an analogous expression can be seen in Mary Shelley's startling figure of the reading monster. Sterrenburg demonstrates how "Frankenstein's Monster . . . rises from the body of the writings on the French Revolution" (152). *Frankenstein* converts the "political monster" of the anti-Jacobins, as in Burke and de Maistre, into the depoliticized, psychological conflict between Victor and his monstrous alter ego. The "formal subjectivity" of Mary Shelley's nightmarish family romance "subverts the clear, definable melodrama of external ideological causes" that characterized both Jacobin and anti-Jacobin discourse in the 1790s. "The world [after 1815] is . . . much more problematic. Monsters are still abroad, but we are no longer quite sure why" (Sterrenburg 157). In part, *Frankenstein* registers Mary Shelley's retreat from the revolutionary radicalism of her husband and her parents, a retreat that she did not fully articulate until 1838.[8] The result is that *Frankenstein* expresses a deep political ambivalence, so that the "hybrid" Monster can be interpreted in both Jacobin and anti-Jacobin terms. Thus, the Monster "suffers the consequences of two symbolic traditions" (Sterrenburg 165).

Frankenstein is so overloaded with ambivalent psychological as well as political meanings that it can be, and has been, interpreted in many conflicting yet persuasive ways. With the French Revolution as general context, Victor can be seen as representing *either* aristocratic oppression *or* Enlightenment rationality and radicalism (given his father's liberal politics and his obvious identification with scientific rationality, the latter interpretation seems more convincing). From the perspectives of psychoanalytic and feminist theory, Victor can also be understood as an abusive or criminally negligent parent of either gender—a father-creator in some sense rivaling God (and therefore a stand-in for Satan), *or* a monstrous mother-figure giving birth to a monster child and then abandoning it.[9] The obscene father of *Otranto*, *The Monk*, and other Gothic romances becomes the obscene son, whose pleasure arises from the destruction of family. But this obscene son is also a victim, who may be variously read as the abandoned child, the oppressed masses, the unconscious or Id to Victor's Ego, or himself a demon or even the devil. Based on his reading of *Paradise Lost*, the Monster likens himself *both* to Adam *and* to Lucifer. To put it mildly, the possible meanings proliferate. As Chris Baldick suggests, this is one of the ways in which *Frankenstein* itself acquires an anti-formal monstrosity, an uncontrollable, irrational excess of signification that transcends the boundaries of normal, comprehensible discourse.

The discursive excess of *Frankenstein* can simultaneously be identified as sublimity, as insanity, and as literary deformity. In her 1831 "Author's Introduction," Mary Shelley famously describes the origin of her Gothic romance in the ghost-story contest with her husband, Lord Byron, and Dr. Polidori, and in the vivid waking nightmare in which "I saw the pale student of unhallowed arts kneeling beside the thing he had put together. I saw the hideous phantasm of a man stretched out, and then, on the working of some powerful engine, show signs of life" (172). As in the example of *Otranto*, nightmare becomes novel through verbal elaboration, with the image of the Monster at its core. The introduction also parallels the main story, both in narrating a creation, a metaphoric birth, and in embedding one story within another, the nightmare within the larger essay. Victor Frankenstein's creation-story thus mirrors Mary Shelley's creation-story. In this labyrinth of mirror-like, embedded stories, Monster and novel become interchangeable. In some sense, so do Monster and novelist. The more obvious parallel is between novelist and mad scientist, both the creators of the Monster. But the central, basic story-within-story of the introduction is the nightmare; and the central, basic story-within-story of the main novel is the Monster's narration. When Mary Shelley ends her introduction by bidding her "hideous progeny [to] go forth and prosper" (173), the identification is complete: the novel itself is the ultimate monstrosity, a transgressive discourse that apparently obeys no literary rules, that is in many ways grotesque, nightmarish, and therefore all the more powerful and effective as a tale of terror that, as Daniel Cottom puts it, "images the monstrous nature of [all] representation" (66).[10]

Frankenstein is, among other things, a novel about two educations or, rather, *mis*educations, Victor's and the Monster's.[11] To the extent that Victor pursues his course of reading and research in isolation and against the advice of his father and his professors, he is a sort of autodidact—willfully so, because he chooses isolation. In contrast, the Monster is perforce an autodidact, in some respects similar to the working-class autodidacts whose autobiographies serve as a rich source of evidence in E. P. Thompson's *Making of the English Working Class*. Victor's education is upper-class, indulgent, liberal in at least two senses. Victor's father is a political liberal, residing in liberal Geneva, and Victor's schooling, with its emphasis on natural science, reflects Enlightenment principles. Yet in isolation, Victor's reading leads him obsessively, regressively backward to Gothic superstition. Reading—and therefore knowledge—is not intrinsically progressive, and even the best educations can backfire.

In his pursuit of the knowledge that will enable him to create life, Victor turns to works of Gothic alchemy and the "exploded systems" of Cornelius Agrippa, Paracelsus, and Albertus Magnus, though his father dismisses their writings as "sad trash" (21).[12] Victor's course of Gothic reading makes him a sort of scientific Quixote figure, though instead of chivalric romances, the texts he consumes are anti-Bibles, like the necromantic "small book" that allows Ambrosio to conjure up the Devil at the end of *The Monk*. At Ingolstadt, he is told again, this time by Professor Krempe, that he has been reading "sad trash," or what might be called Gothic science fiction (perhaps like *Frankenstein* itself):

> "Every minute . . . that you have wasted on those books is utterly and entirely lost. You have burdened your memory with exploded systems, and useless names. Good God! In what desert land have you lived, where no one was kind enough to inform you that these fancies . . . are a thousand years old, and as musty as they are ancient? I little expected in this enlightened and scientific age to find a disciple of Albertus Magnus and Paracelsus." (26)

Professor Waldman, however, whom Frankenstein next consults, is of the different, more sympathetic opinion that modern science has developed out of the "exploded systems" of the past. Therefore, the ideas of the creators of those systems may still be worth studying, if only to avoid their errors.

Through Waldman, Shelley suggests a continuity between medieval alchemy and modern chemistry. But in stressing this continuity, she also renders undecidable whether the Monster's creation is the result of modern science or of black magic. In one direction, her horror story appears to be pro-Enlightenment: Professor Krempe and Victor's father both reject the "exploded systems" of the past as so much superstition. In another, more powerful direction, however, *Frankenstein* is an anti-Enlightenment text. As has often been noted, it offers the paradigmatic science fiction tale of "the dream of reason producing monsters," or in other words of modern science run amock through the overreaching ambition and obsession of the mad scientist. From either direction, moreover, reading—or at least, reading in isolation from human companionship and community—is represented as a dangerous activity, leading to insanity.

The Monster's *Bildungsroman* both parallels and contrasts with Victor's. Learning to speak and to read in isolation, the Monster at least vicariously enjoys the humanizing companionship of Old DeLacey, Felix, Agatha, and Safie. The family circle the Monster longs to join represents everything that Victor, in his obsessive pursuit of the secrets of life and death, has rejected. When his potential adoptive family rejects him, the Monster sets forth on his path of vengeance, destroying Victor's family and friends. As in anti-Jacobin discourse about the Revolution, according to which the *philosophes* conjure up the monstrous mob, *Frankenstein* is a negative family romance for both protagonists.[13]

The story of Victor's pursuit of arcane, in some sense forbidden knowledge involves his self-alienation—loss of self-knowledge, insanity, destruction. The story of the Monster's acquisition of language and literacy is, in contrast, the narrative of his coming to self-knowledge, though for him self-knowledge and self-alienation are identical:

> I had admired the perfect forms of my cottagers . . . but how was I terrified, when I viewed myself in a transparent pool! At first I started back, unable to believe that it was indeed I who was reflected in the mirror; and when I became fully convinced that I was in reality the monster that I am, I was filled with the bitterest sensations. . . . (76)

The Monster recognizes his monstrosity in a moment of reflection like Lacan's mirror-stage, reinforced by his more or less simultaneous acquisition of language.[14] In discovering his own monstrosity, moreover, the Monster also discovers that of the humans who reject him and, indeed, that of human history in general. The Monster eavesdrops as Felix instructs Safie in French by reading Volney's *Ruins* to her, from which he obtains his first "cursory knowledge of history" (80). The other books the Monster accidentally acquires and then reads (*Paradise Lost*, Plutarch's *Lives*, and Goethe's *Sorrows of Young Werther*) deal with cosmic, public, and private themes, and "constitute a possible Romantic *cyclopedia universalis*" (Brooks 210). All three additional texts reinforce the main history lesson he has learned from Volney's *Ruins*, which is also the main lesson of his dawning self-awareness and therefore of his entire education: "sorrow only increased with knowledge" (81). With this melancholy lesson in mind, the Monster declares, romantically if rather incoherently, that it would have been better if "I had for ever remained in my native wood, nor known or felt beyond the sensations of hunger, thirst, and heat!" (81)

From his self-education, Mary Shelley's sympathetically chaotic, homicidal creature develops the reasoning and rhetorical power to challenge his creator, just as Caleb Williams challenges and ultimately defeats Falkland through speaking and writing. Caleb's literacy enables him to forge the weapon—the novel itself —with which he ultimately kills his aristocratic persecutor. So, too, the Monster is in some sense the author of the murderous text in which he is also one of the dual protagonists, the author or narrator of his own tale of terror to Victor, of course, but also the crucial, most vital image in the originary nightmare, *its* cause or "most powerful engine." His transgression of literary, discursive boundaries is rendered possible only through his acquisition of the power of language, his ability, despite great disadvantages, to become both a speaking and a reading Monster.

Though able to read and to speak with great eloquence, the Monster may or may not be able to write. His narrative is (only) an oral one, and so is Victor's to Robert Walton, who then transcribes both oral accounts in his journal and, later, in letters to his sister. As Garrett Stewart notes, however, these letters are "never definitively received by the sister back in England to whom they are addressed" (116).[15] The reader "receives" them, of course, but *Frankenstein* is a tale in which, Stewart suggests, the reader's own identity is questioned or called into crisis. Both *Frankenstein* and *The Last Man* (1826) invoke "an attention whose person-ification they finally obliterate"—in the case of *The Last Man*, quite simply be-cause the narrator of Shelley's apocalyptic tale is also the world's "last author, sole survivor of a universal plague, [who] has no conceivable readers left." But the "conscripted" readers of *Frankenstein* also are not clearly "the solid bour-geois citizen, the stablized monolithic presence" invoked by Dickens, Trollope, and George Eliot (Stewart 115).

As with other Gothic romances, only perhaps more pointedly, *Frankenstein* seems to pose a *caveat lector* question by its own questionable narrative struc-ture: who is reading this "hideous progeny" and with what possibly dire conse-quences? The reader of *Frankenstein* who accepts it at face value—who literally credits the story as true—must be at least as impressionable and irrational as Victor in his imbibing of the "sad trash" of the alchemists, or as the Monster in his first, halting reading lessons. On the other hand, the skeptical reader of *Franken-stein* who sees it for what it is—"hideous progeny," "sad trash," incredible sto-ries-within-story—must, besides doubting what she or he reads, be in some sense an even more doubtful, indeterminate figure than the believing reader. Whether doubting or credulous, why would *any* reader in her or his right mind, *Franken-stein* seems to ask, read its multiple tales of terror? Far more than in most realistic fiction, in Gothic romances the reader is "conscripted" as a sort of shadowy or ghostly extra, just offstage, who may or may not partake of (or believe in) the action, but whose very involvement with the tale is both questioning and called into question. As Stewart says, both *Frankenstein* and *The Last Man* invoke a readerly "attention whose personification they finally obliterate" (115). In *The Last Man*, of course, the obliteration of the implied reader is also the obliteration of reading and writing, of civilization, of humanity. But in both romances, and in Gothic more generally, the critique of Enlightenment rationality involves also a critique of the very motives for reading and writing—indeed, of writing and reading such questionable texts as Gothic romances: the very tale the reader consumes, or, better, the very act of reading the tale turns into a demonstration of the monstrous uses to which literacy can be put.

III

What has seemed ultimately most monstrous and therefore most difficult for readers of *Frankenstein* over the years to accept is precisely the Monster's literacy. The key to the obsessive erasure of that literacy in retellings of *Frankenstein* on stage, in film, and in other popular cultural forms seems to reside in the Monster's evident likeness to that other, collective monstrosity, Burke's "swinish multitude"—that is, to the working-class masses. Like the collective, "many-headed monster" of the crowd in Shakespeare and other Renaissance writers, Mary Shelley's Monster is, after all, multiple, made out of the body-parts of various dead individuals. Whether or not she had Hobbes's trope of society as a gigantic "artificial man" in mind, some such notion is reinforced also by the multiplying narrators in her story (including herself as the ultimate dreamer-author): the novel itself seems to be, or to acknowledge being, a collective creation. Moreover, despite the absence of explicit political references in her nightmare novel, that there is a social-class fantasy at work in its political unconscious has seemed evident to many of its interpreters. Thus, besides Sterrenburg and Baldick, both Franco Moretti and Paul O'Flinn read *Frankenstein* in Marxist terms as an allegory of class conflict. For Moretti, "the literature of terror" in general "is born precisely *out of the terror of a split society*," and in the case of *Frankenstein*, the "sociological fulcrum" is "the creation of the proletariat" during the Industrial Revolution (83, 89; see also Lovell 64–67). For O'Flinn, besides the French Revolution, the more specific context in which Mary Shelley hatched her "hideous progeny" was that of the Luddite machine-breaking rebellion of 1811–1813, the uprising that Charlotte Brontë would later depict in her industrial novel, *Shirley*. Furthermore, as Howard Malchow argues in his study of "Gothic images of race" in nineteenth-century fiction, an equally persuasive interpretation of the Monster identifies him with the oppressed African in discourse about the West Indies and slavery, a connection explicitly invoked in parliamentary debates about abolition (Malchow 33).

Especially in stage versions, the mute Monster, with darkened or, perhaps, Africanized skin color, conjured up the slavery controversy. But this "Calibanized" version of the Monster was still associated with the "wage-slave" at home in Britain. Also identifying the Monster with the working class, Daniel Cottom points to the Caliban-like labor that the Monster performs for the cottagers—only, unlike Caliban's, his labor seems to those he bestows it upon as if "performed by an invisible hand," a trope that echoes Adam Smith's "invisible hand" of the marketplace: "The source of fertility and wealth is described as the labor of a monster that is man's creation, and the class-analysis to which this passage lends itself is carried over to modern economic conditions through . . . Smith's famous image for the unconscious regulation of a laissez-faire market" (Cottom 66).

But Smith's "invisible hand" is not the numerous hands of the working class. In any case, as Chris Baldick demonstrates, the connection between Frankenstein's Monster and the working-class masses was made early and often in the nineteenth century. In her 1848 novel about Manchester factory workers, *Mary Barton*, Elizabeth Gaskell likens them to the Monster, only in doing so she both identifies the creature with his creator and divests him of his education and, indeed, his language:

> The actions of the uneducated seem to me typified in those of Frankenstein, that monster of many human qualities, ungifted with a soul, a knowledge of the difference between good and evil.
>
> The people rise up to life; they irritate us, they terrify us, and we become their enemies. Then, in the sorrowful moment of our triumphant power, their eyes gaze on us with a mute reproach. Why have we made them what they are; a powerful monster, yet without the inner means for peace and happiness? (219–220)

Both Gaskell's identification of the Monster with his maker and her erasure of its education, rendering it inarticulate or "mute," are repeated endlessly in later mass-cultural retellings of Mary Shelley's story. The dumbing down of the Monster actually commenced earlier than *Mary Barton*, however. In *Presumption: or the Fate of Frankenstein*, Richard Brinsley Peake's 1823 dramatic rendering (the first stage version), the Monster has already been silenced, endowed only with "the mind of an infant" (Baldick 59). Similarly, in "The New Frankenstein," a story published in *Fraser's Magazine* in 1838, "what is 'new' about the monster of this tale is really only the established pattern of the stage versions: that it is mute and that its problem is largely one of possessing no soul" (Baldick 141).

But why, when the Monster has been stripped of a soul as well as his education, rendering him wordless, has it been so easy to confuse him with his educated, articulate maker by calling him "Frankenstein"? A simplistic answer is that, because the Monster is nameless, it makes sense to give him his father-maker's name. Also, from a psychoanalytic perspective, the mute Monster of stage and screen has seemed most readily understandable as an emanation of Victor's psyche, his Id personified. The Monster may be Victor's alter ego, his murderous phantom or *Doppelgänger*, his Id or his *petit objet a*, even his "sublime object of ideology," but it is only Victor who is identified with consciousness and, hence, with language.[16] Victor/Ego speaks, reads, and writes; Monster/Id, the Real that remains forever outside the Symbolic Order, cannot. Yet they are the two halves of a divided self. Victor's numerous declarations of guilt for the murders that the Monster commits, coupled with his long bouts of either profound depression or raving lunacy, help to make the conflation easy; and that easy identification of the Monster with its maker, so often replicated in movies, comics, advertising, and television, is both an additional incoherence or monstrosity within the story and a tangent of the proliferating, often contradictory meanings that radiate from it.

Within the novel, the *Doppelgänger* motif that promotes slippages like Gaskell's is reinforced by the dual narratives of Monster and maker. The Monster's narrative is filtered through Victor's, and both are in turn filtered through Robert Walton. That the Monster, though if anything more eloquent and rational than Victor, speaks only through the ventriloquism of Victor (and Walton) encourages both his identification with his creator and the erasure of his demoniac literacy, which is also his ability to represent himself. If the subaltern speaks in Mary Shelley's Gothic romance, it does so only by being spoken for by another, dominant voice—one that, however, attributes to the Monster an amazing literacy and eloquence.

If *Mary Barton* is symptomatic, that the Monster's literacy gets so completely, obsessively erased in his later incarnations has partly to do with middle-class fears of mass, working-class literacy. In *The French Revolution, Chartism*, and *Past and Present*, although he does not allude to *Frankenstein*, Carlyle repeatedly likens the working class to a "dumb," inarticulate, "delirious" monster, Titan, or giant. The French "masses" are "a kind of dim compendious unity, monstrous but dim" (28). Even when "these waste multitudes" appear at Versailles to present a written "Petitition of Grievances," it is a petition "in Hieroglyphics" (28–29). As in Burke's *Reflections*, so in Carlyle's account of revolutionary France: the philosophes and journalists have created a "Paper Age" (23–49), including even "ever fresh Novel-garbage, [which] as of old, fodders the Circulating Libraries" (636). This literate or overly literate culture—"eleutheromaniac Philosophedom" (37)—is, Carlyle thinks, a main cause of the Revolution. "Journalism," as in the case of Marat, is nothing less than the "voice of the People," which Carlyle, perhaps ironically, identifies as "the voice of God" (250). Nevertheless, "the People" or "the masses" are "monstrous," inarticulate, and cannot speak or write for themselves, but must be spoken for by, for instance, the "National Palaver," Parlement (250). Carlyle applies the same rhetoric to the Chartists, who in 1839 presented their Charter to Parliament in writing, with thousands of their signatures affixed to it. Nevertheless, Carlyle calls the Chartists "these wild inarticulate souls, struggling there, with inarticulate uproar, like dumb creatures in pain, unable to speak what is in them!" (*Chartism* 169). There are, it appears, articulate or "speaking classes," and then there are "the masses," to whom the "inarticulate" Chartists belong: "The speaking classes speak and debate, each for itself; the great dumb, deep-buried class lies like an Enceladus, who in his pain, if he will complain of it, has to produce earthquakes" (*Chartism* 222). While Carlyle also insists that "Chartism with its pikes, [Captain] Swing with his tinderbox, speak a most loud though inarticulate language" (191), the stress seems to be on "inarticulate": the "language" spoken is not a written or even, exactly, a spoken one; it is the "language" of events, which are themselves, Carlyle says, "written lessons, glaring in huge hieroglyphic picture-writing, that all may read and know them" (196–197). But this apocalyptic "picture-writing" is, in a sense, the exact opposite of literacy, the undoing or subversion of the hypocritical or myopic reading, writing, and speechifying that goes on among the "speaking classes" and within the walls of their nearly useless institution, Parliament, the "National Palaver."

So Carlyle simultaneously denies articulation to the "giant" working class, while granting it an apocalyptic power to "speak" through events like the French Revolution. These events, in turn, threaten to end altogether the speechifying, treatises, journalism, sermons, and novels of the "speaking" and literate classes. At the same time, nowhere in either *Chartism* or *Past and Present* does Carlyle bother to examine the Charter or any other document produced by the working class. Chartism is simply "delirious Chartism"; trade unionism boils down to "Glasgow Thuggery"; rural discontent equals Captain Swing and rick-burning, and the multiplying miseries of the "dumb," "inarticulate" millions have already marched, burned, and pillaged far down the road toward an English version of the French Revolution, that "frenzied giant" (*Chartism* 166, 194).

In *The Condition of the Working Class in England in 1844*, Engels also does not mention *Frankenstein*, though like Carlyle he emphasizes the monstrosity of both sides in capitalist class conflict. Unlike Carlyle, however, he stresses the learning and, indeed, progressive, vanguard knowledge of a leading segment of the workers. Their radical, working-class literacy, gained for the most part, according to Engels, through self-education, poses a major, immediate, monstrous threat to the bourgeoisie. As Engels narrates it, the story of the proletarian acquisition of literacy and knowledge is one simultaneously of rejection and neglect by the bourgeoisie and of independent struggle, self-education or "the pursuit of knowledge against difficulties," by the workers.[17] "From a moral point of view, as in the physical and intellectual spheres, the workers are neglected and spurned by the possessing classes," Engels declares. Treated like "dumb beasts," the workers "either behave like beasts or are able to maintain their self-respect as human beings only by continually harbouring hatred of the powerful oppressors" (Engels 129). Nevertheless, despite numerous obstacles and, at best, only sham education provided them by the bourgeoisie, "the workers are actually in the vanguard of the national movement":

> Although the average worker can hardly read, let alone write, he nevertheless has a shrewd notion of where his own interest and that of his country lie. He knows, too, where the selfish interest of the bourgeoisie lies. . . . He may not be able to write, but he can at least speak and he can speak in public. (128)

And "speak" he does, of course, mostly in the quotations from parliamentary reports that Engels quotes in his text: workers narrating bits of their experience just as the Monster narrates his experience inside and through the mad scientist's narrative.

Moreover, Engels later points out, "There can be no doubt that the workers are interested in acquiring a sound education," and many of them are doing so mainly through their own reading rooms and "working-class institutes" (272). As a result, "the most important modern works in philosophy, poetry and politics are in practice read only by the proletariat" (272), much to the chagrin of the bourgeoisie, who are "horror-stricken at the very idea of reading anything of a really progressive nature" (272). Engels then provides a list of some of the "progressive" works and their authors, including "such great French materialist philosophers as Helvétius, Holbach and Diderot . . . Strauss's *Life of Jesus* and . . . Proudhon's book on *Property* . . . the poetry of Byron and Shelley [and the works of] Bentham and Godwin" (272–273). In contrast, if the middle classes read any of these writers (except for Bentham), it is only the poetry of Byron and Shelley, and then only in "ruthlessly expurgated 'family' editions . . . prepared to suit the hypocritical moral standards of the bourgeoisie" (272–273).

Despite the "progressive" nature of their self-education, most of the working-class voices in Engels's text are deformed, monstrous. When he quotes from the 1842 parliamentary investigation into the condition of women and children in the mines and other occupations, it is to show how "steeped in ignorance" most workers are (126). Against the claims of their masters and of various middle-class reformers to be doing their best to educate the proletariat, the brutalized workers behave like brutes. "The uneducated worker is wholly ignorant of the simple principles which should regulate the behaviour of human beings towards one another in society" (129). But the response of the workers is a divided one. "Treated like dumb beasts," many of them "become animals as soon as they submit patiently to their yoke, and try to drag out a bearable existence under it without attempting to break free" (129). In contrast, a minority of workers manage to educate themselves and assert their humanity, though as a result of their learning and literacy they become all the more dangerous. Like Mary Shelley's Monster, the more human the workers become, the more they "cherish a burning fury" against their masters (129).

But also as in *Frankenstein*, it takes a monster to make a monster. There is only the single "Frankenstein," the monstrous working class, in *Mary Barton*. In Engels's text, however, as in the Jacobin writings of Tom Paine, William Godwin, and Mary Wollstonecraft, monstrosity pervades class society, and the most powerful monsters are on the bourgeois side of the barricades. These middle-class monsters are versions of Carlyle's Mammon and of his "Steam Demon," straight from "a murky-simmering Tophet" (Engels quotes Carlyle at length [132]). They are cannibal monsters, moreover, threatening or devouring the workers and their families, like the one in Edward Mead's poem "The Steam King," which Engels reproduces from the Chartist newspaper *The Northern Star*. This "monster God" is a "Moloch King," and "children are his food":

> His priesthood are a hungry band,
> Blood-thirsty, proud, and bold;
> 'Tis they direct his giant hand,
> In turning blood to gold. (209)[18]

But again, as do both Carlyle and Marx, Engels stresses that monsters breed monsters and that the bourgeoisie, through the creation of the exploited, brutalized proletariat, is digging its own grave. Though the workers are currently the victims of the monstrous selfishness of the bourgeoisie, the time will come when they will take collective action: "Popular fury will reach an intensity far greater than that which animated the French workers in 1793. The war of the poor against the rich will be the most bloodthirsty the world has ever seen" (334). In relation to mass literacy, Engels draws the obvious moral several times in his account: the more the workers acquire genuine education and enlightenment, the sooner their revolutionary revenge will come.

All of the monsters bred by and in the shadow of the French Revolution are, to greater or lesser extent, enlightened; they are all the Gothic spawn of the Enlightenment. Terror, the phantasmal domain of monsters, proves to be the domain also of literacy and "learning." If in Burke's *Reflections* "the age of chivalry" has given way to that of "sophisters, oeconomists, and calculators" with their "mechanic philosophy" of the gallows (and soon after Burke wrote, of the guillotine, that mechanical monstrosity), these "political Men of Letters" are the ultimate monsters of the Revolution.[19] So, too, in *Frankenstein*, the ultimate monster is the highly enlightened mad scientist. But the Monster that Victor's higher education allows him to create also acquires an education. The Monster learns to speak with such rhetorical force that he seems more rational and articulate than his creator, who plays "the conventional role of the experimenting *philosophe*-scientist," as Sterrenburg puts it; "but [who] raves like a mad demon." In contrast, assigned "the role of the mad, Jacobin demon, risen from the grave to spread havoc abroad," the Monster nevertheless speaks more calmly, rationally, and philosophically than does his creator (Sterrenburg 161).

Even more to the point in terms of middle-class anxiety about mass literacy, the Monster's story dominates that of his maker. While it is true that he speaks (and, in a sense, writes) only through the doubled narration of Victor and Captain Walton, this subaltern's story is the heart and soul, the reason for being, both of the entire novel and of its author's originary nightmare. The disfigured figure of monstrous articulation and literacy *is*, in a figurative sense, the novel—or rather, it is *both* the novel and the reading Monster, ourselves as readers (members of Burke's "swinish multitude," whether we like it or not). Thus do text and Monster imaginatively fuse, transgressing the boundaries of polite, rational literature and discourse and therefore threatening the boundaries of civil society as well, at once the creation and the subversion of enlightenment, a "hideous progeny" haunting modern culture.

4

How Oliver Twist Learned to Read, and What He Read

> The question about everything was, would it bring a blush into
> the cheek of the young person?
> —Charles Dickens, *Our Mutual Friend.*

A fter running away from Sowerberry the undertaker, Oliver rests by a milestone that tells him he has seventy miles to go to London. This isn't surprising, unless one questions how Oliver can read the milestone. It seems unlikely
that a pauper orphan would know how to read—"picking oakum" is the chief
education he gets from the workhouse—and all Sowerberry teaches him is how to
look mournful at funerals.

Perhaps it is Oliver's good fortune that, discounting Fagin's anti-school for
pickpockets, he never attends any school. Throughout Dickens's novels, schools
—from Squeers's in *Nicholas Nickleby* to Gradgrind's in *Hard Times*—are often
places of tyrannical miseducation. Noah Claypole has been to a charity school,
which seems to have taught him nothing but cruelty and low cunning; though
apparently better educated than Oliver, Noah, alias "Morris Bolter," joins the
criminals. But maybe Dickens says nothing about Oliver's schooling because he
takes it for granted. In fact there were schools for pauper children in the late
1830s. Even under the Old Poor Law a pauper schoolmaster might teach in a
parish workhouse: a kindly old man fills that role in the first of the *Sketches by
Boz*. But it was more often the case, as one historian of "schools for the people"
wrote in 1871, that "the only sort of information which the [workhouse] young
had to interest them, was a rehearsal of the exciting deeds of the poacher and the
smuggler, or the . . . adventures of abandoned females" (Bartley 274). On the other
hand, the Benthamite drafters of the New Poor Law of 1834 stressed education as
the key to eliminating pauperism (West 134). Yet well into the 1840s little progress

was made toward providing adequate workhouse schools. Qualified teachers were nonexistent, salaries rock-bottom, and classroom conditions wretched.

Nevertheless, a child in Oliver's circumstances *might* have learned how to read, though probably not very well. An 1838 survey of about five hundred workhouse children ages nine to sixteen showed that 87 percent could read at a minimal level or better, though only 53 percent knew how to write (West 39). More surprising than Oliver's literacy is the fact that the thieves can read. Of course Fagin is literate; he regularly reads *The Hue and Cry*, an actual police gazette containing the latest crime reports.[1] After the Dodger is arrested on only a minor charge, Charlie Bates laments that his friend may never be written up in *The Newgate Calendar*—literary fame of sorts (*Oliver Twist* 390). Even Sikes can read. Although he worries about the Juvenile Delinquent Society's spoiling boys by teaching them to read and write, Sikes learns about Fagin's arrest from a newspaper (447). And when Nancy meets Mr. Brownlow and Rose Maylie at midnight on London Bridge, she tells them that she had almost turned back because of "horrible thoughts of death, and shrouds with blood upon them. . . . I was reading a book tonight . . . and the same things came into the print . . . I'll swear I saw 'coffin' written in every page . . . in large black letters" (490).

In a novel full of improbabilities, a few more may seem insignificant. But books and reading are a central feature of the story, as is more obviously the question of Oliver's education. Will his ultimate teachers be Brownlow and the Maylies, or Fagin and Sikes? It is while Brownlow examines a bookseller's wares that the Dodger and Charlie Bates pick his pocket. It is while returning books to that same bookseller that Oliver is recaptured by the thieves, who make great fun of his apparent bookishness. Between these episodes, Oliver is impressed by the "great number of books" in Brownlow's house—books written, as the narrator says, "to make the world wiser"—and Brownlow tells Oliver: "You shall read them, if you behave well" (145). He adds that Oliver may one day "grow up a clever man [and] write books," although Oliver replies that he would just as soon read them and, perhaps, be a bookseller himself.

I

The motif of books and reading in *Oliver Twist* does not entail a contrast between literacy and illiteracy, but between two dramatically different sorts of reading. The first is represented by Brownlow's library—books "written to make the world wiser." The second, which I shall call criminal reading, is represented by the text that Fagin makes Oliver read just before Sikes takes him to burglarize the Maylies. Fagin insists that Oliver keep a candle burning so that he can read the book, and then locks him up with it. Oliver

> turned over the leaves. . . . It was a history of the lives and trials of great criminals, and the pages were soiled and thumbed with use. Here, he read of dreadful crimes that made the blood run cold; of secret murders that had been committed

by the lonely wayside [and] of men . . . tempted . . . to such dreadful bloodshed as it made the flesh creep, and the limbs quail, to think of. The terrible descriptions were so real and vivid, that the sallow pages seemed to turn red with gore. (196)

Such criminal reading must be part of Fagin's plan to educate—or brainwash— Oliver by "slowly instilling" into the boy's "soul the poison which he hoped would blacken it, and change its hue forever" (185). Fagin's anti-Bible for criminals is probably one of the many versions of *The Newgate Calendar*. Perhaps the first was the *Compleat History of the Lives and Robberies of the Most Notorious Highwaymen, Foot-Pads, Shop-Lifts, and Cheats*, published in 1719. The long list of such books includes *The Tyburn Chronicle* of 1768, *The Malefactor's Bloody Register* of 1796, and George Borrow's *Celebrated Trials* of 1825, down to twentieth-century versions and reprints. In such an anthology of crime, Dickens may have read about Ikey Solomons, the most likely real-life model for Fagin.[2]

The fact that the thieves can read raises the question, much debated in the 1830s and 1840s, about the correlation between crime and education. *What* the thieves read raises the further question about a criminal or underworld culture, the mirror opposite or double of legitimate, bourgeois culture. The idea of criminal versus lawful reading is related to the popular versus high culture dichotomy, and therefore to *Oliver Twist* as a popular crime novel—indeed, to Dickens's entire career as a popular and populist writer. Does *Oliver Twist* belong in Brownlow's improving library, or is it also criminal reading? The debate in the early 1840s about the viciousness of "Newgate novels" made the answer less than clear to Dickens himself (Ford 38–43). Besides being about crime and criminals, Newgate fiction seemed to emulate the lower-class penny fiction and street literature that the respectable, middle-class novel was struggling to transcend.[3] And its very popularity was troubling, as the reception of William Harrison Ainsworth's *Jack Sheppard* demonstrates.

Dickens believed that he was on the side of law and order, but he was unnerved by the public response to *Jack Sheppard*. Ainsworth's Newgate novel began to appear in *Bentley's Miscellany* while *Oliver Twist* was still running its course in that journal. (Ainsworth succeeded his friend Dickens as editor of *Bentley's* early in 1839.) So popular was *Jack Sheppard* that by the autumn of 1839 there were eight stage versions playing in London, including a musical that helped make "flash" songs such as "Nix My Dolly, Pals, Fake Away" hits of the day. In both *Jack Sheppard* and his earlier crime novel *Rookwood*, featuring the exploits of the eighteenth-century highwayman Dick Turpin, Ainsworth seemed to champion "faking" or thieving, and so did much of the London reading and play-going public. Jack Sheppard souvenirs were sold at some theaters, including Sheppard bags containing burglars' picklocks, while the robber's putative grave at Willesden was visited by hundreds of sightseers (Hollingsworth 139–143; Ellis 1:363–380).

"Sheppard-mania," as Keith Hollingsworth calls it, might have passed harmlessly into oblivion, but on 5 May 1840, Lord William Russell was murdered by his valet, who later confessed that reading *Jack Sheppard* had inspired him to slash his master's throat. According to one journal, the murderer's confession proved that "that detestable book, 'Jack Sheppard' . . . is a publication calculated to . . . serve as the cut-throat's manual, or the midnight assassin's *vade-mecum*. . . . If ever there was a publication that deserved to be burnt by the common hangman it is *Jack Sheppard*" (qtd. in Hollingsworth 145–146). The Lord Chamberlain's Office performed its duty of policing theatrical discourse by banning all new plays about Jack Sheppard (though not the eight versions already in performance). Writing of any sort that seemed to sympathize with criminals was suddenly the target of social as well as literary critics. Along with other Newgate novelists such as Bulwer-Lytton, *Punch* accused Dickens of penning "gallows literature." In *Catherine*, his parody of Newgate fiction, which also appeared in *Punch*, Thackeray included Dickens among the writers of criminal literature:

> Breathless to watch the crimes of Fagin, tenderly to deplore the errors of Nancy, to have for Bill Sikes a kind of pity and admiration, and an absolute love for the society of the Dodger [is the result of Dickens's great but misused power as a novelist]. All these heroes stepped from the novel on to the stage; and the whole London public, from peers to chimney-sweeps, were interested about a set of ruffians whose occupations are thievery, murder, and prostitution. (*Catherine* 185)

And after the great popular success of *Oliver Twist*, "the public wanted . . . more sympathy for thieves, and so *Jack Sheppard* [made] his appearance [with] his two wives, his faithful Blueskin, and his gin-drinking mother, that sweet Magdalen!" Thackeray concludes: "in the name of common-sense, let us not expend our sympathies on cut-throats" (186).

Dickens defended himself in the 1841 preface to *Oliver Twist*, arguing that he had not romanticized crime. But his contention that portraying thieves as they really are renders them unsympathetic is feeble. No matter how realistic or even how moralizing, any crime story can be construed, or misconstrued, as teaching vice instead of virtue. Moreover, Dickens anticipated Thackeray's guilty verdict by the very inclusion in *Oliver Twist* of the motif of criminal reading. Dickens himself thus suggested the analogy between his novel and *The Newgate Calendar*. And Fagin's act of giving Oliver criminal reading reflects Dickens's belief that crime stories can make converts.

That Oliver is repelled instead of won over by Fagin's book doesn't gainsay the possibility of such a conversion. The book's "pages were soiled and thumbed with use"; perhaps it has been the main anti-Bible in Fagin's school for pickpockets. Furthermore, Oliver's improbable ability to read it has the paradoxical effect of putting him on the same level, at least educationally, with the criminals; insofar as knowledge is the antithesis of innocence, then Oliver shares something of their guilt as well as their literacy. Clearly, somewhere in Dickens's thinking lurks an equation between crime and literacy, instead of between—as might be expected—crime and illiteracy. On the mythic level, of course, knowledge and guilt have always been equated, as with Fagin's prototype Satan, while everyone knows that "ignorance is bliss." When Dickens represents illiteracy in later novels, he tends to equate it with innocence rather than crime. This is true both of Joe Gargery's painful reading lessons in *Great Expectations* and of Boffin's in *Our Mutual Friend*. In neither novel does Dickens treat learning as an unmitigated blessing. Schoolmaster Bradley Headstone turns homicidal. Joe's illiteracy corresponds to his good-natured innocence, Pip's literacy to his selfish ambition leading, like Victor Frankenstein's, to his alienation from home. Pip compares himself on two occasions to Frankenstein; his monsters are his valet and Magwitch, who ironically is also the creator of that other monster, the "gentleman" named Pip. Other literary allusions in *Great Expectations*, moreover, are nearly all to crime stories; Wopsle, for instance, belabors Pip with lines from *The London Merchant* about an apprentice who murders his master—criminal literature reinforcing Pip's guilt. In these later novels also, then, illiteracy seems less troublesome than criminal literacy or the threat posed by certain types of reading, of which *Oliver Twist* as a Newgate novel is itself an example.

But most liberal Victorians, including Dickens, believed in a direct correlation between crime and ignorance, with education as the main cure: far better to pay for schools than for prisons (see West 121–134). The epigraph to Thomas Beggs's 1849 *Inquiry into the Extent and Causes of Juvenile Depravity* defined crime as "ignorance in action." The Rev. Henry Worsley said exactly the same in his 1849 book, *Juvenile Depravity*: "The causes of ignorance are the causes of crime." And Dickens chimed in with his 1848 *Examiner* article entitled "Ignorance and Crime," advocating state education: "Side by side with Crime, Disease, and Misery in England," Dickens writes, "Ignorance is . . . certain to be found. The union of Night with Darkness is not more certain and indisputable" (1:109). Yet in *Oliver Twist*, Dickens appears to reject the equation between ignorance and crime by making his criminals readers and by pointing to the existence of a criminal literary subculture.

Besides the mythic association of knowledge with guilt, several social and ideological factors help to explain the thieves' literacy. While Dickens and many of his contemporaries believed that ignorance caused crime, they were unable to believe that illiteracy caused crime. Mounting statistical evidence indicated a correlation between criminality and *some* rather than *no* schooling; it became common to admit that criminals were often at least semiliterate, while continuing to insist that they were woefully ignorant. Of course it is comforting to stress the ignorance of criminals: why else do they commit crimes? To acknowledge that criminals know what they are doing—that they are somehow smarter than their victims—*that* is the dangerous proposition. Yet then as now there were educated criminals like Bradley Headstone, and literate, white-collar crimes such as forgery and embezzlement. And then as now criminals often outsmarted their victims, the police, and the courts. In *Oliver Twist*, the Bow Street runners Blathers and Duff are doubly outsmarted. First, they fail to capture Sikes, Toby Crackit, or even Oliver. Second, they are misled by Dr. Losberne, who wishes to protect

Oliver and gets rid of them as quickly as possible. Thus *both* the criminals *and* the respectable bourgeoisie foil the police.

By the late 1830s, statistics had become a flourishing social science, with so-called "moral" or criminal statistics a leading branch. According to Margaret May, the "key breakthrough" in the emergence of the modern concept of juvenile delinquency was a direct offshoot of this development and thus coincided with the publication of *Oliver Twist*. In 1839, the first secretary of the London Statistical Society, R. W. Rawson, demonstrated that "the correlation between age and type of crime was [a] fundamental 'law' of crime." He showed that "criminal activity began early in life and reached a peak between sixteen and twenty-five. . . . Joseph Fletcher, another prominent member [of the Society], concluded that since over half of those sentenced were under twenty-five 'there is a population constantly being brought up to crime'" (May 17). Dickens hated statistical "laws" as much as he hated the New Poor Law, and in the 1830s he satirized societies like Rawson's in both the Pickwick Club and his piece on the Mudfog Association, which appeared in *Bentley's* in 1836. But despite his antipathy to statistics and his obvious resistance to the idea that children could be easily criminalized, Dickens produced a novel in which juvenile delinquency is a major theme.

In 1833 the French statistician A. M. Guerry had contended that education did not lead to a reduction in the crime rate but the reverse. According to Michael Cullen, British social investigators "became obsessed with Guerry's little book" on "moral statistics." Thus in 1835 the economist W. R. Greg tried to refute Guerry, but "like Guerry's French data, at first sight [Greg's Dutch data] showed a direct, not inverse, relationship between the areas of high crime and high education. Greg was forced back on the observation that where there was the greatest quantity of education, then crimes of violence were the least. The overall excess . . . was due to crimes against property" (Cullen 139–140). Similarly, in *Progress of the Nation*, G. R. Porter argued that "although there was a greater proportion of offences in the more enlightened departments [of Guerry's France], the criminals were . . . among the uninstructed. . . . [W]here ignorance abounds, the standard of morals must be low" (Porter 3:211–212). But Porter himself offered figures showing that, while the population of Britain between 1805 and 1841 had increased 79 percent, and while schooling and literacy had also been on the rise, the crime rate had increased 482 percent (3:198)! Porter tried to downplay these distressing figures by showing that crimes committed by illiterates and semiliterates had risen much faster than those committed by literate and well-educated criminals, but the evidence was far from convincing. By shifting the definition of semiliteracy, it was possible to arrive at the opposite conclusion, that education and not ignorance caused crime.

Disagreeing with liberal advocates of education as social cure-all, both radicals and conservatives interpreted the soaring crime rate as a function of education instead of the reverse. On the radical side, Engels insisted that the proletariat were better educated than ever before (though thanks to their own efforts, not to the bourgeoisie), but also that they were more criminal than ever before: "there is more crime in Britain than in any other country in the world." Engels, of course, did not hesitate to see in the rising crime rate a key sign of the pending revolution: "the criminal statistics prove that [the] social war is being waged more vigorously . . . and with greater bitterness every year." The bourgeoisie fail to see, Engels declared, that "the individual crimes of which they read will one day culminate in universal revolution" (Engels 146, 149).

Conservatives also believed that education fomented both crime and sedition. In 1807 Samuel Whitbread's bill, calling for a national system of schools at which all poor children would receive two years of free education, was defeated largely because, as one opponent declared, educating "the poor . . . would be . . . prejudicial to their morals and happiness; it would teach them to despise their lot in life . . . it would enable them to read seditious pamphlets, vicious books, and publications against Christianity" (qtd. in Hammond 49). And at the time of the Reform Bill of 1832, Francis Place, "the radical tailor," could still write: "Ministers and men in power, with nearly the whole body of those who are rich, dread the consequences of teaching the people more than they dread . . . their ignorance" (qtd. in Hammond 46). The gloomy remark of Mr. Flosky (Coleridge) about the "reading public . . . growing too wise for its betters" in Peacock's *Nightmare Abbey* is matched by Dr. Folliott's comment in *Crotchet Castle*: "robbery perhaps comes of poverty, but scientific principles of robbery come of education." In the latter novel, the economist Mr. MacQuedy neatly sums up these views: "Discontent increases with the increase of information" (Peacock 71, 213, 219), which is perhaps a distant echo of the Monster's conclusion in *Frankenstein*: "Sorrow only increased with knowledge."

Thus, despite the dominance among liberals of the wishful view that ignorance caused crime while education cured it, there were many reasons to believe the opposite. Much of the discourse on crime and juvenile delinquency in the 1830s and after expresses a moral panic that, as Foucault might put it, fails to recognize how it produces that which terrifies it. The nearly 500 percent increase in crime from 1800 to 1841 cited by Porter was partly due to increasingly effective methods of surveillance and law enforcement, and thus might have been interpreted as evidence of social progress instead of the reverse. If a further cause of the exponential increase in the crime rate was increased education, as Engels claimed, then that, too, could be construed as the progressive discourse on crime producing crime. Nothing could be more obvious than that the modern disciplines of policing, penology, and education have not eliminated crime. Modern prisons manufacture what Foucault calls "controlled illegality," which is what he means by "delinquency," because he goes on to say that "delinquency [or] controlled illegality, is an agent for the illegality of the dominant groups" (279), an opinion close to that expressed by Engels. In "Crime, Authority and the Police-Man State," historian V. A. C. Gattrell says much the same: "The history of crime . . . is largely the history of how better-off people discipline their inferiors" (245).

Foucault's assertion that prisons produce delinquency offers a corollary to

Marx's wonderfully sarcastic account of the productivity of crime, according to which, so to speak, resistance breeds power. In an appendix to *Theories of Surplus Value*, Marx ridicules definitions of crime that treat it as the antithesis of productive labor:

> A philosopher produces ideas, a poet poems, a clergyman sermons, a professor compendia and so on. A criminal produces crimes. . . . The criminal moreover produces the whole of the police and of criminal justice, constables, judges, hangmen, juries, etc.; and all these different lines of business . . . develop different capacities of the human spirit, create new needs and new ways of satisfying them. Torture alone has given rise to the most ingenious mechanical inventions. . . . (1:387–388)

Whether literate or not, moreover, criminals have been productive of great literature. They have served as inspirations to great writers—Marx names Sophocles' *Oedipus Rex*, Shakespeare's *Richard the Third*, and Schiller's *Robbers*—of course one could add masterpieces by Balzac, Dickens, Dostoevsky, and so forth. Further, Marx says, we have the criminal to thank for breaking "the monotony and everyday security of bourgeois life" (1:387–388). Not that the productivity of criminals was a new idea: Marx was merely embellishing the theme of self-interest in Bernard Mandeville's *Fable of the Bees*, while *The Newgate Calendar* itself declares that Jack Sheppard "found employment for the bar, the pulpit, and the stage" (Kerman 41).

Throughout Victorian criminological discourse, the productivity of crime and the freedom or free will of the criminal are both denied, because they loom as the ultimate threats underlying the very idea of crime. In unconscious, "underworld" ways, crime threatens to *out*-produce and the criminal threatens to be *more* free than the respectable, bourgeois citizen, bound to the ball and chain of law and order. Before the Victorian era, the criminal was often represented as a figure of freedom, strong enough to break through social restraints, to bend the law to his or sometimes her will, supercharged with the charisma of adventure, banditry, rebellion: Jack Sheppard, Jonathan Wild, Dick Turpin, Defoe's *Lives of the Pirates* point the way toward Blake's devils and Byron's corsairs. But by the 1830s various forms of surveillance, mapping, and scientific explanation were making the literary criminal look less like a political rebel than like an object to capture, catalogue, diagnose, and hopefully tame or reform. As Foucault indicates, the biographies of criminals shifted gradually away from the rogue's gallery genres of *The Newgate Calendar* and the condemned man's last words, hawked as broadsides around the public scaffold, to the strange semi-privacy or semi-publicity of police dossiers and the case studies of middle-class reformers.

With the emergence of delinquency, as Foucault contends, crime is pathologized and thus no longer seen as the deeds of freely choosing, unequivocally responsible—as opposed to merely guilty—moral agents. Surveying the history of nineteenth-century criminal psychology, Martin Wiener points to the transition from "the voluntarism of the first half of the century [to] the increasing determinism of later Victorian naturalism" (43). The division between incorruptible Oliver and the thieves, all creatures of their environment, marks the split between voluntarism and determinism. Free will is restricted to the upper classes, an effect more than a cause of the self-congratulatory discourse of bourgeois virtue; the realm of social causation becomes that of the proletariat and the poor. But this wishful contradiction itself gradually gives way to all-inclusive models of hereditary and environmental determinism.[4]

The telos of the pathologization of crime is the perfected robot or "clockwork orange" of present-day behaviorism and sociobiology, descendants of eighteenth- and early-nineteenth-century associationists like Jeremy Bentham. One limit of this development can be seen in social Darwinist criminology toward the end of the 1800s, when craniometry flourished along with the belief that a high proportion of criminal behavior was caused by heredity. Cesare Lombroso elaborated the concept of atavism, claiming that it was possible to identify nearly half of the so-called "criminal class" by their primitive or apelike features: low foreheads, lantern jaws, hairy bodies, prehensile toes. Books filled with mugshots of atavistic heads, faces, and feet became common: with just a panoptical glance, you could spot certain criminals, and in England many suspicious characters were Irish.[5]

II

Those early Victorian officials and reformers most knowledgeable about the lives of criminals often claimed that education rather than ignorance caused crime. In *Reformatory Schools* (1851), Mary Carpenter cited many reports showing, as one put it, that "the proportion of the wholly uneducated in gaol, is [actually] *less* than the proportion [in] the population at large" (31). The warden of Edinburgh Gaol testified that, for the year ending 30 September 1846, the number of prisoners in his charge who could neither read nor write was only "317 out of 4,513 [or less than one-fourteenth]; 292 could read well; 85 could read and write well, and 3 had received a superior education." The safest conclusion from such figures might have been that there was no correlation between crime and literacy, but the warden also observed that "the number of re-commitments of those who can read well, [was] much greater than" among complete illiterates (Carpenter 27).

Narrowing the focus to the Artful Dodger's crowd, juvenile delinquents, produced similar results. According to the evidence gathered from "hundreds of . . . juvenile prisoners," Mr. Cotton, the Ordinary of Newgate, concluded that "juvenile delinquents, as a class, were not destitute of education . . . on the contrary, a very large portion of them had received a considerable degree of instruction" (Carpenter 19). At Wakefield Prison, declared an Inspector of Prisons in 1847, "every care is taken of the boys, and . . . the education given them is such as would qualify them for almost every situation attainable in their state of life, [yet] the frequency of recommitments has not diminished, but . . . increased" (Carpenter, *Juvenile Delinquents* 174). Clever young jailbirds, moreover, often feigned illiteracy in order to be sent to the prison school rather than to the treadmill or the oakum room. They thus swelled the figures for illiteracy; it was of course not possible for illiterates to pretend to read and write, and there were no incentives, at least in prison, for doing so (see Graff 267).

Such revelations made it impossible to think of illiteracy as a cause of crime. But liberal faith in education as a panacea for all social problems ran strong, as it does today. The question was thus reformulated as one of moral or religious ignorance instead of illiteracy, and of improper or even criminal schooling instead of no schooling. For some social observers, no schools would have been better than those which existed. In his 1834 *Blackwood's Magazine* article "Progress of Social Disorganization," Archibald Alison contended that bad schools produced bad—that is, criminal—students. He pointed out that "crime has more than *tripled* in the last twenty years, during which time more has been done for the education of the poor than in the whole previous periods of English history" (Alison 235). What was Malthus's nightmare of the world overrun with population, he wondered, to the far more nightmarish prospect of the world overrun with criminals? The clock could not be turned back, however—Alison did not advocate the abolition of schools—but the criminalization of society would continue to outstrip the population explosion unless education could be placed on a sound religious basis. Otherwise, "the greatest of all blessings," knowledge, would prove to be "the greatest of all curses . . . the Press will become an engine of vast power for the introduction of infidelity, discontent, profligacy, and corruption . . . all the safeguards of religion and virtue will speedily give way, and one unbridled torrent of licentiousness overwhelm the land" (Alison 240).

One of the authorities cited by Alison was the ex-convict Charles Wall, who, in his book *The Old Bailey Experience* (1833), condemned the schools founded by the National Society for Promoting the Education of the Poor for producing graduates "fully qualified to figure on the *pavé* as pickpockets":

> The very calling together so many low-born children daily, without some plan . . .
> for a moral guardianship over them, justifies the assertion, that they are taught
> *immorality*, and . . . *crime*. . . . There is nothing of a mental nature performed
> in [such schools]: a hundred boys at one time are taught to bawl out Lon-lon-
> don-don, London, with a few more words, which leads them . . . to learn just
> enough of reading to enable them to peruse a twopenny life of [Dick] Turpin, or
> Jonathan Wild, proceeding to the lives of the bandits in regular course. (qtd. in
> Alison 232)

Wall's mention of "the lives of the bandits" is one of many occasions when such literature was cited as a direct cause of crime. In a passage cited by Engels, R. H. Horne told the Children's Employment Commission of 1842 about working-class children in the Wolverhampton area who did not know the name of the queen and had never heard of "St. Paul, Moses [and] Solomon," yet who had "a general knowledge of the . . . life of Dick Turpin, the highwayman, and . . . Jack Sheppard, the robber and prison-breaker" (Engels 127). The chaplain of the Preston House of Correction testified in 1847 that over one-third of the nearly fifteen hundred prisoners he had interviewed were "ignorant of the Saviour's name, and unable to repeat the Lord's Prayer." Yet about one-half had "read, or heard read, books about Dick Turpin and Jack Sheppard" (qtd. in Carpenter, *Reformatory Schools* 23). And in Henry Mayhew's *London Labour and the London Poor*, a professional thief declared that, in the cheap lodging houses where he slept, "on Sunday evenings the only books read were such as 'Jack Sheppard,' 'Dick Turpin,' and the 'Newgate Calendar'. . . . These were read with much interest." John Binny, who interviewed this thief, believed that a "very fruitful source of early demoralization is . . . penny and halfpenny romances. . . . One of the worst of the most recent ones is denominated 'Charley Wag, or the New Jack Sheppard, a history of the most successful thief in London.' To say that these are not incentives to lust, theft, and crime . . . is to cherish a fallacy." Binny advocated a strict censorship by the police to end "this shameful misuse of the art of printing" (Mayhew 4:302).

Besides literature directly about crime, there were in the late 1830s many forms of reading that could be interpreted as criminal. In his concern for the "profligacy" of journalism, Alison was reacting, in part, to the so-called "War of the Unstamped Press"—that is, the struggle against censorship and the "taxes on knowledge" waged from 1819 to 1836 by radical publishers such as Richard Carlile, Henry Hetherington, and William Hone.[6] Dickens began his career as both a journalist and a novelist just as this war was winding down: the stamp duty on newspapers was reduced to a penny in 1836 and finally abolished in 1855. The fight against censorship must have given Dickens a vivid conception of the link between criminality and at least certain kinds of political discourse. Between 1830 and 1834, there were perhaps as many as 750 prosecutions for publishing and selling unstamped journals (Wickwar 30). Leigh Hunt, on whom Dickens modeled Harold Skimpole in *Bleak House*, had been jailed for two years (1813–1815) for comments on the Prince Regent he published in *The Examiner*; George Cruikshank could easily have followed him for illustrating such satires as Hone's bestselling *The Political House that Jack Built* (1819). The libel and stamp laws seemed as unjust to reform-minded writers such as Hunt and Dickens as did the poor laws—so unjust that they threatened to make *all* reading and writing criminal.

This is, of course, the general threat implicit in any form of censorship: if one sort of discourse can be outlawed, then it is conceivable that all discourse can be outlawed. Such a paranoid prospect, moreover, seems only to increase the urgency would-be censors feel to fix absolute boundaries between virtuous and vicious, clean and unclean, high and low forms of culture. The literacy of Dickens's thieves reveals just how arbitrary all such boundaries are.[7] As the Gradgrindian prohibition against fairy tales in *Hard Times* indicates, Dickens understood that censorship could criminalize even the most innocent forms of discourse. The evangelicals were much more censorious than the utilitarians, as he also understood. The Society for the Suppression of Vice, founded by members of the Clapham Sect in 1802, was especially sharp after children's books that, it held, were "a most successful channel for the conveyance of infidel and licentious tenets." It sought to eradicate "Infidelity and Insubordination, fostered by . . . the Press, [which has] raised into existence a pestilent swarm of blasphemous . . . and obscene books and prints" (qtd. in Wickwar 36; see also Bristow 32–50). Some evangelicals included all novels in the category of "obscene" and therefore criminal reading.

Dickens detested evangelicalism even more than he detested utilitarianism. Yet with evangelical reformers such as Lord Shaftesbury, he championed the Ragged Schools, the first of which were founded in 1843.[8] Dickens took a special interest in the one in Field Lane, Fagin's Saffron Hill neighborhood, and both he and their founders hoped such efforts would help solve the crime problem. But the struggle against moral darkness was far from easy. In his 1846 *Daily News* essay "Crime and Education," Dickens describes Ragged School children as "low-browed, vicious, cunning, wicked; abandoned of all help but this [the Ragged School]; speeding downward to destruction; and UNUTTERABLY IGNORANT" (1:28). These are, apparently, children fabricated on an entirely different plan from innocent Oliver.

In the Ragged School movement, religious and moral instruction was felt to be more urgent than instruction in reading and writing, and teaching the students not to steal seems to have been the first order of business.[9] At the Field Lane school, Dickens pointed out, the students could not even "be trusted with books," apparently because they would damage or pilfer them; "they could only be instructed orally; they were difficult of reduction to anything like attention, obedience, or decent behaviour" (1:28). Through the 1840s and 1850s, reformers, including Dickens, shifted their hopes from voluntary, charity schools to the far stricter discipline of reformatory and industrial schools, as in Mary Carpenter's work with juvenile delinquents. She began her career by opening a Ragged School in Bristol in 1846, but was soon advocating much more thoroughgoing measures to deal with what she called "the perishing and dangerous classes."[10]

No more than intensifying police and prison discipline, however, did intensifying educational discipline solve the crime problem. And like the strictest schooling, even the purest reading could have effects opposite from those intended. One of the more disturbing accounts of literate juvenile delinquents cited by Carpenter came from a Ragged School teacher:

> The most thoroughly unprincipled and unimpressible boy I ever taught . . . was one who had been long . . . in a Church of England Sunday School, and was thoroughly acquainted with all the facts of Scripture, together with various points of theology, which he would willingly have discussed, had I permitted him. He gloried in having been mentioned in the newspaper as the head of a gang of thieves, and is now in prison. (Qtd. in *Reformatory Schools* 93)

If reading Scripture cannot cure crime, then no reading can. But what if reading Scripture can inspire crime, just as reading *Jack Sheppard* was held to do? This real-life Artful Dodger with theological savvy was only a step removed from the mass murderer whose case Foucault unearthed and published in 1973: "I, Pierre Rivière, having slaughtered my mother, my sister, and my brother. . . ." Rivière was a twenty-year-old peasant who, in June 1835, committed the murders for which he was executed. Foucault found his case fascinating partly because, like Oliver and the thieves in Dickens's crime story, Rivière was surprisingly literate. Though supposedly barely able to read and write, in his teens "he eagerly took to the reading of . . . philosophical works. [And from] irreligion he turned to great piety" (10). Indeed, he claimed that his inspiration to kill his mother, sister, and brother came not from reading crime stories like *Jack Sheppard*, but from reading the Bible. When the judge insisted that "God never orders a crime," Rivière offered a reply worthy of Lewis's Monk or of James Hogg's "Justified Sinner": "God ordered Moses to slay the adorers of the golden calf, sparing neither friends nor father nor son. . . . I was specially inspired by God as the Levites were" (21).

It would be easy to conclude, as the judge does, that Rivière is a madman, but this overlooks the paradox Foucault stresses. Rivière did not just confess orally to the police; he also wrote a forty-page "memoir" explaining how he was the author—*auteur*—both of the murders and of the story of the murders. He even explained that he had planned to write the memoir at the same time that he planned the murders. Both by committing his crimes and by inscribing them in a legible text for a literate audience, Rivière staked his claim to authorship—that is, to the very cultural authority associated with literacy—with the Bible, of course, but also, in the shadowy ways that trouble *Oliver Twist*, with the reading and writing of crime stories. Rivière thus sought a double celebrity, at once criminal and literary, which Foucault has now helped him achieve, just as Norman Mailer's *Executioner's Song*, for better or worse, has immortalized Gary Gilmore. So far from eradicating crime, in this way too, through criminal writing, literacy can be seen to encourage it, to redouble it through representation, just as today the electronic mass media are said to encourage crime by continually representing it. But this is the dilemma of cultural authority in general, which, as Oscar Wilde understood, can and does empower robbers as well as cops—a dilemma manifest in the inextricable doubleness or moral ambiguity of all crime stories and perhaps of all novels, including *Oliver Twist*.

Executioner's songs and celebrations of outlaws like Robin Hood have perhaps always been a mainstay of the sort of popular culture Bakhtin identifies as "carnivalesque." Echoing Bakhtin, Lennard Davis contends that the novel's origins were not just carnivalesque but criminal; he thus ironically appears to agree with those nineteenth-century evangelicals who wished to outlaw all secular fiction. During the Renaissance there emerged a distinctive "news/novel discourse," Davis points out, a blend of fiction and quasi-journalism featuring roguery and crime, as in Robert Greene's "cony-catching" pamphlets, and from this already criminal discourse the modern novel took shape. Contrary to Davis, in *The Novel and the Police* D. A. Miller contends that, in a sense, the novel is the police—or at any rate, the police internalized. Miller is not exactly arguing the case in defense of novels, however, because for him the police are the enemy. Davis and Miller seem to split the truth between them. The novel is often rebellious, vulgar, criminal, perhaps never more so than when it is about criminals, as in *Jack Sheppard* and *Oliver Twist*. But the novel is just as often conservative, even authoritarian—an ideological form of social control—perhaps never more so than when it is about the punishment of criminals, as again in *Jack Sheppard* and *Oliver Twist*. Clearly a single novel can lead a double life by playing both roles in a cultural game of cops and robbers, crime and punishment.

As an embryonic mystery novel, *Oliver Twist* shares in the Manichaean structural doubleness of all mystery novels: secrecy and detection, guilt and innocence, crime and punishment. Its sharp divisions of setting, character, and plot, mirroring this doubleness, Dickens likened to the "streaky bacon" of stage melodrama: "It is the custom on the stage, in all good murderous melodramas, to present the tragic and the comic scenes, in as regular alternation, as the layers of red and white in a side of streaky bacon" (*Oliver Twist* 168). At the level of cultural history, besides the contrast between free will and determinism, the "streaky bacon" of *Oliver Twist* involves the contrast between high and popular culture, legitimate and criminal reading, and its plot is structured to reveal what Peter Brooks calls "the moral occult" of melodrama (5). At the level of biographical or psychoanalytic criticism, it expresses Dickens's notorious duplicity or ambivalence toward his deepest moral themes. "Dickens has always appeared to his readers as a novelist of divided sensibilities," writes John Kucich. "Irrepressibly drawn to rebellious . . . or even murderous displays of passion, Dickens also . . . circumscribe[s] human experience within inflexible moral boundaries" (*Repression* 201).[11]

Thus do theories of the novel as uneasy, divided genre and of Dickens as uneasy, divided self echo the same anxious questions raised by the early Victorian debates about crime and education and about criminal reading. Does fiction about crime prevent or promote it? If certain types of reading promote crime, then how can it be maintained that literacy is beneficial to society or that culture can save us from anarchy? Behind these questions lurks another one, concerning the processes that enforce the criminalization of certain types of literature—in other words, the processes of policing discourse. That these processes usually backfire isn't a pessimistic conclusion. If the ordinary police have not figured out how to stop crime, neither, thank goodness, have the cultural police figured out how to stop the carnivalesque. "The people mutht be amuthed," as Mr. Sleary says; despite Gradgrindism, the circus goes on, and Dickens rightly takes his place in the show.

At the end of his career, Dickens turned criminal—or, at least, criminal reader. For his final tour he composed a reading of the murder in *Oliver Twist*. At first, he could not make up his mind to perform this reading. "I have no doubt that I could perfectly petrify an audience. . . . But whether the impression would not be so horrible as to keep them away another time, is what I cannot satisfy myself upon" (qtd. in Johnson 2:1102).[12] John Forster, for one, objected "because such a subject seemed to be altogether out of the province of reading" (Forster 2:448). Besides, Dickens's health was precarious. Edgar Johnson says that "in deciding to

add the murder of Nancy to his repertoire, he was sentencing himself to death"—
a kind of self-murder by reading (Johnson 2:1104). But Dickens relished petrify-
ing his audiences. During one performance at Clifton in 1868, there was "a contagion of fainting. . . . I should think we had from a dozen to twenty ladies taken
out stiff and rigid" (qtd. in Forster 2:451). Dickens called the Clifton reading "by
far the best Murder [he had] yet done." Indeed, he often spoke of his perform-
ances in the role of Sikes bludgeoning Nancy as "murders" he had committed,
and he joked about his "murderous instincts." "I have a vague sensation of being
'wanted' as I walk about the streets," he declared. "There was a fixed expression
of horror of me, all over the theatre, which could not have been surpassed if I had
been going to be hanged. . . . It is quite a new sensation to be execrated with
[such] unanimity" (qtd. in Johnson 2:1107). Of course this was mock execration,
but it was also the dark, lurid side of the celebrity that had come to him as a
novelist. For Pierre Rivière, execration and celebrity were identical. In both cases,
murder and authorship, as with Caleb Williams, were finally not so far apart.
Though able to read, Bill Sikes didn't write his own crime story as Rivière had
done; Dickens did that for him, and then resurrected Sikes as his favorite criminal
alter ego, the murderer of Nancy over and over again, and the ghostly double of
one of the great authors of his or any other age.

III

Nineteenth-century criminology downplays class and politics to focus instead on the moral deviance of the individual criminal. When the main causes of
criminality are deemed environmental, then education, entailing a minimal politics of individual improvement, is invoked as the cure. When the causes are deemed
biological, then there is no cure except for policing and prison. For early Victorian reformers, crime seems to go either with the neighborhood (working-class,
the slums) or with the race (also working-class, the Irish) or both, and yet also
seems to be a strictly moral and individualistic phenomenon: the illiterate or semi-
literate ignorance and bad habits of uncivilized proles, including drinking, low
company, poor parenting, laziness, no religion, poverty or lack of thrift, and so
on. In such constructions, criminals are simultaneously to blame for their mis-
deeds and seen as the creatures of both environment and heredity. Thus from the
1830s on, poor sanitation and bad housing are frequently represented as causes of
delinquency, as if crime does not also flourish where the drainage is good and
everyone's home is a tidy suburban castle like Wemmick's in *Great Expectations*.[13] In relation to biological determinism, moreover, Henry Mayhew and his
team of interviewers see such a high correlation between those whom they label
"Irish cockneys" and the "criminal class" that the two categories blur into one.
Thus Mayhew's collaborator John Binny can speak of "the felon class of Irish
cockneys" (4:283) without clarifying whether he is referring to a minority of fel-
ons within the larger group, or rather means that the entire group of "Irish cockneys" is felonious. And nowhere does Binny indicate that Irish immigrants to

London might have political reasons to behave rebelliously toward English institutions and to treat the property rights of middle-class English citizens as less than sacred.

In introducing his pre-Darwinian text, Mayhew stresses "race" rather than environment as the key to understanding crime.[14] Migrants and nomads, after all, do not have unchanging environments that can be said to cause their errancy. Mayhew declares that there are "two distinct races of men . . . the wandering and the civilized tribes." And "to each of these tribes," which exist side by side in every society, "a different form of head is peculiar, the wandering races being remarkable for the development of the bones of the face, as the jaws, cheekbones, &c., and the civilized for the development of those of the head" (1:2). Mayhew elaborates:

> Whether it be that in the mere act of wandering, there is a greater determination of blood to the surface of the body, and consequently a less quantity sent to the brain, the muscles being thus nourished at the expense of the mind, I leave physiologists to say. But certainly be the physical cause what it may [he doesn't doubt for a moment that there *is* a "physical cause"] we must all allow that in [the wandering classes] there is a greater development of the animal than of the intellectual or moral nature of man, and that they are all more or less distinguished for their high cheek-bones and protruding jaws—for their use of a slang language—for their lax ideas of property—for their general improvidence—their repugnance to continuous labour—their disregard of female honour—their love of cruelty—their pugnacity—and their utter want of religion. (1:2–3)

"Wandering" for Mayhew means deviant, and deviant means at least latently criminal. The "nomade [*sic*] tribes" in their "purely vagabond" condition are entirely parasitic, "preying upon the earnings of the more industrious portions of the community" (1:2). Yet they are also *too* productive, too prolific both in terms of their own sexuality and physical hardihood and in terms of their direct engagement in trade and economic competition, the main sources of bourgeois value (see Gallagher, "Body" 100–105).

But Mayhew's all-encompassing guilty verdict against the entire category of his necessarily "wandering" street-people (his overzealous panopticism, so to speak) is only the bourgeois, half-baked side of his nomadology, which is at once disciplinary and carnivalesque. Mayhew's "wandering" versus "civilised tribes" thesis is only one gesture, perhaps the least convincing, toward an explanatory positivism that seeks to encompass all social phenomena. But the evidence Mayhew offers subverts that positivism at every turn. Thus *London Labour* ends with elaborate statistical tables, charts, and maps, suggesting a total, scientific surveillance of every nook and corner of England and Wales. The map "Showing the Number of Illegitimate Children in Every 1000 Births in Each County of England and Wales," for instance, implies that all illegitimate children and even births have been accurately tallied and pinned down by location, though many must have gone unreported while they and their parents wandered all over the realm and, through emigration, far beyond. Similarly, for the table "Showing the Relative Degrees of Criminality and Ignorance in the Different Counties of England and Wales," the keywords are those unstable, itinerant terms *relative* and *different*. Middlesex (greater London) is the most literate county but has also one of the highest crime rates. Worcester, edging into the industrial north, is well above average in both crime and illiteracy, while rural Cumberland is well below average in both. The only thing proven by this panoptical graph is the lack of correlation between crime and either literacy or illiteracy, or in other words the incoherence of the graph itself (4:464).

Mayhew and his team of interviewers find that most criminals and street-people have some rather than no literacy. As with Dickens and other middle-class reformers, their main concern is not illiteracy but what they see as moral ignorance. The costermongers, for instance, are in a "brutified state" (1:25), and "only about one in ten of the regular costermongers is able to read" (1:22). Nevertheless, Mayhew provides a section, "The Literature of the Costermongers," in which he declares:

> It may appear anomalous to speak of the literature of an uneducated body, but even the costermongers have their tastes for books. They are very fond of hearing any one read aloud to them. . . . What they love best to listen to . . . are Reynolds's periodicals, especially the "Mysteries of the Court." "They've got tired of Lloyd's blood-stained stories," said one man, who was in the habit of reading to them, "and I'm satisfied that, of all London, Reynolds is the most popular man among them." (1:25)[15]

Even if many of the street-people are illiterate, they still "have their tastes for books." The "low lodging houses" where they often reside sometimes have libraries or reading rooms (1:252), though the reading material they contain tends toward the criminal. Some types of street-people, moreover, including prostitutes and the sizable "tribe" of "street-sellers of stationery, literature, and the fine arts," are more literate than the costermongers. The table purporting to show the "Degree of Education Amongst Prostitutes" indicates that between half and two-thirds of prostitutes arrested in London between 1837 and 1854 were at least semi-literate, "able to read only, or read and write imperfectly" (4:218). Like the prostitutes, the "patterers" or sellers of "literature" ranging from pornography and false reports of crimes, to songs and ballads, and to used books often display considerable education; they

> include many men of respectable connections, and even classical attainments. Among them, may be found the son of a military officer, a clergyman, a man brought up to the profession of medicine . . . clerks, shopmen, and a class who have been educated to no especial calling—some of the latter being the natural sons of gentlemen and noblemen. . . . (1:214)

So much for the salvific effects of literacy, education, or even Arnoldian high culture. Yet like Dickens, Mayhew's ultimate faith lies in education: though all of his street-people may be inherently, through "race," inclined to nomadism and crime, literacy and sound moral instruction will ensure that costermongers, for instance, do not persistently "wander" into the criminal category of "the dangerous classes" (4:273).

Mayhew's most elaborate attempt at scientific analysis is the taxonomy of labor and nonlabor that he offers near the start of volume four. This is neither half-baked, racist anthropology deployed at the expense of the Irish nor an incoherent statistical map or table. It is instead a classificatory grid stretched over the entire social organism (in a sense, over every social organism). Like Balzac in the *avant-propos* to the Human Comedy, Mayhew says that he is writing the "natural history" of labor, and not just of labor but also of nonlabor, of everyone who works and of everyone who doesn't work. Mayhew begins his taxonomy by showing the flaws in previous accounts of the division of labor. He then offers his own, supposedly more scientific classification, ranging from "those who will work," including farmers, manufacturers, shopkeepers, and educators, through "those who cannot work" (the insane, the senile, the incarcerated, the dependent) to "those who will not work," including beggars, prostitutes, and an amazing number and variety of criminals. These three major categories are followed by a fourth, "those who need not work," composed of such types as landlords, fundholders, and "sinecurists."

Under "those who will not work," Mayhew's taxonomy proceeds through the major subdivisions of vagrants, beggars, and "cheats," each with its own ramifications, until it arrives at the tenth subdivision for "thieves and their dependents." "Dependents" is a small surprise, because in what sense can thieves be dependable? Throughout Victorian discourse, as in *Oliver Twist*, vagrancy and thievery are antitheses to family values. Anyway, within this subdivision appears category C, "Those Who Plunder by Manual Dexterity," further subdivided between "Mobsmen" and "Sneaksmen." The latter bifurcates into still more micropolitical categories, including such colorful ones as "Star Glazers," or "those who cut the panes out of shop windows"; "Sawney Hunters," or those who snitch "bacon from cheesemonger's shopdoors"; "Dead Lurkers," or "those who steal coats and umbrellas from passages at dusk, or on Sunday afternoons"; "Skinners," or "those women who entice children and sailors to go with them and then strip them of their clothes"; "Bluey Hunters," or "those who purloin lead from the tops of houses"; and "Mudlarks," or "those who steal pieces of rope and lumps of coal from among the vessels at the river-side" (4:25–26). Similarly, under "Mobsmen" occurs the subheading "Buzzers," the stealers of handkerchiefs and other articles from gentlemen's pockets, and "Buzzers" in turn merits two more subdivisions: "Stook-buzzers," who steal handkerchiefs, and "Tail-buzzers," who steal snuff-boxes and purses.

Mayhew's labels seek to pin down individuals, especially on the vagrant, criminal side of the ledger, to roles or subject-positions and therefore to coherent identities on an apparently stable social map. But his subjects are wandering and, in bourgeois terms, radically unstable. All the colorful labels for the varieties of

beggars and thieves seem only to mimic, in *Beggar's Opera* fashion, the occupa-
tional labels attached to "those who will work." To identify someone as a "stook-
buzzer" or a "dead lurker" is rhetorically no different from identifying someone
else as a shop clerk or a solicitor. The very profusion of names and specializations
among beggars, mobsmen, sneaksmen, and so on implies a productive ingenuity
and energy that more than parallels the legitimate professions. A "bluey hunter,"
for instance, may be a criminal, and therefore the work that he does (his profession, so to speak) is illegal; nevertheless, clambering up on rooftops, prying the
leading off, carting it away, and selling it is a form of work rather than non-work,
definitely a self-help version of making a living. Further, a "stook-buzzer" may
be only an occasional pickpocket; perhaps he has a legitimate job as well; perhaps he engages in many other kinds of theft, so that he is also at times a mudlark,
a dead lurker, a sawney hunter. There is something contradictory in the very idea
of a taxonomy of the "wandering tribe," of people who move about, who frequently shift jobs or roles, who are often unemployed or only erratically self-
employed, as are many of Mayhew's street-sellers, street-performers, street-walk-
ers, and street-robbers. Mayhew's taxonomy is finally only a social-scientific pipe
dream, based on a desire to slow, to stabilize, and to render totally visible and
comprehensible a social realm whose most constant features are flux and incon-
stancy. About the similar classifying system of the eighteenth-century criminolo-
gist Lacretelle, who sought to map crimes and punishments after the natural history model of Linnaeus, Foucault writes: "In theory, or rather in dream, the double
taxonomy of punishments and crimes will solve the problem: but how is one to
apply fixed laws to particular individuals?" (100). Indeed, Mayhew's taxonomy
points relentlessly in the direction of individuals or individuality—or in other
words, of that which cannot be categorized. The web that he weaves, like a Balzac
or Dickens novel, mimes the social totality through microscopic bifurcations and
ramifications that lead not to an overarching theory, taxonomy, or metanarrative,
but to the unique, the radically ungeneralizable, the "novelistic" in Bakhtin's sense
of the word.[16]

The "dangerous individual" always wanders nomadically away from the "fixed
laws" and categorical cages of the bourgeois social scientist.[17] And it is ultimately
the unstable, vagrant individual who gets the last word or perhaps the last laugh
in Mayhew's human comedy. For what is most significant about that survey is not
Mayhew's half-baked anthropologizing, nor his summaries and mappings of statistical information or disinformation, nor his grand taxonomy of labor and nonlabor. It is instead the series of interviews with dozens of London dockers, dustmen,
costermongers, acrobats, flower-girls, chimney sweeps, blind and lame beggars,
prostitutes, burglars, and on and on. Despite editorial tinkering, the voices of
numerous wandering, ordinary and yet eccentric individuals give *London Labour*
a documentary specificity and quasi-objectivity that undermine Mayhew's wishful scientizing.

Mayhew's nomadic subjects elude his scientific strategies and taxonomies,
while often revealing the tactics that enable them to do so. The point is not that

Mayhew's subjects are completely "free" or undetermined in their behaviors, nor that their patterns of resistance (tactics) place them outside the circle of containment and domination (strategies) exercised by bourgeois law-and-order and social science. Vagrancy and criminality are simultaneously inside and outside; the necessary—and in some sense, necessarily *determined*—other of bourgeois legitimacy.[18] But within and through the interstices of that systematizing legitimacy wanders the ever-dangerous individual, capable of lying, capable of committing all conceivable crimes and misdemeanors, and ultimately quite unpredictable.

At the start of one of his interviews with prostitutes, Mayhew's collaborator, minor novelist Bracebridge Hemyng, says of his subject, "I believe she answered my queries faithfully." Claiming that she has to support her seven children and her "bedridden" husband, she describes how she and a couple of her children go out pretending to sell what she calls "hartifishal flowers" in order to deceive the police, and adds that she has been "druv" to prostitution "by poverty." She then tries to beg from Hemyng: "Ain't yer got even a little sixpence to rejoice the heart of the widow?" Hemyng points out that she has just called herself a widow, though she has also said she is a wife with a bedridden husband. "Which are you?" he sagely asks. "Which am I?" replies the prostitute:

> The first I toll you's the true. But Lor', I's up to so many dodges I gets what you
> may call confounded; sometimes I's a widder, and wants me 'art rejoiced with
> a copper, and then I's a hindustrious needle-woman thrown out of work. . . .
> Sometimes I make a lot of money by being a poor old cripple as broke her arm
> in a factory, by being blowed hup when a steam-engine blowed herself hup, and
> I bandage my arm and swell it out hawful big. . . . (4:245)

Which indeed *is* she? Is it even clear that she's a prostitute and not a beggar? To quote another woman interviewed by Hemyng, a former prostitute nicknamed Old Stock who has devolved into a servant at a brothel, "Ah! gay women see strange changes; wonderful ups and downs, I can tell you" (4:248).

While seduction and restricting "circumstances," especially poverty and lack of legitimate employment, figure in most of the prostitutes' life-histories, these factors do not constitute a strictly deterministic set of causes forcing them into prostitution. Indeed, the prostitutes usually tell Hemyng that they have at least partially chosen their deviant way of life. "I wished to escape from the drudgery of my father's shop," says one (4:216), while another—among the most tragic of the seduced and abandoned—says that "if I were to tell you my history it would be so romantic you would not believe it" (4:243). This prostitute is one of several interviewed by Hemyng who, unlike Old Stock, have received "superior educations," but who "have been reduced to their present condition by a variety of circumstances" (4:243), most notably by being seduced and abandoned by their first lovers: "Well, then, I am the daughter of a curate in Gloucestershire" (4:243). Hemyng comments: "Here was a woman endowed with a very fair amount of education, speaking in a superior manner . . . reduced by a variety of circumstances to the very bottom of a prostitute's career" (4:244).

In Mayhew's and Hemyng's bourgeois terms, all prostitutes are "fallen women"; the more "romantic" of their stories, however, usually involve not just loss of chastity, but falls or descents from "higher" social stations and, frequently, good educations. These "romantic" stories are not framed by the same sense of determinism that informs those of working-class women like Old Stock. Even the seemingly unromantic, more deterministic working-class narratives, however, do not stay on the straight and narrow path that the determinism of presumably liberal, utilitarian social science adopts to try to explain them. Like the countless forms of errancy that Mayhew struggles to reduce to a stable taxonomy, the "many dodges" of the prostitutes of *London Labour* evade surveillance and systematization, though in doing so—in common with all crime and vagrancy—they appear to make systemization and surveillance all the more urgent for policing and for the progress of civilization. In stressing this urgency, Mayhew and his middle-class collaborators repeatedly invoke literacy, education, and something like Arnoldian high culture as a cure for that which patently cannot be cured. Indeed, they also declare, as do other Victorian analysts of the accelerating crime rate, that crime increases in direct rather than inverse proportion to a given society's level of civilization. In the case of prostitution, for instance, they assert that it is "an inevitable attendant upon extended civilization and increased population" (4:213).

IV

Just as Dickens, Carpenter, Mayhew, and other reformers could not reduce crime and vagrancy to a set of definite causal explanations or social science "laws," neither could they confidently assert that crime does not pay. On the contrary, there was far too much evidence that it did pay in various ways—that it was a highly productive, often lucrative form of economic activity—to allow for such a conclusion. Anxiety about crime in general was exacerbated by the specter of the free, happy, successful, and even well-educated criminal, of whom there appeared to be many. "But the fact is life's sweet," Old Stock says, "and I don't care how you live. It's as sweet to the w[hore], as it is to the hempress" (4:248). This sentiment seems to be one of the morals, or anti-morals, of the story of the young pickpocket interviewed by John Binny. The chief fascination here is how his narrative subverts bourgeois assumptions about the causes and motivations of crime. The pickpocket isn't an Irishman, he didn't come from the working class, he isn't uneducated, he didn't suffer from child abuse or neglect, and his parents weren't drunkards. On the contrary, there is no way within the terms of either his or Mayhew's discourse to account for his turning to a life of crime except his own stubborn free-will and love of adventure. He didn't even grow up near the mean streets of the city, but in "a little hamlet, five miles from Shrewsbury" (4:317). Moreover, he claims that he grew up in "a very happy" home that was also a religious one: his father was a Methodist minister. And "I was a favourite with my father" (4:317).

Yet from a quite early age, the pickpocket began to reject his father's religion: "I always seemed to have a rebellious nature against . . . religious services . . . they were a disagreeable task to me, though my father took more pains with me than with my brothers and sister. I always rebelled against this in my heart, though I did not display it openly" (4:317). He says that he took to reading the Bible, but mainly to discover flaws in the arguments of his father and his father's minister-friends. "[Their] continual discussions seemed to steel my heart completely against religion. They caused me to be very disobedient and unruly, and led to my falling out with my grandfather" (4:318), who proceeded to cut the boy out of his will. Now convinced that he was the "black sheep" of the family, born with a "quarrelsome disposition," in one difficult moment he threatened to burn down the family house. This threat resulted in the one and only "severe beating" his father ever gave him, and at nine years of age he found himself on the road to London.

The rest of the story reads like Oliver Twist's, only the need to get a living and his falling in with a gang of also homeless boys turned this prodigal son of a preacher into an Artful Dodger. Does he express any regret or even homesickness? No. Does he feel any guilt about his life of crime, of stealing from others mainly by picking pockets (though he engages at times also in shoplifting and burglary)? No. Do his nine jail terms either reform him or make him bitter toward bourgeois justice? No. On the contrary, and despite the jail terms, his narrative might be read as a modest success story, exemplifying that key bourgeois virtue, self-help. His skill at picking pockets keeps him and his various women, the first of whom he shacks up with at age thirteen, in a fair amount of comfort. The work is risky, but therefore exciting. Its only difficult aspect is its uncertainty: at any time he and his partners may be nabbed and jailed, although one lives also in jail, which at least provides food and shelter.

Eventually, at age twenty-three, after his eighth jail term, the pickpocket learns that his father has died and goes home. Reunited with his mother, he thinks of staying on, but "I soon got tired of country life, though my relations were very kind to me." And so he returns to London and his career of artful dodging. After his ninth jail term and a bout of illness, he takes to "pattering" or selling street literature, and he expresses a bit of relief at now having a legitimate source of income, although he is clearly less prosperous than before. As for his father's religion, however, he has cast that aside completely. He ends his narrative this way:

> I am a skeptic in my religious opinions, which was a stumbling block in the way of several missionaries, and other philanthropic men assisting me. I have read Paine, and Volney, and [George] Holyoake, those infidel writers, and have also read the works of Bulwer, Dickens, and numbers of others. It gives a zest to us in our criminal life, that we do not know how long we may be at liberty to enjoy ourselves. This strengthens the attachment between pickpockets and their women, who, I believe, have a stronger liking to each other, in many cases, than married people. (4:324)

Perhaps the pickpocket has rebelled most against his father's religious hypocrisy and loveless marriage. Though he knows his story will shock respectable, bourgeois readers, he is clearly proud of his honesty in living dishonestly. Certainly everything he says contradicts cherished middle-class family values *and also* cherished explanatory mechanisms or social science paradigms. But this is only an extreme instance of the pattern that occurs throughout *London Labour*. Against the voice of bourgeois social science and respectability, there are the proliferating, eccentric, nomadic voices of the street-people, who refuse to stay inside neatly constructed houses, classes, pigeonholes, stereotypes. And Mayhew himself is only partly the social scientist and voice of bourgeois respectability. One gets the feeling that his real project is to let deviance wander free of all rules and regulations, even his own, though to do so he first has to construct his flimsy, pseudo-scientific gantry-work of anthropologizing, taxonomizing, and statistics, a sort of human zoo in which the doors are deliberately rigged to spring open the moment anyone presses against them. As Blake said of Milton, Mayhew was of the devil's party without knowing it.

By privileging the oral accounts of the street-people, Mayhew and his collaborators contradict their own printed discourse. That is to say, Mayhew's street-people, though of course their speech is reproduced in the printed volumes of *London Labour*, speak through and often against the testimony of the written text in which their voices are ventriloquized. As in *Frankenstein*, an ostensibly oral discourse breaks out of literate confinement to express a vitality—monstrous, perhaps, but nevertheless alive—that exceeds the text that conveys it. Much the same contrast between oral vitality and literate tameness or domestication is a feature both of romantic and of realistic fiction. In Scott's "historical romances," for instance, Scotland's past, often expressed through supposedly oral folk songs and tales, is simultaneously both past and more alive than the modern, tepid, literate present. So, too, in much realistic fiction, the trope of "the book of the world" indicates that the stuff of reality is more alive, colorful, significant—in a word, more real—than the written text that tries to reproduce that reality. And in *London Labour*, the voices and experiences of the street-people escape the explanations and moralizings Mayhew and his collaborators apply to them.

Mayhew would be uninteresting if he had put theory before practice, verdict before evidence. But the biographical record suggests that he detested the role of judge and even of jury-member, mainly because of his own familiarity with lawyers, or at least with *one* lawyer, his solicitor father, who sought to bend all seven of his sons to his will by making them also solicitors. It was not easy having a father "who thought law was the finest thing in the world" (qtd. in Humpherys 3); one of Henry's brothers committed suicide; only one became a solicitor. Mayhew turned his legal apprenticeship to his father into a series of minor disasters—crimes in his father's eyes—so that he escaped the law as his profession.

Mayhew didn't threaten to burn the house down and run away as did the pickpocket, but he didn't have to: his father cut him out of his will and virtually banished him. He didn't turn to a life of crime, but instead devoted himself at first to amateur chemistry and comic journalism (again, criminal in his father's eyes). Perhaps chemistry was the inspiration behind his attempts at social taxonomizing, ambitious to discover the social equivalent of the periodic table. But his main claims to fame today are his helping to found the comic journal *Punch* (named for the wife-beating, child-abusing, homicidal street-puppet) and also his construction, if not sole authorship, of *London Labour*. Other projects fizzled or failed; he was often in debt, living on the continent to avoid bill-collectors, and his marriage to comedian Douglas Jerrold's daughter was as unstable as any of the pickpocket's relations with women. Mayhew was himself a bohemian, nomadic type who never settled down to any stable, life-long career.[19]

So *London Labour*, rather than being a triumph of social science positivism, is closer to being a naive nomadology or genealogy. Foucault defines *genealogy* as "anti-science," a way of deconstructing positive knowledges, reified codes, laws, tables, facticities. But a genealogy also, he says, involves the joining of expert knowledge with "naive knowledges" and "popular" memories. What genealogy "really does is to entertain the claims to attention of local, discontinuous, disqualified, illegitimate knowledges against the claims of a unitary body of theory which would filter, hierarchise and order them in the name of some true knowledge and some arbitrary idea of what constitutes a science and its objects." Genealogy gives voice to the "subjugated" knowledges of the people, those for whom and against whom the disciplinary mechanisms of the "human sciences" are deployed. Genealogy involves "a painstaking rediscovery of struggles together with the rude memory of their conflicts"; its ultimate aim is "an insurrection of subjugated knowledges" (*Power/Knowledge* 83, 81).

Just such an imaginary "insurrection," in the form of an ethnography of London nomads or "street Arabs," is what Mayhew achieved. For it is not the voice of the expert, the policeman, or the solicitor that speaks with authority in these pages, but the multitudinous, fractious, contradictory voices of men and women who have tactically chosen not to stay in one place, not to lead lives of respectability, and often enough not to honor "hearth and home," but to roam eccentrically, restlessly, often out of some necessity but often, too, out of some preference for deviance, adventure, freedom. "The ordinary practitioners of the city live 'down below,' below the thresholds at which visibility begins," writes Michel de Certeau:

> They walk—an elementary form of this experience of the city; they are walkers, *Wandersmänner*, whose bodies follow the thicks and thins of an urban "text" they write without being able to read it. These practitioners make use of spaces that cannot be seen; their knowledge of them is as blind as that of lovers in each other's arms. . . . (de Certeau 93)

CHAPTER

5

Poor Jack, Poor Jane

REPRESENTING THE WORKING CLASS AND WOMEN
IN EARLY AND MID-VICTORIAN NOVELS

They cannot represent themselves, they must be represented.
—Marx, "Eighteenth Brumaire of Louis Bonaparte" (1852)

B etween the 1790s and 1830s, a popular, radical press, working-class in ori-
entation, emerged as an alternative to middle-class discourse. The "war of
the unstamped press" in the late 1820s and early 1830s marked a clear, threatening departure from a social situation in which literacy, and literature, had been an
upper-class monopoly. The themes and traditions of radical journals such as William Cobbett's *Political Register* and Henry Hetherington's *Poor Man's Guardian* were extended and brought into national focus by the literature of the Chartist
movement between 1839 and 1848, including its widely disseminated newspaper, *The Northern Star*.[1] The great Chartist petitions of 1839, 1842, and 1848,
each signed by hundreds of thousands of workers, were acts of symbolic literacy
that, along with much else, announced by their very form and prominence a new
dispensation: a working class that knew what was in its best interest and that
could express that interest in written documents that challenged both the written
and unwritten aspects of the British constitution. Yet Carlyle for one treated the
Chartists as "delirious," and the working class in general as a "dumb," "inarticulate" giant, capable of speaking—let alone reading and writing—only through
the mute "hieroglyphic picture-writing" of events (*Chartism* 166, 196).

In Charles Kingsley's Christian Socialist novel *Alton Locke* (1850), the third
Chartist petition is described by old Sandy Mackaye, Kingsley's portrait of Carlyle,
as "the monster-petition." When Alton and John Crossthwaite tell him that they
have not only read the petition but "signed it too!" Mackaye declares that he
made no mistake in calling it a "monster":

> Monster? Ay, ferlie! Monstrum horrendum, informe, ingens, cui lumen ademptum . . . I'll no sign it. I dinna consort with shoplifters, an' idiots, an' suckin' bairns—wi' long nose, an' short nose, an' seventeen Deuks o' Wellington, let alone a baker's dozen o' Queens. . . . (349)

Mackaye is referring to the allegation that many of the signatures on the third petition were counterfeit. But he simultaneously expresses Kingsley's view that the petition itself is a fraudulent representation of the true interests of the working class. In contrast, in his Young England novel *Sybil* (1845), Benjamin Disraeli at least treats the first Chartist petition as a bona fide expression of those interests. When the petition is "carried down to Westminster on a triumphal car, accompanied by all the delegates of the [Chartist National] Convention in solemn procession," the aristocratic protagonist of *Sybil*, Egremont, speaks in favor of giving the Charter serious consideration (340–341), as did Disraeli himself in Parliament in 1839.

For many middle-class commentators like Kingsley, however, the "monster" petitions of the Chartists were somehow the products of a monstrous, out-of-place literacy. When Alton and Crossthwaite visit a group of "slop-working tailors" who are conspiring at full-blown revolution,

> [t]here was a bloused and bearded Frenchman or two; but the majority [of the conspirators] were . . . the oppressed, the starved, the untaught, the despairing, the insane; "the dangerous classes," which society creates, and then shrinks in horror, like Frankenstein, from the monster her own clumsy ambition has created. Thou Frankenstein Mammon! (344)

At least Kingsley does not echo Elizabeth Gaskell in identifying this particular Frankenstein—society—with "her" creature, but the point is just the same here and throughout *Alton Locke*: though they are victims of exploitation and injustice, and though they are increasingly literate, the working class are not equipped to represent their own interests.

In *Mary Barton*, the figure of the ignorant, inarticulate, soulless "Frankenstein" is belied by the literacy of John Barton and the other working-class characters who play prominent roles in that text. Barton's first political act, moreover, is to travel to London as an elected delegate from Manchester to present the first Chartist petition to Parliament. Through the suffering he has both experienced and witnessed, but also through reading *The Northern Star* (123), Barton has become "a Chartist, a Communist, all that is commonly called wild and visionary. Ay! but being visionary is something. It shows a soul, a being not altogether sensual; a creature who looks forward for others, if not for himself" (220). Gaskell of course here contradicts her analogy of the working class as the "soulless" Frankenstein monster just two paragraphs earlier (219–220). The contradiction is basically one between an idea of the working class as incapable of adequate self-expression (more specifically, incapable of political self-representation) and the apparently opposite idea of the working class as all too clamorous, articulate, and capable of representing itself. Like Disraeli, Gaskell sympathizes with the workers when Parliament fails to give the first Chartist petition serious consideration. Also like Disraeli, however, she sees that rejection by Parliament as the catalyst leading from "moral force" to "physical force" Chartism. In *Sybil*, the direct result of the rejection of the 1839 petition is the Plug-Plot riots of 1842. In *Mary Barton*, the result is John Barton's turn from peaceful politics to the trades-union conspiracy that leads to his assassination of Harry Carson. In both cases, and no matter how much blame Disraeli and Gaskell attach to the upper-class rejection of working-class claims, the results are monstrous.

I

In the so-called industrial novels of the early Victorian decades, from Harriet Martineau's *A Manchester Strike* (1832) through George Eliot's *Felix Holt* (1866), workers are shown to have considerable literacy and knowledge, only it is the wrong sort of knowledge. Just how the workers have gained their miseducations and how to provide them with correct knowledge are major preoccupations of middle-class discourse between the two Reform Bills of 1832 and 1867. In novels that express these preoccupations, scenes of instruction have a particular urgency not because those in need of instruction, the workers, have been reading other, inferior novels or romances, but because they have become capable of reading—and often, as both Hannah More and Friedrich Engels insisted, have been reading—Tom Paine, Shelley and Byron, Robert Owen, and other radical writers. As with *The Northern Star* and the three Chartist petitions, moreover, they have become capable of writing and publishing their own literate discourse.

In the 1830s, the debate about mass literacy shifted from whether the "lower orders" should be taught to read and write at all to the questions of what they were reading, what they should read, and how to control their reading. Novels by middle-class writers that feature working-class heroes or heroines generally also offer some version of the main lesson learned by Pip in Dickens's *Great Expectations*: aspirations to transcend or transgress class barriers—to leave the proletariat and rise into the bourgeoisie—are doomed to a tragic outcome. Fictional workers are framed by a rigid social determinism that weakens or ceases to be operative farther up the class hierarchy. Middle-class characters who ape the aristocracy are satirized for snobbery and moral counterfeiting, and so are aristocratic characters (the aristocracy as such is frequently treated as decadent, passé, and fraudulent, so to aspire to become an aristocrat is necessarily a false goal). But above the imaginary line separating the proletariat from the bourgeoisie, class identity is itself treated as a sort of necessary fiction, if not altogether counterfeit, and society for the characters who count—that is, for the upper classes—is seen as a sort of game, a drama or charade, as for example in Thackeray's *Vanity Fair*. Below the line, however, class identity becomes a grim, inescapable reality: melodrama, perhaps, but with tragic, penitential overtones. The factory lad may, by dint of hard work and honesty, become a mechanic with engineering know-how and money enough to emigrate to Canada with his childhood sweetheart, the outcome for Jem Wilson and Mary Barton in Gaskell's novel. He may occasionally also, through sheer force of character and "self-help," become a factory owner, as in Geraldine Jewsbury's *Marian Withers* (1851) and Dinah Mulock's *John Halifax, Gentleman*. But he may just as easily end in tragedy as does Mary Barton's father or, quite differently, Stephen Blackpool in Dickens's *Hard Times*, who falls down an open mine-shaft and later dies from his injuries, too good for the world.

The emergence of fictional realism as a distinct novelistic discourse during this period occurs on two levels: first, the set of literary conventions identified with realism; and second, the reification of the social status quo, notably involving, in industrial novels such as *Mary Barton*, the themes of resignation and class reconciliation. In the school of hard reality, the working-class student learns to accept his station in life (that is, his position in class society) as inevitable, natural, or God-given. In the process, the literacy he has acquired must be deflected from the sort of reading that breeds discontent and focused instead on the edifying lessons of resignation associated with Arnoldian "culture" as the means of achieving one's "best self." In most industrial novels, literacy in general is represented as a distinct improvement over the anarchy or barbarism associated with illiteracy, ignorance, and orality, including demagoguery and extreme versions of political rhetoric. But literacy itself must be tamed, disciplined; and the name for its disciplining—also the name for a disciplined literacy—is *culture*, a category that by definition transcends demagoguery, mere rhetoric, class conflict, political factionalism, and worldly self-interest or calculation.

The years between 1827 and 1836 were the heyday of "the march of mind" and of what one of its pioneers, William Chambers, was to call "the cheap literature movement of 1832." In her *History of the Thirty Years' Peace*, Harriet Martineau, who contributed to that movement throughout her career, writes: "As a winding-up of the improvements of this period, and in rank with the very first, we must mention the systematic introduction of cheap literature, for the benefit of the working-classes. A series or two of cheap works had been issued before, chiefly of entertaining books meant for the middle-classes; and there was never any deficiency of infamous half-penny trash, hawked about the streets, and sold in low shops. The time had now arrived for something very different from either of these kinds of literature to appear" (2:344–348). Landmarks in the cheap literature movement include the founding of the Society for the Diffusion of Useful Knowledge in 1827 and the commencement of *Chambers's Journal* and of the *Penny Magazine* in 1832.[2]

Whether through the SDUK or through other efforts, the aim of the cheap literature movement was to improve the mental and moral condition of the working and middle classes, in part by counteracting the worst effects both of the unstamped radical press exemplified by *The Political Register* and *The Poor Man's Guardian* and of the crude sorts of "neo-Gothic" horror and crime fiction churned out by the Salisbury Square publishers for mainly working-class readers (L. James 12–71). As early as 1821, Charles Knight, who later superintended the publications of the SDUK and edited the *Penny Magazine* and *Penny Cyclopaedia* under its auspices, predicted the rise of a middle-class but still "popular" journalism as an alternative to the working-class radical press:

> A general view of the influence of the Press would lead us to judge that very much of that influence is injurious to the safety of the Government. . . . It is the half-knowledge of the people that has created the host of ephemeral writers who address themselves to the popular passions. If the firmness of the Government, and, what is better, the good sense of the upper and middle classes who have property at stake, can succeed for a few years in providing tranquillity, the ignorant disseminators of sedition and discontent will be beaten out of the field by opponents of [*sic*] better principles, who will direct the secret of popular writing to a useful and a righteous purpose. (Knight 1:260–61)

Although "the ignorant disseminators of sedition and discontent" were not "beaten out of the field" (the war of the unstamped press led to the abolition of the "taxes on knowledge," which had rendered radical publications such as *The Poor Man's Guardian* illegal until 1836), their voices were matched in volume by a swelling chorus of intentionally popular journalism that, while promoting mass literacy, sought to inculcate the virtues of deference, industry, temperance, and political moderation in the working class. According to Henry Brougham's pregnant phrase, "the schoolmaster was abroad in the land" and mighty was the power of his instructional zeal.

Chambers's Journal boasted that it "has done more to wean the people from trash, cultivate their minds, and excite curiosity, than all the [religious] Tract Societies that ever existed" (qtd. in Altick, *English Common Reader* 337). This claim suggests that, although intended to counteract working-class unrest, the cheap literature movement was also intended to counteract the reactionary values of evangelical tract writing, which it in many ways imitated. The SDUK was modeled partly upon the Society for the Promotion of Christian Knowledge, adopting many of its tactics. The apparently inoffensive, nonpartisan writing in the *Penny Magazine* and *Chambers's Journal* disguises how controversial they seemed at the time. To working-class radicals like the readers of *The Poor Man's Guardian*, they were pabulum rather than solid food, and obnoxiously bourgeois pabulum at that. To many conservatives and evangelicals, however, they were dangerous organs of religious skepticism and social discontent. Something of the controversial nature of the cheap literature movement can be seen in Peacock's *Crotchet Castle* (1831), in which the Rev. Dr. Folliott tells the utilitarian economist Mr. Mac Quedy ("son of a Q.E.D.") that he has witnessed too much of "the march of mind":

> It has marched into my rick-yard, and set my stacks on fire, with chemical materials, most scientifically compounded. . . . It has marched in through my back-parlour shutters, and out again with my silver spoons, in the dead of the night. The policeman who was sent down to examine, says my house has been broken open on the most scientific principles. All this comes of education. . . . (Peacock 212)

Yet the promoters of "the march of mind" through the cheap literature move-ment did not think they were sowing the seeds of discontent, but nipping it in the bud. The Chambers brothers believed that they had created "a powerful moral engine for the regeneration of the middle and lower orders of society." They looked to the diffusion of "wholesome and instructive literature" as one of the causes of social peace in the Victorian era, despite occasional "Jacqueries" such as the Char-tist movement. In 1872, looking back over the years between the two Reform Bills of 1832 and 1867, William Chambers wrote:

> The mass of cheap and respectably conducted periodical literature . . . has proved one of the many engines of social improvement in the nineteenth century. Re-ferring to the example of patience which was set by the operatives of Lancashire under the agonizing calamity of [the cotton famine of the early 1860s] a minis-ter of the crown did not hesitate to declare "that to the information contained in the excellent cheap papers of this country he attributed much of the calm for-bearance with which the distressed had borne their privations." (*Memoir* 283)

Whether *Chambers's Journal*, the *Penny Magazine*, or similar cheap publications produced by middle-class teachers of the working class had any such pacifying effect is doubtful, partly because it is not clear that they reached into the working class as far as those teachers claimed that they did.[3] And even if they were widely read by the "lower orders," their apolitical politics and Malthusian lessons of resignation, thrift, temperance, self-help, and sexual restraint do not seem to have hampered the growth of Chartism, trade unionism, and socialism (much less the growth of the working-class population).

But that *Chambers's Journal* and similar "cheap literature" for the masses constituted a mighty "moral engine" for social improvement in the 1830s seemed true to some middle-class observers, although the phrase "moral engine" is re-vealing. Peacock satirized the "Steam Intellect Society"; it almost seemed as if the SDUK and other middle-class producers of "cheap literature" hoped to manu-facture enlightenment in the same way that the factories of Lancashire manufac-tured textiles. The historical significance of the Chambers brothers and Charles Knight is not that they helped to bring about a reign of social peace by convincing the working class of the folly of discontent, but that they were pioneers in the creation of modern mass culture. The success of their journal led the Chambers brothers into related cheap-literature ventures: almanacs, encyclopedias, popular histories, albums, and anthologies good for all occasions and for everyone, ooz-ing with platitudinous noncontroversies. The Chambers brothers were soon run-ning what was quite literally a knowledge factory, mass producing books and periodicals by steam, like bolts of cloth. "With twelve printing machines set to work, there was at length [by the 1850s] a fair average produce of fifty thousand sheets of one kind or another daily. Under one roof were combined the operations of editors, compositors, stereotypers, wood-engravers, printers, book-binders, and other laborers, all engaged in the preparation and dispersal of books and periodi-cals" (*Memoir* 242). Along with Charles Knight, the Chambers brothers were

perhaps the first to show how Coketown factories could produce or at least reproduce Coketown facts.

In general, the cheap literature of the 1830s eschewed fiction for fact. Its
promoters did not always view fiction as a poisonous source of discontent, but
usually did view it as an irrelevant distraction from the didactic task at hand, an
attitude also prevalent in the working-class press (Murphy 62–96). When Harriet
Martineau proposed her *Illustrations of Political Economy* to the SDUK, James
Mill and its other directors felt that it was a mistake to wrap sober, instructive fact
up in fictional packages, and rejected her plan. She had to produce her economical tracts independently, through Charles Fox, who was then editor of the *Monthly
Repository*, and only after their initial great success did the SDUK reverse itself
and offer to publish the series. Referring to the SDUK's rejection of Martineau's
tales, Charles Knight complains that its officers "were . . . as opposed to works of
imagination, as if they had been 'budge doctors of the Stoic fur,' whose vocation
was to despise everything not of direct utility" (2:315). Push-pin, it seemed, really might be as good as poetry—as useful or as useless, depending on your point
of view. *Penny Magazine*'s utilitarian hostility to both fiction and poetry was one
of the reasons for its comparative lack of success. *Chambers's Journal* always
included a story as a sop to its readers, though "no ordinary trash about Italian
castles, and daggers, and ghosts in the blue chamber . . . but something really
good" (qtd. in Altick, *English Common Reader* 333). The *Penny Magazine* was
made of sterner stuff, and although it was illustrated, its antifictional policy seems
to have kept down its circulation.

Whatever the readership of Martineau's *Illustrations*, the success of her series suggests the importance that many attached to popularizing the new science
of economics for all classes. Martineau's economical stories are close in form,
feeling, and, to some extent, political purpose to Hannah More's *Cheap Repository Tracts*, only with God replaced in the scheme of things by Adam Smith's
Invisible Hand. For Martineau, obedient to the Unitarian doctrine of Necessari-
anism, to obey the principles of economics is to obey both God and science.

In her *Autobiography*, Martineau recounts her decision to write a series of
narratives giving practical "illustrations" of the "laws" of political economy, and
also describes the difficulties she had in getting them published. In the days before the passing of the first Reform Bill, some potential publishers found her
project too controversial (162). Also, James Mill for one believed that turning the
abstract laws of economics into stories, fact into fiction, was a mistake (169).
Martineau herself worried about "the practice of making use of narrative as a trap
to catch idle readers, and make them learn something they are afraid of" ("Preface," *Illustrations* 1:xiii)—the practice, of course, of religious tract writers such
as Hannah More.

> We detest the practice, and feel ourselves insulted whenever a book of the *trap*
> kind is put into our hands. It is many years since we grew sick of works that
> pretend to be stories, and turn out to be catechisms of some kind of knowledge
> which we had much rather become acquainted with in its undisguised form.

Despite these reservations, for a "moral science" like political economy, narrative, or illustrating by example, was, Martineau believed, "the best" way to teach that science. Earlier works on economics offered readers the "history" and the "philosophy" of that science, "but we want its *picture*. They give us truths, and leave us to look about us . . . in search of illustrations of those truths" ("Preface" 1:xi).

It was therefore precisely as "illustrations" or "pictures" of the workings of the laws of economics that Martineau wrote her popularizing tales, presumably for readers of all social classes: "We do not dedicate our series to any particular class of society, because we are sure that all classes bear an equal relation to the science . . ." ("Preface" 1:xiv). But in reading *Illustrations*, it soon becomes evident that the main audience—the one to whom most of Martineau's lessons are directed—is the working class, and that her ultimate purpose is to inculcate the virtues of (political) patience, nonviolence, honesty, thrift, self-help, and sexual restraint to limit the size of the labor force. And while "trap" may not be the right metaphor for her little novels, most of them end with a catechism of the economical laws—the morals, so to speak—that they illustrate.

Of all Martineau's "illustrations," *A Manchester Strike* comes closest to the pattern of later industrial fiction both in its somberly realistic depiction of the causes of working-class discontent and in its lessons of resignation and class reconciliation. *A Manchester Strike* is both a document of instruction (like a religious tract) and a story about a scene of instruction that illustrates the taming of several forms of working-class anarchy.

Though the anarchy depicted in *A Manchester Strike* is associated with ignorance, it is not precisely associated with illiteracy. The working-class hero of the tale, William Allen, is chosen to be the leader and "secretary" of the striking union of textile-factory workers because of his integrity but also because of his superior reading and writing skills. Already embodying the moral virtues of patient resignation and nonviolence that Martineau is partly illustrating, Allen serves less as a leader of the strike than as an honorable mediator between the workers and the masters. Again (though Martineau does not use the word in her tale), it is Allen's evidently superior culture that situates him midway between the workers and the masters, already on the path to the moral and economic truths articulated by the chief middle-class pedagogue in the story, the plain-spoken master Mr. Wentworth.

The general plot of *A Manchester Strike* is one of working-class anarchy brought into conformity with the set of economic principles that Martineau summarizes after the end of the story, like the moral tacked on to an Aesopian fable. The principles themselves are all the corollaries of the main point, based on the wages-fund doctrine of orthodox political economy: "The rate of wages in any country depends . . . not on the wealth which that country contains, but on the proportion between its capital and its population" (134). Workers cannot gain an increase in their wages by striking; this only wastes both the fixed wages-sum that the manufacturers have at their disposal to pay the workers and also the even more limited funds a union can gather from contributing unions in other places while the strike is in effect. But the workers can improve their lot, including their wages, by the Malthusian method of "adjusting the proportion of population to capital" (136)—that is, of limiting their numbers through abstinence from breeding, or, in other words, from the sorts of sexual activity (she names only "early marriage" as the culprit) that Martineau, like Malthus before her, identifies as a sort of blind incontinence.

A Manchester Strike is thus as much an illustration of sexual as of political economy. The tale opens with Allen following his lame, eight-year-old daughter, Martha, home from the factory and carrying her up the stairs to their third-floor, two-room apartment in an obviously overcrowded tenement, "occupied by many poor families":

> Barefooted children were scampering up and down these stairs at play; girls nursing babies sat at various elevations, and seemed in danger of being kicked down as a drunken man or an angry woman should want to pass; a thing which frequently happened. . . . (3–4)

Though an honorable fellow, Allen himself has hardly practiced sexual restraint, because besides Martha he has fathered at least "four or five little ones" (4). The indefinite number of these "little ones," presumably all younger than Martha and therefore too young to be sent to the factory to work, reproduces the population pressure within the apartment characteristic of the tenement and, beyond it, of working-class Manchester in general. Who is to blame for the scenes of overcrowding in the streets, in the tenements, but also at the factory gates, except the workers themselves? Not the masters, not even when they are thoroughly obnoxious and exploitive. According to Martineau, echoing Malthus, only the workers have it in their power to control their destiny.

As Catherine Gallagher notes, when Allen assumes the leadership of the striking union, he knows in advance both what the outcome of the strike and what his own fate will be. The other workers choose him both because of his steadfast but modest honesty and because of his literacy (he has much correspondence to keep up with the unions in other locations). He accepts that leadership with a grim foreknowledge of the future, playing his role "in the tradition of tragic stage heroes" (Gallagher, *Industrial Reformation of Fiction* 57). The strike fails because, as the honest master Mr. Wentworth repeatedly explains to the strikers, it erodes both the union's funds and the capital from which wages are paid when all are at work. Allen and several of the other workers know this already because they have been through other strikes. Allen shoulders his duty, however, because he knows he is the best man for the job and because most of the other workers know it as well. But the result—again, one he knows in advance—is that, once the strike is over, Allen is left unemployed. Several of the masters blacklist him because of his role as strike leader, and even the sympathetic Wentworth can barely continue to employ those workers who have been with him the longest.

Added to this bleak outcome, not just for Allen and the strikers but also, according to Martineau, for the masters, is the dreary subplot of little Martha,

Allen's lame daughter. In chapter 6, entitled "Night and Morning," Martha works the late shift at the factory (the adult workers, including her father, are out on strike, but the children have continued to work—as if a factory could be kept in operation by eight-year-olds and a couple of adult overseers). Martha's painful, bandaged knees, which barely support her, are just one affliction. Another is the oppressive heat in the factory, which causes her to doze off. A kindly overlooker wakes her, but does not reprimand her. She works on till the dawn.

In contrast to the antifactory propaganda of the Ten Hours Movement, which sought to limit the hours, improve the working conditions, and raise the age-limits for the employment of factory children, Martineau's depiction of Martha suggests no criticism of child labor.[4] It isn't even clear that Martineau thinks Martha should not be working the late shift or, because of her lameness, working at all. Instead, Martineau represents Martha's plight, like her father's, as pathetic but unavoidable. The natural workings of the laws of economics produce these pitiful scenes, and only strict obedience to those laws—not ones drawn up by interfering government—can improve the lot of workers like the Allens. Those laws, which produce scarcity and hardship in the short run, will lead to prosperity in the long run, once they are understood and followed by all, workers and masters alike. "The political economy that Martineau developed," writes Gallagher, "was a popular but peculiar blend of optimistic, providential beliefs and pessimistic, mechanical doctrines; it forced the ideas of the economists into the mold of a theodicy. Her providential beliefs implied that the gloomy determinism pervading the working-class characters' lives would lead ultimately to the greatest good for the greatest number" (55).

Lessons in resignation addressed mainly to the working class, *Illustrations* follows several of the theses of orthodox, capitalist economics to their logical but narrowest extremes. John Stuart Mill declared that Martineau "reduces the laissez-faire system to absurdity as far as the principle goes, by merely carrying it out to all its consequences" (qtd. in Webb, *Harriet Martineau* 120). At the same time, Martineau was entirely sincere and benevolent in her edifying and popularizing aims. "I have been awakened from a state of aristocratic prejudice," she could write, "to a clear conviction of the *Equality of Human Rights*, and of the paramount duty of society, to provide for the support, comfort, and enlightenment of every member born into it" (qtd. in Webb, *Harriet Martineau* 123). But her democratic sympathies are curiously paralyzed, snarled in a tragic vision of scarcity and hardship that she acquired both because of her father's financial ruin in the bank crisis of 1825–1826 and from her reading of Malthus and Ricardo. Hard work, sexual abstinence, obedience to middle-class employers, and patience in the face of adversity are all that she proposes to improve the condition of the working class.

Perhaps the thorniest problem for the sympathetic Malthusian who, like Martineau, wished "to enlighten the people" arose from the vicious circle of population and charity. It was a terrible paradox of political economy that charity, however well-intentioned, was apt to create distress rather than relieve it, because it fostered improvidence and overpopulation. Yet how could one oppose charity and still claim to sympathize with the people? Martineau, "teacher of the people," had the painful duty of illustrating the principle that "all arbitrary distri-bution of the necessaries of life is injurious to society, whether in the form of private almsgiving, public charitable institutions, or a legal pauper-system" (*Cousin Marshall* 130). Distress is caused by the attempt to relieve it; the same economic laws that cause poverty also cause progress, and, although Martineau does not realize it, her vision of society inexorably binds one to the other. She and her family, as well as much of the rest of the middle class, had both prospered and suffered through early industrial capitalism, and she expected the working class to do the same. That the suffering was real she knew by experience. But she also knew, or thought she knew, that violations of economic laws only produced worse suffering, while obedience to them would ultimately bring prosperity to both "men and masters." The only kind of charity that is not "injurious to society" is the sort that teaches people how to better their lot through their own efforts, and that charity, of course, Martineau generously extends through her tales of reification.

II

Middle-class novelists who portray working-class movements, including trade-unionism and Chartism, often resort to the figure of the outside agitator to explain working-class discontent. The outside agitator is always portrayed as a class traitor and parasite who employs his own considerable literacy to mislead the working class or the poor. In "The Soul of Man under Socialism" (1891), with his usual flair for insightful paradox, Oscar Wilde declared:

> What is said by great employers of labour against agitators is unquestionably true. Agitators are a set of interfering, meddling people, who come down to some perfectly contented class of the community and sow the seeds of discon-tent amongst them. That is the reason why agitators are so absolutely necessary. Without them . . . there would be no advance towards civilisation. (232)

The "bloused and bearded Frenchman or two" conspiring with the Irish tailors in *Alton Locke* are examples of outside agitators. In *Hard Times*, Slackbridge, the trade union organizer—that is, as far as Dickens is concerned, agitator—is an equally obvious example, and so is the socialist Stephen Morley in Disraeli's *Sybil* (1845).[5] There are, moreover, outside agitators in other industrial novels, from Charlotte Elizabeth Tonna's *Helen Fleetwood* (1841) to Charles Reade's *Put Yourself in His Place* (1870), always treated as corrupting innocent or igno-rant working-class communities with false rhetoric and sometimes with secret conspiracies.[6] The outside agitator is, in other words, a false teacher of the people and is always contrasted to a genuine teacher. Moreover, the outside agitator is often characterized by his oratorical abilities; the genuine teacher, on the other hand, is usually a man of the book, whether the book is the Bible or, as with Mr. Wentworth in *A Manchester Strike*, the book of Adam Smith. The outside agitator preys on ignorance and illiteracy; the genuine teacher practices literacy and at least points his working-class students down the long road that leads to culture.

Well before his assassination of Harry Carson at the secret behest of his trade union committee, John Barton has become "chairman at many a trades' union meeting; a friend of delegates, and ambitious of being a delegate himself; a Chartist, and ready to do anything for his order" (61). To be a "delegate" would have involved traveling to other locales or at least supporting union organizing elsewhere, just as Barton travels as a Chartist delegate to London to help present the petition of 1839 to Parliament. It is not clear whether Gaskell is referring to Barton or to the general class of outside agitators when she writes:

> For there are never wanting those who, either in speech or in print, find it in their interest to cherish such feelings [of vengeance] in the working classes; who know how and when to rouse the dangerous power at their command; and who use their knowledge with unrelenting purpose. . . . (61)

Though there is no outside agitator in *A Manchester Strike*, Allen's rival for leadership of the union, a worker appropriately named "Clack," almost fills that role. Like Slackbridge in *Hard Times*, Clack is a demagogue whose only qualification for leadership is his speaking ability—he is above all an "orator" with "a very high opinion of his own powers of persuasion" (23, 17). Martineau offers a crude but therefore clear contrast between the noisy demagogue and rhetorician on the one hand, and the quiet "secretary" of the union, Allen, on the other. Throughout the story, Allen is identified with literacy and writing rather than with oratory and noise.

Through Clack, and also through the blacklisted worker Bray, who with his daughter Hannah has become a street musician, the deaf Martineau aligns orality—noise in general, it seems—with social disorder, anarchy, and ignorance. In her spare, parsimonious stories, where the leading economic force is scarcity, the antithesis to noise and anarchy, or more specifically to rhetoric and demagoguery, is precisely the spare, orderly text before the reader, or in other words the printed page that conveys the unyielding truths of economic orthodoxy. One must, it seems, be a reader to gain access to those truths or "laws," no matter how popularized into "pictures" or "illustrations." The minimal literacy necessary to read Martineau's *Illustrations* can thus be understood as a first stage in a modern, utilitarian pilgrim's progress both to the secular salvation that comes through individual culture and to the social harmony that obedience to the laws of political economy will bring. For Martineau, mass literacy is not a threat, but the necessary gateway through which the masses must proceed on their pilgrimage to culture and social harmony.

In later, more complex industrial fictions, the same equations between orality and anarchy on the one hand and literacy, culture, and social order on the other are operative and yet overwritten or contradicted in ways once again revealing mass literacy as a source of anxiety and perhaps anarchy rather than a clear, unambiguous social good. In at least two cases, moreover, *Alton Locke* and George

Eliot's *Felix Holt* (1866), the figure of the outside agitator becomes fused or confused with that of the genuine teacher of the people. Both Kingsley's and Eliot's
working-class protagonists become, not exactly intentionally, outside agitators
who are arrested for inciting riots that they seem to be leading. Yet both had
hoped to convey to the rioters the same general lessons that Martineau illustrates:
resignation, nonviolence, and class reconciliation. Their self-entrapments in the
role of outside agitator are symptomatic of the contradictory ideological impulses
that inform all industrial novels by middle-class authors. In both cases, moreover,
their quixotic attempts to lead working-class rioters express the anxiety that literacy—or, more exactly, culture in the Arnoldian sense—is insufficient to cure
the social anarchy stirred up by illiterate, or at least ignorant, masses.

Like John Barton, Alton becomes a Chartist. He also becomes a poet of the
people, comparable to "the Corn-Law Rhymer" Ebenezer Elliott and to the author of *The Purgatory of Suicides*, Chartist poet Thomas Cooper. The exercise of
his extraordinary literacy—his poetic talent—on behalf of "the suffering millions"
(270) gives him a political and literary prominence that, however, is deflated when
he is attacked as "a time-server, a spy, [and] a concealed aristocrat" in the pages
of *The Northern Star*. The author of the attack, the editor of the Chartist newspaper, is one "Mr. O'Flynn," Kingsley's caricature of Chartist leader Feargus
O'Connor. Often represented in middle-class discourse as an Irish arch-outside
agitator, O'Connor is described by Kingsley as a dangerous demagogue with (according to Kingsley's stereotyping) an Irishman's inconsistency, lack of moral
principle, and oratorical verbosity.

Stung by O'Flynn's attack, Alton is eager to prove his solidarity with Chartism
by traveling as a "deputation"—that is, as an outside agitator—to a rural district
where the starving peasants are "going to have a great meeting" to inquire into
their "rights and wrongs" (277). Once there, Alton listens to a number of illiterate
(dialect) and inflammatory speeches by the peasants, and these incite him also to
turn orator:

> I explained the idea of the Charter, and begged for their help in carrying it out.
> . . . I went on, more vehement than ever, to show them how all their misery
> sprung (as I then fancied) from being unrepresented—how the laws were made
> by the rich for the poor, and not by all for all—how the taxes bit deep into the
> necessaries of the labourer, and only nibbled at the luxuries of the rich. . . . (297)

And so forth. When this part of his speech is met with demands for "bread,"
Alton, no longer the genuine teacher of the people but now clearly the outside
agitator, responds: "'Go, then,' I cried, losing my self-possession between disappointment and the maddening desire of influence . . . 'go . . . and get bread! After
all, you have a right to it. No man is bound to starve . . .'" (298). Alton's own
speech becomes increasingly inflammatory, until he is drowned out by the "roar
for 'Bread! Bread!' My hearers had taken me at my word . . ." (298). One could
ask why they should *not* have taken him at his word, or more generally how
Kingsley could simultaneously declare his sympathy for Chartism and the op-

pressed laborers of Britain and yet renege on the logical conclusions of that sympathy, virtually on every page of his novel? As Rosemarie Bodenheimer notes, "Kingsley does not know what he thinks, and Alton is created in his image. . . . Alton is wrong when he acts like a part of the working class and wrong when he aspires beyond it" (136, 139). Alton is, in short, a character expressive of a sort of political hysteria and incoherence; like Kingsley's faltering attempts to sympathize with Chartism and the working class, Alton's faltering attempts to claim allegiance to that social class (his class of origin, of course) land him inexorably in the role of outside agitator. And it must have been difficult, if he perceived the irony at all, for Kingsley not to identify his very novel, together with all of his other efforts on behalf of his version of "Christian Socialism," with outside agitation.

In any event, responding to Alton's rhetoric, the starving peasants attack a nearby farm, grab as much food as they find, and set fire to its hay-ricks and stables. The riot becomes a miniature French Revolution when "the more ruffianly part of the mob" invade the farmhouse and vandalize its furniture while looting it of anything they can carry away. Alton, however, presumably not taking himself at his word, has been frantically trying to stop the violence, but "I was answered by laughter, curses, frantic dances, and brandished plunder":

> Then I first found out how large a portion of rascality shelters itself under the wing of every crowd; and at the moment, I almost excused the rich for overlooking the real sufferers, in indignation at the rascals. But even the really starving majority, whose faces proclaimed the grim fact of their misery, seemed gone mad for the moment. The old crust of sullen, dogged patience had broken up, and their whole souls had exploded into reckless fury and brutal revenge. . . . (301)

Just as he mimes Carlyle in the character of Sandy Mackaye, Kingsley here echoes Carlyle's account (and perhaps Burke's) of the invasion of the Tuileries by the French revolutionary sansculottes. His attempt to distinguish between "the real sufferers" and the "ruffianly part of the mob," moreover, echoing similar middle-class attempts (particularly those of the Benthamite poor-law reformers of the 1830s) to distinguish between the deserving and the undeserving poor, is typical of the crowd psychology in much middle-class Victorian discourse, a sort of despairing divide-and-conquer strategy. But a parallel contradictory division afflicts Alton as both the inciter of the riot (the outside agitator) and the first person on the scene who attempts to prevent it. Though he hasn't exactly intended to be such a Doppelgänger, so lacking in "self-possession" (297), one frequent synonym for *culture*, Alton is almost as much a divided self as Frankenstein and his monster. From Kingsley's perspective, one itself divided by extreme ideological bad faith, justice is served when Alton is arrested as a leader, or at least fomenter of the riot, and jailed for three years.

During his time in prison, Alton strives after culture, both to produce the great poetry he feels he can write and to become a genuine teacher of the people.

His course of reading is both severe and exemplary. True, Alton evades the censorship of the prison chaplain by learning French and getting Sandy Mackaye to smuggle in copies of Proudhon and Louis Blanc (324). And he interprets the Bible in a distinctly political, democratic way that the chaplain would not have approved (323). But by the end of his jail term, Alton has also learned his lesson: no longer the outside agitator, his new acquisition of literary, historical, and scientific culture equips him to be, far more than before his penitential experience, a man of culture, a poet, and a genuine teacher of the people.

"The frenetic history of Alton's class oscillations and betrayals," writes Bodenheimer, "is partially controlled by another, more rigidly allegorical structure that might be called the novel's family romance" (145). Alton's first mentor, Sandy Mackaye, dies with the last gasp of Chartism. Alton finds another, higher mentor—fairy godmother, as Bodenheimer puts it—in the aristocratic Eleanor Staunton, who presides over Alton's delirious evolutionary dream, his conversion to Christian Socialism, his emigration, and his death. "Eleanor replaces Sandy because social reform must come from the upper classes and from a redeemed Church of England" (Bodenheimer 145). Alton's self-contradictions and failures, like the failure of Chartism, convey the incoherent message that all workers who take up politics in order to represent their own interests are outside agitators. In contrast, it takes an aristocratic, angelic outsider like Eleanor Staunton to bring about genuine reform, which is always a reform of the individual heart.

More coherently or at least clearly than in *Alton Locke*, the motif of the outside agitator in industrial fiction reaches a climax or, perhaps, crisis in Eliot's *Felix Holt*. Once again, as in *Alton Locke*, the protagonist himself becomes, albeit partly against his will, just such an agitator. But virtually every literate character who engages in politics in Eliot's novel can be seen as an outside agitator, both because Eliot treats politics in general as external to and disruptive of communities like Treby Magna and because literacy as such is somehow alienating. Only Felix is capable of turning literacy to genuinely constructive use, and that is because he is the working-class incarnation of literacy's transfiguration into the higher category of culture. At the same time, the very distance of culture—again, in the Arnoldian sense—from working-class values and behaviors (construed as ignorance and anarchy, if not exactly as illiteracy) means that all attempts to diffuse it among the masses will seem like versions of outside agitation and may, in any case, do as much harm as good. Both Alton Locke and Felix Holt personify the grotesque transformation of culture into its opposite—into outside agitation, into anarchy—at the hands of the "soulless" and unreasoning Frankenstein's monster, the working-class mob.

At Duffield, where Felix has gone to watch the pre-election shenanigans of the various candidates in the first election after passage of the Reform Bill of 1832, he listens to a powerful speech by a red-headed "trades-union man" (300) who says that "the greatest question in the world is, how to give every man a man's share in what goes on in life"—an assertion that Felix loudly cheers "in his sonorous voice" (297). But Felix disagrees when the speaker says that "if we working men are ever to get a man's share, we must have universal suffrage, and annual Parliaments, and the vote by ballot, and electoral districts" (299). As far as Felix is concerned, mere voting, if it is ignorant voting, will not give "every man a man's share." Eliot's word for what the working-class "man" must have before he is granted the vote is *culture*, which Felix almost translates into *wisdom*: there is no sense and a lot of danger in extending the franchise to voters who are the opposite of wise—who are "ignorant" and therefore either "wicked" or susceptible to the "wickedness" of others.

That Felix, though a working man of sorts, is also a man of culture is evident even in his appearance. At the start of his speech in response to that of the Irish trade-unionist, his "face had the look of habitual meditative abstraction from objects of mere personal vanity or desire, which is the peculiar stamp of culture, and makes a very roughly-cut face worthy to be called 'the human face divine'" (300). He has rejected his father's patent medicine business as he rejects all other forms of "cant," false culture or false rhetoric, and instead taken up the honest trade of watch-repairing. But Felix's true vocation is that of teacher. To Esther Lyon, he seems often like "an angry pedagogue," though she comes to realize that he is only trying to bring her around to her "best self" (224), a phrase that foreshadows Arnold's *Culture and Anarchy*. That much of his teaching of Esther involves strictures against her reading of Byron and of French novels reinforces his role as advocate of whatever higher forms of literacy he and Eliot, like Arnold, identify with the ideal category of culture. From his first meeting with Esther, he attacks her favorite forms of reading as frivolous: "Byron's poems! . . . What! do you stuff your memory with Byron, Miss Lyon?" (61). At one point, Felix himself alludes to Shakespeare's *Tempest*, only to recollect that Esther's adoptive father, the dissenting minister Rufus Lyon, considers Shakespeare irreligious or nonserious. Rufus has "looked into" Esther's volume of Shakespeare's plays, but then "forbore the reading, as likely to perturb my ministrations" (226–227). Eliot's thought here is not that Rufus is even more the man of culture than Felix, but that he, as Arnold might put it, over-Hebraizes. There is a hierarchy of literature (and therefore culture) and for Eliot, Shakespeare is near the apex of that hierarchy. Moreover, even the Bible can be misread or too narrowly construed: Rufus is close to being a man of culture, but his dissenting religious views place him in the camp that, in *Culture and Anarchy*, Arnold identifies as "illiberal." In any event, Esther is a version of the female Quixote, and it is Felix's pedagogy and example that weans her from Byron and French novels and gives her instead a "vision" of what her life might be.[7] Felix "was like no one else to her: he had seemed to bring at once a law, and the love that gave strength to obey the law" (227). Evidently the "law" for Eliot is very different from the laws of England—the legal tangles of the inheritance plot and the machinations of lawyer Matthew Jermyn suggest the misuse of literacy and a fraudulent version of culture—and also different from the "laws" of economics "illustrated" by Martineau. The higher "law" that Felix represents is exactly that which Arnold identifies with culture: the "pursuit of perfection," the recognition of "right reason and the will of God."

Felix tells Esther that he wants to be a "demagogue," but "a demagogue of a new sort; an honest one, if possible, who will tell the people they are blind and foolish, and neither flatter them nor fatten on them" (224). This is at least part of the teaching that he had hoped to deliver to the Sproxton miners before his lesson was interrupted by the election agent, Mr. Johnson. It is also the main substance of the speech he gives to the election-day crowd—a speech about "power":

> I'm a working man myself, and I don't want to be anything else. But there are two sorts of power. There's a power to do mischief—to undo what has been done with great expense and labour, to waste and destroy, to be cruel to the weak, to lie and quarrel, and *to talk poisonous nonsense*. That's the sort of power that ignorant numbers have. . . . Ignorant power comes in the end to the same thing as wicked power; it makes misery. It's another sort of power that I want us working men to have, and I can see plainly enough that our all having votes will do little towards it at present. I hope we, or the children that come after us, will get plenty of political power some time. (249; my italics)

The phrase "to *talk* poisonous nonsense" signals that Eliot, at least in *Felix Holt*, is more anxious about the influence of oratory on "ignorant numbers" than about poisonous reading. All of the speeches given by the political campaigners in the novel, perhaps including Felix's speech, are wide of the mark: either mere foolishness like Mr. Brooke's election speech in *Middlemarch* or forms of oratory more likely to delude than to enlighten the masses. In Felix's strictures about Esther's reading and elsewhere (for example, in "Silly Novels by Lady Novelists"), Eliot expresses her concern over the lack of moral seriousness and also of realism in much of the literature of her time. But in *Felix Holt*, the equation between oratory and working-class disorder (noise, shouting, uproar) appears to be the same as that in *A Manchester Strike, Alton Locke*, and, indeed, in *Culture and Anarchy*, where Arnold describes the predilection of workers to "practice an Englishman's right to do what he likes; his right to march where he likes, meet where he likes, enter where he likes, hoot as he likes, threaten as he likes, smash as he likes" (85). For Eliot as for Arnold, noisy "rowdyism" is the antithesis of culture, or of that slow, quiet, historically reverent literacy that depends on a silent reading and understanding of both the printed page and tradition.

Before the working class gains "political power," Felix believes (and Eliot agrees), "ignorant power" must be replaced by education, by the ideal power that comes with culture. Felix does not get around to describing that ideal power, however, except in negatives—in terms of what it is not, apart from the ability to recognize "public duty" (250). Meanwhile, "suppose there's a poor voter named Jack, who has seven children, and twelve or fifteen shillings a-week wages, perhaps less. *Jack can't read* . . ." (251; my italics). So the route to virtuous power— that is, the power of culture—comes down to literacy. After the first Reform Bill of 1832, few or none of the new voters, the "ten-pound householders," were actually illiterate. And in 1866, when *Felix Holt* was published, on the verge of the passage of the second Reform Bill (1867), illiteracy, as opposed to mere ignorance, which can hardly be measured, had declined even further. But Felix nevertheless invokes the specter of "poor Jack," the illiterate voter, though otherwise—in Felix's strictures about Esther's reading, in the obvious deficiencies of the speeches made by the political campaigners, and in the legal and illegal entanglements of the inheritance plot—Eliot worries much more about what she considers to be the abuses of literacy.

In *Felix Holt*, those who sow the seeds of discontent and disorder among the perhaps otherwise innocent, though ignorant, workers all qualify as outside agitators. For Eliot, the role of outside agitator acquires a sort of infinite expandibility: anyone from the upper classes who pretends to represent the working class is doomed to failure, less because workers or the masses are ignorant and destructive than because they are different, incomprehensible, and unrepresentable by anyone except one of themselves. The character Felix Holt is a sort of utopian, wishful figure for Eliot—her version of what an ideal representative for, and representation of, the working class might approximate. That Felix is not a particularly probable or believable character does not negate the fantasy of representation produced by Eliot's quite genuine political and cultural idealism. In a sense, Felix is nobody because nobody could be Felix: like Horatio Alger, he is too good and honest to be real or even realistic. So he only represents the ideal image or "best self" of what Eliot hoped the working class might become. Meanwhile, there are illiteracy, ignorance, anarchy, political and legal machinations—all the stuff of reality that Felix transcends and that Eliot rejects in favor of culture.

Nevertheless, even Felix is, in relation to the Sproxton miners, an outside agitator, though he is trying only to teach them lessons of patience, temperance, and nonviolence similar to Martineau's lessons of resignation and class reconciliation. He is merely striving to be an ideal "demagogue." But the role of outside agitator most obviously fits Mr. Johnson, the electioneering charlatan or vote-hustler from London, hired by lawyer Jermyn, who has himself been hired by Harold Transome, the newly returned prodigal son and supposed heir to the Transome estate and also the Radical (quondam Tory) candidate for North Loamshire. In several senses, Jermyn is also an outside agitator: as his employer's secret antagonist; as a lawyer; as a lawyer seeking to blackmail both the Transomes and the Durfeys; and as an electioneering agent himself, seeking, partly through employing Johnson, to manipulate the vote. And so is Harold Transome a sort of outside agitator, or at least an interloper, a figure of homelessness at home: this prodigal son and false heir has spent years in the Orient, especially in Smyrna, acquiring a second fortune, a Greek wife, and a semi-savage (or just spoiled?) semi-semitic or semi-oriental son.

Other characters in *Felix Holt* also fit the outside agitator role. These include the candidates in the field against Transome: Durfey the Tory, Garstin the Whig, and also their electioneering agents. And there is the red-headed "trades-union man" who appears out of nowhere, makes his impressive speech, and then disappears. Felix's speech follows and responds to that of the Irish union organizer. As a piece of imagined oratory, Felix's speech is thoroughly inept, and yet Felix, apparently because of his manly stature, fearless honesty, and "sonorous voice" (246), makes himself heard and even applauded. He tells the workers in his audience that they are drunken, ignorant louts who don't deserve the vote. His speech is rhetoric in the literal sense of spoken language, oratory: honest rhetoric, of course, attempting to counteract those who "talk poisonous nonsense." But there is also printed or literate "poisonous nonsense": Esther's novels, the labyrinth of legal documents in which the inheritance plot is snarled, the counterfeit election placards that Johnson manufactures and that, with Maurice Christian's inveigling, the illiterate Tommy Trounsem plasters on the walls of Treby Magna. Felix—and Eliot—run up against the difficulties that anyone encounters who attempts to combat "cant" or the false uses of language, whether spoken or written: they must use words to fight words, and though culture may be invoked as a higher, ideal category, the actual contents of that category cannot be fixed or rendered absolute; they are instead socially constructed and relative.

Felix's lengthy oration expresses his anxiety, and clearly Eliot's as well, about the nefarious impact "ignorant numbers" (read: the masses) are likely to have on government and society if allowed to vote. He has much to say about the damage to "public opinion" that the hypothetical voter "poor Jack" will do because of his illiteracy. "Jack can't read," says Felix; "I don't say whose fault that is—he never had the chance to learn . . ." (251). Felix imagines "poor Jack" being corrupted and misled by "a smart stranger"—that is, an outside agitator—very much like Mr. Johnson, who has been busily "treating" the Sproxton miners. But as the example of Mr. Johnson suggests, the main political plot line of the novel doesn't concern what men like "poor Jack" do when they vote, but what they already do without being able to vote. "Ignorant numbers," plied with free beer, show up at the polls to cheer and to hoot candidates, to intimidate voters, to create public disturbances. This is exactly the outcome that Felix had hoped to prevent by his abortive lessons to the Sproxton miners.

The election riot that ensues, like the bread riot in *Alton Locke*, finds the protagonist, the man of culture, trapped in the middle of it. Unlike Alton, whose speech actually incites the riot, Felix's oratory has had no such inflammatory effect. Nevertheless, Felix's heroic attempt to quell the violence, or at least to prevent the worst of it from occurring, involves his "assuming the tone of a mob-leader" (266) and to some extent even acting like one:

> Felix was perfectly conscious that he was in the midst of a tangled business. But he had chiefly before his imagination the horrors that might come if the mass of wild chaotic desires and impulses around him were not diverted from any further attack on places where they would get in the midst of intoxicating and inflammable materials. . . . He believed he had the power . . . to carry the dangerous mass out of mischief till the military came to awe them. . . . (268)

Felix does not have that "power," however, any more than he has earlier had the pedagogic, rhetorical, or cultural power to win the Sproxton miners to more sensible behavior. For his efforts, which allegorically are those of culture attempting to raise the ignorant masses to a vision of their "best self," Felix, like Alton, is imprisoned for inciting to riot. Eliot agrees with Arnold that culture is the only conceivable cure for the anarchy of class conflict, and yet her novel expresses deep pessimism about the very possibility of such a cure. Once again, as in Kingsley's fantasy, culture, descending or intruding from above into the lower reaches of the class hierarchy, itself appears to be a form of outside agitation. The antithesis of culture proves to be politics in general, which means that it is inapplicable in reality to the very problems that, ideally, it is meant to solve.[8]

Just as the early Victorians had worried that transforming illiteracy to literacy was not solving but was instead exacerbating the crime problem, so Eliot worries that culture—the only conceivable solution, given her conservative strain of mid-Victorian liberalism—will not prevent anarchy. In his self-chosen vocation as a teacher of the Sproxton miners, at least, Felix is a failure. Apart from the working-class boy whom he takes under his wing, the only person Felix's pedagogy clearly affects is, of course, Esther, and it is Esther's newly discovered power of culture—identical in the trial scene to her newly found voice, her rhetoric— that empowers her to give the testimony that releases Felix from prison. As in several other examples of industrial fiction (*Sybil, North and South, Shirley*), Felix and Esther, both now identified with the ideal power of culture, go forth into freedom and into their new life together, but with no greater power over "ignorant numbers" than they had at the start.

III

In her industrial novel *Shirley* (1849), Charlotte Brontë employs the motif of the outside agitator to suggest that Luddism was a conspiratorial movement not only against the interests of manufacturers like Robert Moore, but also against the interests of the working class. As the honest worker William Farren tells Shirley Keeldar and Caroline Helstone,

> there is many an honest lad driven desperate by the certainty that whichever way he turns, he cannot better himself, and there is dishonest men plenty to guide them to the devil: scoundrels that reckons to be the "people's friends," and that knows naught about the people, and is as insincere as Lucifer. I've lived aboon forty year in the world, and I believe that "the people" will never have any true friends but theirsel'n, and them two or three good folk i' different stations that is friends to all the world. (367)

In his pursuit of the leaders of the machine-breakers, Moore reaches the same conclusion. Despite his early arrest of the Rev. Moses Barraclough, a local Methodist preacher and tailor, as one of the leaders, Moore concludes that the real culprits "were strangers: emissaries from the large towns. Most of these were not members of the operative class: they were chiefly 'downdraughts,' bankrupts, men always in debt and often in drink—men who had nothing to lose, and much— in the way of character, cash, and cleanliness—to gain" (431). The *declassé* backgrounds of *Shirley*'s outside agitators suggest the conspiratorial, paranoid view of revolution expressed by many conservatives and liberals from 1776 and 1789 forward. Brontë wrote and published *Shirley* just as the Chartist movement was climaxing, and in the excitement and fear generated by the continental revolutions of 1848.[9]

After the nightime attack on his mill, which he heroically defends with the help of the military and the local clergy, Moore pursues the outside agitators to London, sees that the "four ringleaders" are arrested, attends their trial, and makes sure that they are transported. Apart from the attempt on Moore's life by the crazy, alcoholic, "Antinomian preacher," Michael Hartley, whose motive is not clearly explained, Luddism disappears from the novel. With Moore's recovery and the rescinding of the Orders of Council in 1812, his business begins to prosper. He has also learned the lesson that Caroline has attempted to teach him from the start, that he should not behave toward the workers as Coriolanus behaved toward the Roman plebs. At the end, a kinder and gentler Robert Moore, now married to Caroline, witnesses the fulfillment of his "extravagant day-dreams" of social progress and prosperity for everyone connected with his mill. The narrator comments:

> The other day I passed up the Hollow, which tradition says was once green, and lone, and wild; and there I saw the manufacturer's day-dreams embodied in substantial stone and brick and ashes—the cinder-black highway, the cottages, and the cottage gardens; there I saw a mighty mill, and a chimney, ambitious as the tower of Babel. (739)

Though the allusion to Babel adds a note of ambivalence to this otherwise nearly utopian picture of industrial peace and prosperity, Moore almost single-handedly has managed to quell Luddism. After the Luddite period, Brontë suggests, class conflict gave way—or should have given way (and this is her implicit criticism of the Chartist movement)—to the recognition that the interests of workers and their middle-class masters are identical. The industrial aspect of Brontë's novel offers a plot of class reconciliation and social progress based on technological advancement and free trade, a version of the triumph of the bourgeoisie and the taming of the proletariat. As Terry Eagleton notes, moreover, the triumph involved the at least momentary unification of the upstart industrial bourgeoisie with the gentry against the working-class Luddites. Shirley Keeldar is herself partly an incarnation of that ruling-class unity because she is the landowner on whose property Robert Moore's mill is located; she is thus simultaneously a member of the gentry and, as she likes to assert, a manufacturer. In political terms, as Eagleton notes, *Shirley* thus expresses a "curious blend of Gaskellian liberalism and Wellingtonian reaction" (46), which means that from neither perspective is it clearly sympathetic to the workers.

It is not the case, however, that Brontë portrays the Luddites as completely ignorant of their interests and bamboozled by the outside agitators. Despite faulty spelling, the Luddites who waylay the waggons carrying the first shipment of machinery to Moore's factory leave an elaborate, threatening note. Further, the individual working-class characters in the novel—William Farren; Michael Hartley; Joe Scott, the foreman at Moore's factory—are all literate, articulate advocates of their various political and social opinions. Thus, when Moore accuses Joe and his fellow workmen of being "savages," Joe replies:

> I reckon 'at us manufacturing lads i' th' north is a deal more intelligent, and knaws a deal more nor th' farming folk i' th' south. Trade sharpens wer wits; and them that's mechanics, like me, is forced to think. (68)

Joe adds that he likes reading, "and I'm curious to knaw what them that reckons to govern us aims to do for us and wi' us." Moreover, he claims that he is not unusual, but that "there's many 'cuter nor me" (69). Given this picture of working-class literacy and intelligence, it is not clear why, assuming that Luddism was not in their interest, the workers should fall prey to the outside agitators. On the other hand, if Luddism was in their interest, and the workers knew this, they wouldn't have needed outsiders to rouse them to action.

Further, much as Alton Locke and Felix Holt become unwilling outside agitators, Moore the manufacturer is the ultimate outsider in *Shirley*. A Belgian, he has wound up running a mill in Yorkshire, on Shirley Keeldar's property. As an industrialist, Moore is also, for better or worse, the disrupter of England's green and pleasant land, which is one implication of the ambivalent passage about "the tower of Babel." Brontë treats Moore both as a hero—the one manufacturer brave enough to stand up to the Luddites—and as an interloper.[10] Though the future belongs to industry, Brontë in various ways criticizes mill owners and capitalists for being, at least at the time of the Napoleonic Wars, unpatriotic profit-mongers. Moore the outsider and despoiler of England's rural past must himself be humbled and tamed, partly by Michael Hartley's bullet and partly by the two heroines, Caroline and Shirley.

At the same time, women in *Shirley*, as in all the Brontës' novels, are also outsiders, alienated by a patriarchal system that offers them few outlets for their intelligence, emotions, and dynamism. Prohibited by her uncle from socializing with Moore, Caroline longs for change, and she eventually asks for permission to seek work as a governess.

> At last the life she led reached the point when it seemed she could bear it no longer; that she must seek and find a change somehow, or her heart and head would fail under the pressure which strained them. She longed to leave Briarfield, to go to some very distant place. She longed for something else. . . . (208)

Caroline does not leave, however; instead, her restlessness finds its match in Moore's ambition. Brontë emphasizes the comparison, not between the alienation of women and that of the working class, but between the desire expressed by Caroline, which is partly the longing to do meaningful work in the world, and Moore's equivalent desire to struggle through difficulties, represented mainly by Luddism, for the sake of social progress.[11]

Nevertheless, just as both Caroline's and Shirley's longings seem to exceed the conventional ending in marriage, there is something inexplicably excessive about Luddism, an inarticulate energy and violence that makes it comparable to, for instance, Shirley's fantasies about "the first woman." This is not Milton's Eve, she tells Caroline, but "a woman-Titan" (360). Milton's Eve was modeled upon "his cook" (359), whereas the genuine Eve, whom Shirley identifies with Nature, was the mother of Titans. "I say, there were giants on the earth in those days: giants that strove to scale heaven. The first woman's breast that heaved with life on this world yielded the daring which could contend with Omnipotence" (360). There is here, as also in Shirley's identification with manliness (she bears a man's name; she is an "esquire," or master of an estate; she is "Captain Keeldar" and a "tigress" as ready to stand up against the Luddites as her tenant, Robert Moore), a rebelliousness that would seem to align Shirley with the Luddite rebellion. But Brontë avoids acknowledging that women and workers have similar injustices to rebel against, by making Shirley, as Moore's creditor and landlord, also an industrialist (another manly role), by giving her conservative political opinions, and by showing her as adamantly opposed as is Moore to the Luddites.

But that there is something rebellious—revolutionary, even—smoldering within the hearts and minds of Charlotte Brontë's heroines was commonly recognized by many of her first readers. For instance, in her 1855 *Blackwood's Magazine* essay, "Modern Novelists—Great and Small," Margaret Oliphant approvingly calls the "furious love-making" of *Jane Eyre* "a wild declaration of the 'Rights of Woman' in a new aspect. . . . Here is your true revolution. France is but one of the Western Powers; woman is the half of the world" (312). Oliphant thinks that *Jane Eyre* and *Villette*, along with *Wuthering Heights*, offer "revelations" of both women's and men's passions and desires that ordinarily "lie below the surface of life," and she seems to echo the reviewer of *Jane Eyre* for the *Christian Remembrancer*, who declared that "every page burns with moral Jacobinism" (90). But of course Jane Eyre is no more explicitly a Jacobin than Shirley Keeldar is a Luddite. And as do the marriages that conclude *Shirley*, the ending of *Jane Eyre* draws whatever has been transgressive or "wild" about both the heroine's and Mr. Rochester's behavior back into the fold of conventionality: "Reader, I married him" (574).

Though this declaration announces the final taming of both heroine and hero, it is nevertheless the lowly orphan and governess Jane who addresses the reader, whether female or male, and whose passionate life has enough "interest" for her to record it and publish the account as an irregular "autobiography."[12] The question of literacy—not just of reading and writing, but of *who* reads and writes, and *what* gets read and written—is central to all of Charlotte Brontë's novels, but perhaps especially, given what Mark Hennelly calls its "preoccupation with the problematic phenomenology of reading" (694), to *Jane Eyre*. Despite hardships— the selfishness of the Reeds, the evangelical tyranny of Mr. Brocklehurst, and so on—Jane succeeds in acquiring an excellent education and becomes first a governess and then a schoolteacher herself. Though an avid and impressionable reader, moreover, at no point does she appear to be a female Quixote, seduced by romantic reading, and the same can be said of both Caroline Helstone and Shirley Keel-dar.[13] True, reading in chapter 1 of *Jane Eyre* is represented as an escape from the exclusions visited upon Jane by Mrs. Reed and the Reed children, and Bessie the nurse is also in the habit of feeding "our eager attention with passages of love and adventure taken . . . from the pages of Pamela, and Henry, Earl of Moreland" (5). But, left to her own devices, Jane chooses quite different, nonfiction books to read: Bewick's *History of British Birds* and Goldsmith's *History of Rome* (4, 8).

If Jane Eyre as a reader is not a female Quixote, neither does she follow the path of evangelical righteousness marked out for her first by Mr. Brocklehurst and later by St. John Rivers. Hers is a serious, secular cultivation. Throughout her story, Jane manages to be a passionately imaginative but disciplined reader, and at the novel's end her new role as Rochester's wife is also one of serious, passion-ate, but, it appears, secular reading. Her husband, she declares, saw both nature and "books through me":

> . . . never did I weary of gazing for his behalf, and of putting into words the effect of field, tree, town, river, cloud, sunbeam—of the landscape before us . . . and impressing by sound on his ear what light could no longer stamp on his eye. Never did I weary of reading to him. . . . (577)

Needless to say, Jane takes reading seriously; after all, it is this activity—read-ing—more than any other that allows her to follow both the romance and the vocation plots of her life story to their logical conclusions, and then to write her irregular account of those plots.

When, with Rivers's assistance, Jane begins her second career as a village schoolteacher, her aim is to provide her students with the literacy to acquire a similar cultivation. Most of the "coarsely-clad little peasants" whom she teaches are illiterate at first (458), but "several farmers' daughters . . . could already read, write, and sew; and to them I taught the elements of grammar, geography, history, and the finer kinds of needlework" (467). Similar scenes of instruction occur in *The Professor*, *Shirley*, and *Villette*. Having gained their own educations, some-times against difficulties, Brontë's heroines discover their vocations as teachers, helping others achieve literacy and culture. Especially in *Jane Eyre* and *Villette*, scenes of instruction can be understood as foreshadowings of Arnold's doctrine of culture, similar in this respect to *Felix Holt*. But literacy and culture, and with these the moral gravity that Brontë associates with artistic imagination, are first and foremost the achievements and attributes of her heroines, giving them the necessary mental and emotional equipment both to oppose and to domesticate (and, of course, to marry) their male antagonists, lovers, and, in Shirley's case, former teacher. Though an industrial novel of sorts, *Shirley* is less concerned with bringing culture to the workers than with the heroines' taming of the middle-class men in their lives, Robert and Louis Moore; and *Jane Eyre* has little to do with the working class, but much to do with how a poor girl, herself almost work-ing class, manages to use her education to tame a member of the squirearchy, Mr. Rochester.

As Penny Boumelha notes, for Charlotte Brontë's heroines, a plot of *Bildung* and vocation leads teleologically from being taught, often by men, to teaching—to taking charge of the instruction of others. But the plot of vocation conflicts with two other story-lines: that of romance, leading to marriage, and that of desire, over and above both vocation and romance (20). The plot of desire, Boumelha suggests, is in effect an anti-plot, consisting of impulses and wishes that cannot be roped back into social conventionality as dictated either by vocation (the governess plot) or by romance (the marriage plot). Bertha Mason, "the madwoman in the attic," represents just such an uncontainable, unplottable or unsocializable excess. To many critics, she has seemed to be a sort of improbable, if not altogether impossible, quintessence of otherness.[14] Insofar as "female desire" exceeds the plots of vocation and romance, the chief way that Brontë accommodates it is through her own and her heroines' ability to express it. But because Bertha Mason exists outside of the rules of society and reason—metaphorically as pure flame or passion or anger—she does not, cannot, express her own excess. Both Jane Eyre and Lucy Snowe, however, compromise between passion and reason, alienation and socialization, self-assertion and submission. They are thus enabled—indeed, in a sense, culturally empowered—to write their irregular autobiographies, though part of the irregularity corresponds to the often dreamlike passages and events that seem to express whatever exceeds the double plots of vocation and romance.

Though all of Charlotte Brontë's heroines are private poets or artists, the plot of vocation focuses almost exclusively upon teaching; novel-writing is never represented as a possible career. The novels themselves (at least those narrated by their heroines, *Jane Eyre* and *Villette*) stand in for the something in excess; they *are* the transgressive results of their author's efforts to express female desire, or that which cannot be contained within the conventional logics of either romance or vocation. And though her adoption of a male pseudonym, like that of her sisters and of other women novelists and poets throughout the eighteenth and nineteenth centuries, is ordinarily understood as a conventional act of deference to patriarchy, it can also be understood as another form of transgression—a transvestite wish, at least, like Shirley's manliness, to make gender performative or malleable, an also excessive expression of female desire that seeks to escape the rules of patriarchy.

The chief result of Jane's own education is, of course, the story of her life—the story we read. And her struggle to help others gain literacy can be understood as directed toward the voicing and recognition of those "millions" who are "condemned to a stiller doom than mine," the "millions" of women who "are in silent revolt against their lot" (132). Here Brontë does identify the "lot" of women with that of the working-class "masses," though her emphasis is upon women:

> Nobody knows how many rebellions besides political rebellions ferment in the masses of life which people earth. Women are supposed to be very calm generally: but women feel just as men feel; they need exercise for their faculties, and a field for their efforts as much as their brothers do; they suffer from too rigid a

restraint, too absolute a stagnation, precisely as men would suffer; and it is narrow-minded in their more privileged fellow-creatures to say that they ought to
confine themselves to making puddings and knitting stockings. . . . (132–133)

Jane, of course, does not allow herself to be so confined; her own use of literacy,
her writing of her irregular autobiography, is her primary act of rebellion and
self-assertion, one that Brontë clearly intends to be exemplary for readers of both
genders.

Charlotte Brontë's novels all push against the limits of patriarchy and prudery, but none of them is quite so overtly transgressive as her sister's masterpiece,
Wuthering Heights. Thus, while Sandra Gilbert and Susan Gubar read *Jane Eyre*
as ambivalently transgressive, they read Emily's astonishing rewriting of *Paradise Lost* as a "Bible of Hell." In the first act of rebellion by Catherine and Heathcliff
recorded in *Wuthering Heights*, the youngsters throw the "good books" Joseph
has foisted upon them "into the dog-kennel," Catherine "vowing" that she "hated
a good book" (26). The books are evangelical tracts, *The Helmet of Salvation* and
The Broad Way of Destruction. The primary recorder of this rebellion against
"good books," moreover, is none other than Catherine herself, writing in the margins of another book that Lockwood discovers in the closet where he is to sleep:

> Catherine's library was select, and its state of dilapidation proved it to have
> been well used, *though not altogether for a legitimate purpose*; scarcely one
> chapter had escaped a pen-and-ink commentary—at least, the appearance of
> one—covering every morsel of blank that the printer had left. (24; my italics)

In contrast to Jane Eyre's more conventional, Arnoldian literacy, Catherine
Earnshaw turns reading and writing into acts of self-assertion that, Gilbert and
Gubar note, allude to the rebellions both of Frankenstein's literate Monster and
of the ultimate incarnation and master of earthly knowledge, Satan. Catherine's
rebellion against "good books" is not a rebellion against books in general, but
specifically against Joseph's evangelical tracts. Catherine's "select" library,
moreover, has "been well used," presumably both well read and overwritten, so
that the books have become palimpsests, as if Catherine were struggling to write
her own book. She is at least the author of this early, highly suggestive narrative
fragment (embedded, of course, in Lockwood's main narrative), one that, besides
presenting herself and Heathcliff as blasphemous rebels against "good books,"
nevertheless establishes the importance of reading and writing, for Catherine at
least, as means of self-expression and rebellion.

Catherine's rebellious use of literacy is soon contrasted, however, to
Heathcliff's "degradation" through Hindley's abusive treatment of him. Forced
to work like a slave or an animal, Heathcliff loses "the benefit of his early education," including "any love for books or learning" (84). That Heathcliff manages
somehow to rise above his degradation and to gain additional education (or experience, at least) during his three years' absence is a measure of his will power.

But, as part of his revenge, he then treats Hareton in the same abusive manner that Hindley had treated him. Heathcliff keeps Hareton from learning to read and write, teaches him to curse like Caliban, and "to scorn everything extra-animal as silly and weak." As a result, Heathcliff tells Nelly, "he'll never be able to emerge from his bathos of coarseness and ignorance. I've got him faster than his scoundrel of a father secured me, and lower; for he takes a pride in his brutishness" (267).

In contrast to Hareton's "brutish" miseducation by his "devil daddy," Catherine Linton receives an excellent education from her father. Nelly tells Lockwood that "curiosity and a quick intellect urged her into an apt scholar; she learnt rapidly and eagerly, and did honour to his teaching" (232–223). The opposition between Hareton's ignorance and Catherine's education is magnified toward the end of the novel, in part by another scene of destructive rebellion against books. Catherine tells Lockwood that Heathcliff has destroyed all of her books, except for a "secret stock" of them preserved by Hareton, who has been using them to struggle toward literacy. In this episode, Catherine mocks Hareton for his theft and his "blunders" at reading and writing. "The young man," Lockwood says, "evidently thought it too bad that he should be laughed at for his ignorance, and then laughed at for trying to remove it" (364–365). Hareton responds by dealing with Catherine's books exactly as her mother and Heathcliff had dealt with Joseph's "good books" in the opening account of rebellion. Hareton, according to Lockwood, "gathered the books and hurled them on the fire. I read in his countenance what anguish it was to offer that sacrifice to spleen—I fancied that as they consumed, he recalled the pleasure they had already imparted, and the triumph and ever increasing pleasure he had anticipated from them . . ." (366). Lockwood goes on to guess that the chief "incitement" to Hareton's "secret studies," the chief source of his anticipated pleasure, is Catherine's respect and affection: "Shame at her scorn, and hope of her approval were his first prompters to higher pursuits" (239).

For Hareton, then, the pathway to literacy and the "higher pursuits" of culture is also the pathway to love and reconciliation. When Lockwood pays his next visit to Wuthering Heights, six months after Hareton's burning of Catherine's books, he discovers Hareton engaged in a reading lesson, with Catherine as his rough but doting teacher. Lockwood listens as Catherine gets Hareton to read the word "contrary" correctly, and then to reread a longer passage:

> The male speaker began to read—he was a young man, respectably dressed, and seated at a table, having a book before him. His handsome features glowed with pleasure, and his eyes kept impatiently wandering from the page to a small white hand over his shoulder, which recalled him by a smart slap on the cheek, whenever its owner detected such signs of inattention. (372)

The battle of the books in *Wuthering Heights* leads to this ultimate scene of instruction, which is also the scene of Hareton's transformation from peasant "brutishness" and illiteracy to some approximation, at least, of middle-class culture and respectability.[15] Hareton, it seems, is well on his way to becoming another

Edgar Linton, if not another Lockwood. As later in Arnold, in both *Jane Eyre* and *Wuthering Heights*, the solution to social "anarchy" and class conflict lies in right though not religious reading—that is, in a secular literacy that has the power to reshape the "brutish" and dangerous working class after the "respectably dressed," well-spoken, and nonviolent image of the bourgeoisie.

6

Cashing in on the Real in Thackeray and Trollope

And yet in very truth the realistic novel must not be true,—but just so far removed from truth as to suit the erroneous idea of truth which the reader may be supposed to entertain.

—Anthony Trollope, *Thackeray*

The thematic and metaphoric connections between money/commodification and realistic fiction go back at least as far as Defoe. In contrast to the more or less aristocratic "romance," Defoe's decidedly bourgeois novels are all about gaining and losing "fortunes" in the monetary sense. "That Robinson Crusoe, like Defoe's other main characters . . . is an embodiment of economic individualism hardly needs demonstration," writes Ian Watt. "All Defoe's heroes pursue money . . . and they pursue it very methodically according to the profit and loss book-keeping which Max Weber considered to be the distinctive technical feature of modern capitalism" (63). But what was true for Defoe is equally true for both Thackeray and Trollope. Enumerating both real wealth and debts, Thackeray's *Vanity Fair* and Trollope's *The Way We Live Now* can both be read as fictionalized account-books: their characters' "fortunes" depend less on moral virtue than on real wealth gained or lost, or at least on financial credit temporarily gained or lost.

The equations between fiction and money, literary imagination and fiscal credit, and the novel and other commodities in Thackeray and Trollope are simultaneously basic to their practice of narrative realism and a powerful source of their own resentment against that practice. They saw themselves as the manufacturers of commodified amusements for a degraded marketplace or readership that scarcely deserved to be called literary. Though Thackeray in particular worried about working-class semi-literacy, as in his 1838 review "Half-a-Crown's Worth of Cheap Knowledge," both he and Trollope imagined the mainly middle-class, novel-reading public, and more specifically the readers of their own novels, as doing something analogous to eating candy or drinking punch.[1] "Novels are sweets," Thackeray declares. "All people with healthy literary appetites love them; almost all women;—a vast number of clever, hard-headed men." But as with sweets, it is possible to overindulge, as does the "lazy idle boy" Thackeray once observed novel-reading at Chur: "He is taking too great a glut of [novels]. . . . He is eating jelly until he will be sick" (6). And Trollope echoes Thackeray, on this as on many other issues: "So it is with the novel. It is taken because of its jam and honey" (Thackeray 202).

Trollope goes on to note, however, that novel-reading is also a serious business because "the bulk of the young people in the upper and middle classes receive their moral teaching chiefly from the novels they read" (203); therefore, it is urgent to pay attention to something more than the "jam and honey" that they contain. Besides sweetness, novels also provide, or should provide, light, both *dulce* and *utile*: "unlike the honest simple jam and honey of the household cupboard, [the novel] is never unmixed with physic. There will be the dose within it, either curative or poisonous" (202). Here again, of course, is the novel as *pharmakon*, either wholesome or toxic. Trollope's ambivalence points explicitly to his view that there are (morally) good and bad novels, but that ambivalence may also be understood as suggesting that there are good and bad ways of consuming novels, or in other words that the same novel may be "curative" to one reader and yet "poisonous" to another.

Along with metaphors of eating for reading, the merchant's account book remained a central paradigm for realistic fiction from Defoe onward, down at least as far as such late-Victorian and Edwardian realists as George Gissing (*New Grub Street*), H. G. Wells (*Tono-Bungay*), and John Galsworthy (*The Man of Property*). But why should money even more than food be the baseline for establishing an illusion of reality? As Marx understood, money was at once the ultimate commodity (and therefore, the ultimate object of the false worship he anatomized at the outset of *Capital* as "commodity fetishism"), the ultimate measure of at least economic value, and the ultimate expression of the reification of all values under bourgeois hegemony. The great nineteenth-century realistic novelists, including Thackeray and Trollope, often seem to be depicting the social realm as exactly the congealed, monetarized, and alienated realm that Marx analyzed. Realistic fiction from Balzac (or even Defoe) down to Gissing and Galsworthy simultaneously valorizes and condemns money as the measure of all values. To reduce everything to reality means to de-idealize, to puncture the balloon of romance, to be anti-Platonic, and so forth. In terms of both economic and cultural value-hierarchies, moreover, it also means to equate the high with the low, or at any rate with the common—the mediocre, the middling, the quotidian, the ordinary.

I

The reduction to the ordinary—realism as the fictional but not necessarily critical mirror of everyday reality—raises simultaneously questions of the status of the realistic novel as literature (or high culture) and of the moral purpose of reading it. Because of its equivocal status as commodity and as (mere) mirror of reality, the realistic novel, unless it is explicitly critical of reality from an idealistic standpoint that violates its claim to realism, cannot logically claim to be a superior form of writing or a better source of moral instruction than the idealistic forms of fiction (usually identified with romance) that it often appears to critique.

Moreover, since the equation of high with low implicit in fictional realism can be understood to elevate the low just as readily as to deflate the high, the logic of realism is not that of the lowest common denominator; it is rather the logic of the general equivalent, which is the value form that can serve as the measure of all values—that is, money. At once the scandal and the glory of bourgeois consciousness, money as the ultimate yardstick of values is also the ultimate yardstick of reality in realistic fiction. From the perspective of the bourgeois "science" of values, capitalist economics, money is the glory of modernity because it rationalizes, universalizes, and objectifies the otherwise subjective realm of values. From the perspective of the critics of orthodox economics such as Marx, money is the scandal of bourgeois ideology precisely because it reduces or reifies all values—and, indeed, human beings themselves as commodities—into the almighty signs of the dollar, the pound, the franc, the deutschmark. The realistic novel is a literary, rhetorical structure constructed uneasily, perhaps unrealistically, over this monetary faultline.

The description of life among Fleet Street publishers, editors, and hack writers in Thackeray's *Pendennis* suggests that almost anyone with sufficient literacy and in want of money, including penniless Irishmen like Captain Shandon, can turn a penny by producing subliterary poems, essays, and novels and palming them off on the credulous reading public as literature. From his cell in debtors prison, Captain Shandon founds the *Pall Mall Gazette* with an appeal to "the gentlemen of England" to uphold the "ancient monarchy" and the Church (*Pendennis* 348–349). Political articles appear in the new journal that the reading public judges to be by great statesmen, but that are instead either by Shandon or by Pen's friend, Warrington (374). Pen himself writes "impertinent" reviews for the journal, characterized more by youthful "dash and flippancy" than by sound knowledge or taste (377). The same sense of dishonesty, of counterfeiting genuine culture, carries over to the publication of Pen's novel, *Walter Lorraine*, which is the double or analogue for Thackeray's novel, *Pendennis*. Reading *Walter Lorraine*, Warrington tells Pen: "All poets are humbugs, all literary men are humbugs: directly a man begins to sell his feelings for money he's a humbug" (434).[2]

All literature produced for money, including his own novels, Thackeray suggests, is counterfeit: "When you want to make money by Pegasus (as he must, perhaps, who has no other saleable property), farewell poetry and aërial flights; Pegasus only rises now like Mr. Green's balloon, at periods advertised beforehand, and when the spectators' money has been paid" (*Pendennis* 380). Thackeray does not quite say that selling one's private "feelings for money" is the modern, Fleet Street equivalent of selling one's soul to the devil, but that metaphor is perhaps implicit in his depiction of the petty squabbling and literary posing among the Fleet Street characters whom Pen encounters. For instance, at publisher Bungay's dinner, Wagg tells Pen about Percy Popjoy's novel, plagiarized from "an old magazine story written by poor Buzzard years ago" (372). The plagiarist, however, wasn't Popjoy, but hack writer Bob Trotter, who "fished [the story] out and bethought him that it was applicable to the later elopement; so Bob wrote a few chapters *à propos*—Popjoy permitted the use of his name, and I dare say supplied a page here and there—and 'Desperation, or the Fugitive Duchess' made its appearance" (372). Wagg adds that "the great fun is to examine Popjoy about his own work, of which he doesn't know a word," and he proceeds to praise to its supposed author "a capital passage . . . where the Cardinal in disguise, after being converted by the Bishop of London, proposes marriage to the Duchess's daughter" (372). When Popjoy responds gratefully, adding that the passage is "a favourite bit of my own," Wagg whispers to Pen: "There's no such thing in the whole book. . . . Invented it myself. Gad! it wouldn't be a bad plot for a High Church novel" (372).

Here, as with Pen's amateurish, autobiographical *Walter Lorraine*, Thackeray continues the practice of parodying novels and satirizing both novelists and novel-readers with which he began his own literary career. In *Catherine*, he had satirized Newgate novels such as *Paul Clifford*, *Jack Sheppard*, and *Oliver Twist*. In "The Professor," *The Yellowplush Papers*, and *A Shabby Genteel Story*, he satirized Byronism, "silver fork" or "fashionable" novels like Bulwer-Lytton's *Pelham*, and also bourgeois realism like his own. In *Barry Lyndon*, he satirized both Irish novels and historical romances such as Scott's (as he did a few years later in his sequel to *Ivanhoe*, *Rebecca and Rowena*). And in *Novels by Eminent Hands*, he satirized works by G. P. R. James, Bulwer-Lytton, Disraeli, Mrs. Gore, Cooper, Charles Lever, and himself (*Crinoline* "by Je-mes Pl-sh, Esq.," mocks Thackeray's own *Yellowplush Papers*). As Trollope remarks, "No writer ever had a stronger proclivity towards parody than Thackeray, and we may . . . confess that there is no form of literary drollery more dangerous" (194). What Trollope does not fully recognize, perhaps, is the danger that Thackeray's parodic bent poses to fiction in general, and more specifically to the novel. Just as the neoclassical satirists whom Thackeray emulated (Pope, Swift, Gay) often wrote mock-epics, Thackeray wrote mock-novels. A novel was merely a commodified form of artistic or literary sham, which if well done could be a decent form of amusement, but which was also in some basic way antithetical to the great literature of the past (cf. Shepperson 206–233).

In several of his early mock-novels, Thackeray creates author-characters who are at best semi-literate, like Charles Yellowplush with his servant's-eye-view of the "fashnabble" world and his comic misspellings and malapropisms. Orphaned, Yellowplush was, through the goodness of "a benny-violent genlmn," placed in "the Free School of Saint Bartholomew's the Less," where he received "sicks years" of education (169). It is on the basis of this semi-literacy, as Thackeray conceives it, that Yellowplush sets up shop as "a littery man" who (like Thackeray) publishes his "papers" in *Fraser's*. Yellowplush declares to his fellow servants who have read and been astonished by his first article:

"I am . . . a littery man—there is no shame in it in the present instins; though, in general, it's a blaggerd [blackguard,] employment enough. But it ain't my *trade* —it isn't for the looker of gain that I sitt penn to paper—it is in the saycred caws of nollitch. . . ." (166)

Yellowplush goes on to say that the "exolted class which *we* have the honour to serve . . . has been crooly misreparysented. Authors [of fashionable novels such as Bulwer-Lytton, named later in Yellowplush's speech] have profist to describe what they never see" (166). Yellowplush's "saycred caws" is therefore to set the deluded readers of fashionable novels straight about "the aristoxy" (167).

Similarly, though Barry Lyndon comes from the "exolted class" that Yellow-plush chronicles, and is therefore apparently better educated than Thackeray's footman-author, he is a vivid instance of unreliable narration: his fictional autobi-ography is largely the product of Irish blarney. Barry Lyndon, moreover, also frequently alludes to novel-reading as a less-than-serious, disreputable, distract-ing activity. Thus, he describes his six weeks of education (considerably shorter than Yellowplush's): "at taw, prison-bars, or boxing, I was at the head of the school, but could not be brought to excel in the classics." On the other hand, "in the matter of book-learning, I had always an uncommon taste for reading plays and novels, as the best part of a gentleman's polite education" (14). Barry Lyndon's semi-literacy—his mere six weeks of formal schooling—does not prevent him, in an age of semi-literacy, from writing his inflationary life story and palming it off on a credulous reading public, itself (Thackeray seems to believe) only semi-literate.

When Thackeray describes novel-reading in his early mock-novels, it is al-ways as a frivolous activity that somehow takes the place of more literate, more serious, or more rational forms of reading. In *A Shabby Genteel Story*, George Brandon says that Mrs. Gann is a great reader "of the fashionable novels, in every word of which she believes" (296). And in *The Yellowplush Papers*, the Shum sisters are "great slatternly doddling girls [who] was always on the stairs, poking about with nasty flower-pots . . . or sprawling in the window-seat with greasy curl-papers, reading greasy novels," while their mother "was such a fine lady, that she did nothink but lay on the drawing-room sophy, read novels, drink, scold, scream, and go into hystarrix" (171). Thackeray's own resentment or self-con-tempt at making his living through novel-writing is evident in such remarks, as well as in the generally parodic and satiric quality of all of his fictions. As An-drew Miller notes, for Thackeray novels, including his own, "are inadequate for the significance he wants them to carry and he, as a result, stands estranged from the products of his own labor" (15).

Thackeray's early story "The Professor" is as good an example of his mock-novel practice as any. The romantic, novel-reading Adeliza Grampus, daughter of an oyster-monger, falls in love with the mountebank dancing instructor, Roderick

Dandolo, who poses both as a "professor" and as the thirty-eighth Count of Dandolo. "[I]s it not passing strange that one of that mighty ducal race should have lived to this day, and lived to love *me*? But I, too," Adeliza tells her friend Miss Binx, "am . . . a daughter of the sea." The narrator continues:

> The fact was, that the father of Miss Adeliza Grampus was a shell-fish monger, which induced the young lady to describe herself as a daughter of Ocean. She received her romantic name from her mother, after reading Miss Swipe's celebrated novel of *Toby of Warsaw*; and had been fed from her youth upwards with so much similar literary ware, that her little mind had gone distracted.

Like Mrs. Gann and the Shums, in other words, Adeliza Grampus is a female Quixote. Her oyster-mongering father had been forced to send her from home "at fifteen, because she had fallen in love with the young man who opened natives [oysters] in the shop, and had vowed to slay herself with the oyster-knife" (114).

The reduction of literature to food and reading to eating is the main satiric trope in "The Professor." When Dandolo receives a letter from Adeliza with no less than three postscripts, "he literally did what is often done in novels, he *devoured* them" (120). And his own letter in response moves from high romance to the bathos of hunger and, even more absurdly, of the seafood that Adeliza has sent him along with her letter:

> Hear my tale! [writes Dandolo.] I come of a noble Italian family. . . . We were free once, and rich, and happy; but the Prussian autograph [autocrat] has planted his banner on our towers,—the talents of his haughty heagle have seized our wealth, and consigned most of our race to dungeons. I am not a prisoner, only an exile. (121)

Dandolo continues: "I have wrestled with misfortune in vain; I have struggled with want, till want has overcome me. Adeliza, I WANT BREAD!" This declamation then leads to the pathetic final paragraphs of what turns from a love letter into a begging letter:

> The kippered salmon was very good, the anchovies admirable. But, oh, my love! how thirsty they make those who have no means of slaking thirst! My poor grandmother lies delirious in her bed, and cries in vain for drink. Alas! our water is cut off; I have none to give her. The oysters was capital. Bless thee, bless thee! angel of bounty! Have you any more sich, and a few srimps [sic]? My sisters are *very* fond of them. . . . Half-a-crown would oblige. . . . (121)

The bathetic declension in Dandolo's letter, and in the story as a whole, through misspellings, malapropisms, and bad pronunciation, from love to food and finally money, is the same pattern to be found in Thackeray's later fiction.

At the climax of "The Professor," Dandolo shows up at the Grampuses' oyster shop, eats enough shellfish and drinks enough booze to serve at least four people, and racks up a bill amounting to £1 5s. 9p. This bill is itemized in the text:

	s.	d.
Two lobsters at 3s. 6d. 7		0
Sallit 1		3
2 Bottils Doubling Stott 2		4
11 Doz. Best natifs 7		4
14 Pads of Botter 1		2
Bredd (love & 1/2) 1		2
Brakitch of tumler 1		6
1	5	9

Here, of course, the account-book basis of Thackeray's fictional realism is explicitly rendered. When Mr. Grampus demands payment of this bill, the professor declaims, "in a voice of thunder": "What a flat you are . . . to think I'm a-goin' to pay! Pay! I never pay—I'm DANDO!" (126).

Adeliza, who has gone for a glass of brandy and water for the deceiver, returns just in time to see Dando "tipsy and triumphant, bestriding the festal table, and yelling with horrid laughter" (126) while her father rushes off in search of the watchman. Realizing the truth at last, Adeliza faints, and when her parents manage to revive her with vinegar and soda-water, she is "restored . . . to life, but not to sense. When Adeliza Grampus rose from that trance she was a MANIAC!" Such is the dire fate of this female Quixote; but, asks the narrator, "what became of *the deceiver?*"

> The gormandizing ruffian, the lying renegade, the fiend in human shape, escaped in the midst of this scene of desolation. He walked unconcerned through the shop, his hat cocked on one side as before, swaggering as before, whistling as before: far in the moonlight might you see his figure; long, long in the night-silence rang his demoniac melody of "Jim Crow"! (126)

In the morning, an inventory is made at the oyster shop, and "a silver fork, a plated ditto, a dish, and a pewter-pot" are missing.

But this is not quite the end of the tale, because the narrator-author, "Goliah Gahagan," first adds a paragraph of moralizing sentiment about "the folly of sickly sentiment" and "the *meanness* of gluttony" (129), and then follows this up with a begging passage of his own: "NOTE.—Please send the proceeds as requested per letter; the bearer being directed not to give up the manuscript without" (129). The final words of the tale, in short, seem to convert it into a begging letter, on one level little different from Dandolo's fishy love letter about "the kippered salmon" to Adeliza, which ends with "half-a-crown would oblige" (121). Thackeray's mock-novel formula is one of words turning into either food or money, though as *begging* words they can just as easily be understood as equaling either hunger or debt (or both, since food and money are equated).

Given the reigning vanity of Vanity Fair, writing—even writing the novel *Vanity Fair*—is a vain endeavor. As has often been noted, like the Augustan satirists whom he admired and took as models, Thackeray repeatedly writes himself into a *caveat lector* corner: this is a "novel without a hero," declares the subtitle in mock-epic fashion; Vanity Fair—or *Vanity Fair*—is mere play, mere theatrical entertainment, declares the "Before the Curtain" preface; "I" the novelist am merely "the Manager of the Performance," the puppeteer pulling the strings that give "the puppets" the mere semblance of motion and life. The fair and puppet-show metaphors at once reveal the dissembling of most of the characters (they are all masquerading) and the theatrical, illusory nature of the whole (social reality as masquerade). But the narrator's insistence on theatricality means that he cannot insist on his own narration as offering objective, slice-of-life realism. Instead of mirroring everyday reality in all its solidity and detail, *Vanity Fair* suggests that such solidity and detail are, at best, a transient mirage. In offering that revelation, however, the novel itself threatens to dissolve into "a mobile army of metaphors," showing its own "truths [to be] illusions about which one has forgotten that this is what they are" (Nietzsche 46–47).[3]

Just as the society *Vanity Fair* depicts is a charade, so is the novel, because in a society in which both written and spoken language are ordinarily shallow, hypocritical, or deceitful, the novel written from within that society, whether it provides a truthful representation or not, will perforce also be shallow, hypocritical, and so on. "The world is a looking-glass," says the narrator, "and gives back to every man the reflection of his own face" (11). Is the reflection critical or merely narcissistic? In order to be critical, Thackeray suggests that it must be the latter: whether the looking-glass is the novel that Thackeray, echoing John Bunyan, names *Vanity Fair* or the self-confirming world that the novel names, people will see what they want to see, pay the price for the performance, and come away entertained but not necessarily wiser. That the specular relation of *Vanity Fair* to the world it reflects is a fetishistic one follows: the commodity-form of the novel, as Andrew Miller points out, mirrors exactly, but presumably without any transcendence, whether aesthetic or philosophical (the omniscient puppeteer ironically claims to have no more wisdom than his puppets), the increasingly commodified realm of Victorian capitalism.

As even his most admiring critics, including Trollope, acknowledge, for Thackeray the novel is a facile form of writing that the author exchanges for money in a none-too-sophisticated marketplace. "The demand [for novels] being what we know it is," Thackeray writes in "A Lazy Idle Boy," "the merchant must supply it, as he will supply saddles and pale ale for Bombay or Calcutta" (7). The novelist is simply a tradesman who can start from nothing—no capital, minimal education, and no apprenticeship: "Literature and politics have this in common, that any ignoramus may excel in both. No apprenticeship is required . . ." ("Fashionable Authoress" 570). This is a claim that Trollope, both in his monograph on Thackeray and in his *Autobiography*, echoes almost verbatim. In the former, Trollope declares that Thackeray, after the loss of his Indian fortune, was attracted to literature as "a business which . . . requires no capital, no special education, no training, and may be taken up at any time without a moment's delay. If a man can command a table, a chair, a pen, paper, and ink, he can commence his trade as literary man" (10), which is just what both George Warrington and Arthur Pendennis do in *Pendennis*. There are at least four forms of self-denigration involved in Thackeray's and Trollope's claims of the *easiness* of undertaking the "business" or "profession" of literature. First, there is the Gissing-like class resentment involved in exchanging what others, at least, may still consider to be literature or art for money, thus reducing literature to a mere commercial enterprise. Second, there is the further sense—false modesty, no doubt—that one needs no genius, talent, or exceptional education to engage in this enterprise. And third, there is the more general contempt for a society and culture that has produced a novel-reading public incapable of distinguishing high or true literature from the commodified form of the novels they so readily purchase and consume as the latest form of mass entertainment. Finally, with other realists, Thackeray and Trollope share the open secret that their novels are not reality but fictions instead, which seemingly reduces the novelist to a purveyor of lies rather than truths.

When the narrator of *Vanity Fair* directly addresses his readers, he usually genders them female, but sometimes also male (Flint 247–248). According to the narrator, the female reader will be inclined to credit, to emote, even to weep over the sentimental aspects of the story, as does Amelia Sedley: "the silly thing would cry over a dead canary bird or over a mouse that the cat haply had seized upon, or over the end of a novel were it ever so stupid" (5). In contrast, the male reader will react differently:

> All which details [about Amelia's "sensibility"], I have no doubt JONES who reads this book at his club, will pronounce to be excessively foolish trivial twaddling and ultra-sentimental. Yes, I can see Jones at this minute (rather flushed with his joint of mutton and half-pint of wine,) taking out his pencil and scoring under the words "foolish twaddling" &c., and adding to them his own remark of *"quite true."* Well he is a lofty man of genius, and admires the great and heroic in life and novels, and so had better take warning and go elsewhere. (6)

"Jones" is the figure for the (male) reader that Garrett Stewart calls Thackeray's "hypocrite lecteur" (49–54), while Amelia and most other female readers in his stories are variations on Charlotte Lennox's Arabella, the original "female Quixote."

Though both Becky Sharp and Amelia Sedley are novel-readers, the shrewd and cynical Becky is, needless to say, closer to the skeptical, unsentimental male reader like "Jones" than to Amelia.[4] And Becky's initial act of rebellion—throwing Dr. Johnson's *Dictionary* out of the coach window as she and Amelia leave the Miss Pinkertons' academy—is hardly one of illiteracy or even of miseducation, but can instead be construed as a rejection of all forms of literate culture that do not serve her immediate self-interest of getting ahead in the world. Like Defoe's Moll Flanders and Roxana, Becky's main reading interest has to do with the bottom line, the text of money. In direct contrast to sentimental Amelia, Becky is a better representative of the class of hard-nosed *homo economicus* or bourgeois businessmen than even Amelia's father, who of course goes bankrupt. Like Defoe's money-conscious heroines, Becky is an extraordinary example of that key, usually male, bourgeois virtue, self-help, whereas the meek and mild Amelia is in constant need of male help.

When the widowed Amelia, feeling guilty about her father's bankruptcy, spends a little money for some good books for her beloved son, Georgy, she purchases *The Parent's Assistant* and *Sandford and Merton*. She then writes in each, "in her neatest little hand, 'George Osborne, A Christmas gift from his affectionate mother.'" The narrator adds: "The books are extant to this day, with the fair delicate superscription" (462). Thackeray apparently does not think much of these "good books," though more approvingly than of those that Mrs. Kirk, "disciple of Dr. Ramshorn," supplies Amelia. These are evangelical tracts: "three little penny books with pictures, viz., the 'Howling Wilderness,' the 'Washerwoman of Wandsworth Common,' and the 'British Soldier's best Bayonet'" (270). Neither Amelia nor her son seem to get much help from any of these "good books"—or if they do, the narrator never tells us so. Nevertheless, Amelia, though prone to reading and crying over sentimental novels, is also a reader in search of "good books," whereas Becky throws Johnson's *Dictionary* from the coach, preferring altogether different forms of textuality.

In contrast to Amelia's timid but genuinely "affectionate" gift to her son, with her supplemental "fair" and "delicate" but apparently enduring, genuine "superscription[s]" inside the covers, Becky eventually cajoles the young Sir Pitt Crawley to get her "presented to her Sovereign at Court" (473). Unvirtuous women seeking "a character for virtue," the narrator remarks, all seek the monarch's benediction, because "from that august interview they come out stamped as honest women" (473). The narrator continues:

> And as dubious goods or letters are passed through an oven at quarantine, sprinkled with aromatic vinegar, and then pronounced clean—many a lady whose reputation would be doubtful otherwise and liable to give infection, passes through the wholesome ordeal of the Royal presence, and issues from it free from all taint. (473)

On this "royal" occasion, Becky receives "a certificate of virtue" from the Lord Chamberlain—a document which, despite or because of its monarchical cachet, fits into the proliferating category of phony or counterfeit writing that threatens to overwhelm the novel: begging letters, IOUs that are never paid, adulterous love notes, altered wills, eviction notices, and of course novels.

There are many sorts of "dubious goods" as well as "letters" throughout *Vanity Fair*, some of them penned by Becky herself.[5] When the Miss Pinkertons, Becky's and Amelia's former teachers, provide "the indefatigable pursuer of truth," Mrs. Bute Crawley, with various "juvenile letters and petitions" written by Becky to her feckless French father, "imploring" his financial support or "declaring her . . . gratitude" (191), the narrator reflects that "in Vanity Fair there are no better satires than letters" (191). Given the foolishness, deceitfulness, immaturity, and silliness of letters in general, the narrator declares,

There ought to be a law in Vanity Fair ordering the destruction of every written document (except receipted tradesmen's bills) after a certain brief and proper interval. Those quacks and misanthropes who advertise indelible Japan ink, should be made to perish along with their wicked discoveries. The best ink for Vanity Fair use would be one that faded utterly in a couple of days, and left the paper clean and blank, so that you might write on it to somebody else. (192)

The narrator's target here is not just personal letters, but *"every written document,"* which must include his own "written document," the novel. Not only is the novel itself interwoven with numerous personal letters by Becky and many other characters, but the only exception the narrator makes to "every written document" is "receipted tradesmen's bills." In other words, the only "written documents" that can be trusted in Vanity Fair and that deserve to be preserved are statements of monetary indebtedness, even though most of these go unpaid (Becky and Rawdon notoriously live on "nothing a year" for several years). Novels, on the other hand, including *Vanity Fair*, would seem to be no different—at least, no more creditworthy—than the sorts of begging letters that Becky, her husband, and some of the other characters write in search of money. If Vanity Fair—that is, society—is counterfeit, then so is its supposedly creditworthy reflection, *Vanity Fair*.

II

Conventional theories of literary realism presumably explain how words can best represent reality. In contrast, poststructuralist theories of literary realism presumably explain how words cannot (never already) represent reality. But both of these presumptions are simplistic. Poststructuralists do not deny that words can represent reality, because that's what words ordinarily do; what they deny is that representations can or should ever be mistaken for presences (or for reality). Similarly, the theories that I have here labeled "conventional," including those generated by realist fiction-writers, often seem poststructuralist *avant la lettre*. It would be strange indeed for any writer in any age not to recognize the difference between words and reality, which is the main reason why there is "always already" a "failure of mimesis."

Mimesis of course "fails" because it is mimetic—it is only (ever eternally) an imitation of the real, never the real stuff—the *Ding-an-sich*. In *Dickens and Reality*, John Romano declares that "the failure of literature faithfully to represent the real is the defining preoccupation of realism. . . . For the novelist's preoccupation with the novel's failure of mimesis inevitably finds expression in the novel's form, which is, then, the form of frustration" (94). But if Romano is correct, there must be a goodly number of frustrated forms of failure, perhaps nearly as many as correspond to literary and artistic works through the ages (and not just those dubbed "realistic"), because most works are in some sense or to some degree mimetic. The question vis-à-vis novelistic realism then becomes, what is "the form of frustration" specific to it as a set of rhetorical, fictional conventions?

My answer to this question is a double one. First, the realistic novel is a "form of frustration" because the closer it appears to come to effacing the distinction between itself and reality, the more duplicitous it becomes. To put this paradox in its simplest terms, the truer a realistic fiction seems, the falser it is (the more it corresponds to "the erroneous idea of truth which the reader may be supposed to entertain," as Trollope says in the epigraph to this chapter). In contrast, those literary forms that exaggerate, thematize, or otherwise stress their artifice—their difference from reality—realistically or honestly declare their fictive status. And second, the realistic novel is a "form of frustration" because, as a commodity exchangeable for money, in its own terms its ultimate value is no more or less than the price that it sells for in the literary marketplace. Its materialistic premises, including its emphasis on the power of money over its characters' lives and "fortunes," define and limit its status as a commodity. That is to say, its own thematization of money and commodification undermines the possibility of its transcending the marketplace, or of its achieving a high cultural value distinct from its exchange value. These two forms of frustration together distinguish realistic fiction from all other literary forms. Moreover, especially because money serves as the baseline—the chief yardstick or measure—of reality in most realistic fiction, and also because money ("the root of all evil") is invariably treated as a false or counterfeit measure of true value, these two generic markers tend to fuse or to operate as if identical: duplicitous realism as fool's gold or counterfeit money. Of all Victorian novelists, Thackeray and Trollope seem to have been most aware of this metaphoric nexus, and also—at least prior to George Gissing—of the literary frustration or dead end of a fictional realism that, the more it achieves its goal of accurate, documentary mimesis, the more tautological, uncritically narcissistic, and duplicitous it becomes.

Writers of realistic fiction start from the always-already frustrated assumption and sometimes assertion that their works will provide the closest possible approximation to reality—that they will adopt, mimetically speaking, the least frustrated of all artistic and literary forms or methods. The frequent post-1839 comparison between photography and realistic fiction implies that realists believe their fictions can rival photography in achieving documentary accuracy (perfect empiricism: seeing is believing or, rather, is ocular proof, tautologically speaking, of what one has seen). But the photograph, like the "human document" dramatized or melodramatized by Émile Zola and the Goncourt brothers, itself is doomed to exactly the same sort of mimetic failure that Romano emphasizes: only the most naive viewer would ever mistake a photograph for the reality it portrays.

Yet, does either the photograph or the human document express frustration, as Romano suggests? Part of the illusory or trompe l'oeil quality of both photography and "human documents" (including both realistic or Zolaesque naturalist fiction and all of the kinds of documentation admissible as evidence in the human sciences) may be the failure of either the photograph or the document to express frustration: though photographers and human scientists can emphasize the artifice of their forms or modes, such an emphasis can also strike the viewer or reader as inappropriate. On the other hand, it is possible to construe certain structural features of both photographs and documents as expressing a kind of frustration: nineteenth-century photographs, for example, were often posed or staged because of the time-lapse involved in producing an image on early silver plates. So Matthew Brady's pictures of the Civil War were much more after-the-fact than were televised images of the Gulf War coming from cameras inside the snouts of so-called "smart bombs" (though in those images there were no corpses, in contrast to Brady's pictures of corpse-strewn battlefields). More often than not, the photograph or the document (the confession, the transcript, the interview, the ethnographic "thick description," the "objective" news story, history *wie es eigentlich gewesen*, the "genealogy") betrays little or no frustration. Their particular forms of failure, as opposed to frustration, reside in their claims, or at least the various impressions they deliver, that the difference between them and reality is the slightest possible—almost nonexistent. In this manner, as the realistic novelists, painters, and photographers of the nineteenth century recognized, the photograph is an especially uncanny form because it is such a deeply duplicitous form. A photograph fails, of course, to correspond exactly to the reality it depicts; but unless the photographer works to produce special effects, expressive of artifice, the photograph also fails to express frustration about the inevitable failure of mimesis that is a defining characteristic of all forms of representation.

In nineteenth-century realistic fiction, the frustrating failure of mimesis is often most evident when money is the theme or when money is at stake. Then a novelist's debts to the real are apt to seem most irredeemable and the novel itself most insolvent. Recognition of the novel's commodity status—that is, of the novel's exchangeability through the literary marketplace into money—was the primary theme or trope through which writers of realistic fiction registered their frustration with the always-already failure of mimesis. Extending Romano's argument, John Vernon, in *Money and Fiction*, points to the connected failures of mimesis involved in both money and the realistic novel. Money appears to be wealth, but is instead always a form of debt; realistic fiction appears to be reality, but is instead always a form of deception, of artifice disguised (doubly artificial, like money) as reality. "The failure of money," writes Vernon, "the fact that paper money is money but at the same time the absence of money, parallels in the realistic novel the failure of mimesis, which can never be a pure, homogeneous extension of its world" (19). The frustration derives from the failure: the discourse in question does not correspond to (or, more precisely, is not identical to) the reality that it purports to be (as opposed to, more modestly, describes or represents).

A realistic novel such as Trollope's *The Eustace Diamonds* expresses frustration in regard to its inevitable failure of mimesis both by covertly insisting on its faithful duplicity and by taking money to be the ultimate measure of the real. The title itself represents the already commodified, monetarized form of that failure, whereby the novel promises more than it can possibly deliver: the novel of course *is not* the Eustace diamonds. Like its heroine (or rather, antiheroine), Lizzie Greystock/Eustace, the novel is "paste" rather than "diamond" or "real stone" (628); or again, it is paper (as in its own material pages, as in paper money, or, even better, as in IOUs) rather than gold. It can only pretend to be "as good as gold" (309)—that is, truth-telling—by acknowledging that it is not gold or diamond or real stone: it is mere paste or paper or imagination. Frustratingly, it both does and does not acknowledge that it is paper rather than gold, fiction rather than fact. That the diamonds—a most valuable commodity and therefore emblematic of the real—vanish (that the novel is precisely the history of their multiple disappearances) marks Trollopian realism as covertly based upon absence rather than presence. The diamonds are the novel's version of the Lacanian *objet petit a*, a fetish-object around which all of the desires of all of the characters circulate.[6] It is also a commodity valued precisely at £10,000, and yet the money disappears from the text (or, perhaps, into the text because, like the story that Trollope tells, the money that he enumerates inside that story never "really" exists) along with the diamonds. Even when "the diamonds are seen in public" (188), draped around Lizzie's neck, they are of course imaginary—"realistically" speaking, nonexistent.

The legal subplot of *The Eustace Diamonds* reaches its climax in the trial in London from which both the diamonds and the person ultimately responsible for their disappearances are absent. Lizzie successfully absents herself from the trial; she escapes to "her" castle in Scotland and then feigns illness in order to get a doctor's certificate that excuses her from appearing in court. But there is a subtler climax, featuring the law and the lawyer characters. Mr. Camperdown, who out of loyalty to the Eustace family (despite its various defections from its own cause) has tried to reclaim the diamonds from Lizzie for the family estate, consults the guru of the Inns of Court, "Turtle" Dove, who renders several opinions about the status of the diamonds, beginning with the opinion that diamond necklaces (probably) cannot be claimed as heirlooms. But Dove's final opinion on the matter is a special dash of cold water for Camperdown's failing cause: "Spare her [i.e., Lizzie Eustace]," writes Dove; "There is no longer any material question as to the property, which seems to be gone irrecoverably. It is, upon the whole, well for the world, that *property so fictitious* as diamonds should be subject to the risk of annihilation" (695; my italics). Not only do the diamonds, the ultimate metaphor for the real in Trollope's novel, get stolen (first by Lizzie, presumably) and then doubly stolen, only to disappear irrecoverably from the possession of the Eustace estate (they are last "seen in public" around the neck of a Russian noblewoman), they are identified by the ultimate legal expert in the novel as a troublesomely "fictitious" form of property not unlike the novel itself. Dove's opinion (or legal fiction) is a tremendous weight of frustrating failure for Mr. Camperdown; nobody else—not even Lizzie—seems to mind nearly so much (except possibly the robbers, including the viperous Jew Mr. Benjamin, who, in Trollope's antisemitic mode, seems to have been the ultimate thief—that is, the ultimate scapegoat who goes to jail instead of the beautiful, remarkable, but totally duplicitous Lizzie Eustace).

Lizzie is a "liar" (passim), an upperclass "snake" (54), and a gold-digger whom Trollope explicitly compares to Becky Sharp in *Vanity Fair* (57). There-fore, of course, like the "fictitious" diamonds that she in the first instance steals (according to the narrator's own legal opinion), she cannot be the true center or heroine of any story worth telling. "But why should one tell the story of creatures so base?" asks the narrator, a half-ironic question that he does not answer (354). The novel commences with a confession of its frustrating failure to identify a hero or heroine whose story is worth narrating: "We will tell the story of Lizzie Greystock from the beginning," reads Trollope's second sentence, "but we will not dwell over it at great length, as we might do if we loved her" (39). But this assertion, the second in the novel, is itself duplicitous because the narrator/author proceeds to tell Lizzie's story in detail and at length (ca. eight hundred pages' worth!). Further, the one character in the novel who appears to be an analogue for the novelist himself is the antiheroine, Lizzie. We are told repeatedly, from chap-ter 1 to the very end of the novel, that Lizzie is a liar—a talented liar, but still a liar. But what distinction can be drawn between Lizzie's lies and the very fiction, albeit "realistic," that she inhabits? Like Trollope, Lizzie knows how to tell a good story (and she makes a good story). "What is a broken promise?" Lord George Carruthers asks Lizzie. "It's a story," she realistically replies (617). Even Lizzie's reading of poetry, novels, and sundry other literature involves lying in the sense of image-making (quite apart from the fictitiousness of the texts she reads): she is always "skipping, pretending to have read, lying about books, and making up her market of literature for outside admiration," just as Trollope makes up his "market of literature for" public consumption (51).

If Trollope's novel concerns an antiheroine who flirts with criminality, it con-tains no one else the narrator thinks is worth calling a "hero" or "heroine." Frank Greystock, Lizzie's cousin and equivocating lover, two-times his poor but honest fiancée, Lucy Morris, for most of the story. Frank turns out pretty well, but while he equivocates, with money or, rather, the absence of money as well as Lizzie on his mind, he "must be little better than a mean villain" (354). Frank is certainly no "[King] Arthur—a man honest in all his dealings" (355). Moreover, even Frank's true and faithful paramour, Lucy Morris, is herself "a treasure—a treasure though no heroine" (61). This antiheroic or mock-epic metaphor ("treasure") in regard to Lucy is a sort of verso image of the diamonds' absence and "fictiousness." First, Lucy the penniless governess is forthrightly presented by the narrator as honest: in contrast to Lizzie, Lucy tells the truth (to her cost, as when she twice tells Lord Fawn what she thinks of his condemnations of her equivocating fiancé). Lucy's honesty means that she is "a treasure" in one meaning of that metaphor: she is creditworthy. But Lucy is also "a treasure"—that is, "as good as gold" (314)—precisely because she doesn't possess treasure or gold or diamonds: Lucy is poor. "There was no doubt about Lucy being as good as gold;—only that real gold, *vile as it is*, was the one thing that Frank so much needed" (314; my italics). So Lucy is "as good as" something real that is also "vile." Here the narrator seems to stumble: "gold," the "diamonds," or "treasure" seem to be the main obstacles in the way of upright, honest behavior ("gold" corrupts); yet the one character in the novel who seems most sympathetically virtuous, Lucy Morris, is only "as good as" that which corrupts. The narrator is unable or unwilling to offer metaphors for Lucy's goodness that clearly distinguish her from Lizzie's "vileness" or from that very reality that her fiancé Frank most craves: namely, money, even though Lucy is valuable (honest) only because she lacks value (money).

"A treasure though no heroine," the penniless but honest Lucy sheds tears as good as "diamonds," though they don't fall (212). She herself is "as good as gold," though not as good as "real gold," which is "vile" (314). Lucy is "real," and therefore can hold "her ground" because she is like a "diamond":

> You may knock about a diamond, and not even scratch it; whereas paste in rough usage betrays itself. Lizzie, with all her self-assuring protestations, knew that she was paste, and knew that Lucy was real stone. (628)

So the most honest, honorable character in the novel—the character closest to being a "real" heroine, though no one is heroic—is also hard to distinguish from that most valuable and presumably real, but continually and ultimately vanishing and "fictitious," piece of property for which the novel is named, "the Eustace diamonds."

The novel itself—so named—has just the same equivocal status as Lucy. It is presumably honest, truth-telling, etc. Thus, the narrator "scorns to keep from his reader any secret that is known to himself" (514); the narrator, he himself insists, is as honest and forthright as Lucy Morris. But just as the very title of the novel involves the frustrating untruth that the novel is not the diamonds, so the narrator, in abjuring mysteries, secrets, and especially the sorts of "lies" that Lizzie tells, is thoroughly compromised, duplicitous.[7] Although *The Eustace Diamonds* is a sort of inside-out "sensation novel," whose plot seems to reverse the mysteries or secrets involved in Wilkie Collins's *The Moonstone* or Mary Elizabeth Braddon's *Lady Audley's Secret*, it replays many of the features of these popular novels while keeping the "fictitious" diamonds within narrative reach, revealing within a few pages of their various disappearances exactly where they are and, consequently, are not, which is never where they ought to be.

The narrator also usually declares when Lizzie has strayed from the straight and narrow path of honesty, which is most of the time; but here again he is self-compromising. Revealing Lizzie's lies, the narrator simultaneously condemns her for dishonesty and admires her storytelling talent. Moreover, insofar as Lizzie's lying is just an extreme version of what most people do most of the time (the realist demonstrates that the world at large is dishonest, antiheroic, corrupt, disappointing) the narrator, despite his duplicitous or just fictitious avowals to the contrary, is not exempt from this general rule of normal duplicity. Realism capitalizes upon "the erroneous idea of truth which the reader may be supposed to entertain." Realism as exemplified by *The Eustace Diamonds* is an extended version of the liar's paradox, whereby assertions of the type "This statement is a lie" are simultaneously true and untrue, and through their very ambiguity become self-canceling or self-condemning.

After reiterating that "the chronicler states [that] he scorns to keep from his reader any secret . . . known to himself" (514), the narrator proceeds to cloud the entire story in legal ambiguity, secrets of a sort. After the second robbery in which the diamonds are (really?) stolen from Lizzie's desk, the narrator asserts that Lizzie "had, in fact, stolen nothing" (515)—this, after asserting throughout that her initial appropriation of the diamonds was tantamount to theft. But this assertion also is one of many occasions in which it is difficult or impossible to distinguish what the narrator is claiming Lizzie thinks or believes from what the narrator himself thinks or believes. The slippages between narrative point of view, Lizzie's thoughts, and Lizzie's normal mode of lying are so frequent that it is finally impossible to keep the narrator's opinions and Lizzie's lies entirely separate. Lizzie as "liar" is a consummate storyteller, a composer of "fiction" (429); Trollope as storyteller and composer of realistic fiction must therefore also be a liar. This is not to suggest that Trollope is a self-condemning Platonic poet: there is nothing Platonic about *The Eustace Diamonds* or any other Trollopian or, for that matter, realistic fiction by other novelists. Platonism condemns the storytelling of the poets for being thirdhand imitations of ideal forms; the material realm is only secondhand imitation and therefore already a kind of lie, less honest or real than the ideal realm. In contrast, for fictional realism, there is nothing beyond material reality to represent. But like the diamonds, material reality, even though everywhere, turns out to be nowhere. Trollope, Thackeray, and other realists frustratedly condemn their own fictions, at least metaphorically, exactly for imitating the real—for being, like Lucy Morris, "as good as gold"—which is automatically to condemn them as lies and as commodities exchangeable for "vile" money. Like Lucy, they may be more or less "true," but they are definitely not either gold or diamonds—not "real stone" after all, or if they are, then they must be something "vile."

Trollope's realism frustratingly fails because it consists of patterns of reification that it cannot overcome. It is largely a poetry of money and commodities that reduces characters' motives to money and then, metaphorically, reduces the characters themselves to monetary forms or commodity-status. Lizzie as gold-digger, like Thackeray's Becky Sharp, is a near-prostitute who rises to the top of the social pyramid. Both Lizzie and Becky are versions of Defoe's "fortunate mistress," although without Roxana's final note of contrition. Becky even appears to get away with poisoning Jos Sedley for the life insurance she had cajoled him into purchasing in her name—the final counterfeit text in the text of *Vanity Fair*. But Lucy Morris, though the reader can tell where the author's sympathy lies, is in metaphoric terms no better than Lizzie (she is "as good as gold," she is "treasure," and yet she is penniless) because Trollope's realism—fictional realism in general—reduces all values to money and all things, including characters, to the status of commodities. Lizzie is worthless because of her facility for acquiring money; Lucy is worthless because she is poor.

Has Trollope finally any clear way of distinguishing between his realistic yet fictitious novel and Lizzie Eustace's lies? In "making up" her own "market in literature" (51), Lizzie reads everything from "French novels" (121) to Sir Walter

Scott (whom she accuses of lying like herself [697]) to Byron, Shelley, and other "romantic" poetry such as Tennyson's *Idylls of the King* (208–209). Her taste for romantic poetry, suggesting that she is another female Quixote, is identified at several points in the narrative with her propensity for lying. In regard to Mr. Emilius, for example, whom Trollope represents as "a nasty, greasy, lying, squinting Jew preacher" and "an impostor" (710), his eloquence counts for much with Lizzie as it does also, presumably, with the churchgoing public who have made him a popular preacher. Lizzie understands that "something of what he said was false, [but] she liked the lies. There was a dash of poetry about him; and poetry, as she thought, was not compatible with humdrum truth" (711). But the identification of poetry with lies, which presumably involves the contrasting identification of the realistic novel "with humdrum truth," is doubly frustrating. Reality disappoints or is disillusioning and anti-romantic because it is "humdrum." Depicting such disappointment, the realistic novel means to be understood as truth-telling, but it is nevertheless fictitious—a form of lying minus the poetry or the romance that Lizzie finds attractive. Lizzie "liked lies, thinking them to be more beautiful than truth" (762); but this seemingly veracious statement (and every sentence in *The Eustace Diamonds* that is not inside quotation marks is apparently such a truthful statement) is obviously untrue because fictitious.

Lizzie is a liar, but there is also a general domain of lying that is indistinguishable from public opinion and therefore from "the erroneous idea of truth which the reader may be supposed to entertain." In chapter 17, entitled "The Diamonds Are Seen in Public," the narrator says: "The general belief which often seizes upon the world in regard to some special falsehood is very surprising" (188). The "lies" about Lizzie and the diamonds that the chapter enumerates, ranging from club-room gossip to Lady Glencora Palliser's hyperbolic version of events (inflating the value of the diamonds to £24,000, for instance), are no different in kind from Lizzie's own fabrications. More importantly, they are no different in kind from the novel itself, despite the narrator's claim to be providing the truth. The novel's difference from public opinion dissolves for three reasons. First, it consists in part of the "lies," rumors, and gossip-mongering that it purports to transcend (chapter 17 is literally composed of such "lies"). Second, just as the "lies" that seize hold of public opinion depend upon "credit" or "general belief," so too a realistic novel depends upon the general illusion that it is realistic—accurate, probable, truthful—and therefore creditworthy. And third, to be a success in the literary marketplace, the novel depends upon public opinion in the sense of consumer demand, or, in other words, upon that general domain of falsehood that chapter 17 both participates in and illustrates.

But the realm of public opinion, and therefore of the reading public, is also the thoroughly commodified realm of the marketplace. Here the account-book aspect of *The Eustace Diamonds*, as well as of Trollope's other novels and, indeed, of his *Autobiography*, comes to the fore, with the narrator offering such worldly wisdom as this: "it is nicer to be born to £10,000 a year than to have to wish for £500" (60). Lizzie, of course, is born into genteel poverty, because her father the Admiral "died greatly in debt;—so much so that it was a marvel how tradesmen had trusted him" (40). Lizzie's career of lying about money starts with her first lies regarding the jewelry she manages to salvage from her bankrupt inheritance, and this is also where the novel starts. Her inherited debts represent an absence of money that both causes and corresponds to her main talents: lying and using her beauty (for Trollope and his Victorian readers, not much different from prostitution) to get what she wants, which is money. As a character whose lying generates money, Lizzie is again analogous to the novelist, whose *Autobiography* is largely an account book detailing his own rise from poverty (his father, too, was an impecunious debtor) to bestsellerdom and its near-analogue, prostitution (*"Diamonds*, 1873, £2500"—*Autobiography* 313).

In telling the story of the £100 he received as an advance for *Barchester Towers*, Trollope writes: "I am well aware that there are many who think that an author in his authorship should not regard money,—nor a painter, or sculptor, or composer in his art" (*Autobiography* 90). But why, Trollope continues, should authors, artists, or musicians be expected to transcend worldly concerns like making a living when other professional men, including even clergymen, are not expected to do so? Novelists and their families must eat. And novels are first and foremost commodities to be sold in the literary marketplace. Nevertheless, in offering his statement of income from his various novels over the years, Trollope declares: "It will not, I am sure, be thought that, in making my boast as to quantity [including quantities of money], I have endeavoured to lay claim to any literary excellence" (*Autobiography* 313). Indeed, the thoroughgoing realist cannot lay claim to being "literary" at all because realism purports to obliterate the very distinction between literature and reality. In striving to erase this distinction, the realist, especially if he achieves bestsellerdom, doubly obliterates the "literary" by producing commodities equivalent to so many sums of money.[8]

The equation between realistic fiction and money is the basic theme of Trollope's bourgeois success story in the *Autobiography*, his version of Samuel Smiles's 1859 bestseller *Self-Help*. But "vile" money is the antithesis of literature (or high culture) from the genteel, quasi-aristocratic perspective that Trollope always admired and often emulated (by fox hunting, for instance). And it was partly Trollope's honesty both about the monetary side of his success in the literary marketplace and about the "methodical," calculating way he went about "manufacturing" novels that, Gissing declared in *The Private Papers of Henry Ryecroft*, led even "'the great big stupid'"—the reading public—to demote him to relative oblivion (*Ryecroft* 138–140).[9] From Gissing's perspective, this is one judgment that the "stupid" reading public, with its "vulgarity unutterable," got right: Ryecroft (and therefore Gissing) categorizes Trollope as "an admirable writer of the pedestrian school" (138).

This is a description, however, that fits Gissing just as well as it does Trollope—as Gissing must ironically have known. After all, in *Ryecroft*, *New Grub Street*, and elsewhere, Gissing even more relentlessly than Trollope pursued the realistic paradigm in relation to authorship by simultaneously practicing and declaiming against the reduction of literature to a mere trade, anatomizing the mercenary "vulgarity" of the literary marketplace even as he fashioned his own modestly successful career within and through that marketplace. It is thus no accident that Ryecroft's bitterest condemnations of the "degraded" condition of modern authors and authorship seem to apply quite realistically to Gissing himself:

> There has come into existence [Ryecroft believes] a school of journalism which would seem to have deliberately set itself the task of degrading authorship and everything connected with it; and these pernicious scribblers (or typists, to be more accurate) have found the authors of a fretful age only too receptive of their mercantile suggestions. (139)

If there is a difference between Trollope's and Gissing's realistic accounts of the "methodical" and "mercantile" aspects of modern authorship, it is that Trollope accepts those aspects and is even grateful for them; Gissing, however, loathes them, even as he, too, capitalizes upon them.

As Jacques Derrida suggests in his analysis of Baudelaire's short story "Counterfeit Money," the ultimate analogue (and *reductio ad absurdum*) of nineteenth-century fictional realism is not just filthy lucre, but counterfeit money. Turning the basic formula of realism (novels "as good as gold") inside out, Derrida writes: "Counterfeit money can become true capital" (124), just as Trollope managed to transform his fictions into £70,000.

> Everything that will be said, in the story, of counterfeit money (and in the story of counterfeit money) can be said of the story, of the fictive text bearing this title. This text is also the coin, a piece of counterfeit money provoking an event and lending itself to this whole scene of deception. . . . It is as if the title [and here it is possible to substitute *The Eustace Diamonds* for "Counterfeit Money"] were the text whose narrative would finally be but the gloss or a long note on the counterfeit money [the Eustace diamonds] of the title. . . . (*Given Time* 86)

One implication of Derrida's argument is that, in contrast to Walter Benn Michaels, Jean-Joseph Goux, and some other theorists, there is no clear divide, corresponding to the modern abandonment of the gold standard for money, between nineteenth-century realist fiction (language supposedly "as good as gold") and modernist fiction. Derrida suggests that Goux's analysis of André Gide's *Les faux monnayeurs*, with its central analogy of fiction and counterfeit money, tends itself "to naturalize and de-fictionalize gold-money" in a way that Baudelaire's nineteenth-century story already problematizes (Derrida 110 n. 1). In relation to economic history, it is also the case that there is no simple correspondence between an era when money was on the gold standard and fictional realism because many currencies (including the pound and the dollar) went on and off the gold standard at various times during the nineteenth century and after. But the key point here is that nineteenth-century realists, including both Thackeray and Trollope, often already, well before Gide, metaphorized their novels as counterfeit money.

The equation between realistic fiction and (counterfeit) money was reduced to its bare minimum (or absurdity) in a *Household Words* article by W. H. Wills called "Review of a Popular Publication." The bestseller under review is the bank note, which Wills praises for "the power, combined with the exquisite fineness of the writing. It strikes conviction at once. It dispels all doubts, and relieves all objections" (426). Wills's article offers an interesting contrast to Baudelaire's "Counterfeit Money": instead of metaphorizing its own text as counterfeit or fictitious, it stakes its claim to realism or truth on the equation between paper money (presumably based upon the gold standard) and a bestselling novel. But by identifying bank notes with novels, Wills reveals the unhidden secret of realism: the commodification of all value-forms, and therefore cultural degradation, deflation, and disillusionment. There is ultimately nothing more highly prized (more real) in *The Eustace Diamonds* than the Eustace diamonds, and yet they (though "real stones") are themselves mere "paste," merely "fictitious," and forever vanishing or vanished (along with the £10,000 they are supposedly worth). The ultimate measure of all values is the general equivalent or universal commodity-form of money, but it is "vile" or valueless; there is nothing other than reality, but its legibility is problematic, its text a counterfeit.

7

Novel Sensations of the 1860s

> Just as in the Middle Ages people were afflicted with the Danc-
> ing Mania and Lycanthropy . . . so now we have a Sensational
> Mania. . . . From an epidemic . . . it has lately changed into
> an endemic. Its virus is spreading in all directions, from the
> penny journal to the shilling magazine . . . to the thirty shillings
> volume. . . .
> —J. R. Wise, "Belles Lettres," *Westminster Review*, 1866

Noting the "moral panic" aroused by the "sensation novels" of the 1860s, Ann Cvetkovich links this reaction to the critical response to novels in general: "The success of the novel has to be told as a counternarrative to the Victorian belief in progress" (22). This is so if only because fiction, no matter how realistic, always implies the inadequacy of the reality that it supplements and often explicitly critiques. In the context of skeptical, often pessimistic reaction to mass literacy, the more specific history of reaction to novels and novel-reading can be understood as a diffuse moral panic extending over two centuries.[1] But the general anxiety is punctuated by the controversies aroused by specific kinds of fiction—Gothic romances, Newgate novels, penny dreadfuls—none exceeding in intensity the uproar over sensation novels. The writers of Gothic fiction—"terrorists," as they were sometimes called—aimed to inspire terror in their readers, but *The Castle of Otranto*, *The Mysteries of Udolpho*, and even *The Monk* could be given a dose of quasi-philosophical cultural capital through the theory of the sublime. In contrast, the sensation novels of the 1860s seemed intended mainly to produce thrilling sensations in readers with few if any philosophically, socially, or morally redeeming features; they thus anticipated today's mass-market thriller. The archbishop of York was perhaps not far from the mark when, in an 1864 sermon, he declared that "sensational stories . . . aimed at this effect simply—of exciting in the mind some deep feeling of overwrought interest by the means of some terrible passion or crime." He believed that this "overwrought interest" almost literally struck home because sensation novels "want to persuade people that in almost every one of the well-ordered houses of their neighbours there [is] a skeleton shut up in some cupboard." W. Fraser Rae, who quoted the archbishop in the *North British Review*, added that sensation novels were "one of the abominations of the age" (202).

In reviews of sensation fiction throughout the 1860s, metaphors of moral corruption, disease, and poison proliferate. In 1863, Dean Henry Mansel opined in *The Quarterly Review* that sensation novels belong "to the morbid phenomena of literature." Such novels are "indications of a wide-spread corruption, of which they are in part both the effect and the cause; called into existence to supply the cravings of a diseased appetite, and contributing themselves to foster the disease" (482–483). For Mansel, sensation novels are "poison," like "those French novels devoted to the worship of Baal-Peor and the recommendation of adultery" (486). Along with disease and poison, sensation novels also purvey filth and excrement, polluting the minds of the reading public and befouling the national culture. In sensational language, Mansel asserts that "there is something unspeakably disgusting in this ravenous appetite for carrion, this vulture-like instinct which smells out the newest mass of social corruption, and hurries to devour the loathsome dainty before the scent has evaporated" (502).

Mansel, Rae, and the archbishop of York represent the hysterical extreme, but even the most positive reviewers of sensation fiction treat it as subliterary. While some reviewers commend Wilkie Collins, Mary Elizabeth Braddon, and other sensation novelists for providing new thrills, they rarely suggest that their fictions offer anything more than mere entertainment. The novelists themselves, moreover, often acknowledge that there is something cheap or degrading about producing a "sensation" among the reading public. On the cusp of the transition from early industrial production toward consumerism and consumer society, a transition also marked by the development of marginalist economics in the 1870s, sensation fiction seems to capitulate to the desires of the mass reading public in a self-conscious manner that distinguishes it from earlier writing and publishing practices.

Both critics and novelists in the 1860s use *sensation* in a way that dissociates it from the epistemological empiricism that informs fictional realism from Defoe to Trollope. Instead of a basic unit of sense perception, *sensation* now means some extraordinary shock or thrill to the reader's nervous system, with no specific or necessary truth content involved in the transaction. Nevertheless, shocks or thrills can have epistemological implications. In the discourse about sensation fiction, the novel becomes, metaphorically, a weapon or missile, aimed at the mind or, rather, the nerves of the reader. The reification of the novel implied by metaphors of physical assault indicates a cynical, designing objectivity on the part of the producer (the writer, the publisher); the supposedly blasé or jaded subjectivity of the reader-consumer registers the "sensation" as pleasurable wound, or an injury without consequences. This cultural formulation is the mirror-opposite of that involved in the contemporaneous phenomenon of French impressionist painting, in which the painter attempts to register, as objectively as possible, his or her subjective "impression" or "sensation" of a scene.

The formula for many sensational bestsellers emphasizes plot rather than character, theme, style, or other aspects of fiction. As in melodrama, plot in sensation fiction usually produces versions of secular revelation by stripping away surface appearances, the stuff of quotidien experience. The implication, that everyday phenomena as sensed by everyday persons should not be mistaken for reality, runs counter to the common-sense empiricism that informs earlier novelistic realism. The anti-realistic tendency of *sensation* among British novelists and critics in the 1860s is also quite different from the way that word was just beginning to be used in French aesthetic discourse. Starting in the 1860s, *sensation* and *impression* were often used synonymously by painters and art critics in France to refer to what Camille Pissaro called "the unique sensation" a scene or a fleeting moment made on the artist. The point was to capture such impressions or sensations on canvas, which might or might not produce a similar impression in the viewer (Paul Smith 21–24).

But the aim of the impressionists was not to create a sensation or make an impact on the viewer by any means available. When Braddon likens *Lady Audley's Secret* to a Pre-Raphaelite painting (47), she is cannily correct because the assumptions informing both Pre-Raphaelitism and sensation fiction are closer to symbolist aesthetics than to the extreme, albeit extremely subjective, epistemological and methodological realism involved in impressionism. In contrast to both Pre-Raphaelitism and symbolist aesthetics, however, and despite its challenge to naive empiricism, sensation fiction remained stubbornly materialistic by equating both "sensation" and novelistic success with bestsellerdom, the monetary bottom line. The "nervous system" of the familiar, bourgeois, and quotidien, but also abstract and alienating, reading public was the quite material target of the sensation novelists. And that they often hit the target is proven by their equally material achievement of bestsellerdom. The ultimate scandal, according to both novelists and critics, was the capitulation by the novelists to the demand for "cheap" thrills or sensations on the part of the reading public. Giving the public what it wanted, the sensation novelists of the 1860s managed, it appeared, to bridge the widening gap between writers and readers, but at the expense of artistic gravity and greatness. The ultimate mystery, however, is that there is no mystery: the archbishop was right, though there was no reason for him to get so upset about it.

I

The emergence of sensation fiction is usually dated from 1860, when Collins published *The Woman in White*, a bestseller soon followed by Mrs. Henry Wood's *East Lynne* (1861) and Braddon's *Lady Audley's Secret* (1862). Though sensational ingredients continued to characterize much fiction down to 1900 and beyond, critical reaction to sensation novels began to wane toward the end of the 1860s, marking that decade, at least in literary terms, as one of sensationalism.[2] It is not possible, however, to pinpoint elements of sensation fiction that cannot be found in novels both earlier and later than the 1860s, or to distinguish it in any absolute sense from what Peter Brooks calls "the melodramatic imagination," both on stage and in novels. Moreover, in the 1860s *sensation* and *sensational* were attached—usually with a dash of sarcasm—to many phenomena other than novels, so that the words connoted the newness, fast pace, and shock of modernity. There were "sensation dramas" at least as early as Dion Boucicault's melodramatic hit of 1861, *The Colleen Bawn*, and also "sensational" advertisements, products, journals, crimes, and scandals. Theatrical "sensations" such as Boucicault's or Tom Taylor's *The Ticket-of-Leave Man* (1863), which features the professional detective and master disguise artist Hawkshaw, suggest the connection between stage melodrama and the sensation novel that foreshadows the relationship between best-sellers and the cinema today. In his analysis of sensation fiction for the *Spectator*, Richard Holt Hutton states what was often literally the case: "The melodrama of the cheap theatres is an acted sensational novel" (932).[3]

As with melodrama, so with the sensation novel: violent and thrilling action; astonishing coincidences; stereotypic heroes, heroines, and villains; much sentimentality; and virtue rewarded and vice apparently punished at the end. However, according to Winifred Hughes, "with the rise of the sensation novel, melodrama . . . lost its innocence" (71). Because of its moral, epistemological, and sexual ambiguities, the sensation novel was felt to be dangerous by many of its first critics, while stage melodrama usually seemed less threatening. Traditional melodrama celebrated virtue and domesticity, but the sensation novel seems to question them, at least by implication. Of course the subversive tendencies of novels such as *Lady Audley's Secret* are reined in by their endings, which restore order, reward virtue, and punish villainy just as does melodrama. But for many pages of suspenseful novels such as *East Lynne*, *Armadale*, and *Uncle Silas*, the outcome is in doubt, the evidence circumstantial and incomplete, the detectives faltering, and the innocent bedeviled by their villainous adversaries.[4]

In content, the sensation novel deals with crime, but not in remote or unfamiliar settings, as Gothic had tended to do. Newgate fiction often belongs to the "urban mysteries" subgenre associated with G. W. M. Reynolds's enormously popular *Mysteries of London*, and, as in the burglary episode in *Oliver Twist*, crime moves closer to home. But crime in sensation novels usually occurs in apparently proper, bourgeois, domestic settings, and the criminals are often, like Lady Audley, members of the family. Moreover, whether gentleman amateur like Robert Audley in *Lady Audley's Secret* or official policeman like Sergeant Cuff in *The Moonstone*, the figure of the detective emerges in sensation fiction as a clear, formulaic role, the character who follows the trail of evidence to the solution of those "most mysterious of mysteries," as Henry James called them, "the mysteries which are at our own doors" (593).

As the detective pries into domestic, familial secrets, he or she seems at times to foreshadow psychoanalysis. Whether amateur or professional, the detective operates as a sort of super-reader, a person more capable than the average reader of novels of deciphering the clues that, like pieces of a puzzle or even like Freudian dreamwork, lie scattered around the narrative present. As if second-guessing the author, the detective reconstructs the fragmented text of the past—the buried story of the crime or crimes. As super-reader, moreover, the detective seems to mediate between the novelist and the anonymous, ever-increasing "outlying mass of average readers," the "unknown public" that Wilkie Collins, for one, both viewed with trepidation and sought to entertain (Lonoff 66–78).

The emergence of the detective seems to be linked to a weakening or defaillancy of narrative authority, which in turn may be linked to a paradigm shift in modes of observation. If in *Vanity Fair* and *The Eustace Diamonds* fictional realism enters a logical cul-de-sac of reification (though it remained for Gissing to sound the death-knell in *New Grub Street*), in the sensation fiction of the 1860s it approaches a related, though almost antithetical, dead end. The sensation novels of Collins, Braddon, Wood, Reade, and others all start from the assumption that empiricism and its corollary, fictional realism, are inevitable, hegemonic, the only sensible, accurate way to understand and portray the world. Yet they recycle elements of the Gothic romance and attempt to render their novels as thrilling as theatrical melodrama. To the increasingly sophisticated and demanding novel-reading public of the 1860s, the Gothic and melodramatic seemed distinctly mass-cultural, at the opposite end of the taste hierarchy from high art. That public, however, according to many of the first, anxious reviewers of sensation fiction, was also all too ready to seek in the latest fiction mere amusement, tawdry thrills or "shocks" to stimulate its otherwise jaded "nervous system." The sensation fiction of the 1860s is thus an odd hybrid, neither modern nor exactly Victorian, neither realistic nor romantic, neither high cultural nor clearly low, a subgenre whose uncertain, liminal status posed and still poses reading problems, while also posing, according to its first critics, various moral and cultural dangers to its readers. For many of those critics, the main danger was simply the reduction of reading to thrill-seeking; within some sensation novels, novel-reading is similarly reduced to mere entertainment, as in Robert Audley's predilection for yellow-backed "French novels" in Braddon's first best-seller.

In contrast, however, in sensation fiction other sorts of reading—metaphorically, reading the text of reality or of the past—acquire a new, ambiguous complexity that contradicts the straightforward empiricism of most realistic fiction. Sensation novels register the post-Darwinian shift, "arbitrary as it is, and imprecise," in George Levine's words, "between Victorianism and modernism," a transition "from belief in [empirical] observation as authority to deep distrust of it" (Levine 235). Both observation and reading—or the observation of observation, to paraphrase Levine on the situation of readers of Victorian novels—are treated in sensation fiction with a pleasurable paranoia that, in the 1880s and 1890s, would be reified in the formulaic plots and stock characters of the modern mystery-detective novel. The detective serves as an expert observer or reader of clues, one who is able to read differently from the (mere) novel-reader.[5] The latter is reduced to hankering after both thrills and facts, while the distinction between the two—

thrills and facts—blurs: the ultimate thrill is the final revelation of the criminal truth, a revelation provided by the detective, who after reading the clues can narrate the final, coherent story of the crime and effect a restoration of order. In this way, sensation novels are always allegories of reading that, on one hand, install a new professionalism or expertise while, on the other, validating the contested concept of novel-reading as mere pleasure, mere entertainment. From now on, they suggest, only experts can do the serious business of reading the book of the world. But for ordinary readers, there are newspapers and sensation novels.

While reality seems no longer open to casual scrutiny or observation, but instead requires the expertise of detectives or scientists to fathom, the sensation novel ironically threatens to reduce reality to mere surfaces, mere superficiality. In a sense, sensation fiction claims the best of both worlds—both the romance and the novel—but does so superficially or cynically, unwilling to affirm either without equivocation. There are mysteries whose depths must be plumbed by detectives, but the solutions, like the crimes that generated the mysteries in the first place, are secular, material, and tawdry. Detection—the super-reading involved in pursuing the clues to these mysteries—becomes an exciting game of trivial pursuits, a kind of chasing after the obvious (or so the solution seems, once the game ends). Novels such as *Vanity Fair* and *The Eustace Diamonds* push fictional realism to an epistemological limit by simultaneously rejecting and mourning, parodying and hankering after, the romantic narratives that their sometimes Quixote-like characters try to imitate or believe, yet invariably fall short of or find deficient. Fictional realism spells disillusionment, in part through its insistence that reading is never reality. Yet it paradoxically insists both on its own status as reality—the novel named *Vanity Fair* is no different from the society named Vanity Fair—and on the deceitfulness, fictionality, and superficiality of that reality. The problem with reality (whether in a realistic novel, in a sensation story, or in reality) is that there is nothing below or above it, neither subterranean nor transcendental, to give it meaning. Despite its (cynical) recreations of romance, the sensation novel arrives at the same result. What you see or read is all you get, a world of mere appearances, mere surfaces without depths, the postmodern condition *avant la lettre*.[6]

Sensation fiction manages to be both realistic and romantic (or melodramatic), both superficial and cynical, often by mimicking the daily news. The crimes in sensation fiction are sometimes drawn from the newspapers of the day, while newspapers serve as important analogues within many sensation novels for the novels themselves. Hence, they were sometimes referred to as "newspaper novels," a phrase implying their ephemerality. In the sensation novel, the Gothic is brought up to date and so mixed with the conventions of realism as to make its events seem possible if not exactly probable. But by sensationalizing modern life, the novelists discovered that they were making fictions out of the stuff that filled the newspapers every day. Indeed, on one level they could even claim that to sensationalize was to be realistic. In *Victorian Studies in Scarlet*, Richard Altick points out that "every good new Victorian murder helped legitimize and prolong the fashion of sensational plots" (79). Historically there is a direct relationship between the sensation novel and sensational journalism, from the extensive crime reporting in the *Times* and the *Daily Telegraph* to such early crime tabloids as the *Illustrated Police News*. Collins based some of the details of *The Moonstone* on the sensational news stories of the Constance Kent murder in 1860 and the Northumberland Street murder in 1861. As Dickens modeled Bucket on Inspector Field, so Collins modeled Sergeant Cuff on Inspector Whicher, the chief detective in the Kent affair. With some justice, Dean Mansel complained about the emergence of "the criminal variety of the Newspaper Novel, a class of fiction having about the same relation to the genuine historical novel that the police reports of the 'Times' have to the pages of Thucydides or Clarendon" (501). All a writer of a sensation novel needed to do, said Mansel, was to "keep an eye on the criminal reports of the daily newspapers," which would virtually write his fiction for him.

Mansel's outcry against the "Newspaper Novel" comes especially close to Charles Reade. Of all the sensation novelists, Reade was most dependent on the newspapers, just as he was also the most involved in stage melodrama. When the *Times* criticized his *A Terrible Temptation* (1871), partly for its portrayal of the "scarlet woman" Rhoda Somerset, Reade wrote two letters to the editor protesting that he had merely "dramatized" facts reported by that newspaper. Indeed, all of his best novels, he said, were inspired by the *Times*: "For 18 years, at least, the journal you conduct so ably has been my preceptor, and the main source of my works—at all events of the most approved." Reade proceeds to list several of his works that the *Times* inspired.[7] Reade is incensed that his favorite newspaper should complain about the subjects of his novels when he takes those subjects straight from its pages. Those who dismissed his novels as melodramatic, crude, or worse, had first to show that the facts were not melodramatic, crude, or worse. He was simply a writer of "romances founded on facts."

Several features of newspaper publishing distinguish the 1860s from earlier decades. The abolition of the final "taxes on knowledge" by 1861 facilitated a proliferation of inexpensive newspapers, including new dailies in the provinces as well as in London.[8] The dramatic increase in news and newspaper-reading, making them a regular feature of everyday life, was also facilitated by advances in printing technology such as the Hoe rotary press and stereotyping, by telegraphy, and by improved rail and postal service. By 1870, there were a dozen morning and evening newspapers in London alone, and the circulation of several of these, including the aptly named *Daily Telegraph*, established in 1855, quickly outstripped that of the *Times*.[9] Moreover, besides politics, much of the space in these new dailies was devoted to reporting "sensational" crimes. As Altick points out, by the 1860s "newspapers had taken over the proprietorship of English murder" from the earlier publishers of broadsides such as James Catnach (*Victorian Studies in Scarlet* 66). Among the new newspapers, the *Daily Telegraph* "excelled in murder reporting," but even the *Times* "lavished attention on court cases, whether for murder or divorce" (Altick 61). In another development, a new women's press emerged in the 1860s in connection with magazines if not with newspapers. This women's press, centered in journals edited and sometimes owned by women, was, according to Elaine Showalter, "both feminist and activist in its principles" (155). A number of women authors of sensation novels invested their earnings "in their own careers, publishing and editing magazines and retaining book copyrights. Mrs. Wood edited the *Argosy*, Braddon edited *Belgravia*, Charlotte Riddell edited *St. James Magazine*, and Florence Marryat edited *London Society*" (Showalter 156).

Newspaper-reading becomes a central feature quite early and prominently in *Lady Audley's Secret*, when, on his return from Australia, George Talboys by chance peruses "a greasy *Times* newspaper" in which appears the obituary for his wife, "Helen Talboys, aged 22" (25). This news item ends chapter 4 in melodramatic, headline fashion; the next chapter, entitled "The Headstone at Ventnor," begins with an account of the impact reading the obituary has on George:

> When George told the governess on board the *Argus* that if he heard any evil tidings of his wife he should drop down dead, he spoke in perfect good faith. . . . The suddenness of the blow had stunned him. In this strange and bewildered state of mind he began to wonder what had happened, and why it was that one line in the *Times* newspaper could have so horrible an effect upon him. (25)

Though reading the obituary does not kill George—an outcome that makes him feel guilty because it contradicts what he told the governess—it nevertheless delivers a quite physical shock to his nervous system. That reading can be dangerous, even life-threatening, is thus physically demonstrated by what happens to George. That this information, the obituary, which "stuns" him with its "blow" is *mis*information, a fiction in the guise of a matter-of-fact news item, compounds the idea that reading can be dangerous by adding the possibility that the latest news, even in a respected newspaper like the *Times*, may be false. It is possible, Braddon suggests, that reading an erroneous notice in a newspaper could kill someone. George withstands the "blow," but at the end of the chapter he unwittingly compounds the falsehood of the obituary by having a stonemason carve a "brief inscription for the headstone of his dead wife's grave"—an inscription that duplicates the misinformation in the *Times* and that forms the melodramatic last words of chapter 5.

In both cases, moreover—the *Times* obituary and the epitaph carved in stone— the novel itself headlines misinformation, asking the reader (no matter how suspicious) to believe, at least for the moment, that Helen Talboys lies buried in the grave at Ventnor. Braddon's text thus aspires to the condition of the "greasy *Times* newspaper" in at least two ways: first, by capitalizing upon "sensationalism," it aims to deliver shocks or "blows" to its readers that, though pleasurably vicarious and voyeuristic, will mimic the shock George Talboys experiences in reading the obituary; and second, if it succeeds in shocking or stimulating its readers through sensationalism, it doesn't matter whether it does so through truthful or fraudulent means, through information or misinformation, fact or fiction, any more than it matters, in terms of sales, whether a newspaper headline is fact or fiction. The idea that journalists could manufacture the news, creating events by publicizing them, was already in the air.[10]

Lady Audley puts both the telegraph and the railway to sensational use to mystify her husband, Robert Audley, and the reader. Like the latest newspaper headlines, in Braddon's novel the most modern, instantaneous communications medium, the telegraph, carries deceit or helps to multiply secrecy, rather than the reverse. The electrified messages sent by Lady Audley have the effect of electrifying—or, at any rate, of stimulating—her detective nephew into action. Nevertheless, in contrast to the newspaper and the telegraph, the chief clues that Robert stitches together are the scraps of handwriting that reveal Lady Audley and Helen Talboys to be the same person. In *Lady Audley's Secret*, at least, the up-to-date, electrical, public forms of communication seem untrustworthy; the truth is conveyed by the most old-fashioned, private form of written communication, handwriting (cf. Welsh, *George Eliot and Blackmail* 56).

In Braddon's best-seller, the superficiality of news and newspapers with their possibly misleading headlines is read against the buried or hidden story that can be recovered only through detection. The fragments of the buried story that Robert uncovers, revealing that Helen Talboys is not buried at Ventnor but is instead alive and well as Lady Audley, consist mainly of examples of his false aunt's handwriting. But in all mystery-detective stories, as in the Gothic romance motif of newly discovered (sometimes newly unburied) manuscripts, there is a textual doubling, a second narrative that is brought to the surface of the main one. In *Dead Secrets*, Tamar Heller explores the motif of "buried writing" both in Collins's novels and more generally in the "female Gothic" tradition that Collins at once resisted and adopted. While the female Gothic may be one "dead secret that is alternatively repressed and resurrected" by Collins (Heller 12), perhaps another one is the waning of significance in all forms of written communication, including any sense of genuine profundity or transcendence, registered by sensation novels. The search for an Ur-text or primary, written document or clue that unlocks the mystery proves to be an inadequate substitute for the (impossible) presence and immediacy of oral, face-to-face communication, although this inadequacy is often compensated for after the facts, both of the crime and of its detection, by the seemingly oral confession of the criminal. It may be that the more sensational, instantaneous, or telegraphic written communication became, the more it revealed the nonidentity of all forms of communication with any ultimate truth, wisdom, or presence. Plumbing the depths to bring the buried texts to the surface reveals also their superficiality and banality, which is at the same time their newsworthiness: yesterday's buried text becomes today's headliner.

Winifred Hughes points out that Reade's obsessive insistence on the factual basis of his stories implies a lack of faith in the authority of fictive imagination. A similar difficulty in claiming authority marks the narrative structures of many other sensation novels. Because they blended romance with realism, the melodramatic with the domestic and contemporary, improbable or striking events with probable settings and characters, sensation novels posed difficulties for their writers as well as their readers. Murders and conspiracies do not lurk down every dark street, in the shadows of every dark house. Or do they? Newspapers suggested otherwise, and how could a sensation novelist who relied on the daily news fail to be realistic? Here is one way in which the conventions of fictional realism become punctuated by question marks. Braddon indicates part of the creed of the sensation novelist when she makes Robert Audley tell his villainous aunt:

> "What do we know of the mysteries that may hang about the houses we enter? If I were to go to-morrow into that commonplace, plebeian, eightroomed house in which Maria Manning and her husband murdered their guest, I should have no awful prescience of that bygone horror. Foul deeds have been done under the most hospitable roofs; terrible crimes have been committed amid the fairest scenes, and have left no trace upon the spot where they were done. . . . I believe that we may look into the smiling face of a murderer, and admire its tranquil beauty." (94)

The reference to Maria Manning helps to emphasize the plausibility of Lady Audley, who is herself an incarnation of this creed: her outward beauty—the blonde, blue-eyed, childlike but also coquettish stereotype of female loveliness and innocence—masks bigamy, homicide, insanity.

In a review entitled "The Enigma Novel," a writer in the *Spectator* for 28 December 1861 declared: "We are threatened with a new variety of the sensation novel, a host of cleverly complicated stories, the whole interest of which consists in the gradual unravelling of some carefully prepared enigma" (Page 109). Not every tale that has come to be labeled a sensation novel involves a mystery. Reade, for example, rarely withholds the sources of villainy from his readers, while, as Kate Flint notes, the novels of Rhoda Broughton "derive their sensationalism from explicit situation, rather than from mystery" (292). Nevertheless, sensation fiction in general implies that domestic tranquility conceals heinous desires and deeds, and frequently these are identical to the heroines' (or villainesses') desires and deeds. As Elaine Showalter puts it, "For the Victorian woman, secrecy was simply a way of life," and the secrets in sensation novels written by women, at least, seem often to concern "women's dislike of their roles as daughters, wives, and mothers" (Showalter 158).

Just as much as the introduction of sex and violence, about which the first reviewers of sensation novels raised a great hue and cry, the introduction of mystery into a narrative that otherwise follows the conventions of domestic realism posed disturbing questions on both the thematic and structural levels. On the former level, there is the questionable relation of mysteries of crime, bigamy, and other skeletons in family closets to religious mystery. By metaphoric sleight of hand, the Gothic romance seemed to turn secular mystery into a version of religious mystery.[11] In *Uncle Silas* (1864) and elsewhere, Sheridan Le Fanu perpetuates the supernatural elements of Gothic at least as metaphors (Silas Ruthvyn as werewolf or vampire, for example), while Collins, Braddon, and Wood link speculations about fate and coincidence to the accidental turnings of their plots, thus offering versions of what Brooks calls "the moral occult" in melodrama. Everything that happens in *The Moonstone* can be interpreted as the fulfillment of the curse that follows the diamond, while everything that happens in *Armadale* seems predestined either because it is wildly coincidental or because it has been foreshadowed by Allan Armadale's dream. And in *Lady Audley's Secret*, Robert refers repeatedly to "the awful hand of fatality" (134) that points his way to the solution of the mystery. Robert also sermonizes to Lady Audley about "Providence," whose rule ensures that life is not a mere game of chance and that "wicked secrets are never permitted to remain long hidden" (177). The worldly-wise narrator, on the other hand, whose female persona is thoroughly conversant with gambling, horse-racing, adultery, and homicide, never sermonizes about Providence. Rather than crediting Providence with the outing of Lady Audley's multiple secrets, the narrator credits Robert's patient, empiricist piecing together of "circumstantial evidence." The sensation novel thus both domesticates and secularizes the apparently higher (or, at any rate, more romantic) mysteries of the Gothic romance. Ironically, just as novel-writing waxes sensational in the 1860s, it is also in a sense growing tamer. Sensation fiction infuses romantic elements into realism, but in doing so it reduces romance to fit Biedermeier frames.

Nevertheless, sensation novels did not seem tame to their first readers. Especially when they dealt with bigamy, they seemed to be a British equivalent of the suspect "French novels" that Robert carries about with him and often reads in the novel that *Punch* called *Lady Disorderly's Secret*. One reviewer of Collins's *No Name* mistakenly declared the sensation novel to be "a plant of foreign growth":

> It comes to us from France, and it can only be imported in a mutilated condition. Without entering on the relative morality or immorality of French and English novelists, one may say generally that, with us, novels turn upon the vicissitudes of legitimate love and decorous affection; while in France they are based upon the working of those loves and passions which are not in accordance with our rules of respectability. (Page 134–135)[12]

This hardly gives British fiction prior to the 1860s its due with regard to the illegitimate and indecorous. But subjects were broached in sensation novels that many good Victorians thought inappropriate, and that these subjects seemed to be addressed sensationally rather than seriously made them all the more disreputable. Perhaps the greatest sensation was the discovery (though hardly unknown before the 1860s) that crime paid in fiction, as Count Fosco in *The Woman in White* says it pays in life. In his review of *Aurora Floyd*, Henry James declares: "The novelist who interprets the illegitimate world to the legitimate world, commands from the nature of his position a certain popularity" (594).

In sensation fiction, an apparent disintegration of narrative authority, caused by the introduction of secular mystery and the withholding of information from the reader, signals the crisis of observation, and therefore of fictional realism, that both Welsh and Levine note. Collins's narrative fragmentation is one way that the weakening of narrative authority is registered. The multiple, conflicting first-person narrations in *The Woman in White* and *The Moonstone* resemble the frame-story patterns in *Frankenstein*, James Hogg's *Confessions of a Justified Sinner*, *Wuthering Heights*, and other Gothic-inflected texts. But Collins otherwise subscribes to the empiricist epistemology of realist fiction, which conventionally calls either for one continuous first-person narrator presumably of sound mind or for an omniscient, third-person narrative perspective. Divided among various narrators, *The Woman in White* and *The Moonstone* seem to be realistic novels without centers, fictional panopticons whose wardens have gone missing.[13]

If narrative fragmentation is one way that the disintegration of narrative authority is registered, another is the worldliness and duplicity of a narrative persona like Braddon's in *Lady Audley's Secret*, an exaggerated version of the duplicitous realism practiced by the narrators of *Vanity Fair* and *The Eustace Diamonds*. Early in her story, Braddon intrudes as narrator to make the same point that her hero makes about crime and mystery "amid the fairest scenes." One remarkable feature of this narrative interpolation is its appearance out of context, well before the reader learns that any crime has occurred. Prior to this passage, George Talboys and Robert Audley are quietly fishing. After it, they return quietly to their rustic inn. Given the pastoral context, the narrative interpolation seems all the more abrupt, gratuitous, shocking, like its subject matter:

> We hear every day of murders committed in the country. Brutal and treacherous murders; slow, protracted agonies from poisons administered by some kindred hand; sudden and violent deaths by cruel blows, inflicted with a stake cut from some spreading oak, whose every shadow promised—peace. In the county of which I write, I have been shown a meadow in which, on a quiet summer Sunday evening, a young farmer murdered the girl who had loved and trusted him; and yet, even now, with the stain of that foul deed upon it, the aspect of the spot is—peace. No species of crime has ever been committed in the worst rookeries about Seven Dials that has not been also done in the face of that rustic calm which still, in spite of all, we look on with a tender, half-mournful yearning, and associate with—peace. (36)

This passage is a microcosm of the sensation novel—indeed, of all mystery-detective novels—not just in its content, but in its structure of abrupt revelation. And not only is fiction like this, but so is life, Braddon says: peace masks violence; innocent appearances cloak evil intentions; and reality itself functions as a mystery until the sudden revelation of guilt, which is always lurking in the shadows. The passage is also, of course, proleptic; before the reader knows about specific crimes, Braddon jingles the keys to the mystery, all of which are in the narrator's possession. The narrator says, in effect, that the reader is ignorant both about the ways of the world and about the story to come. But if the narrator knows the buried truth, the story can proceed only if she withholds what she knows—only if, so to speak, she colludes with Lady Audley by protecting her secret or, rather, secrets—from Robert Audley, and therefore from the reader, for most of the novel. All-knowing, the narrator shares both truth and secrecy with the criminal, while an aspect of narrative authority, associated both with honesty and with realism, is transferred to the figure of the detective.

The narrator of Braddon's best-seller either withholds information or scatters it as hints, clues, and emphatic gaps in the text, as when Lady Audley orders her maid to send what would be, if revealed, an incriminating telegram: "'And now listen, Phoebe. What I want you to do is very simple.' It was so simple that it was told in five minutes, and then Lady Audley retired into her bed-room" (39). But it is not told at this time to the reader. The central mystery, the disappearance of George Talboys, involves the same pattern. The narrator seems willful, capricious, when George and Robert view Lady Audley's "pre-Raphaelite" portrait and George gives no clear sign of recognition (47). When George then wanders away from Robert, not to reappear until the end of the novel, the same sense of narrative willfulness arises. George disappears into a gap in the text that, in literal terms, turns out to be the well into which his bigamous wife has pushed him.

II

The sensation novel detective functions partly as a substitute for the more forthright, credible narrative personas of realistic novels. Like their prototypes, Inspector Bucket and Sergeant Cuff, most fictional detectives have as part of their professional equipment a sort of reduced omniscience, similar to Vautrin's worldly knowledge in Balzac: they are familiar with society, crime, and criminals, but about the causes of the particular crime in a story they are at first as much in doubt as the reader. They do not have a solution but they know how to arrive at one. They can read the clues that the no longer trustworthy narrator-authors place in their paths, leading toward a restoration both of social order and of some semblance of narrative omniscience, usually through a final retelling, by the detective, of the buried criminal narrative.

The early, naive development of omniscient narration basic to realistic fiction breaks down partly from the intrusion of mystery into it, but also partly from the recognition of the conventional—and logically preposterous—nature of omniscience. Within Jane Austen's compass of "two or three families in a country village," omniscient narration proceeds without apparent difficulty. Within Dickens's London, it begins to seem more artificial or fantastic, both because the idea of a narrative persona knowing everything about such a vast place implies something close to supernatural authority, an uneasy fit in fiction purporting to be realistic, and because Dickens wants to reveal the "mysteries" of the city while still rendering them mysterious. Dickens's occasional experiments with narrative structure—the double narration of *Bleak House*, for example—can be understood as attempts to deal with these contradictions. So, too, can the more radical experiments in Collins's novels: the multiple narrations of *The Woman in White* and *The Moonstone*, the odd mixture of narrative patterns and effects in *No Name* and *Armadale*. Collins offers something close to multiple narration in *Armadale* by interjecting correspondence without authorial comment (the letters between Lydia Gwilt and Maria Oldershaw), long passages of dialogue in which characters recount their life stories (the opening confession of Allan Armadale), condensations of long periods of time as viewed through the memories of a single character (the Rev. Mr. Brock's recollections in the first chapter of the second book), and Lydia's diary at the end of the tale. At the same time, the supposedly omniscient narrator of *Armadale* does not often intrude into the story either to moralize or to speculate about events.

The strange world of the Armadale doubles and of the dream that comes true seems to exist in a kind of vacuum. Because of the dream and the heavy doses of coincidence, everything in *Armadale* seems to be laden with a preternatural, if not clearly supernatural, significance. Because of the unobtrusiveness of the narrator, this potential significance is never explained, even while the reader, along with the characters, witnesses the unraveling of the secular mysteries that constitute the plot. The story's emphasis on "fate" or "destiny" does not finally point beyond the labyrinthine windings of its plot to something more than accident or chance. When Collins does at last intrude as narrator, presumably to explain the higher mysteries to which the secular mysteries gesture, it is only in an appendix in which he gives no answers: "My readers will perceive that I have purposely left them, with reference to the Dream in this story, in the position which they would occupy in the case of a dream in real life—they are free to interpret it by the natural or the supernatural theory, as the bent of their own minds may incline them" (597). Collins simply dodges the questions about dreams and predestination that his novel has so elaborately raised. The passage thus suggests an abdication of omniscience and a backhanded acknowledgment of the diminished stature of the narrative persona in contrast to, say, the more authoritative narrators of George Eliot's novels.

As in *Armadale*, the introduction of mystery—the self-conscious withholding of any important information from the reader—necessarily both diminishes and complicates the role of narrator. The narrator must seem either to connive with criminals, thereby sacrificing moral legitimacy, or to suffer a kind of structural amnesia, only recovering something close to omniscience as a version of memory or recapitulation at the end of the story. The diminution, perhaps even criminalization, of the narrator is also linked to a diminution of the kind of knowledge hidden and recovered: he or she now holds the keys only to a secular mystery, ordinarily of the criminal, most sordid kind, and can no longer make any very credible or consistent claim to be able to unlock the higher mysteries of life. The equivocations and silences of both Braddon's and Collins's narrative personas suggest these transformations of metaphysical-religious knowledge into the solution of a crime puzzle and of the omniscient narrator into a collaborator with his disreputable character doubles, the criminal and the detective.[14]

The detective, moreover, is not always clearly opposed to the narrator, trying to recover what the narrator secretes. In sensation fiction, detectives are sometimes unsuccessful, presiding over stories as apparent substitutes for defaillant narrators and yet leading the reader down several false paths before someone else discovers the true one. Sergeant Cuff, for example, solves only parts of the mystery in *The Moonstone*, stirs up some false leads, and then disappears from the story until near the end. Similarly, in Taylor's melodrama, *The Ticket-of-Leave Man*, the master detective Hawkshaw fails even to recognize the criminals, though he has tangled with them in the past and though they are right under his nose. And in W. S. Gilbert's comic opera spoof, *A Sensation Novel in Three Volumes*, the Scotland Yard investigator, Gripper, seems mainly bent on delaying the solution of mysteries and allowing criminals to escape. Disguised as a North American Indian, Gripper says:

> When information I receive that Jones has been a-forging,
> And on the proceeds of his crime is prodigally gorging,
> Do you suppose I collar my friend and take him to the beak, m'm?
> Why, bless your heart, they wouldn't retain me in the force a week, m'm.
>
> In curious wig and quaint disguise, and strangely altered face, m'm,
> Unrecognised I follow my prey about from place to place, m'm;
> I note his hair, his eyes, his nose, his clothing and complexion,
> And when I have got 'em all into my head, I set about detection. (Gilbert 22–23)

And thus Jones slips through Gripper's fingers. Gilbert is right: fictional detectives often seem to collude with both criminals and narrators, functioning as much to blow smoke in the reader's eyes as to provide solutions. They thus further erode the apparently diminished powers of the narrators. Their roles are largely dictated by the central structural ambiguity upon which all mystery and detective fiction is based, an ambiguity suggested by telling a secret: you must first be a party to holding the secret in order to tell it.

Despite the air of preternatural significance in a novel such as *Armadale*, mysteries in most sensation novels do not clearly connect with anything higher than a particular case of arson or bigamy or murder. The mysteries in *Bleak House* point to the larger mysteries of community and isolation, love and selfishness in the society that Dickens anatomizes. But the mystery of *The Moonstone*, even though serious issues of crime and poverty, religious hypocrisy, the law, and the empire are evoked, does not explicitly point beyond itself to larger issues. And unlike the Dedlocks and their followers in *Bleak House*, who represent everything that Dickens thinks is wrong with the decaying aristocracy of the 1850s, Sir Percival Glyde and Count Fosco in *The Woman in White* are not bearers of social or even very weighty moral messages. Sir Percival is a stereotypic melodrama villain from whose career of deceit and crime Collins asks us to draw only the most obvious of morals. Count Fosco is more interesting as a character, but the shadowy Italian politics that destroy him at the end of the novel are only a deus ex machina to bring on his just deserts. Collins is not interested in saying anything about secret societies, Mazzini, or the Orsini affair. He does not even take the occasion to deplore the terrible conditions in private insane asylums, as Charles Reade does in *Hard Cash*.[15]

The mysteries in *Lady Audley's Secret, Uncle Silas*, and *The Moonstone* do not connect with larger themes or issues. In each case, though much that is violent and terrifying occurs, the mystery turns out to be soluble, unlike the larger mysteries raised by *Bleak House* and *Our Mutual Friend*. The worst evils that can be perpetrated by individuals are unmasked, but the instant of their revelation is usually also the instant of their exorcism. The paradox is that sensation novels—and mystery-detective novels after them—conclude in ways that liquidate mystery: they are not finally mysterious at all. The insoluble is solved; guilt is displaced onto others, in a sense onto scapegoats whom the reader is glad to see brought to justice. The innocent, meanwhile, remain innocent and are rewarded with happy endings. In "The Guilty Vicarage," W. H. Auden describes the process:

> The magic formula is an innocence which is discovered to contain guilt; then a suspicion of being the guilty one; and finally a real innocence from which the guilty other has been expelled, a Cure effected, not by me or my neighbors, but by the miraculous intervention of a genius from outside who removes guilt by giving knowledge of guilt. (The detective story subscribes, in fact, to the Socratic daydream: "Sin is ignorance.") (Auden 158)

Auden suggests the ritual nature of mystery-detective fiction, with the detective as priest performing the exorcism. But the pattern is not fully developed in sensation novels, which are more flexible and various than modern detective novels and, as T. S. Eliot pointed out in his essay on Collins and Dickens, closer to serious fiction. Their structures are consequently less reassuring; the detectives in them, for example, are often not Auden's "genius from outside," but a character or characters directly involved in the story. Indeed, Sergeant Cuff, the prototype of later professional sleuths, is not the main detective in *The Moonstone*. That role belongs to Franklin Blake, the apparent protagonist, who turns out also to have stolen the diamond. And the piecemeal process of detection often depends heavily on luck and coincidence, as in *Oliver Twist* (the most striking coincidence in *The Moonstone*, of course, is also the most baffling: that Franklin Blake himself is the thief).

The paradox of Franklin Blake, or of the detective in pursuit of himself, points to the essence of later mystery novels. Most serious novels—manifestly in a Bildungsroman, for example—involve a search for self-knowledge and the struggle of the protagonist to stake out an identity and a career in the social wilderness. In sensation and later mystery-detective novels, however, just as the intractable problem of evil is reduced to a neatly soluble puzzle on a personal level, so the search for self-knowledge is short-circuited. The unraveling of the mystery, as in *The Moonstone*, in which Franklin Blake works his way through the labyrinth of clues and false leads only to discover that he himself has stolen the diamond, mimics self-revelation but moves in the opposite direction. The mystery revealed exonerates both the protagonist and the reader from guilt: Franklin's act was unconscious; the real villain is his rival, Godfrey Ablewhite, who is murdered by the convenient Indians, the rightful owners of the gem.

III

Although crimes are solved and both mystery and guilt exorcised from sensation novels, there is often another "enigma"—another, even more buried because taboo sort of mystery—one that the tidy solutions of the detectives cannot solve. One sensational aspect of *Lady Audley's Secret* is its title character's multiple identities and aliases, through which she manages to escape poverty and marry into the aristocracy—a fantasy of class mobility and insecurity that was a staple of nineteenth-century fiction and melodrama. On this sociological level, as Ronald Thomas notes, the secrets of sensation novels involve "class anxiety and instability" (482).[16] But a second, even more sensational aspect of Braddon's bestseller concerns the way Lady Audley crosses class boundaries by exploiting the appeal of her angelic beauty and therefore of her sexuality.

As has often been noted, Braddon's demonic woman masquerading behind blonde, childlike innocence challenges the "angel in the house" stereotype. Hers seems to be the opposite of a physical sexuality, however: she is an almost bodiless incarnation of cold, ruthless calculation. Elaine Showalter is thus surely correct in her contention that, "as every woman reader must have sensed, Lady Audley's real secret is that she is *sane* and, moreover, representative" (167). Lady Audley is a proto-feminist who, without being mad, "moves out of the dollhouse and into the madhouse" (Showalter 180). But her ultimate secret—her supposedly hereditary madness—hints also at a contrary, though buried, passionate side of her character that aligns her story with the excessive, nonlinear anti-plots of female desire in *Jane Eyre* and *Villette*. Her final incarceration in the madhouse in Belgium seems as desolate and wasteful as the deaths-by-passion of Catherine and Heathcliff in *Wuthering Heights*. It is not just that she has committed criminal acts in a perfectly sane, rational manner; the buried side of her personality—her deepest secret—is one that escapes reason and domestication altogether. That her madness is linked to sexual passion, moreover, is suggested early in the story by her "pre-Raphaelite" portrait:

> No one but a pre-Raphaelite would have so exaggerated every attribute of that delicate face as to give a lurid brightness to the blonde complexion, and a strange, sinister light to the deep blue eyes. No one but a pre-Raphaelite could have given to that pretty pouting mouth the hard and almost wicked look it had in the portrait. (47)

The narrator's description of the portrait continues for two more paragraphs, detailing her "crimson dress [that] hung about her in folds that looked like flames" and "her fair head peeping out of the lurid mass of color as if out of a raging furnace" (47).

This is, of course, a version of the woman-as-demon or "beautiful fiend" (Braddon 47) familiar not only in Pre-Raphaelite painting and poetry, but throughout Romantic and Victorian culture—a version, in short, of the femme fatale. The "adventuress," as Sally Mitchell notes, is a key character in sensation fiction; these are "Becky Sharp's children," in pursuit of "money, position, power and security" any way they can get it, which usually means marriage and "sex without love" (Mitchell 76). But the adventuress in sensation novels is never merely a coldly calculating gold-digger. She behaves in impulsive, passionate, willful ways that often involve her in extramarital sexual adventures. Frequently entailing adultery and sometimes bigamy, as in *Lady Audley's Secret*, the mysteries of sensation fiction, true to the "mode of excess" that Brooks identifies with melodrama, usually also at least hint at a hidden, steamy, or perverse sexuality that may itself never be described or explained, but that lends a titillating, dreamlike, quasi-psychoanalytic element to novels otherwise as different as Wood's *East Lynne* and Charles Reade's *Griffith Gaunt*.[17]

The sexual dimension of the "mode of excess" in sensation fiction seems to point relentlessly, regressively back through a kind of self-deconstructing family romance to primal scenes that are simultaneously the solutions of the main mysteries and never revealed, buried within infantile energies that, as in dreams, are at once expressed and concealed. Bigamy, that staple of sensation fiction, seems often to be nearly as horrific as incest, a surrogate or double for that most unspeakable of sexual crimes.[18] Even in those sensation novels whose plots do not hinge upon bigamy, there is often a stress upon sexual irregularities, adultery, forced marriages, and marriages formed under false pretenses. But rather than striking forthright blows in favor of divorce-law reform and greater sexual freedom, sensation novels usually merely exploit public interest in these issues.

In his psychoanalytic interpretation of *The Moonstone*, Albert Hutter perhaps grants too much to mystery-detective fiction when he likens it to the process of psychoanalysis itself.[19] While such fiction may act as a bridge between dreams "and literary experience in general," it also, in reducing mystery to a soluble level, undercuts any search for self-knowledge. Nevertheless, *The Moonstone*, according to Hutter, can be read "as an expression of primal scene fears and wishes, that is, as an expression of the conflicts of the child who witnesses parental intercourse," in part because it is a novel "built around a visual tension . . . the characters watching a crime committed in a bedroom at night, not understanding it, and suffering because they are forced into a new view of a loved object" (203–204). Obsessive curiosity and voyeurism characterize all mystery-detective stories, but the primal-scene thesis fits best where the mystery is confined to "the secret theatre of home" (see Jenny Bourne Taylor) and the voyeurism is a matter of life and death to the voyeur, as in both *Lady Audley's Secret* and *Uncle Silas*, for example, and also in much Gothic fiction. Such a thesis involves interpreting both the victims, including corpses, and the villains as surrogate parent figures, seen dimly through the childhood memory of the fearful vision (whether real or imagined) that both misconstrues the parental intercourse as an act of violence and secretly wishes it to be such an act. In *Uncle Silas*, which has, if anything, even more "visual tension" and horror related to that tension than does *The Moonstone*, the Bluebeard and vampire-werewolf metaphors attached to Maud Ruthvyn's uncle point toward the regressive pattern suggested by the primal-scene thesis, although it is Silas's son, Dudley, who aims at marrying Maud, seducing her, or having her any way he can. The terrific finale points even more clearly in the same direction:

Maud watches from the shadows as Dudley drives home the strange pick axe, with its "longish tapering spike," meant for Maud herself, time after time into the breast of Mme. de la Rougierre, who is in Maud's place in bed. Maud sees the body heave with "a horrible tremor" and "convulsions," "the arms drumming on the bed," until "the diabolical surgery was ended" (426–427). It is a "sensation scene" to match anything in Boucicault's plays—anything in the entire literature of sensation, in fact—for its combination of grisly terror with erotic suggestion.

Nevertheless, Maud's situation as terrified voyeur makes it difficult to explain the scene either in terms of Foucauldian surveillance—Maud's gaze is hardly that of the detective or policeman—or in terms of the male scopophilia associated with pornography and, as Laura Mulvey contends, with the cinema in general. It may be true, as Fredric Jameson claims, that "the visual is *essentially* pornographic" (*Signatures* 1); in this way, sensation novels seem tailor-made to convert into film scripts. They operate obsessively, albeit regressively, to see, to render visible, what is unseen or hidden within "the secret theatre of home." Though in some sense they are, as D. A. Miller believes, extensions of the long arm of the law, surveillance within them threatens to turn at any moment into the pornographic gaze that, at least in Victorian terms, itself needs policing. And when the gaze belongs to the innocent heroine, as in the case of Maud Ruthvyn, but more generally in the tradition of female Gothic from *Mysteries of Udolpho* through *Jane Eyre* and beyond, the primal scene becomes one of masochistic horror: Maud witnesses what might have been her own sexual violation, her own murder, or both.

That surveillance, or the gaze of the detective-policeman, cannot be neatly disentangled from the pornographic gaze in any sensation novel suggests their duplicity, their doubleness. Reality in sensation fiction, as in later detective stories, seems Manichaean, radically split between the warring forces of good and evil. Hutter notes that Collins "adopts . . . the device so common to the Victorian novel of splitting hero and villain and giving one the crime and punishment so that the other may be free to enjoy his rewards without guilt" (202–203). While this may call into question the analytic power of all fiction where such character splitting occurs, it also suggests why it means very little to say that detective fiction follows the pattern of psychoanalysis. It only mimics that pattern, just as it mimics aspects of serious fiction; character splitting by sensation novelists like Collins is quite different from that by more realistic novelists such as George Eliot. If the world according to *The Woman in White* is Manichaean, double, the world according to *Middlemarch* is much more complicated, morally ambiguous, and symbolically undecidable. Reflecting the influence of Gothic, the proliferating Allan Armadales; Anne Catherick as ghostly double-goer in *The Woman in White*; and the multiple lives, two husbands, and at least two personalities of Lady Audley hark back to such double-goers as Frankenstein and his Monster, Ambrosio and Rosario in *The Monk*, and Robert Wringhim and Satan in James Hogg's *Confessions of a Justified Sinner*. These patterns can be partly explained as expressions of narcissistic regression; they are also instances, as Slavoj Žižek says of *film noir*, of the failure of "the paternal metaphor." If *Uncle Silas* can be said to have a serious theme, it is precisely that failure. In such moments as the horrific primal scene witnessed by Maud, the Symbolic Order capitulates to the Imaginary, complexity and ambivalence to duality and the seeming clarity of trauma. In place of the "traditional father—guarantor of the rule of Law . . . who exerts his power as fundamentally *absent*, whose fundamental feature is not an open display of power but the threat of potential power—we obtain an excessively *present* father . . ." (*Enjoy* 158). This is "the obscene, uncanny, shadowy double of the Name of the Father," the embodiment of "radical evil" who is also "a kind of 'master of enjoyment'" or *jouissance*—the chief actor in the psychodrama of the primal scene.

In sensation fiction as in *film noir*, the femme fatale like Lady Audley is perhaps a double or disguise for the appearance of the obscene father; she is, according to Žižek, "nothing but a lure whose fascinating presence masks the true traumatic axis of the *noir* universe, the relationship to the obscene father, i.e., the default of the paternal metaphor" (*Enjoy* 160). Žižek might have added that, in the sensation novel as in the *noir* universe, *seeing is believing but only at the level of trauma*, which is also the level of the phantasmal, the uncanny, and the sensational; words fail just at the moment the curtain goes up on the primal scene and the obscene father takes the stage, signaling the failure of both the Law and the Symbolic Order. The sensational is from this perspective always in excess of language, to be experienced, like the Real for Lacan, only as a blow or shock that cannot be communicated through either writing or speech. Žižek suggests that the appearance of the obscene father is even more scandalous than anything directly attributable to the femme fatale, including her sexuality (or, applying the Victorian metaphor, her demonism). But, besides the traumatized observer, there are always two actors in the primal scene, and insofar as the femme fatale is always a sort of double (whether mask or shadow) of the obscene father, a villainess like Lady Audley evokes the entire erotic register of the sensational—that is, of the sexual and the sado-masochistic—as do villains such as Count Fosco, Uncle Silas, and Dracula.[20]

The development of the sensation novel marks a crisis in the history of literary realism, in part because of its challenge to the naive empiricism or observation that serves such realism as its epistemology. As the omniscient narrator—that shadowy incarnation of the "paternal metaphor," the Symbolic Order, and the Law—disappears, abdicates authority, or proves untrustworthy, the work of detection begins, for the reader as well as for the detective. The first discovery—one that immediately problematizes observation—is that seeing involves more than meets the eye, or in other words that seeing is no longer believing. The material surfaces of things, even in that most familiar of settings, the bourgeois home, themselves become double, treacherously unstable, disguises for the most buried, traumatic secret, the once-seen and not-yet-seen. In such a world, where everything threatens to become a clue—a sign pointing excessively, obsessively to *the* hidden meaning—everyone is a suspect, even (or rather perhaps especially) that most familiar of law-givers, *pater familias*, whose hypocritical, cynical presence may at any moment transmogrify into the more phantasmal and yet substantial, monstrous form of the obscene father. Though sensation novels, like later mystery-detective novels, strip the world of one sort of simplicity or naivete—that expressed in those realist novels that subscribe to some version of the empiricist credo "seeing is believing"—they substitute another: the binary vision of the Imaginary, the Manichaeanism that splits the universe into the figures of absolute good and evil.

Perhaps the deepest secret of the sensation novel is that there is a seeing beyond seeing, a double vision that can, by a new kind of expert, professional looking (detecting the clues), discern realities behind appearances. That these hidden realities, however, as in Gothic romances, point still further to something regressive, and especially to some variation on primal-scene psychology, marks them as sensational in another way, anticipating much modern mass culture, including *film noir*—whereby the double-seeing of the detective-voyeur becomes a kind of perverse, ambiguous wish-fulfillment, expressing the desire to be both the law-giving father and his obscene double, both angel-in-the-house and her demonic self, both adult and child, both knowledgeable or in-on-the-real-facts-of-the-case and eternally innocent. The ultimate secret—and scandal—of *Lady Audley's Secret*, as of other sensation novels, is that it encourages the reader in her or his own radical doubleness, without deciding the issue.

Surveillance or pornography? That is the question. Beyond the innocent though absolutist eye of the realist author, narrator, and reader, says the sensation novel, there is another, second way of seeing and therefore of reading. But that second way of reading/seeing is neither self-evident nor safe. If it isn't exactly pornographic (at least, not in Victorian sensation fiction), neither is it the police. The detective and the pornographer, the victim and the villain, innocence and experience walk through the menacing, secretive front door of Audley Court together, in collusion. Who has stolen the moonstone is, for most of Collins's great, complex exercise in the simplification of—or regression from—realistic fiction and the Symbolic Order, the fetishistic question that drives the narrative toward its final solution. In the case of *The Moonstone*, of course, the solution is that the main detective in the story, and the character who comes closest to being the protagonist, Franklin Blake, has, while somnambulating, stolen the diamond and secreted it so that it won't be stolen. Both detective and culprit, both the Name of the Father and his obscene opposite, Franklin Blake in his doubleness foreshadows that of the heroes of later mystery-detective stories, including *film noir* versions, in which the detective, even if he remains law-abiding and commits no crimes, is invariably implicated in or tainted by the guilt of whatever shady business occurs. These patterns are not simply ways of expressing the universality of guilt; they also express the radical, regressive doubleness whereby the law-giving father gives way, if only momentarily, in some brief but shimmeringly traumatic primal-scene vision, beyond simple empiricism, to his obscene shadow.

Through their reinscriptions of Gothic motifs, sensation novels suggest that the ultimate buried truths of experience are phantasmal. Yet they also insist on the radical materiality of those truths—indeed, on the physically traumatic nature of truth, like the "blow" that reading the *Times* headline gives to George Talboys—because they insist on "sensation." That insistence on the physical, however, can in turn be understood as expressing a new kind of anxiety about the mass readership for novels. The assault on the "nervous system" of the reading public that the "sensation mania" seemed to involve implies an uncertainty about how best to capture the attention of readers. To write a sensation novel means, in part, to construct a fiction that will deal its readers blows or shocks. To reach Collins's Unknown Public, new, more powerful stimulants, it seemed, had to be scripted into novels.

The sensation novelists were, more than earlier generations of authors, acutely aware that novels are commodities, which to succeed—that is, to sell—must compete with other novels and forms of popular entertainment in an abstract, impersonal marketplace. As much as its regressive psychological tendencies, its status as mass-cultural commodity—*mere* entertainment—caused the writers of sensation fiction to join their most severe critics in devaluing what they wrote. In *The Doctor's Wife*, her version of *Madame Bovary*, Braddon offers an elaborate, parodic account of the works of sensation novelist Sigismund Smith, while elsewhere she frequently writes in disparaging terms about her own stories.[21] In a letter to Bulwer-Lytton, for example, Braddon declares: "The amount of crime, treachery, murder, slow poisoning, and general infamy required by the halfpenny reader is something terrible. I am just going to do a little parricide for this week's supply" (qtd. in Wolff 126). Braddon refers here to the stories she wrote, not just for the penny-novel journals that Collins's Unknown Public reads, but for her husband's *Halfpenny Journal* (Wolff 119). Braddon, however, writes in the same disparaging way about her greatest successes, *Lady Audley's Secret* and *Aurora Floyd*. In her correspondence with Bulwer-Lytton, she wonders if "the sensational [can] be elevated by art, & redeemed from all its coarseness?" And she confesses:

> I have learned to look at everything in a mercantile sense, & to write solely for the circulating library reader whose [palate] requires strong meat, and is not very particular as to the quality. (Qtd. in Wolff 155)

Part of the controversy aroused by sensation novels stems from the tendency of their authors to devalue them, as Braddon does here: they see themselves as producing inferior fiction for mass consumption. At best, echoing their critics, they think of themselves as mere entertainers, striving to capture public attention through the latest sensation, like the writers of newspaper headlines. And they regard their readers with a patronizing contempt—these are readers who ought to know better, or who ought to have better ways of spending their time—like the contempt Thackeray expresses for consumers of "greasy novels" or that which Collins expresses for the Unknown Public, the three million or so consumers of penny-novel journals who, he says, despite their literacy, must nevertheless be taught "how to read" (263).

Recognition of the commodity-status of the sensation novel, moreover, renders it mysterious on another level, distinct from the enigmas of plot and theme—mysterious, that is, just as Marx declared all commodities to be mystifying "social hieroglyphics." The sensation fiction of the 1860s seems simultaneously to acknowledge its commodity-status and the abstractness and distance between author and audience, story and mass marketplace, while trying to eradicate that distance through shocks and blows, thrills and shivers—through, in other words, striving for an immediate albeit impossible physicality or direct contact with its increasingly distant, unknown, and uncontrollable readership.

At the same time that George Eliot was investing the novel with a new philosophical gravity, the sensationalists were breaking down the conventions of realistic fiction and pointing the way to the emergence of later popular forms and perhaps also to later, more conscious assertions of the need to go beyond realism into all those mysterious areas of life and art that supposedly omniscient narrators seem not to know or to recognize. Although anything "sensational" is by definition not to be taken too seriously, the word itself points to a source of immediate excitement or surprise, the realm of the unexpected. Most sensation novels confine their voyeuristic, primal-scene revelations to family circles, but of course the family was the mainstay of bourgeois, Victorian values. Sensation novels were therefore both immensely popular and deeply unsettling to their first readers. They stripped the veils from Victorian respectability and prudery, exposing bigamists and adulterers, vampires and murderesses. They did so not by pushing the conventions of realistic fiction to its reified limits, as Zola was beginning to do in France, but by destabilizing those conventions, importing Gothic elements back into contemporary settings, reinvesting the ordinary with mystery (albeit only of the secular, criminal variety), and undoing narrative omniscience to let in kinds of knowledge—suspicions, at least—that realistic fiction had banished. In place of the empiricist realism that strives for objective, direct mimesis, the sensation novel substitutes a different measure of reality, based on primal-scene psychology, that reads objective appearances as question marks or clues while insisting that the traumatic kernel of truth lies hidden, smuggled away behind the appearances. But this destabilizing of simple empiricism is also felt to be regressive, inferior to traditional realism: the sensation novel never directly challenged the dominance of more serious, realistic fiction, and sensational authors and narrators seem forever to be backing away from the deepest truths in their stories, thereby abdicating or undermining their own authority, offering their works as mere entertainment.

With the sensation fiction of the 1860s in mind, T. S. Eliot remarked, "[W]e cannot afford to forget that the first—and not one of the least difficult—requirements of either prose or verse is that it should be interesting" (417–418). Whatever else they are, sensation novels are certainly that. In his defense of literary sensationalism in *Belgravia* (a journal edited by none other than Mary Elizabeth

Braddon), George Augustus Sala launched an assault on "the dolts and dullards and envious backbiters" for whom "everything is 'sensational' that is vivid, and nervous, and forcible, and graphic, and true." If these "anti-sensationalists" had their way, Sala declared, then life itself would be a sorry affair, for they would establish a new reign of dullness: "Don't let us move, don't let us travel, don't let us hear or see anything; but let us write sonnets to Chloe, and play madrigals on the spinet, and dance minuets, and pray to Heaven against Sensationalism, the Pope, the Devil, and the Pretender; and then let Dulness reign triumphant, and Universal Darkness cover all" (457–458). Sala's sensational protest points forward to the fuller, more profound rebellions of the decadent and modernist writers who, influenced by both impressionism and symbolism, wrote the final epitaphs both for the safer kinds of realism and for the Victorian pieties of hearth and home.

CHAPTER

8

The Educations of Edward Hyde and Edwin Reardon

> What is more vulgar than the ideal of novelists? They won't
> represent the actual world; it would be too dull for their readers.
> —Rhoda Nunn in Gissing's *The Odd Women*

I

On 25 January 1886, the *Times* reviewed a "sparsely-printed little shilling volume" entitled *The Strange Case of Dr Jekyll and Mr Hyde*. According to Charles Longman, this review initiated the story's immense popularity, although the tale was packaged from the start to be a best-seller (Maixner 205). Dr. Thomas Scott recalled Robert Louis Stevenson's annunciation one morning that "I've got my shilling shocker." This, said Scott, was "the period of the shilling shockers," and at a time before Stevenson's "success was ensured, when he was in financial difficulties," his publishers had been "urging him, much against his inclination, to write such a book" (qtd. in Masson 269). Yet Stevenson had been quite willing to publish earlier stories in popular formats. "The Body Snatcher" had appeared in the 1884 Christmas extra of the *Pall Mall Gazette*, which "advertised it in the streets in a way as horrible as the story itself" (Hammerton 318).

For Longman's part, *Jekyll and Hyde* was deliberately formatted as a "shilling shocker" aimed at the 1885 Christmas market, though because completed too late it was withheld from the booksellers until the new year (Swearingen 99). For his part, because of "financial fluctuations," Stevenson had been "racking [his] brains for a plot of any sort" ("A Chapter on Dreams"). Despite being able to fall back on his father, Stevenson desperately wanted to earn his living as a writer. Producing a shilling shocker for Longmans might disagree with his sense of the higher aims of literature, but it agreed with his desire for financial independence and popularity.

"The wheels of Byles the Butcher drive exceedingly swiftly," Stevenson wrote apologetically to F. W. H. Myers. Therefore, "*Jekyll* was conceived, written, re-written, re-re-written, and printed inside ten weeks" (*Letters* 2:294). What Stevenson meant by "Byles the Butcher" was perhaps his "initial monetary impulse" (Swearingen 99). The "white-hot haste" with which he produced the story, Stevenson hoped, would help to excuse some of the solecisms Myers detected in it. Paradoxically it could perhaps also explain or excuse its astonishing popular success. Other stories that Stevenson labored over and considered more serious might never be best-sellers; but popularity and seriousness seemed antithetical to him. Despite lavish praise by Myers and others, Stevenson's own statements about the story tend to be defensively ironic. Instead of a masterpiece that would win the unconditional approval of the most discriminating readers, he had produced a "Gothic gnome," a "fine bogey tale." Through the revision prompted by his wife Fanny, he had converted the tale into a "moral allegory," but the revision had perhaps only given it another source of appeal to the mass readership who, both he and Longmans believed, were the real arbiters of the late-Victorian literary marketplace.

In part because of his deep-rooted ambivalence toward that marketplace, Stevenson responded ambivalently to *Jekyll and Hyde*, at times referring to it as if it were a despised double, or at least the unwanted spawn of the weaker, Hyde-like side of himself, as in the Byles-the-Butcher letter, or in his account of its genesis in "A Chapter on Dreams," according to which his "Brownies" invented Hyde while his waking or rational self supplied the "morality." Such ambivalence suggests that *Jekyll and Hyde* can be read, in part, as a kind of Gothic version of George Gissing's *New Grub Street*. It has always been read as an "allegory" about good and evil, about "the war in the members" and the "double nature" of human nature. But it can also be read as an unconscious "allegory" about the commercialization of literature and the emergence of a mass consumer society in the late-Victorian period.

"I had long been trying to write a story on [the] strong sense of man's double being," declares Stevenson in "A Chapter on Dreams." The various accounts of the genesis of the "fine bogey tale," including Stevenson's, are all marked by an ambivalence or doubleness that stems from the fundamental contradiction between the sense of literature as a high calling and the desire for popular fame and fortune. According to Stevenson, "one of those financial fluctuations" caused him to feel a sort of panic.

> For two days I went about racking my brains for a plot of any sort; and on the second night I dreamed the scene at the window, and a scene afterwards split in two, in which Hyde, pursued for some crime, took the powder. . . . All the rest was made awake, and consciously, although I think I can trace in much of it the manner of my Brownies. The meaning of the tale is therefore mine, and had long pre-existed. . . . ("A Chapter on Dreams")

Nevertheless, Stevenson's sense of ownership, or of authorial control, of the story is itself ambivalent: "Mine, too, is the setting, mine the characters," he adds. "All that was given me was the matter of three scenes, and the central idea of a voluntary change becoming involuntary." Though he owns or controls most of the story, it, too, has its "involuntary" aspect.

The division of labor between Stevenson's waking self, who supplied the "meaning" and who owns the characters, and his "Brownies," who supplied, through his dream, the central "scenes" and "manner" of the story, itself points to "man's double being." Stevenson's account applies the chief message of *Jekyll and Hyde* to the history of its production, as does Mary Shelley's account of the nightmare genesis of her "hideous progeny," *Frankenstein*. As personifications of the mind's dream-life, the Brownies are Stevenson's doubles, creatures hidden inside the waking personality who beg comparison with the "dwarfish" or "gnome-like" Mr. Hyde. Stevenson says that, in the division of labor that produced the tale, he took care "of the morality, worse luck!" because "my Brownies have not a rudiment of what we call a conscience" ("A Chapter on Dreams").

A similar division of labor is evident in the accounts by Fanny Stevenson and Lloyd Osbourne, except that in these Fanny plays the role of "conscience" or supplier of "meaning" and "morality." They both indicate that the first draft, itself written in "white-hot haste," was tossed into the fire because of Fanny's reaction to it. Stevenson had apparently written a mere "crawler" or tale of terror, without any more serious intention than to entertain, but Fanny thought that "it was really an allegory."

> The morning after her husband had the dream . . . he came with a radiant countenance to show his work to his wife, saying it was the best thing he had ever done. She read it and thought it the worst. . . . At last . . . she put her objections to it . . . in writing, complaining that he had treated it simply as a story, whereas it was in reality an allegory. After . . . seeing the justice of her criticism, with characteristic impulsiveness he immediately burned his first draft and rewrote it from a different point of view. . . . (Sanchez 118)

It is not altogether apparent what Fanny meant by "allegory" and "story," but Osbourne added, "In the first draft Jekyll's nature was bad all through, and the Hyde change was worked only for the sake of a disguise" (65). In other words, the sharp moral antithesis—the struggle between the mostly good, outward self (Jekyll) and the evil, hidden self (Hyde)—was not a feature of the first draft. The "allegorization" that Fanny demanded apparently changed a horror story *tout simple* into one about the warfare between good and evil, giving it a religious or philosophical gloss. Whether or not this transformation made *Jekyll and Hyde* a better work of art, it probably did make it seem more serious and respectable and may therefore also have helped to attract a broader spectrum of readers than a mere shilling shocker would have. Instead of just a crawler, it became, so to speak, a crawler with a purpose.

If this interpretation is correct, then Stevenson's own explanation of why he burned the first draft acquires an intriguing ambiguity. According to Osbourne, both he and Fanny "cried out at the folly of destroying the manuscript," but Stevenson "justified himself vehemently. 'It was all wrong,' he said. 'In trying to save some of it I should have got hopelessly off the track. *The only way was to put temptation beyond my reach*'" (65; my italics). What was the "temptation" that led to the burning of the first draft? The simplest reading is that it was merely to make life easier for the writer by relying on a botched job. But "*it was all wrong.*" Perhaps there was a further temptation to produce a story in which the evil side of human nature would go unchallenged by the good—a story lacking "conscience" that would cater to the most sensation-hungry and therefore also "popular" tastes of readers. But the allegorization of *Jekyll and Hyde* may also have helped make it a popular success by rendering it just as respectable as it was "wrong" or criminal.

The Jekyll/Hyde split between "allegory" and mere "story" is similar to the other, more familiar dichotomies of Stevenson's life and work. There are, for example, the conflicts between bourgeois respectability and bohemianism, engineering and art, and Calvinism and free thought that marked Stevenson's troubled relations with his family. As for his art, his letters and essays reveal his vacillations between "realism" and "romance." In each case, Stevenson affirms the creative energy or vitality of what he simultaneously regards as the lower, less serious or less moral half of the antithesis. Stevenson defines most of his fiction in terms of romance or "the novel of adventure" and therefore criticizes the various realisms as both drab and pseudo-scientific. But his defenses of romance often lack conviction. He is aware that "English people of the present day are apt . . . to look somewhat down on incident [in fiction], and reserve their admiration for the clink of teaspoons and the accents of the curate" ("A Gossip on Romance"). But he associates romance or the fiction of "incident" and "adventure" with daydream, escapism, and childhood rather than with any visionary or romantic qualities that would both transcend and see more deeply into reality than the rational, realistic mind. At the end of "A Humble Remonstrance," for example, he calls Sir Walter Scott both "a great romantic" and "an idle child," as if these phrases were synonymous. Perhaps the universal, timeless appeal of "romance" seemed unconsciously problematic to him because of its kinship to that contemporary popular or mass appeal—the appeal for instance to mere "sensation" in the sensation novels of the 1860s—which he believed he should resist.

What Andrew Noble describes as "Stevenson's ambivalent relationship to his audience and to money" (21) shows up throughout his letters and essays. When some of his well-wishers looked askance at the publication of *Treasure Island* in *Young Folks*, Stevenson wrote angrily to W. E. Henley:

> To those who ask me . . . to do nothing but refined, high-toned, bejay-bedamned masterpieces, I will offer the following bargain: I agree to their proposal if they give me £1000 . . . and at the same time effect such a change in my nature that I shall be content to take it from them instead of earning it. If they cannot manage these trifling matters, by God, I'll trouble them to hold their tongues, by God. . . . Let them write their damn masterpieces for themselves. . . . (Calder 172)

This is the sort of difficulty expressed by the struggling writers in *New Grub Street*, whose efforts to write what they consider serious literature are not marketable, although other, less serious forms of writing—the kinds of "journalism," for example, that Jasper Milvain cynically masters and markets—achieve high levels of popular success.

For Stevenson and Gissing alike, the choice was not between being read and going completely unread, but between producing popular or unpopular kinds of writing. Earlier writers and publishers, from the eighteenth century through the 1830s, had necessarily aimed their works at smaller, more uniform and predictable, more clearly middle-class or upper-class readers. The market for penny fiction aimed at the working class, catered to by Edward Lloyd, G. W. M. Reynolds, and others, seemed quite distinct through mid-century (Louis James 28–44). But by the 1880s, the massification and yet also diversification of the literary marketplace, facilitated by the evolution toward nearly universal literacy by the end of the century, pulled both Stevenson and Gissing in contradictory directions. On one hand, B. G. Johns, in an 1887 *Edinburgh Review* essay entitled "The Literature of the Streets," reported sales of "sensational novels in serial form" in excess of "two million copies a week, with individual titles selling from ten to sixty thousand each" (Altick 308). On the other, as Stevenson's publishing *Treasure Island* in *Young Folks* shows, it was possible to write "popular" stories for quite specific sectors of the mass readership, such as middle-class boys. But was it still possible, both Stevenson and Gissing wondered, to write and publish literary "masterpieces"?

Late-Victorian critics and educators did much moralizing about the sad state of popular taste and the semi-literacy of the mass readership, though given the massive increase in reading material of all sorts and in reading as a form of leisure activity, the complaints seem contradictory. Johns asserted that it was "a disgrace to our boasted civilisation" that "a nation like England, which spends millions on the education of her children, and boasts of teaching every poor boy and girl to read, should provide for them no fiction but of an infamously worthless kind" (61). Johns is thinking partly of the "cheap literature, hideous and ignoble of aspect" that Matthew Arnold also deplored, including "the tawdry novels which flare in the book-shelves of our railway stations, and which seem designed . . . for people with a low standard of life" (Arnold, "Copyright" 126). But he also has in mind the "garbage of the 'Penny Dreadfuls,'" which is, he believes, especially "poisonous" to the newly literate or semi-literate masses. Such "depraved" street literature is criminal, according to Johns, both because it deals with crime and because it stimulates "foul aims" and "vicious" behavior in readers. Johns ranks Stevenson among the writers of "healthful" fiction, but he goes on to say, "The worst of modern novels are too often among the most popular."

Framed by these mass cultural trends and anxieties in the 1880s, Stevenson's resuscitation of older "romance" forms of story-telling can be understood as an effort to mediate between an ideal of literature as high culture and a desire for mass-market success (Veeder, "Introduction" xii–xiii). A similar effort is evident in the work of other late-Victorian "romancers" such as H. Rider Haggard and H. G. Wells. Equating fictional realism with serious or high culture as opposed to nonserious, low, popular, or mass culture, both Stevenson and Gissing saw the handwriting on the wall for the realist novel. Suicidally (in a metaphoric sense), Gissing chose the doomed realist paradigm, while Stevenson nervously pursued the apparently more "popular" direction of romance. According to Fredric Jameson:

> It is in the context of the gradual reification of realism in late capitalism that romance once again comes to be felt as the place of narrative heterogeneity and of freedom from that reality principle to which a now oppressive realistic representation is the hostage. Romance now again seems to offer the possibility of sensing other historical rhythms, and of demonic or Utopian transformations of a real now unshakably set in place. . . . (104)

As Jameson also notes, however, the late-Victorian romance that emerged between the breakdown of realism and the rise of modernism tended toward "popular . . . or mass culture," sharing "the commercialized cultural discourse of what, in late capitalism, is often described as a media society" (206). Jameson diagnoses Conrad's *Lord Jim* as "schizophrenic" because of its unresolved tension between mass cultural "romance" and high cultural "modernism," and a similar diagnosis, though in terms of "romance" and "realism," applies to Stevenson's fiction.

If the "utopian" search for a "salvational future" is less evident than "demonic . . . transformations" in late-Victorian writing, that is perhaps because "romance" from the outset seemed both highly mannered—a recasting of obsolete conventions—and itself "hostage" to the new, seemingly progressive and affluent, but apparently also degraded and degrading, industrialized mass market for literature. What Stevenson specifically resurrected in *Jekyll and Hyde* was the old Gothic message about the evil within, given a scientific spin by the "powders" that Jekyll concocts in his laboratory, as a mass cultural entertainment or "shilling shocker." The writer of "healthful" fiction, according to B. G. Johns, was himself concocting something close to the "poisonous," "depraved" "garbage of the 'Penny Dreadfuls.'" But by reviving the antiquated conventions of romance, Stevenson hoped that he could cater to the reading masses while also satisfying his own ideal of a serious literature that would have universal or timeless appeal. But Hyde, the evil within Jekyll, surfaces within the Stevenson romance as an oblique, unconscious condemnation of the same fictional stratagems that sensationalize and commodify literature in order to gain mass-market success. As the educated Frankenstein created his reading Monster, so the educated Dr. Jekyll creates his: Hyde as personification of the reading masses. Stevenson's discovery of Hyde first within himself as dream, alter ego, and literary invention (another version of Mary Shelley's "hideous progeny") involved the author/creator in a subtle form of cultural damnation.

On numerous occasions, Stevenson defends romances on the grounds of their universality, but without explicitly equating such universality with mass-market appeal. "The great creative writer shows us . . . the apotheosis of the day-dreams of common men," particularly in the form of the "romance" or "adventure novel" ("A Gossip on Romance"). But if Stevenson could view the "day-dreams of common men" positively, he could also treat the "gross mass of mankind" with Arnoldian contempt, an attitude that frequently caused him to disparage his own work because of its popularity. Thus he considered *The Black Arrow* mere "tushery" and *St. Ives* a mere "tissue of adventures," with "no philosophic pith under the yarn" (Eigner 5). *Treasure Island* might be better than these potboilers (which had no great popular success anyway), but it was also no more than an "elementary novel of adventure," written for the boy readers of *Young Folks*. "The truth is I am pretty nearly useless at literature," he declared late in his career. "My skill . . . was a very little dose of inspiration, and a pretty little trick of style . . . improved by the most heroic industry. So far, I have managed to please the journalists. But I am a fictitious article and have long known it" (*Letters* 4:327).

Stevenson was indeed a "fictitious article"—the hero-storyteller whose stories formed key episodes in a picaresque career. His "heroic industry" in the face of disease and death, his fabled bohemianism, his South Seas adventures—these also were chapters of the Stevenson romance, the story of the constructed self, the author as hero, that can be read between the lines of such clearly fictitious (or, perhaps, factitious) stories as *Jekyll and Hyde*. By the 1880s, the writer as personality or celebrity had, along with his or her books, become an important commodity that publishers and critics sought to market (see Bowlby 29, for example). From the outset of his career, Stevenson was taken up by such author-peers or writerly colleagues as Leslie Stephen, Sidney Colvin, and Andrew Lang, for whom, as Jenni Calder notes, "literature . . . had grown demoralised, and needed to be rescued" (87). Stevenson appeared to them as a potential rescuer, though his mass-cultural ventures, including *Jekyll and Hyde*, threatened more demoralization. But for his critics and admirers, even those stories and essays most removed from autobiography arranged themselves as episodes in a version of that quite typical modern genre—the Carlylian saga of "The Hero as Man of Letters." *Jekyll and Hyde* can thus be read as a palimpsest between or beneath whose lines the knowing reader will discern the well-advertised originary dream, the incineration of the first draft, and the subsequent allegorization of the story at Fanny's behest.

Stevenson's "Gothic gnome," in other words, mirrors the story of an exemplary struggling author, torn between the desire to produce "masterpieces" and the knowledge that popular success lay in the contrary directions of both "shilling shocker" and "moral allegory." For the supposedly undiscriminating mass readership, the story could still be consumed as "crawler" plain and simple, though this was also a palimpsest in which the form of the Gothic thriller was overwritten by the modern patterns of the detective story and science fiction (Hirsch; Lawler). For a supposedly more sophisticated sort of reader, there was the moral allegory about good and evil; *Jekyll and Hyde* apparently served as the subject of numerous late-Victorian sermons. But for the discriminating elite such as Henry James and Edmund Gosse, there was also the heroic, self-pitying story of its writer's struggle against adversity, which involved the adversity of having to cater to the literary mass market of the late-Victorian age. It is just such a self-pitying story, minus the heroism, of various writers' struggles within and against the literary mass market that George Gissing offers in *New Grub Street*.

II

Stevenson's ambivalence toward his "audience and money" shows up dramatically in a letter he wrote to Edmund Gosse in 1886. "What the public likes is work . . . a little loosely executed," Stevenson tells Gosse. "I know that good work sometimes hits; but, with my hand on my heart, I think it is by an accident." So if an author wants to succeed, the trick is *not* to produce really "good work," but something less than "good," something suitable to the inferior intellectual level and aesthetic taste of the mass audience. Stevenson realizes "that good work must succeed at last; but that is not the doing of the public; they are only shamed into silence or affectation." He adds emphatically, "I do not write for the public"; nevertheless, "I do write for money, a nobler deity; and most of all for myself. . . ." Just how writing for money could mean anything other than writing for the public, Stevenson does not explain, much less how money can in any sense except an ironic one be noble and godlike. Stevenson continues with a paragraph in which the note of self-pity is unmistakable:

> Let us tell each other sad stories of the bestiality of the beast whom we feed. What he likes is the newspaper; and to me the press is the mouth of a sewer, where lying is professed as from an university chair, and everything prurient, and ignoble, and essentially dull, finds its abode and pulpit.

Stevenson's diatribe against "the press" causes him to wax misanthropic, but his general misanthropy is immediately directed back to "that fatuous rabble of burgesses called 'the public,'" and he adds, "God save me from such irreligion" as respecting the public; "that way lies disgrace and dishonour." But how, then, to account for his own success with the public, except through repudiating that success or treating it as something shameful? Stevenson tells Gosse: "There must be something wrong in me, or I would not be popular" (*Letters* 2:281).

The contempt that Stevenson here expresses toward "the public" and his own popularity is similar to that expressed by Gissing in *New Grub Street*. Both believed that the commercial exploitation of a new, qualitatively inferior (as they saw it) mass readership with "a low standard of life" was undermining "good work." For both, an ideal of high culture was opposed to a social reality dominated by "journalism" or "the press" and by the transformation of literature into a mere "trade."

Stevenson's ambivalence toward his own popular success implies that there must be "something wrong in" any story that succeeds with "the public." Obviously there is "something wrong in" *Jekyll and Hyde*, and on a literal level that is Hyde himself, whose physique and criminal propensities make him virtually a stereotype of what Arnold in *Culture and Anarchy* called "the populace," if not exactly of "that fatuous rabble of burgesses called 'the public.'" Though not straight from "the mouth of a sewer," Hyde belongs to the slums of "darkest London." When not at home with or within Jekyll, he lives in the "blackguardly surroundings" of Soho (48), where Utterson travels with Inspector Newcomen as through "a district of some city in a nightmare":

> As the cab drew up before the address indicated, the fog lifted a little and showed him a dingy street, a gin palace, a low French eating-house, a shop for the retail of penny numbers and two-penny salads, many ragged children huddled in the doorways, and many women of many different nationalities passing out, key in hand, to have a morning glass. . . . (48)

The literature of Soho is even cheaper than its food; the "penny numbers" are no doubt identical to the penny-novel journals that Wilkie Collins's "Unknown Public" were already reading in 1858. But this "dismal quarter" with its "muddy ways, and slatternly passengers" (48), is not illiterate; among the "penny numbers" in the shop, perhaps, a "slatternly" reader with a "low standard of life" could purchase a copy of a "shilling shocker" entitled *The Strange Case of Dr Jekyll and Mr Hyde*.

The Soho neighborhood haunted by Hyde is the haunt also of the "dangerous" or "criminal classes." Though such biased class language does not occur in the story, these phrases were current from the 1840s forward.[1] Moreover, the newly national system of elementary education, established after the passage of Forster's Education Act of 1870, was viewed by the 1880s by many commentators to be already at least a partial failure. While it was indeed improving the literacy rate, it did not seem to be moralizing the masses, decreasing the crime rate, or leading the reading public to abandon "the garbage of 'Penny Dreadfuls'" or (to Stevenson) the sewerlike newspaper press in favor of "the best that has been thought and spoken" down through the ages.

In an 1894 article for the *Nineteenth Century*, Joseph Ackland attributes "the decay of literature" directly to the success of Forster's Education Act in universalizing elementary education and increasing literacy. Of the many benefits that its supporters believed Forster's Act would provide, writes Ackland, "[i]t was with reason expected that multitudes who hitherto had occupied their leisure with degrading excitements would find in reading a more agreeable and more elevating amusement" (412). It was also thought that "literature" would benefit from the discovery and training of "genius," thus "swelling the ranks of writers" (413). But the actual results, as Ackland measures them, contradict these high hopes. Ackland provides a statistical survey of the increase of literacy and also of book publication rates from 1869 to 1892, the latter broken down into categories of "learned," educational, and recreational works (the recreational category Ackland labels "The Fiction, &c, Group"). His numbers show a decline in the areas of learned and educational works, though also a "growth of the demand for fiction"

(420). Among other sorts of reading, the newspaper press was growing but also, Ackland believed, declining in quality, in part through catering to "the love of gambling and sensationalism inherent in human nature" (421). New, hugely popular newspapers such as the *Family Herald* were dependent on fiction as much as on factual reporting, while the factual reporting tended to be "scrappy and sensational" (421). Ackland's conclusion is not, however, that the new system of elementary education is a complete failure or should be abandoned but only that its promise has yet to be fulfilled. The new mass readership that it has helped to create, Ackland thinks, has demanded "fiction" instead of "the best books," thus "undermining the growth of solid literature" (420–421). When "the shackles of ignorance were struck off there was a rush to the Elysian fields of fancy and pleasure"; the masses must be led instead toward "voluntary acceptance of the nobler servitude to knowledge and reason" (423). Sounding rather like Dickens's Mr. Gradgrind, Ackland adds:

> The imagination which craves for fiction must be trained to find in the marvels of science and the deductions of philosophy the only fascinations which will yield abiding satisfaction. With this object some national effort to advance secondary and technical education, and to make the connection between elementary schools and the Universities a reality, ought to be vigorously undertaken. (423)

Ackland dates the "decay of literature" quite specifically to 1885, the year before publication of *Jekyll and Hyde*. Meanwhile, in 1876, Cesare Lombroso had published his influential study of the hereditary nature of crime and "moral insanity," arguing that much criminal activity could be explained in terms of physical and mental "atavism." Lombroso also argued that, "contrary to general belief, the influence of education on crime is very slight" (149). His chief work, *L'uomo delinquente*, was not translated into English until 1911, but his basic ideas had gained currency by the 1880s through social scientists and evolutionary psychologists such as Stevenson's friend James Sully (Block 463).

Hyde himself is, of course, an atavistic creature, whose "dwarfish . . . ape-like" appearance reflects the stereotype of the Irish hooligan. As Perry Curtis describes the stereotype, "Paddy" was "childish, emotionally unstable, ignorant . . . primitive . . . dirty, vengeful, and violent" (53). He was also "ape-like" and often stunted in growth or "dwarfish." Curtis quotes a letter by Charles Kingsley describing "white chimpanzees" in Ireland, and in 1845 James Anthony Froude found much of that country's population "more like tribes of squalid apes than human beings" (Curtis 84, 85; see also Malchow 126–129). The threat of Fenianism and the Irish Home Rule controversy, which was to split the Liberal party in 1886, form the political context of Stevenson's *The Dynamiter* (1884), and help to explain Hyde's stereotypically Hibernian traits. Though originally belonging to Utterson, the "heavy cane" with which Hyde "clubs" Sir Danvers Carew might easily have been a shillelagh, and the brutal murder of an M.P. in Stevenson's "crawler" must have caused many readers to recall the 1882 Phoenix Park murders in Dublin. The theme of the increasingly dangerous "Irish Frankenstein," often employed by English caricaturists, has both Celtic and Gothic overtones, which Stevenson's portrayal of Hyde also reflects.[2]

Nevertheless, *Jekyll and Hyde* does not deal explicitly with any contemporary political themes or controversies. The allegorization prompted by Fanny did not involve making the story more topical but perhaps the reverse. Hyde is an emanation of Jekyll's "transcendental medicine" or of Stevenson's nightmare, rather than of either a social class system that spawned criminality or an imperial domination that had shackled Ireland for centuries. Whatever the "moral" of the story—and at first it had none—it concerns good versus evil in the abstract, not the politics or the police of late-Victorian society. The novella's anachronistic style and ahistoricism help it to seem timeless and universal, while also obscuring the literary sleight of hand that sneaks Hyde into the heart of the respectable bourgeoisie (or, better, into the heart of a respectable, bourgeois doctor). Jekyll's metamorphosis is a matter of certain unbelievable "powders," not of politics nor even of science. But the mass-cultural format of the first edition promised topical reality enough to the "populace"—in other words, to the same readers who would have responded to the newsboys whom Utterson hears "crying themselves along the footways: 'Special edition. Shocking murder of an M.P.'" (53).

Stevenson as popular author of a "shilling shocker" shares in the criminal popularity or populace-like nature of Hyde. The statement "There must be something wrong in me, or I would not be popular" is itself, in a sense, the formula of *Jekyll and Hyde*. There is "something wrong in" the story—that is, Hyde—and this "something" accounts for its popularity. Further, the story was "wrong" not only because Hyde was "in" it as well as within Jekyll, but because the germ of it was still the "crawler" that perhaps did nothing more than pander to the low tastes of "that fatuous rabble . . . the public." Fanny, after all, told its author that the first draft was "all wrong"; it needed to be rendered morally acceptable, even though allegorization did not necessarily move it closer to the sort of masterpiece by which Stevenson longed to gain permanent, as opposed to merely popular, recognition. The story was "wrong" because it was immediately and immensely popular; more than anything else he had written, *Jekyll and Hyde* made Stevenson's fame and fortune. Hyde was thus both a chief cause of his creator's popular success and an ironic, albeit perhaps unconscious, image of that popularity: the "ape-like," atavistic image of "the populace," the mass reading public. For Hyde, after all, is a reader—he is literate, just as Bill Sikes and the other criminals in *Oliver Twist* are literate—and, even more significantly, he is a writer, an author of sorts.

Despite his degenerate nature, Hyde retains at least one of Jekyll's upper-class traits. Though his hands are smaller, more gnarled, yet stronger than Jekyll's, Hyde's handwriting is identical to Jekyll's; Hyde therefore tries to disguise it by slanting it differently. "When, by sloping my own hand backwards, I had supplied my double with a signature," says Jekyll, "I thought I sat beyond the reach of fate" (87). One might say that this is the only education Hyde needs because, despite his "ape-like," "deformed" physique and personality, he is just as literate as Jekyll. When Jekyll transforms into Hyde while dozing on a bench in Regent's

Park, Hyde's ability to write in Jekyll's hand is what rescues him from discovery and capture by the police. "Then I remembered that of my original character, one part remained to me: *I could write my own hand*; and once I had conceived that kindling spark, the way that I must follow became lighted up from end to end" (93; my italics). Just as handwritten clues provide the strongest evidence for the continuity of Lady Audley's identity through her metamorphoses, so the single item that does not change through Jekyll's metamorphosis into Hyde is handwriting, though *what* gets written changes dramatically.

Hyde's slanted handwriting proves a poor disguise.[3] Utterson shows the "murderer's autograph" to his head clerk, Guest, who compares it with Jekyll's handwriting and declares, "There's a rather singular resemblance; the two hands are in many points identical; only differently sloped" (55). Further, more often than not the disguise is dropped, as in the Regent's Park episode or in the privacy of Jekyll's laboratory. On these occasions, Hyde writes like Jekyll. And he also makes use of Jekyll's library. In Jekyll's quarters, Hyde apparently entertains himself by reading whatever is available. Given Jekyll's sober, upper-class tastes, however, such reading material is far removed from penny dreadfuls or shilling shockers. "There were several books on a shelf; one lay beside the tea things open, and Utterson was amazed to find it a copy of a pious work for which Jekyll had several times expressed a great esteem, annotated, *in his own hand*, with startling blasphemies" (71; my italics). In his narrative, Jekyll speaks of "the ape-like tricks that [Hyde] would play on me, scrawling *in my own hand* blasphemies on the pages of my books" (96; my italics).

Works of theology are, perhaps, an odd sort of reading for a mad scientist, let alone for his demonic double. Within the terms of the Stevenson romance, however, they perhaps correspond to "moral allegory" as the obverse of "crawler" or "shilling shocker." In any case, Utterson is also in the habit of sitting down by the fire after his solitary, abstemious dinners with "a volume of some dry divinity on his reading-desk" (35). In the chapter where this is mentioned, however, Utterson neglects such "dry," pious reading for a more intriguing although distressing sort— the "holograph" will that Jekyll has drawn up and entrusted to the lawyer. Or did Hyde draw up the will? In his narrative, Jekyll says, "I next drew up that will to which you [Utterson] so much objected" (86), but the "I" is ambiguous in this context. Because they share the same handwriting, it is impossible to know whether Jekyll or Hyde authored the will. Utterson cannot know, since he "had refused to lend the least assistance in the making of it." Similarly, Utterson can't tell whether Jekyll or Hyde wrote the check for ninety pounds to recompense the trampled girl and her family, though no doubt Hyde was its author because he obtains it so quickly. Enfield thought it might prove to be "a forgery," but on the contrary "the cheque was genuine" (32). The ambiguous, perhaps double authorship of several pieces of writing within the text mirrors its double nature as "story" and "allegory," shilling shocker and tale with a "conscience," at once criminal and morally improving.

Among the various recommendations by which Myers hoped to help Stevenson turn a near-masterpiece into the genuine article, one concerned the improbability of Hyde's retention of Jekyll's handwriting. "I think you miss a point for want of familiarity with recent psycho-physical discussions," Myers told Stevenson. "Handwriting in cases of double personality . . . *is not* and *cannot be* the same in the two personalities. Hyde's writing might look like Jekyll's done *with the left hand*, or done when partly drunk, or ill; that is the kind of resemblance there might be. Your imagination can make a good point of this" (Maixner 215). But through the motif of identical penmanship, Stevenson makes a deeper, much more interesting point about cultural authority. Though their values are several worlds, or at least social classes, apart, Jekyll and Hyde share the same ability to express those values, and they do so even in the same "hand" or with the same "signature." Though Jekyll, like all mad scientists, menaces society through his overcultivated, overambitious intellect, Hyde menaces society not just by his criminal violence but by his ability to write checks and letters, draw up wills, and pen blasphemies in books of "divinity." Further, though he apparently does not write his confessions (he leaves that up to Jekyll), let alone a culturally blasphemous shilling shocker, Hyde is nevertheless the hero or antihero of just such a shocker—one that was, perhaps, purely "evil" until allegorized. And this shilling shocker, bearing "Satan's signature" (40) as its central image (Utterson reads that "signature" in Hyde's face), helped to establish Stevenson's literary celebrity and success story. As the Brownies (Stevenson claimed) were the authors of the originary nightmare, so the uncannily literate Edward Hyde was in an important way the author of the Stevenson romance.

When Utterson and Inspector Newcomen enter Hyde's Soho residence, they discover something quite different from its "blackguardly surroundings." The rooms Hyde uses are "furnished with luxury and good taste." They are evidently the rooms of an epicure who takes pleasure in art. "A closet was filled with wine; the plate was silver, the napery elegant; a good picture hung upon the walls, a gift (as Utterson supposed) from Henry Jekyll, who was much of a connoisseur; and the carpets were of many plies and agreeable in colour" (49). Stevenson seems almost to be illustrating Oscar Wilde's thesis, in "Pen, Pencil, and Poison," that "there is no essential incongruity between crime and culture" (98). Perhaps Hyde retains more of Jekyll's traits than just his handwriting. Or is the evidence of epicureanism pure Hyde, whereas Jekyll, like Utterson, adheres to a routine of abstinence and "dry divinity"? Whatever the case, the Soho flat is not some Fagin's roost in the underworld slums, but a setting that implies sensual enjoyment, perhaps libertinism, of an apparently upper-class sort. Further, there is more evidence of Hyde's reading in the apartment—unless it is Jekyll's reading—or perhaps it is evidence of his/his writing. The rooms, says Utterson, appeared to have been "recently and hurriedly ransacked," while on "the hearth there lay a pile of grey ashes, as though many papers had been burned" (49).

What "papers" would Hyde, or perhaps Jekyll, need to burn? The scientific texts and records of their transformations appear to have been left in Jekyll's laboratory. There would be no occasion to bring works of theology to Soho, unless Hyde so enjoyed writing blasphemies on their pages that he couldn't resist bringing some along. Perhaps the papers are business or legal documents such as the will; the only item that can be rescued from the ashes is "the butt end of a green cheque book" (49). Or perhaps the papers represent some confession of Jekyll's (or Hyde's?)—a first draft of his final narrative, which, as Jekyll writes it, is in imminent danger of destruction. "If my narrative has hitherto escaped destruction, it has been by a combination of great prudence and great good luck. Should the throes of change take me in the act of writing it, Hyde will tear it in pieces" (97).

Whatever the burned pages may represent within the context of the story, within the context of the Stevenson romance the associations between high culture and the furnishings of the Soho apartment and between Hyde's incineration of "papers" and Stevenson's incineration of his unallegorized first draft point to the buried theme of cultural authority. If Hyde shares Jekyll's handwriting, he also shares Stevenson's. He is the shadowy, demonic double of the author, bent on complete bohemian, artistic license and also on the desecration of art, for whom the ultimate "temptation" is to live or at least to write stories "all wrong"—"blasphemies," "forgeries," stories of and about pure evil, though perhaps allegorized to make them seem respectable—calculated only to thrill the ignorant masses into granting them a meretricious popularity. Such stories could be purchased as penny numbers in Soho, from newsboys hawking papers on the streets, from Longmans as shilling shockers, or perhaps even transmuted into sermons about the duality of human nature. Their heroes and readers alike might be Edward Hydes, and so also might their authors, who would write and sign themselves with "Satan's signature." "This was the shocking thing," Jekyll declares, "that the slime of the pit seemed to utter cries and voices" (95). His distress echoes Stevenson's in regard to "the bestiality of the beast whom we feed. What he likes is the newspaper; and to me the press is the mouth of a sewer, where lying is professed as from a university chair" (*Letters* 2:281).

Hyde's writing produces lies or half-lies, forged checks that are genuine, and blasphemies in Jekyll's "own hand," scrawled in revered texts. Within the larger context of the Stevenson romance, Hyde lurks in a shadowy borderland between a criminal literature of the slums—penny numbers, shilling shockers—and the moral allegory Fanny urged her husband to write, while the authentic masterpiece that Stevenson dreamed of writing hovered outside his range like a mirage. What renders Hyde especially menacing in these cultural terms, however, has perhaps less to do with the Stevenson romance than with the late-Victorian politics of education and literacy. Hyde's ability to write in Jekyll's "hand" renders him dangerous in a more insidious way than his violence. "We must educate our masters," as Robert Lowe had argued at the time of the Second Reform Bill.[4] The Third Reform Bill had passed in 1884, but the hope that mass literacy would hold back the barbarous anarchy or the criminal degeneracy that the upper classes had always feared the "lower orders" would visit upon society and culture seemed, perhaps, even less realistic than it had in 1867 or 1832.

Jekyll and Hyde insists on the dualism of human identity, and yet, as Peter Garrett, Jerrold Hogle, and other critics have argued, that insistence may itself conceal a deeper fear of incoherence, anarchy, or dissolution on both a psychological and a political level. Jekyll claims that he has discovered "the thorough and primitive duality of man," but then goes on to confess:

> I say two, because the state of my knowledge does not pass beyond that point. Others will follow, others will outstrip me on the same lines; and I hazard the guess that man will ultimately be known for a mere polity of multifarious, incongruous and independent denizens. (82)

In this passage, the unity and even duality of the self give way to something like Arnold's account of "anarchy": the conflict of classes, and of "ordinary selves" or individuals within those classes, pulling centrifugally, perhaps disastrously, against the unity both of the body politic and of the "Best Self." Certainly Jekyll's political metaphor for the "multifarious, incongruous" disunity of individual identity reinforces my contention that Stevenson's story expresses, at least subliminally, anxiety about the masses and the consequences of mass literacy. From this perspective, Hyde is not so much the symmetrical double of Jekyll as a figure for the "multifarious, incongruous," and dangerous disunity of "the populace," "the lower orders," or "the masses." For Stevenson, Gissing, and many other late-Victorian intellectuals, popular or mass culture and mass literacy themselves threaten a sort of cultural entropy or abjection, the swamps or sewers of mediocrity or vulgarity into which, they feared, excellence—high intelligence, literary and artistic aura— was sinking.[5]

To this interpretation, Garrett Stewart objects that it confuses Hyde as a figure for mass literacy or the mass reader with *Jekyll and Hyde* itself as a popular-cultural artifact (Stewart 364). But Stevenson's anxieties about mass literacy are registered both in his own equivocal, defensive statements about the story and in the figure of Hyde himself, not so much as a reader but as a writer or author of various forgeries, blasphemies, and perhaps even Jekyll's will. In this regard, Ronald Thomas's contention that Jekyll writes himself out of the narrative—that *Jekyll and Hyde* is, in a sense, a late-Victorian tale about the postmodern theme of "the death of the author"—is suggestive. Who is to say, in fact, that Hyde is not the author of Jekyll's "confession" and therefore of the central narrative that we read? But forgeries and blasphemies are more obviously the genres in which Hyde, as author, exercises his considerable literacy, a literacy that, like his handwriting, is the simulacrum of Jekyll's.

Hyde's literacy is a nightmare version of the writing on the wall for supposedly civilized, respectable, Victorian Britain. When Jekyll discovers that he can no longer control the transformations and that Hyde is instead seizing control of him, he declares, "This reversal of my previous experience, seemed, like the Babylonian finger on the wall, to be spelling out the letters of my judgement" (88). In an early, somewhat perplexed review, James Noble wrote:

"The Strange Case of Dr. Jekyll and Mr. Hyde" is not an orthodox three-volume novel; it is not even a one-volume novel of the ordinary type; it is simply a paper-covered shilling story, belonging, so far as appearance goes, to a class of literature familiarity with which has bred in the minds of most readers a certain measure of contempt. (Maixner 203)

But by "most readers," did Noble mean the reading masses? Or did he just mean "most readers" like himself—well-educated, upper-class, and elitist? His uncertainty about both the format (popular) and the readership of *Jekyll and Hyde* (also popular) mirrors Stevenson's own anxiety about the reception of his moralized "crawler." For Stevenson, to be a popularly acclaimed author was both desirable and monstrous; he felt he must have "something wrong in" himself both to imagine Hyde and to write, publish, and prosper from *Jekyll and Hyde*. Though the original story may have deserved to burn, this particular shilling shocker had been plucked out of the flames of its imaginary damnation by allegorization, and it was, many of its reviewers believed, as near to being a masterpiece as anything its author had yet written.

III

Like Stevenson, Edwin Reardon in Gissing's *New Grub Street* longs to write masterpieces. Also like Stevenson, Reardon finds that the exigencies of the literary mass marketplace have rendered masterpieces impractical, perhaps impossible, because unprofitable. To succeed as a novelist, one must aim to be popular; but that aim contradicts the ambition to achieve literary excellence. In *New Grub Street*, as in Gissing's earlier novels focused on the slums, socialism, and interclass relations, the conflict between "Culture and Vulgarity" (Poole 75) leads to the defeat of the former. *Demos* (1886), published in the same year as *Jekyll and Hyde*, illustrates the failure of socialism, represented by Richard Mutimer, because of the literal, apparently unalterable, vulgarity of "Demos." So, too, in *The Unclassed* (1884) and *The Nether World* (1889), the impossibility of community is also the impossibility of making culture work in the class-harmonizing way that Arnold advocated in *Culture and Anarchy*. And *Thyrza* (1887) seems almost to be a self-conscious rewriting of Arnold: the efforts of its idealistic protagonist, Walter Egremont, "to bring some humanising 'culture' into the lives of Lambeth working-men through his evening lectures" lead only to a disillusioning failure that, Gissing suggests, is "inevitable" (Poole 76). Gissing's final portrait of an Arnoldian "Best Self," living for literary culture, is Henry Ryecroft, who, rather than attempting to change "the vulgarity unutterable" of the masses, escapes to the countryside to live alone with his books and his good but semi-literate housekeeper (*Ryecroft* 139).

Again in *New Grub Street*, vulgarity defeats culture. For Reardon, achieving popularity is just as impossible as writing a masterpiece, largely because—like Stevenson and like Ryecroft—he has nothing but contempt for the sort of litera-

ture that succeeds in becoming popular. I am not suggesting that Gissing took
Stevenson for his model for Reardon; rather, both Reardon and Ryecroft represent the dilemma of the late-Victorian author as experienced by Stevenson and
Gissing, and by many others as well—the thousands of literati, journalists, and
would-be authors that seemed, from about 1870 forward, to be jostling and competing together for literary fame and fortune in an abstract, alienating marketplace.[6] Expanding partly through increased literacy, and partly through increased
book, newspaper, and journal production, the mass market for print seemed paradoxically all the more alienating the more the demand for publications of all sorts
accelerated. Cataloguing the many forms of literate and literary culture both published and advertised in the literary journals of the day, including the many cheap
reproductions of the works of "classic authors" now available to "the multitude,"
Ryecroft wonders if this isn't proof positive of the progress of civilization and the
diffusion of culture at least within Britain? No, he says, because if you compare
the bookish contents of the literary journals with "your daily news-sheet," the
difference will be stark. In the newspaper, the space devoted to "the material
interests of life" simply crowds out intellectual culture; and there "you have a
gauge of the real importance of intellectual endeavour to the people at large":

> No, the public which reads, in any sense of the word worth considering, is very,
> very small; the public which would feel no lack if all book-printing ceased to-
> morrow, is enormous. (*Ryecroft* 59)

Once more, of course, the question posed by Ryecroft—and Gissing—is not one
of literacy versus illiteracy but of two kinds of literacy, dividing those who read
books from those who read only, at best, newspapers.

Like Joseph Ackland, Gissing might worry that books of a "learned" and
"educational" sort were on the decline, but he was well aware that the production
of both newsprint and novels was soaring. A novel bemoaning the semi-literacy
of the masses, *New Grub Street* is nonetheless populated by journalists and novelists all making their livings, or struggling to do so, from the reading public,
despite its deficiencies. Gissing's failed novelists and men-of-letters are not isolated geniuses menaced by the crowd or the tyranny of the majority; rather, they
are the crowd—ordinary men and women who have gained enough literacy to
aspire to authorship and literary fame and fortune. Moreover, the Darwinian
struggle for survival among Gissing's author-characters apparently has more to
do with their sheer numbers—a sort of overpopulation by competing intellectuals—than with the "vulgar" inattention to their literary wares by the reading public. Ryecroft describes this condition of excessive literacy:

> Innumerable are the men and women now writing for bread, who have not the
> least chance of finding in such work a permanent livelihood. They took to writ-
> ing because they knew not what else to do, or because the literary calling tempted
> them by its independence and its dazzling prizes. They will hang on to the squalid
> profession. . . . Hateful as is the struggle for life in every form, this rough-and-

tumble of the literary arena seems to me sordid and degrading beyond all others. (*Ryecroft* 52)

The overpopulation of writers is, of course, linked both to mass education and to the overproduction of journals and books of all sorts. The three-volume novel maintained by the circulating library system dominated by Mudie's retarded the proliferation of cheaply produced novels and paperbacks. But the demise of the "triple decker" system in 1894, as Nigel Cross points out, fostered an increase in the writing and publication of new, shorter novels by "shrinking the novel-form . . . to one- or two-volume works. A diligent manufacturer of fiction could write at least two short novels in the time it took to write a three-decker" (Cross 207; for a detailed account of the end of the three-volume system, see Griest 156–212). For some novelists, the end of the three-volume novel also spelled liberation from the tyranny of Mudie's Select Library, and hence from the sort of moral censorship or Mrs. Grundyism they attributed to Mudie's. George Moore, seeking to emulate Zola's naturalism in his early novels, had his first effort, *A Modern Lover* (1883), in effect banned by Mudie's because "two ladies in the country . . . disapproved of the book, and on that account he [Mudie] could not circulate it" (Moore 4–5). Moore fought back first in "A New Censorship of Literature," published in the *Pall Mall Gazette* in 1884, and then a year later in his pamphlet *Literature at Nurse, or Circulating Morals*, published by Henry Vizetelly, who was also beginning to publish English translations of Zola's novels. Attacking Mudie's as a "monopoly," Moore declared:

> the character for strength, virility, and purpose, which our literature has always held . . . is being gradually obliterated to suit the commercial views of a narrow-minded tradesman. Instead of being allowed to fight, with and amid, the thoughts and aspirations of men, literature is now rocked to an ignoble rest in the motherly arms of the librarian. That of which he approves is fed with gold; that from which he turns the breast dies like a vagrant's child; while in and out of his voluminous skirts run a motley and monstrous progeny, a callow, a whining, a puking brood of bastard bantlings. . . . Into this nursery none can enter except in baby clothes; and the task of discriminating between a divided skirt and a pair of trousers is performed by the librarian. Deftly his fingers lift skirt and under-skirt. . . . (18)

And so forth.

Moore's assault on Mudie's and the three-volume system did not single-handedly result in its demise, but he nevertheless contributed to that result. His critique, moreover, is not directed against mass literacy, "vulgarity unutterable," or the supposedly debased taste of working-class readers, but instead against the hegemony of bourgeois respectability as represented by Mudie's. He is, of course, championing his own brand of Zolaesque naturalism, with its explicit depictions of seduction, adultery, and other sexual behaviors. He is also championing the right, and presumably the ability, of adult readers to make up their own minds about novels, without the intervention of a "narrow-minded tradesman" like Mudie.

For his part, Gissing saw Mudie's merely as a reflection of public taste. Though he sympathized with Moore, he also opined that "[i]f you abolish the library system tomorrow, you are no nearer persuading the 'two ladies in the country' (typical beings!) to let this or that work lie on their drawing room tables." Gissing saw in Moore himself "a strain of vulgarity" that made him "shudder," and he condemned *A Modern Lover* as "unspeakable trash" (qtd. in Griest 84). Gissing was happy enough to publish *New Grub Street* in the standard three-volume format. Nevertheless, Reardon's literary struggles have partly to do with his inability to fill up three volumes. And Jasper Milvain declares that the three-volume format, which Mudie's and other commercial libraries insisted upon but which the reading public could not afford to buy rather than borrow, is "a triple-headed monster, sucking the blood of English novelists" (235). Responding to Milvain's comment, Reardon asks: "For anyone in my position . . . how is it possible to abandon the three volumes? It is a question of payment. An author of moderate repute may live on a yearly three-volume novel" (236). If the system is altered, he goes on to say, it would "throw three-fourths of the novelists out of work" (236). Part of Gissing's irony here is apparently that Reardon himself is an obvious victim of the vampirism of the triple-decker mode. In any case, Gissing clearly felt that that mode was cumbersome, confining, and, like the realism that he practiced, soon to become passé. The three-volume format was, nevertheless, the obsolescent mode to which Gissing himself adhered.

One-volume novels, unmediated by Mudie's and the other, less dominant commercial libraries, rapidly became standard after 1894. So did "newspaper novels," though not in the sense that that phrase had been applied to the sensation novels of the 1860s for imitating newspapers: the phrase now meant works of fiction published through newspaper syndication. This pattern had begun to develop in the 1870s, and one of the most famous (or infamous) sensation novelists, Mary Elizabeth Braddon, had led the way through the stories (*Lucy Davoran*, 1873; *Taken at the Flood*, 1874) that she wrote for the Tillotson Newspaper Syndicate.[7] Both shorter novels and short stories, such as Conan Doyle's tales of Sherlock Holmes and H. G. Wells's brief "scientific romances," also became standard publishing formats in the *Strand*, the *Graphic*, and other late-Victorian magazines.

In his study of Gissing, Adrian Poole claims that these changes in the format and production of fiction were related to an "acute crisis" (20) of narrative confidence among late-Victorian writers. Though some novelists agreed with Moore in welcoming the demise of the triple-decker and the decline of Mudie's hegemony as liberation, just as frequently the changes in novel-publishing were identified with mass-cultural degeneracy, the triumph of commodification or the decline in cultural authority of literature, of authors in general, and of the cultural elites capable of recognizing and rewarding literary excellence. Part of Gissing's pessimism stems from his ambivalence about these changes. His own novelistic practice leans ambivalently, nostalgically back toward Dickens, Mudie's, three volumes, and mid-Victorian realism, while it also looks forward, albeit pessimistically, toward the versions of modernist and avant-garde liberation from the constraints of "the masses"—in effect, the constraints not of working-class readers, but of bourgeois respectability and the hegemony of Mudie's—that Moore at least anticipated.

In *New Grub Street*, the late-Victorian crisis of narrative authority is projected onto readers—that is, onto the *literate* masses—in a *caveat lector* manner that implies: you probably will not want to read this novel, but even if you do read it, you either won't like it or won't understand it. Just as Gissing's failed novelists are the products of late-Victorian mass education and literacy, so must be the readers of his novel. And, as Gissing's version of cultural original sin, vulgarity must inevitably be the result both of his characters' writing, especially if it succeeds in the marketplace (popularity as the ultimate damnation), and of most of his readers' experience of his novel. According to Henry Ryecroft, "Democracy is full of menace to all the finer hopes of civilisation" (*Ryecroft* 53); but by the 1890s, democracy was in charge, at least in deciding what counted as popular, profitable reading. *New Grub Street* hardly suggests that the future will lead back to illiteracy, but rather that increasing literacy—and the overproduction and Darwinian competition among novels, journals, and newspapers—spells the death of genuine culture.

The crisis in narrative authority, pointing toward the categorical rupture between high and mass culture in modernist literature, is evident in the works of many late-Victorian novelists and intellectuals. Instead of the qualified optimism about the future of democracy that Arnold identified with the diffusion of culture, that diffusion itself is often viewed as a threat to culture and, indeed, to "all the finer hopes of civilisation." And in fiction, as Poole points out, instead of the older, progressive, hopeful sense of the possibility, at least, of reconciling desire with actuality, the inner life of the individual with external circumstances, expressed in much early and mid-Victorian fiction, there emerges, in novelists as various as Gissing, Stevenson, Hardy, Wells, and Conrad, "a sharp polarisation between will, success, vulgarity and pragmatism on the one hand, and will-lessness, failure, imagination and self-consciousness on the other" (Poole 21). The isolated consciousness of characters in novels by all of these writers seems often to be that of the weak individual trapped in the powerful crowd, struggling to confront or to escape the "whirlpool" of London, the prejudice of public opinion, the petty vulgarity of the petite bourgeoisie, the slums of the Jago and East End, or the customs and superstitions of Egdon Heath, only to be defeated, either pulled down to the level of the crowd or doomed to expire like a member of an elite but unfit species.

For Gissing, moreover, books—at least, good ones—share the fate of the isolated individual. If life is a "battle" in *New Grub Street* (122), it is largely because of the new, Darwinian or Malthusian battle of the books caused by an expanding market for publications of all sorts, including fiction. It is not Reardon but the successful Jasper Milvain who says: "The struggle for existence among books is nowadays as severe as among men" (493). Jasper is describing to his sister his two, contradictory reviews of Harold Biffen's novel, *Mr. Bailey, Grocer*, one for a journal called the *Current* and the other for the *West End*. Both reviews are favorable, though one more so than the other, and Jasper tells Dora, "I half believe what I have written." But he also believes that "most people will fling the book down with yawns before they're half through the first volume. If I knew a doctor who had many cases of insomnia in hand, I would recommend 'Mr. Bailey' to him as a specific" (492).

In this conversation, Jasper adds a version of Gissing's main theme, that in the 1890s it no longer pays to write good literature. "A really good book," he tells Dora, "will more likely than not receive fair treatment from two or three reviewers . . . but also more likely than not it will be swamped in the flood of literature that pours forth week after week" (493). The world of *New Grub Street* is one in which books destroy books and journals destroy journals, while the "Literary Machine" works overtime to feed the great, culture-cannibalizing maw of "the mass of readers" (188). Slaving away for her father in the tomb of culture, the British Museum ("valley of the shadow of death"), Marian Yule comes across "an advertisement in the newspaper, headed 'Literary Machine,'" and wonders:

> had it then been invented at last, some automaton to supply the place of such poor creatures as herself, to turn out books and articles? Alas! the machine was only one for holding volumes conveniently, that the work of literary manufacture might be physically lightened. But surely before long some Edison would make the true automaton; the problem must be comparatively such a simple one. Only to throw in a given number of old books, and have them reduced, blended, modernised into a single one for to-day's consumption. (138)

In this moment of dystopian science fiction, Gissing through Marian Yule imagines the complete mechanization, and reification, of writing—*Reader's Digest*, perhaps, *avant la lettre*. But he also imagines his own novel as a kind of literary machine, grinding up the literary projects of his failed realists and enslaved, embittered journalists like Marian for the easy digestion of readers whom he simultaneously counts himself among and despises. Novelistic realism, Gissing suggests, only limps along like a clumsy machine because great, beautiful, original literature is exhausted, lost in an era of commercialized, mechanical reproduction and waning or nonexistent cultural aura.

This is not to say that all books and writers, either in *New Grub Street* or in Gissing's own experience, are ground up in the publishing mills. But those that succeed—Jasper Milvain is a case in point—are either able to compromise by recognizing that literature has become a mere trade and adapting to that fact of modern life, or are only capable in the first place of churning out popular sorts of writing. But Gissing's bleak vision of an elite, minority culture swamped by a commercialized, mass culture of debased and debasing vulgarity fails to acknowledge several features of the new regime in publishing and its mass readship. While there were more readers than ever before—indeed, an increasingly imperial, global audience for novels and other sorts of books produced by British publishers—

and while it is also the case that many mediocre novelists managed to write best-sellers, it is not true that writers of aesthetic and intellectual merit were excluded from the expanding literary marketplace. Though never as successful as, say, Marie Corelli or even Thomas Hardy, Gissing nevertheless found publishers and also a modest amount of public acclaim for his novels. As V. S. Pritchett long ago remarked, much of the ironic pathos of Gissing's career stems from the fact that his "failure is . . . the source of his persisting fame" (Pritchett viii). This paradox—contradiction, rather—says, in effect: cultural pessimism sells; to berate the mass reading public with its semi-literate vulgarity is to tell it, or some segment of it, at least, what it wants to hear. To tell it, moreover, that your own novels are both too refined and too realistic for its debased taste is a backhanded way of advertising those very novels. There is a sort of secular evangelism in Gissing's cultural pessimism: rather than to eternal perdition, he condemns the vast majority of readers, including his own, to eternal vulgarity; those chosen for the salvation of cultural refinement and good taste can be only a tiny remnant out of the vast sea of literate humanity: this remnant may even prove to be the select readers of *New Grub Street.*

The new literary marketplace that emerged in Britain from about 1870 forward was not simply one of massification by a degraded, homogeneous reading public. It was instead far more diversified, as well as larger, than the literary marketplace had been, say, in the 1830s, when Dickens was starting his career (McAleer 12–41). If, as Poole says, "Dickens provided for Gissing an image of transcendant integration" (123–124) with his readers, that is partly because Dickens's readership was less rather than more diverse than that of the 1890s. Dickens was, at least, much more comfortable with his middle-class audience than was Gissing, who seems to have assumed that all readers, except for a few close friends, would inevitably misunderstand him. Gissing certainly felt that "the masses" of working-class readers would misunderstand him, if they read him at all. Harold Biffen and Reardon, both failed novelists, visit their peer in literary failure, Mr. Sykes, who tells them: "The working classes detest anything that tries to represent their daily life" (416). At the outset of his career, Biffen himself, Sykes tells Reardon, "had an idea of writing for the working classes; and what do you think he was going to offer them? Stories *about* the working classes!" (416). Nothing was better calculated to fail than such realism—a realism close, of course, to Gissing's own. Even Dickens, says Sykes (named, no doubt, after Bill Sikes), "goes down only with the best of them, and then solely because of his strength in farce and his melodrama" (416).

Whether or not Gissing intends Sykes's commentary on the working-class reader as a criticism specifically of the new "mass of readers" coming through the recently nationalized school system, Sykes attributes the failure of his own career as a would-be novelist to just the same cause that destroys Reardon, if not Biffen. Sykes says that his "writing was too literary by a long chalk" to become popular; on the other hand, when "for a whole year [he] deliberately strove to write badly" he did not succeed (415). Reardon himself had struggled painfully to finish his novel *On Neutral Ground*; the title suggests what Gissing seems to have felt about his own efforts at novelistic realism, that they were neither here nor there, neither doomed to be popular nor fated ever to be recognized, by the limited number of genuinely cultivated, sensitive readers capable of such recognition, as great literature.

Sykes's comment about the working-class reader's response to realism says something about the works of *all* of the failed novelists in *New Grub Street*. They are all, like Gissing, realists; and realism for Gissing is a form of truth-telling that can never be popular because it will forever reveal vulgarity and other human failings where it finds them. The literary agent Whelpdale says that he "was a poor devil who had failed as a realistic novelist" (248) and so has set up shop instead both as an agent and as a teacher of other would-be novelists.[8] Whelpdale tells Reardon and Biffen that he is writing "an author's Guide" and that he also intends "to advertise: 'Novel-writing taught in ten lessons!'" (179).

> The first lesson deals with the question of subjects, local colour—that kind of thing. I gravely advise people, if they possibly can, to write of the wealthy middle class; that's the popular subject, you know. Lords and ladies are all very well, but the real thing to take is a story about people who have no titles, but live in good Philistine style. I urge study of horsey matters especially. . . . (249)

Apparently Whelpdale did not follow this formula for popular success when he failed as a "realistic novelist"; it seems likely that his failure is related to Sykes's: like Gissing in *Demos*, *The Nether World*, and *Thyrza*, Whelpdale made the honest—that is, realistic but not practical—mistake of portraying the working- and lower-middle-class mass readership as it really is, in all its vulgarity and inability to recognize genuine culture when it sees it.

While Gissing attributes Whelpdale's and Sykes's—and his own—mistake to an honesty that doesn't cater to wish fulfillment but instead portrays the masses in all their unseemly, albeit semi-literate, coarseness, he does not recognize the contradiction that invests any attempt at a strictly mimetic rendition of reality. As in *Vanity Fair* and *The Eustace Diamonds*, Gissing's ideal, an unflinching literary realism, is self-defeating. If it fulfills the (ironic) ambition to produce a perfect simulacrum of Vanity Fair, Thackeray's novel cannot also transcend—in the sense of function as social critique—the reality that it depicts. The same is true of Gissing's realism in *New Grub Street* and elsewhere, which suggests still another reason why he sensed that his own novelistic practice was inadequate; it was outmoded precisely because such eminent *and* popular realistic predecessors as Thackeray and Trollope, not to mention such eminent French writers as Flaubert and Zola, had already run the gamut of its conventions and its contradictions. While it seems evident that, as Fredric Jameson contends, Gissing's *ressentiment* was fueled by his liminal, petit-bourgeois status, and that such *ressentiment* characterizes a number of other late-Victorian and Edwardian writers (Hardy, Wells, Galsworthy, and Joyce, among others), it was exacerbated by Gissing's sense that he was trapped within the cul-de-sac of a reified realism whose heyday was over.

If high cultural, literary art must in some sense always stand in critical contrast to a reality that it does not simply mirror, then such art cannot be the sort of "ignoble realism" that Harold Biffen advocates and practices in *Mr. Bailey, Grocer* and that Gissing himself practices in *New Grub Street* and elsewhere. As one review of Biffen's novel suggests, the result of any completely faithful rendition of grovelling reality is just "grovelling realism" (522).

Even more than *On Neutral Ground* and *Margaret Home*, two of Reardon's failed novels, Biffen's novel about "the day-to-day life of that vast majority of people who are at the mercy of paltry circumstance" (173–174) operates as a self-conscious reductio ad absurdum that mocks the very form of honesty— the "ignoble" or "grovelling realism"—that Gissing himself practices. While Gissing certainly expresses *ressentiment* about his own experience of social-class marginalization, he also expresses *ressentiment* about the general failure of realism, which is not a failure to make an impact on vulgar or semi-literate readers, but instead the logical impossibility of being simultaneously a faithful representation of and a critical distancing from the social reality that it depicts. The "mirror in the roadway" is in the roadway, and in danger of being trampled into the mire.[9]

Biffen's account of *Mr. Bailey, Grocer* doesn't suggest the failure of the working-class reader to comprehend his novel; it suggests instead the failure of his novel to do anything except offer "an absolute realism in the sphere of the ignobly decent" (173). Biffen tells Reardon:

> The field, as I understand it, is a new one; I don't know any writer who has treated ordinary vulgar life with fidelity and seriousness. Zola writes deliberate tragedies; his vilest figures become heroic from the place they fill in a strongly imagined drama. I want to deal with the essentially unheroic. . . . (173)

Biffen is not exactly aiming at an account of working-class life; a grocer, after all, no matter how "vulgar," is a petit-bourgeois shopkeeper. Nor is a woman (Mrs. Bailey) who has "saved forty-five pounds out of a cat's-meat business," which sum induces Mr. Bailey to marry her so that he can set up as a grocer, clearly working class. Whether working or lower-middle class, however, Mr. Bailey's is the realm of "the decently ignoble," as Biffen explains to Reardon (244). Biffen equates his practice of realism both with "low-class life" and with "honest reporting," or in other words with a merely newspaper-like accuracy, similar to the "human documents" that Zola and the Goncourt brothers claimed to emulate or even produce in their naturalistic novels. The "true story of Mr. Bailey's marriage and of his progress as a grocer," Biffen predicts, will be "a great book—a great book!" (244). But precisely because it will be a great book in terms of the conventions of fictional realism, now identified merely with journalistic accuracy or "honest reporting," it will necessarily be a failure with even the most cultivated, intelligent readers, as Biffen himself recognizes by insisting that its main effect will be boredom. "The result," he tells Reardon, "will be something unutterably tedious. Precisely. That is the stamp of the ignobly decent life. If it were anything *but* tedious it would be untrue" (174). The collapse of art into reality, as opposed to the transformation of reality into art, could hardly be more complete or more disillusioning.

At this moment of abysmal tedium, Biffen adds: "I speak, of course, of its effect upon the ordinary reader" (174). But it isn't clear that it is just "the ordinary reader" who is liable to find *Mr. Bailey, Grocer* tedious. Later, Reardon either joins ranks with "the ordinary reader" or else *Mr. Bailey, Grocer* proves to be "tedious" even to sensitive, cultured readers—that is, to Reardon. The most pleasurable aspect of the friendship between Biffen and Reardon stems from their conversations about Greece and therefore, in Arnoldian fashion, about classical Greek culture, completely at odds with vulgar, modern, British culture. Biffen, however, is also in the habit of reading to Reardon chapters of *Mr. Bailey, Grocer* after he finishes writing them. On one occasion, when Biffen offers to read a "new chapter of 'Mr. Bailey'" to his feverish, already dying friend, he adds: "It may induce a refreshing slumber" (402).

If Reardon does not represent the sensitive, cultivated reader and writer, alienated from the vulgar masses of the semi-literate but nevertheless reading public, then nobody does. Yet he both detests his own literary productions and, if Biffen is right, might be put to sleep by *Mr. Bailey, Grocer*. But this is exactly the result that Biffen has earlier declared he intends: tedious reality is—well, tedious. Again, Jasper tells his sister that he would recommend Biffen's novel as medicine to any doctor "who had many cases of insomnia in hand" (492), though *Mr. Bailey, Grocer*, *Neutral Ground*, and *Margaret Home* are analogues for *New Grub Street* itself, an intensely self-conscious novel or anti-novel about Gissing's sense of his own inevitable failure both to achieve mass popularity and to attain high or elite literary status.

New Grub Street, in other words, is a sort of manifesto against itself, an extreme instance of a novel declaring itself to be, if not harmful to its readers' mental health, then even worse—utterly innocuous, tedious, and irrelevant to any important cultural concern. Its cynicism and bitterness about the incompetence of the reading public to recognize and support high cultural values is entirely self-implicating, logically claustrophobic. It is a declaration of why, at least in the 1890s, the dead-end, albeit deadpan, realism Gissing practiced no longer made sense (if it ever had) either aesthetically or commercially. *New Grub Street* is itself a sort of "newspaper novel"—"honest reporting," but supposedly nothing more—whose most "sensational" moments are the deaths of its two most central failures, the twin (though hardly demonically double-going) deadbeat realists, Harold Biffen and Edwin Reardon. Though not exactly deaths by boredom through reading each other's failed novels, these are, in a sense, deaths by realism—that is, by a novelistic practice that simultaneously repudiates and reproduces the mass or popular "vulgarity" that it makes its ironic but (Gissing insists) necessarily tedious theme.

To paraphrase Jameson's argument about *ressentiment*, Gissing wasn't angry with the world merely because he felt exiled or hung up between respectable, middle-class status and the working class that he simultaneously identified with and scorned. He was also resentful because he sensed the logical trap that novelistic realism had laid for him and, indeed, for the other novelists of his generation, while not quite being able to see his way out of the impasse into the coming era of literary modernism—the era of James Joyce and Virginia Woolf. The "ordinary reader" whom none of the failed novelists in *New Grub Street* can please, like the apelike, dwarfish Hyde as an implicit figure for the "populace" and therefore for the popularity that Stevenson both courted and despised, serves partly as a convenient scapegoat for a fictional tradition at the end of its tether, a realism that no longer believed in itself.

CHAPTER

9

Overbooked versus Bookless Futures in Late-Victorian Fiction

I' th' commonwealth I would by contraries Execute all things; for no kind of traffic Would I admit; no name of magistrate; Letters should not be known. . . .
— Gonzalo in Shakespeare's *Tempest*

That old pagan world, of which Rome was the flower, had reached its perfection in . . . poetry and art—a perfection which indicated only too surely the eve of decline. As in some vast intellectual museum, all its manifold products were intact and in their places, and with custodians still extant, duly qualified to appreciate and explain them.
— Walter Pater, *Marius, the Epicurean* (1885)

Foregrounded in several late-Victorian romances, including *Jekyll and Hyde* and *Picture of Dorian Gray*, the problematic of literacy involves a "Gothic of reading," as Garrett Stewart puts it, in which novels are figured as not merely "parasitic," but "vampiric." "Neogothic" texts such as Stevenson's and Wilde's are "horror stories in which plotted monstrosity becomes an image of generic perversity" and in which the reader is drawn into "the drama" of his or her "own grotesque metamorphoses" (Stewart 344–345). But a "Gothic of reading" seems just as evident in much late-Victorian realistic fiction as in romances. "Novels about the production of textuality," writes Stewart, "tend to entail a metanarrative of reading concerned with reading's own nervous perversity, its surrogate pleasure and pain, its psychosomatic risks rather than institutional stability, less its humanist reach or stretch than its parasitic grasp" (347). And no late-Victorian novel is more concerned with the production or overproduction of textuality than *New Grub Street*.

For Gissing, mass literacy is inherently excessive, parasitic on legitimate culture, and "vampiric" in its effects on sensitive individuals such as Edwin Reardon and Henry Ryecroft. Its most monstrous effect is evident in the neurotic inaptitude for dealing with reality of all of Gissing's failed writers and intellectuals. Whether viewing those writers and intellectuals as members of an endangered elite or as themselves part of the danger, part of the vast majority, Gissing treats the rise of the literate masses as the death of literature, or perhaps more exactly as the death of the author, figured in the literal deaths of two of his failed novelists, Reardon and Biffen. Further, Marian Yule's dystopian image of the "Literary Machine" points to a mindless overproduction, a glut of printed matter, corresponding to that other, greater menace of an indiscriminate, vulgar, mass readership: not too few books and readers, but, as Old Father Time says in Hardy's *Jude the Obscure*, "too meny"—Malthus's nightmare applied both to publishing and to the reading public.

Like *New Grub Street*, Hardy's last novel also depicts characters—Jude Fawley and Sue Bridehead—whose excessive literacy or bookishness has unsuited them for living. Gissing's and Hardy's overbooked characters are symptomatic of what both novelists see as the negative results of the nearly universal literacy Britain had achieved by the 1890s, or, in other words, of the pessimistic paradox of too much culture leading to decadence, a pathology that Nietzsche was also diagnosing and that Freud would later analyze, in *Civilization and Its Discontents*, in terms of excessive repression. In at least two other fin-de-siècle novels, moreover, William Morris's *News from Nowhere* (1891) and H. G. Wells's *The Time Machine* (1895), the overbooked or overcultivated present leads even more dramatically to its antithesis in bookless futures. As romances, Morris's and Wells's narratives more closely fit the "Gothic of reading" that Stewart identifies than do Gissing's and Hardy's, but all four deal with what might be called the vampirism of too much of a good thing, literacy. The waning of literacy and gradual disappearance of books in Morris's utopian romance are signs of health rather than the reverse. However, in Wells's dystopian world of the Elois and Morlocks, albeit some 800,000 years into the future, not only have books and the ability to read them disappeared, but language itself is on the wane.

I

For Gissing, mass literacy, though of course he doesn't advocate returning to mass *il*literacy, is a cultural catastrophe. Yet as Walter Allen notes, Gissing often suggests that "the sole end of life [is] that men and women should read" (Allen 346). This is literacy and Arnoldian culture gone over the edge of sanity, however, because *both* Gissing's sensitive readers (Walter Egremont, Edwin Reardon, Henry Ryecroft, and the rest) *and* "the mass of readers" are, according to his pessimistic vision, failures. As consciousness seems only to bring pain and misery in Hardy, so reading only brings pain and misery, including weakened eyesight, in Gissing, even though he also looks to it (that is, to literacy and Arnoldian culture) as the only possible salvation from the commercialization, industrialization, massification, and therefore vulgarization of reading. There is no more a way out for the doomed writers and readers in the literate and literary wasteland of *New Grub Street* than there is for the doomed slum dwellers of London's East End in Arthur Morrison's *A Child of the Jago* (1896). For Morrison's illiterates, reading is an impenetrable mystery; most of them think that "school-going was a practice best never begun" (Morrison 91).

In *New Grub Street*, however, Jasper Milvain's phrase for the British Museum, "the valley of the shadow of death," implies the defeat of all past culture by culture, not by its lack. The British Museum is a mausoleum for dead books, equally as overcrowded—swamped in excessive print—as New Grub Street itself. The double indemnity that Gissing's pessimism entails—a damned if you do, damned if you don't position regarding the alleged benefits of literacy and culture—is perfectly captured when, early in *New Grub Street*, John Yule declares: "I should like to see the business of literature abolished" (20). Ironically, instead of responding with his usual cynicism, Jasper takes the view of the cultural idealist and optimist, insisting that "literary production" in general "helps to spread civilisation."

> "Civilisation!" exclaimed John [Yule] scornfully. "What do you mean by civilisation? Do you call it civilising men to make them weak, flabby creatures, with ruined eyes and dyspeptic stomachs? Who is it that reads most of the stuff that's poured out daily by the ton from the printing-press? Just the men and women who ought to spend their leisure hours in open-air exercise; the people who earn their bread by sedentary pursuits, and who need to *live* as soon as they are free from the desk or the counter, not to moon over small print." (20)

It isn't clear, of course, that Gissing exactly agrees with any of his characters. But John Yule's indictment of reading in general—not just novel-reading—equates it with cultural as well as physical decadence. Just as Carlyle in *Past and Present* had claimed that "the Unconscious is the alone Complete" (119), and just as Nietzsche in "The Use and Abuse of History" argued that a nation or culture that is too wrapped up in historicizing, too self-conscious, is diseased and decadent, so Gissing portrays society as in an advanced state of decline not in spite of literacy and literature, but because of them. The sensitive, cultured souls—Reardon, Biffen, Marian Yule—are just as unhealthy as the vulgar masses, only they are aware of the cultural epidemic that Gissing identifies with too much culture, with excessive reading and writing.

Hardy's similar cultural pessimism is nowhere more evident than in the scene in which Jude Fawley incinerates his books.

> At dusk . . . he went into the garden and dug a shallow hole, to which he brought out all the theological and ethical works that he possessed. . . . He knew that, in this country of true believers, most of them were not saleable at a much higher price than waste-paper value. . . . Lighting up some loose pamphlets to begin with, he cut the volumes into pieces as well as he could, and with a three-

pronged fork shook them over the flames. They kindled, and lighted up the back of the house, the pigsty, and his own face, until they were more or less consumed. (172)

Unlike Catherine and Heathcliff's attack on "good books" in *Wuthering Heights*, aimed at Joseph's evangelical tracts, Jude's book-burning represents his rejection of culture and literacy in general, both secular and religious. In a sense, Jude only repeats Arabella's earlier attack on his precious books (56–57). But, through his exclusion from the university at Christminster and his troubled relations with Sue, he has also come to the realization that the truth of experience isn't contained in any of the books he has read. The book of the world and the world of books, he concludes, are radically different, even antithetical.

Like the university—"Sarcophagus College," "a place full of fetichists and ghost-seers" (120)—all books for Jude come to represent death, not life. Outside the walls of the colleges, Jude experiences Christminster as a necropolis, haunted by the ghosts of the great dead whose written words he has admired and loved in books, but now hears as spectral voices. Though an autodidact, he knows their voices more familiarly—as familiar spirits—than do the scholars in their cloistered, both unreal and exclusionary, mausoleum of culture. Shut out from that bookish realm of death, Jude accepts Sue's judgment upon it. Christminster, she tells him, "is an ignorant place, except as to the townspeople, artizans, drunkards, and paupers":

> *"They* see life as it is, of course; but few of the people in the colleges do. You
> prove it in your own person. You are one of the very men Christminster was
> intended for when the colleges were founded; a man with a passion for learning,
> but no money, or opportunities, or friends. But you were elbowed off the pave-
> ment by the millionaires' sons." (120)

Christminster, "city of light" (22), for Jude and Sue proves to be a city of dreadful night. Though "the tree of knowledge grows there" (22), it is a killing knowledge. Better not to know, not to be conscious of what happens, if life merely produces suffering and death. In Hardy's bleak vision, illumination means disillusionment; both Jude and Sue echo in a variety of ways the Monster's conclusion in *Frankenstein*: "Sorrow only increased with knowledge."

"Sarcophagus College," the metaphor of cultural institution as mausoleum, is most evident in *New Grub Street* through the experience of Marian Yule. Toiling away for her father in "the valley of the shadow of books," Marian thinks: "This huge library, growing into unwieldiness, threatening to become a trackless desert of print—how intolerably it weighed upon the spirit!" (138) In the "gloomy" reading-room, Marian "could scarcely see to read; a taste of fog grew perceptible in the warm, headachy air."

> Such profound discouragement possessed her that she could not even maintain
> the pretence of study. . . . She kept asking herself what was the use and purpose
> of such a life as she was condemned to lead. When already there was more good

literature in the world than any mortal could cope with in his lifetime, here was
she exhausting herself in the manufacture of printed stuff which no one even
pretended to be more than a commodity for the day's market. What unspeakable folly! To write—was not that the joy and privilege of one who had an
urgent message for the world? Her father, she knew well, had no such message;
he had abandoned all thought of original production, and only wrote about
writing. (137)

Like Reardon and Biffen, Marian is a victim of overcultivation. Her father, Alfred
Yule, can only write about writing, because the modern world has become so
dependent on reading and writing that there is, in a sense, nothing but reading and
writing. At the end of the nineteenth century, culture—literacy, education, literature—appear to both Gissing and Hardy a historical trap, leading nowhere except
to the painful disillusionment of the cultured individual. If in *Jude* the only text
worth reading is the book of the world, according to the claustrophobic, biblio-
centric vision of *New Grub Street*, there is no longer any external book of reality
to turn to, because all experience has been swamped by commodified printed
matter, entirely overwritten by the bookish but also money-grubbing culture of its
novelists, publishers, critics, and readers. For Gissing, culture at the end of culture has killed off reality by converting everything into "a trackless desert of
print," or at least into secondhand, belated, self-entrapped writing. *Il n'y a pas
de hors-texte*—for Gissing as for Derrida, "there is nothing outside the text" (*Of
Grammatology* 158).

The dead and deadening "valley of the shadow of books" in *New Grub Street*,
the British Museum or its equivalent, turns up as a striking image of the self-
defeating tendency of culture in both *News from Nowhere* and *The Time Machine*.
Morris composed his utopian fantasy in reaction against the cheery, technological
optimism of Edward Bellamy's *Looking Backward* (1888). In the year 2000, Julian
West, Bellamy's time-traveller, finds that, so far from being problematic or pathological, mass literacy and book-culture have been perfected. Visiting a public
library with his hosts, West marvels both at the profusion of new books and at
their accessibility. "I judge, then," he says to Dr. Leete, "that there has been some
notable literature produced in this century." Dr. Leete replies:

Yes. . . . It has been an era of unexampled intellectual splendor. Probably humanity never before passed through a moral and material evolution, at once so
vast in its scope and brief in its time of accomplishment, as that from the old
order to the new in the early part of this century. When men came to realize the
greatness of the felicity which had befallen them, and that the change through
which they had passed was not merely an improvement in details of their condition, but the rise of the race to a new plane of existence with an illimitable vista
of progress, their minds were affected in all their faculties with a stimulus, of
which the outburst of the medieval Renaissance offers a suggestion but faint
indeed. There ensued an era of mechanical invention, scientific discovery, art,
musical and literary productiveness to which no previous age of the world offers anything comparable. (116)

The paradoxes of an overbooked future, of literary culture as a form of entrapment, or even of the progress of civilization leading to decadence, are not within the ken of Dr. Leete's—or Edward Bellamy's—relentlessly upbeat imagination. In contrast, Morris offers a vision of a future that is at once optimistically progressive and learning to do quite well without book-culture, thank you—a post-literate society that is growing into a paradoxically healthy state of illiteracy, equated with pastoral innocence.

II

As socialist daydream, *News from Nowhere* stands in opposition to the literature and art produced under the regime of industrial capitalism, including Morris's own literature and art. Morris the artist declares that art is impossible under capitalism and thereby condemns his own work. Like *New Grub Street, News from Nowhere* is a thoroughly self-reflexive and self-implicating anti-novel. However, instead of resentfully reproducing while satirizing the conventions of a cumbersome and obsolescent fictional realism as does Gissing, Morris depicts a future society in which fiction is unnecessary, because the book of the world gives more pleasure than any merely printed book.

Morris's stance as an artist is always self-effacing, not from false humility but partly because of his belief that genuine art is impossible under "plutocracy." Throughout his career, he rejected the role of romantic poet-prophet; in *The Earthly Paradise*, for instance, the poet is only an "idle singer of an idle day."[1] There is a prophetic element in Morris's socialist poetry, but it comes from Marxism rather than from divine revelation or inspired genius. And what is true of Morris's poetry is also the case with his fiction; if he is able to speak prophetically, as he does in *A Dream of John Ball* and *News from Nowhere*, that is because of his solidarity with the working class and his acceptance of history as revealed by Marx. At the end of *News from Nowhere*, awakening in bed in his house "at dingy Hammersmith," the narrator, Guest, echoes Keats's "Ode to a Nightingale" by wondering if he has been dreaming. "Or indeed *was* it a dream?" he asks, concluding that "if others can see it as I have seen it, then it may be called a vision rather than a dream" (228). If instead of being merely a private, egoistic dream, Morris's utopian romance is a collective vision shared by others, it is so because the future belongs to socialism.

In "Art under Plutocracy" and elsewhere, Morris develops the Ruskinian theme that, under ideal conditions, art and labor are identical:

And first I must ask you to extend the word art beyond those matters which are consciously works of art, to take in not only painting and sculpture, and architecture, but the shapes and colours of all household goods, nay, even the arrangement of the fields for tillage and pasture, the management of towns and of our highways of all kinds; in a word, to extend it to the aspect of all the externals of our life. For I must ask you to believe that every one of the things that goes to make up the surroundings among which we live must be either beautiful or ugly. . . . (164–165)

Under capitalism, the separation of art from labor and life means that the artist has acquired a sense of himself as a special person, set above the masses; the "artist" sells his elitist wares to the rich, while the "artisan" declines into the status of skilled or unskilled wage-slave or even pauper. In healthy ages in the past, says Morris, "the best artist was a workman still, the humblest workman was an artist" (166). Morris's position is the antithesis of Gissing's almost Nietz-schean pessimism about the inevitable vulgarity and shallowness of any cultural form that becomes popular. For Morris, the only great art is "popular art," shared by all the people. And the only way to achieve genuinely "popular art" is through the revolutionary creation of a democratic, egalitarian society.

Morris's romantic Marxism seems to render all of the poetry and art of the nineteenth century null and void: "popular art" under "plutocracy" is impossible. For Morris, when writers and artists manage to express democratic attitudes, as do Dickens and Whitman, some truth and aesthetic power come through. But these successes are scattered and ineffective, and Morris recognizes that his own work has not been "popular art" either:

> In spite of all the success I have had, I have not failed to be conscious that the art I have been helping to produce would fall with the death of a few of us who really care about it, that a reform in art which is founded on individualism must perish with the individuals who have set it going. Both my historical studies and my practical conflict with the philistinism of modern society have *forced* on me the conviction that art cannot have a real life and growth under the present system of commercialism and profit-mongering. (Qtd. in Thompson 98)

So Morris, like many of the novelists surveyed in this study, arrives at a position that involves the belittlement of his own artistic activities, largely because the age itself makes it impossible for those activities to succeed.[2] At the same time, his interpretation of Marxism involves imagining the utopian conditions that will make "popular art" possible—or rather, that will be "popular art."

News from Nowhere is Morris's fictional demonstration that, in the communist society of the future, "art" as it has been known throughout the history of civilization will cease to exist because "popular art" and everyday labor will be identical. Forms of substitute gratification will be unnecessary because life will be gratifying. And *News from Nowhere*, in which Morris imagines utopia itself as "popular art," is not "art" in the ordinary sense of that term. It is certainly not a novel in the tradition of Dickens, Trollope, George Eliot, and Gissing.

Even critics sympathetic to Morris have often treated *News from Nowhere* as a not-quite-serious daydream or romance, at once unbelievable and only vaguely related, if at all, to Marxism. So Philip Henderson writes:

> It would be an insult to Morris's intelligence to suppose that he really believed in the possibility of such a society, where the only work that appears to be going on is a little haymaking at Kelmscott. . . . In reality it is an Arts and Crafts Utopia with very little relation to anything that we know as communism, though in its account of "How the Change Came" Morris makes use of Marxist analysis. (328)

Henderson, however, overlooks both the utopian elements in Marx and Engels and the logically consistent significance that Morris gives to "Arts and Crafts." It is only the reign of "organized greed" that has so diminished the status of "Arts and Crafts" that they seem trivial rather than universal, mere hobbyhorses rather than the entire category of nonalienated labor. And while Morris casts his utopian fiction into the shape of a dream-vision romance, he clearly considers it a possible future, consistent with his understanding of Marx. The main elements of this future—abolition of classes, of the state, of private property, and of money; the flexible, rational use of machinery; labor rendered "attractive" or merged into the categories of art and play; the decentralization of cities and of working sites; freer relations among the sexes—are all themes in Marx and Engels. Among the ten points about the future given in the *Communist Manifesto*, the ninth, the "gradual abolition of the distinction between town and country," begs for pastoral speculation like *News from Nowhere*. Far from being a mere "Arts and Crafts Utopia," in Henderson's trivializing sense, *News from Nowhere* is a quite precise depiction of the future according to Marx.

News from Nowhere can be read both as an example of "popular art" before its time and as a declaration of the impossibility of "popular art" in the present. In contrast to Dr. Leete's account of the flourishing condition of literature in *Looking Backward*, moreover, several inhabitants of Morris's happy future indicate that the literature that they produce is either about the past and has therefore only a kind of "antiquarian" interest, or else that it is not as interesting as that which was written in the past. So Clara asks old Hammond:

> How is it that though we are interested with our life for the most part, yet when people take to writing poems or painting pictures they seldom deal with our modern life, or if they do, take good care to make their poems or pictures unlike that life? Are we not good enough to paint ourselves? How is it that we find the dreadful times of the past so interesting to us—in pictures and poetry? (131)

The answer is that dwellers in utopia are too good to "paint" and their communal life too pleasurable to need the vicarious pleasure provided by literature. The flourishing of "popular art" means that the great book of reality is open for all to read, without reading the dreary books of the past.

This idea is also expressed when Guest talks to Ellen's grandfather, a wrongheaded old "grumbler" who likes to argue that past times and other countries may be happier than the socialist utopia in which they live. The old man bases his argument on literary evidence:

> Well, sir, I am happy to see a man from over the water; but I really must appeal to you to say whether on the whole you are not better off in your country; where I suppose . . . you are brisker and more alive, because you have not wholly got rid of competition. You see, I have read not a few books of the past days, and certainly they are much more alive than those which are written now. . . . There is a spirit of adventure in them, and signs of a capacity to extract good out of evil which our literature quite lacks now. . . . (174)

The old man's argument provokes a rebuttal from his highly un-Victorian grand-daughter: "Books, books! always books, grandfather! When will you understand that after all it is the world we live in which interests us . . ." (175).

Having suggested that the literature of the past is based on unhappiness, Ellen criticizes nineteenth-century fiction in particular, because that is what her grand-father thinks most "alive." The status of *News from Nowhere* as an anti-novel, opposed especially to novelistic realism from Defoe to Gissing, becomes explicit in her remarks:

> As for your books [says Ellen], they were well enough for times when intelli-gent people had but little else in which they could take pleasure, and when they must needs supplement the sordid miseries of their own lives with imaginations of the lives of other people. But I say flatly that in spite of all their cleverness and vigour and capacity for story-telling, there is something loathsome about them. Some of them, indeed, do here and there show some feeling for those whom the history-books call "poor," and of the misery of whose lives we have some inkling; but presently they give it up, and towards the end of the story we must be contented to see the hero and heroine living happily in an island of bliss on other people's troubles; and that after a long series of sham troubles (or mostly sham) of their own making, illustrated by dreary introspective nonsense about their feelings and aspirations, and all the rest of it; while the world must even then have gone on its way, and dug and sewed and baked and built and carpen-tered round about these useless—animals. (175–176)

By "dreary introspective nonsense," Ellen sums up and attacks what, Morris be-lieves, virtually every work of fictional realism concerns. The novel as a genre, she suggests, is based on bourgeois individualism with its cult of personality and its massive blindness to the larger questions of freedom, justice, and equality. Even those novels that deal with the lives of the working class evade real social issues and wind up with the bourgeois hero and heroine living happily ever after on the foundation of "other people's troubles."

In his reading of *News from Nowhere*, Lionel Trilling finds it difficult to imag-ine a world liberated from struggle and aggression. According to Trilling, Morris's romance offers a regressive pattern of social life based on "childhood and rest." Trilling agrees with Morris in condemning aggression as it expresses itself in economic competition and war. But isn't aggression also, he asks, the very basis of "the humanistic tradition," the indispensable motive for the strivings of indi-vidual genius, and the source of "great art"? "There are no geniuses in *News from Nowhere*," Trilling proclaims. That may be so, but neither has Morris's future society degenerated into what Marx called "the idiocy of rural life." While ag-gression is largely absent from their lives, art surrounds Morris's utopians, and so does work of a pleasurable sort because the two have grown indistinguishable. What is missing is "great art" along traditional lines, the unique creations of indi-vidual geniuses. Morris's category of "popular art" entails the complete abolition of what Walter Benjamin calls the "aura" of high cultural forms. Neither Trilling nor Morris can disentangle the humanistic "great art" of the past from its economic and social roots, but Morris envisions another sort of art, not based on "misery," including the distinctly literate and literary misery experienced by Gissing's and Hardy's overbooked characters. Morris is both opposed to Trilling's brand of common-sense, liberal realism and completely uncompromising: if history is incapable of producing widespread happiness, or a social formation that at least approximates the utopia of "popular art" depicted in *News from Nowhere*, then history had better cease altogether. Speaking of the utopian right to beautiful surroundings, Morris says that "if every civilized community cannot provide such surroundings for all its members, I do not want the world to go on; it is a mere misery that man has ever existed" ("How We Live" 22).

The art created and enjoyed by the characters in *News from Nowhere* is "popular" in several ways. For one thing, the distinction between "artist" and "artisan" or worker has been abolished: labor has become "attractive labor," and everyone is an artist. The products that the characters make, the tasks that they perform, and the communal relations among them reflect Morris's ideal of nonalienated labor. At the same time, the objects Guest observes that are most like the art he is familiar with—architecture, paintings, friezes, books—are qualitatively different from "art under plutocracy." Thus, Guest describes a baked-clay frieze on the outside of the guest house in which he awakens: "The subjects I recognised at once," he says, "and indeed was very particularly familiar with them" (53). He does not mention what these subjects are—to do so would spoil the point: they are subjects so familiar, so fully shared and collective, that even strangers can recognize them on first sight. The same mythic universality is evident in the "wall pictures" at the Bloomsbury Market, whose subjects "were taken from queer oldworld myths and imaginations which in yesterday's world only about half a dozen people in the country knew anything about . . ." (100). But old Hammond tells Guest that nowadays "everybody knows the tales." Further, the tales are not heroic legends, but fairy tales, and this also Guest finds both strange and familiar: "Well, I scarcely expected to find record of the Seven Swans and the King of the Golden Mountain and Faithful Henry, and such curious pleasant imaginations as Jacob Grimm got together from the childhood of the world, barely lingering even in his time: I should have thought you would have forgotten such childishness by this time" (130).

But in growing up into utopia, humanity has also grown up or regressed into a second childhood, in the positive sense that all of the innocent pleasures and wonders of childhood have been restored to it. Dick responds to Guest's surprise by telling him that the fairy tales in the murals are "very beautiful" and that "when we were children we used to imagine them going on in every wood-end, by the bight of every stream: every house in the fields was the Fairyland King's House to us" (130). But if there is no need for fantasy in utopia, why do Morris's utopians engage in highly luxuriant fantasizing? Morris's point seems to be that the borders between imagination, desire, and reality are fading, no longer important. In any case, unlike adult, bourgeois novels, fairy tales are close to being unmediated daydreams; as naive or primitive folk narratives, they are for Morris one sort of "popular art."

Morris depicts a society that has rid itself of what Herbert Marcuse, in *Eros and Civilization*, calls "surplus repression," and that can afford to be childlike in its customs and pleasures. In "The Society of the Future," Morris anticipates Marcuse by arguing that art under socialism will be based on abolishing asceticism or excess repression:

> I feel sure that no special claim need be made for the art and literature of the future: healthy bodily conditions, a sound and all round development of the senses, joined to the due social ethics which the destruction of all slavery will give us, will, I am convinced, as a matter of course give us the due art and literature, whatever that due may turn out to be. Only, if I may prophesy ever so little, I should say that both art and literature . . . will appeal to the senses directly, just as the art of the past has done. (200)

By "the art of the past," Morris means something like Gothic art, or at least art that preceded the rise of bourgeois capitalism, for he continues:

> You see you will no longer be able to have novels relating the troubles of a middleclass couple in their struggle towards social uselessness, because the material for such literary treasures will have passed away. On the other hand the genuine tales of history will still be with us, and will, one might well hope, then be told in a cheerfuller strain than is now possible. (200)

In referring to novels as "literary treasures," Morris is being ironic; he criticizes the whole genre as expressing the struggle of the bourgeoisie toward "social uselessness." In *News from Nowhere*, it is not stories from modern novels, but rather such "genuine tales of history" as the King of the Golden Mountain that Guest sees on the walls of Bloomsbury Market.

Predominant in *News from Nowhere* are useful "handicrafts" such as weaving, building, and haymaking, but several of the characters are also writers, among other roles, and the texts they produce again underscore the anti-novel status of Morris's utopian romance. Bob the weaver and old Hammond are both historians or "antiquarians," but as that term suggests, history is not seen as an especially crucial or serious activity, and Morris deliberately makes it inaccurate (old Hammond, for example, is not sure whether to say "Gladstone" or "Gladstein" [139]). In a society governed by the pleasure principle, history is a study of questionable utility: why should dwellers in utopia bother to recollect the doleful follies of the past? Morris's thinking seems contradictory here, however. Hammond believes that it is vital to study history as a means of avoiding past mistakes; further, the study of the past is one of the more pleasurable activities of several of the characters. The British Museum may be "an ugly old building" by utopian standards, but it is also full of "wonderful collections . . . of all kinds of antiquities, besides an enormous library with many exceedingly beautiful books in it, and many most useful ones as genuine records . . ." (86). For Morris, history consists of human follies and crimes, but it is—like the future—full of beauty to set against the ugliness of modern civilization. In *A Dream of John Ball*, this contradiction is especially apparent, for there the medieval world is portrayed as more beautiful than the present, even though it has produced the serfdom and tyranny against which Ball is rebelling, without clearly producing the hope for a socialist future. The narrator tries to explain to John Ball what he—or his descendants, at least —have to look forward to in the future, and that is, first, the wage-slavery of capitalism.

In *News from Nowhere*, Boffin, ironically named after Dickens's illiterate "golden dustman," writes novels, an activity that seems even more out of place in Morris's anti-novel than does the study of history. The word *novel* always appears with a qualification attached; Boffin is described by Dick as a writer of "reactionary novels" or "antiquarian novels"—the two phrases are synonymous. Of course there is no reason why Boffin should not write novels if he enjoys doing it, but it seems unlikely that he is producing public art, or pleasing anyone more than himself. Apart from Boffin and Ellen's grandfather, most of the characters think that novels are outmoded and decadent. When Bob the weaver tries to question Guest, Dick upbraids him: "You remind me of the radical cobblers in the silly old novels, who, according to the authors, were prepared to trample down all good manners in the pursuit of utilitarian knowledge" (56). And when Guest indulges in a moment of self-pity, Ellen, who has already expressed her opposition to novels, says: "Do you know, I begin to suspect you of wanting to nurse a sham sorrow, like the ridiculous characters in some of those queer old novels that I have come across now and then" (217). It is possible to write novels in Morris's utopia, but it is an "antiquarian" activity that most of the characters find at least faintly ridiculous. While not capitulating to her criticism of novels and novel-reading, Ellen's grandfather ironically reveals that she is right. After she concludes by saying, "I love life better than death," he replies: "Well, for my part I like reading a good old book with plenty of fun in it, like Thackeray's 'Vanity Fair'. Why don't you write books like that now?" (182). The answer to his question, at least in utopia, is self-evident: novels like Thackeray's are beside the point "now" because life is no longer a Vanity Fair.

III

Just as Morris's utopia is a response to Bellamy's *Looking Backward*, so H. G. Wells's *Time Machine* is a response to *News from Nowhere*. The world of the Elois, at least, some 800,000 years into the future, is a parody and critique of Morris's "Arts and Crafts Utopia." Beautiful, childlike innocents who dress in "bright, soft-coloured robes" and who live and dine in a communal hall "richly carved" with images that the Time-Traveller thinks are like "old Phoenician decorations" (26–27), the Elois are also illiterate. Their world may be a "social paradise," a new "Golden Age" (40), or so the Time-Traveller believes before he discovers the Morlocks; but it is also one in which not only are reading, writing, books, and literature defunct, but language itself is threatened with extinction. The Elois still have a language of sorts, but it is "excessively simple—almost exclusively composed of concrete substantives and verbs."

> There seemed to be few, if any, abstract terms, or little use of figurative language. Their sentences were usually simple and of two words, and I failed to convey or understand any but the simplest proposition. (39)

Whether the other species—the Morlocks—that humanity has devolved into has any language the Time-Traveller does not learn. They have, however, something like industrial technology in their underworld abattoir or flesh-mine. But they show, if anything, even fewer signs of the human intelligence that Wells associates with language, literacy, and literature than do the Elois.

Given the disappearance of language, one would expect books to have entirely vanished from the false Eden of the future. But that is not quite the case. The Time-Traveller explores the ruins of a building that he calls "the Palace of Green Porcelain," a place that, if not the British Museum, seems to be "some latter-day South Kensington" Museum (60–61). Passing through various galleries of paleontology, natural history, and machinery, the Time-Traveller comes upon something like a library, draped with "brown and charred rags" that he recognizes as "the decaying vestiges of books":

> They had long since dropped to pieces, and every semblance of print had left them. But here and there were warped boards and cracked metallic clasps that told the tale well enough. Had I been a literary man I might, perhaps, have moralized upon the futility of all ambition. (63)

The Time-Traveller does, in fact, moralize upon the futility of all civilization, not only in this contemplating-the-ruins scene, but in his conclusion that he is witnessing "the sunset of mankind" as the ultimate outcome of human progress:

> For the first time I began to realize an odd consequence of the social effort in which we are at present engaged. . . . The work of ameliorating the conditions of life—the true civilizing process that makes life more and more secure—had gone steadily on to a climax. One triumph of a united humanity over Nature had followed another. Things that are now mere dreams had become projects deliberately put in hand and carried forward. And the harvest was what I saw! (31)

That "harvest" is the result of an immense contradiction undermining, apparently, the entire effort of "the true civilizing process." At some point in evolutionary time, progress turns into its opposite, into regression, backward to the childish innocence of the Elois and the atavistic cannibalism of the Morlocks. "I grieved to think how brief the dream of the human intellect had been," the Time-Traveller reflects. "It had committed suicide" (72).

Whether or not the illiteracy of the Elois, the weakening of language and reason, and the obliteration of book-culture in Wells's Darwinian version of the dialectic of Enlightenment is a direct commentary upon Morris's critique of novels and his depiction of the lapse of literacy in *News from Nowhere*, their opposed fantasies of bookless futures, one utopian and the other dystopian, are just as symptomatic of anxieties about mass literacy as Gissing's and Hardy's bookish pessimisms. Wells, of course, echoes those pessimisms, both in *The Time Machine* and elsewhere—for instance, in his fantasy about the destruction of book-culture in the near future in *The War in the Air*. And in *The Outline of History*, like Gissing's Henry Ryecroft, Wells treats mass literacy, with its untrained appetite for mindlessly chauvinistic, war-mongering journalism, as a main cause of the disastrous war-making of the twentieth century (*Ryecroft* 73–74; Carey 118–134).

According to Ryecroft, the chief "characteristic and peril of our time" is "the host of the half-educated" (61). The enormous reading public with their "semi-education," he opines, may think that they read books, but "hardly will a prudent statistician venture to declare that one in every score of those who actually read sterling books do so with comprehension of their author" (60). Here Gissing, like many other late-Victorian intellectuals, arrives at a casting-pearls-before-swine argument that marks one limit of pessimism about mass literacy: though the masses can now read, and though "sterling books" can be set before them, there is no guarantee that they will read those "sterling books" in the right manner, "with comprehension of their author" (60). Like *New Grub Street*, *Henry Ryecroft* is in part a mournful catalogue of the many reasons that Gissing sees for the failures of democracy and mass literacy—failures caused in the first instance by the impossibility, he believes, of the diffusion of high, Arnoldian, literary culture downward to the masses.

At various moments in his "papers," Ryecroft mentions at least five related but more or less distinct reasons why neither democracy nor mass literacy can succeed. First, most people, even though they can attain basic literacy, remain only "half-educated"; they cannot or do not attain culture or wisdom (this is a version of the tautological claim that most people are average or below average in some respect, whether in vice or virtue, ignorance or intelligence). Second, most individuals are basically decent and even reasonable as individuals, but herded into crowds—the masses—they lose whatever virtue and independent rationality they had. This is a key theme in the writings of fin-de-siècle "crowd psychologists," such as Gustave Le Bon and Gabriel Tarde, who contend that individuals in crowds revert, via a sort of collective "contagion," to barbarism or savagery. Third, too much literacy and print-culture is productive only of cultural mediocrity or worse; both too many writers and readers and too many books swamp the few "sterling books" that (perhaps) continue to be written and published. Fourth, the "bookish leisure" that Ryecroft and Gissing most value is attainable only by a tiny minority who can both afford and appreciate such leisure (*Ryecroft* 114); the specialness of that cultivated leisure would in any case be quite spoiled if too many people indulged in it, like too many people trampling through a private garden. And fifth, authorship has become simultaneously too "easy" and a "profession" that almost anyone can enter:

> I surmise [Ryecroft declares] that the path of "literature" is being made too easy. Doubtless it is a rare thing nowadays for a lad whose education ranks him with the upper middle class to find himself utterly without resources, should he wish to devote himself to the profession of letters. And there is the root of the matter; writing has come to be recognized as a profession, almost as cut-and-dried as church or law. . . . (137)

In contrast to Gissing, Walter Besant held that the reason there were so many aspiring but failing authors in New Grub Street was that authorship was not accorded the same respect and did not have the sort of organization that the other "professions" had. If thousands of hack writers were struggling in the obscurity and lower depths of literature, that was because publishers in particular exploited them without mercy. "No worker in the world," Besant asserted, "not even the needlewoman, is more helpless, more ignorant, more cruelly sweated, than the author" (Besant 314). But give authors a professional organization to protect their rights and to maintain literary standards, Besant thought, and all would be well. His view of New Grub Street was, no doubt, overly sanguine, just as Gissing's was overly dour. But Besant is surely correct in his assessment of the "immense enlargement of independence" available even to modestly talented writers through the expansion of literacy, of monthly magazines and weekly journals, of mass-circulation dailies, of new publishers, and of new retail outlets for books, rivaling Mudie's, like Boots' pharmacies that had begun to operate as bookstores and circulating libraries (Besant 325–326). "A literary man of the present day may carry on all his literary work—all that he can do—for as many hours of the day as is good for him, together with as much journalistic work as will suffice to render him independent of his publisher," Besant goes on to say (326–327). The "profession" of authorship needs to develop protections against the rapacity of publishers, a key reason why Besant organized the Society of Authors in 1883, also known as "Besant's Society" (Keating 27). But Besant does not suggest that it needs also to develop protections against the "vulgarity unutterable" of the reading public.

From Gissing's perspective, Besant's view of authorship as a "profession" must itself have seemed "vulgar," a version of the barbarism of mass culture and not a defense against it. Nevertheless, by the 1890s, literacy had become nearly universal, and the consumption of books, newspapers, advertisements, and many other products of print-culture had both grown to genuinely mass proportions and become bewilderingly diverse—a regime of reading and writing that intellectuals, including novelists, were no longer sure they could influence, let alone control or in some sense dominate. Like the motif of the poisonous book in Wilde's *Picture of Dorian Gray*, the theme of too much literacy—of humanity becoming overbooked, or of the very success of culture leading to a sort of collective suicide—that Gissing, Hardy, Morris, and Wells all express points to that pathology of reading that is often evident in earlier novels as anxiety about novels but that also points ahead to the modernist reification of the antithesis between high and mass culture.

For the history of fiction, that antithesis has entailed situating the vast majority of novels on the debased, commercial, mass-cultural side of what Andreas Huyssen calls "the great divide," but also situating a small minority or elite of fiction on the other side, in the domain of "great art." With such modernist novelists as Conrad, Joyce, Lawrence, and Woolf, the ambiguous status of the novel that characterizes it as a genre from Defoe to Hardy comes to an end, or at least enters a sort of truce: most novels may not be art; but some novels and a small number of novelists belong in the pantheon, with the very greatest writers and artists of the past. Nevertheless, the claim of modernist fiction to high cultural status entails rejecting or demoting ordinary novels as commercial, mass-cultural detritus. Peter Keating points out that when Joyce and Lawrence portray themselves as aspiring young novelists, they "focus entirely on the development of the Artist and dispens[e] entirely with commercialism. Stephen Dedalus and Paul Morel are Artists alright, but they have nothing to do with publishers, editors, agents . . . [and] they are not even shown writing books" (Keating 86).

The demarcation of modernist, high cultural fiction from the ordinary novels of the past is also evident in Virginia Woolf's famous remark: "On or about December, 1910, human nature changed" (194). The remark comes in "Mr. Bennett and Mrs. Brown," Woolf's repudiation of the conventions of Victorian and Edwardian novelistic realism. Woolf acknowledges that "after the creative activity of the Victorian age it was quite necessary, not only for literature but for life, that someone should write the books that Mr. Wells, Mr. Bennett, and Mr. Galsworthy have written."

> Yet what odd books they are! Sometimes I wonder if we are right to call them books at all. For they leave one with so strange a feeling of incompleteness and dissatisfaction. In order to complete them it seems necessary to do something— to join a society or, more desperately, to write a cheque. (201)

Writing a "cheque," at least, might be more effective than writing another novel on the pattern of *The Old Wives' Tale* or *The Man of Property*. Woolf imagines the three Edwardian novelists riding in a railway carriage with Mrs. Brown, and failing to observe her in any adequate way. All three see something-or-other quite intensely, but what they see is irrelevant to capturing Mrs. Brown's "character" in language. During the ride, "Mr. Bennett" for one "has never once looked at Mrs. Brown in her corner," though he and his fellow novelists "have looked very powerfully, searchingly, and sympathetically out of the window; at factories, at Utopias, even at the decoration and upholstery of the carriage; but never at her, never at life, never at human nature" (205). They are all three, Woolf would later declare in "Modern Fiction," "materialists":

> It is because they are concerned not with the spirit but with the body that they have disappointed us, and left us with the feeling that the sooner English fiction turns its back upon them, as politely as may be, and marches, if only into the desert, the better for its soul. (285)

And march it did, of course, through the modernist novels of Woolf herself, and also of Joyce, Lawrence, Dorothy Richardson, and many other writers who emerged after "December, 1910."

In his 1901 essay "The 'Average Reader' and the Recipe for Popularity," Bennett complains that "the division of the world into two classes, one of which has a monopoly of what is called 'artistic feeling,' is arbitrary and false. Everyone is an artist, more or less . . ." (51). In contrast to Gissing, Bennett does not chafe at the "democratisation of literature" that has characterized late-Victorian culture (46), and he rejects the "dilettante spirit which refuses to see the connection between art and money" (47). But in doing so, he is rejecting the modernist stance that he does not foresee and that Woolf would later articulate—a stance opposed to the "materialism," both commercial and epistemological, that he champions.

As a successful novelist, playwright, and critic, Bennett is, perhaps, not much different in his self-satisfaction, cultural good cheer, and moderate cynicism from Jasper Milvain in *New Grub Street*, who recognizes that literature has become a branch of commerce and who accommodates himself to that fact of modern life. For Bennett as for Milvain, modernity is not characterized by the demise of genuine culture, much less by the disappearance of books and literacy, but by their proliferation, and above all by the triumph of the novel:

> Unnecessary to go back to the ante-Scott age in order to perceive how the novel has aggrandised itself! It has conquered enormous territories even since *Germinal*. . . . Were it to adopt the hue of the British Empire, the entire map of the universe would soon be coloured red. Wherever it ought to stand in the hierarchy of forms, it has, actually, no rival at the present day as a means for transmitting the impassioned vision of life. (Bennett 16)

In objective, common-sense terms, Bennett is right: the period from 1870 to 1901 was an age both of geographical and of cultural imperialism—the era of what Edmund Gosse called "the tyranny of the novel." Never before had there been so many readers, nor so many novels, nor so many literary journals, libraries, bookstores, and publishers—nor so much opportunity for even a mediocre novelist to gain popularity and a decent livelihood through fiction-writing. From Bennett's comfortably mercantile perspective, like Trollope's in *The Autobiography*, the woes of Gissing's failed novelists must have been caused by their inability to take advantage of the ever-growing demand for fiction rather than by some imagined incompatibility between art and the masses, or even between refined literary taste and the unrefined, perhaps unliterary, perhaps only semi-literate taste of the reading public. The aspiring novelist must, Bennett thinks, aspire to make money and therefore to achieve popularity, and not shun these things, as if they were antithetical to art.

"There is a numerous band of persons in London," Bennett declares, "who spend so much time and emotion in practising the rites of the religion of art that they become incapable of real existence. Each is a Stylites on a pillar" (49).

These worshipers of art, Bennett continues, in terms exactly antithetical to Woolf's later critique, fail to capture life in their own artworks, because they despise life: "They never approach normal life. They scorn it. They have a horror of it" (49). Bennett does not recognize, however, that the sense of frustration and failure expressed by many more-or-less successful late-Victorian and Edwardian writers—Gissing, Stevenson, Hardy, Morris, Wells, Wilde, Conrad, Woolf—may have less to do with the alleged inability of the mass reading public to appreciate great literature than with their suspicion that the novel-form itself, or at least novelistic realism as practiced by their great Victorian predecessors, has played itself out. Like both Besant and Gissing, Bennett sees no new techniques for expressing "real existence" on the horizon. But Gissing's failed novelists write themselves into corners that they themselves acknowledge to be literary dead ends *before* their novels reach the mass reading public. Hardy's Jude Fawley and Sue Bridehead both come to the realization that even the highest literary culture—Arnold's "best that has been thought and written" over the ages—is not solacing, much less salvational, as they try to cope with the book of the world they are living. And contemplating "the decaying vestiges of books" in the ruins of the Palace of Green Porcelain, Wells's Time-Traveller sees them as symbolizing "the futility of all ambition." Like *News from Nowhere, The Time Machine* is a fantasy partly about the future death of all books; but also like Morris's utopia, the very form of Wells's dystopia implies the death of a certain kind of book—the realist novel as practiced by Dickens, Thackeray, Eliot, Gissing, Hardy, and Wells himself in works like *Tono-Bungay*. The resurrection of the Gothic romance form—the old-new paradigm or subgenre to which *Jekyll and Hyde, Picture of Dorian Gray, The Time Machine, Dracula,* and *News from Nowhere* all belong—is itself symptomatic of the felt inadequacy, on the part of many late-Victorian novelists, of the old realist paradigm.

The story of modernist experiments in fiction has often been told. But after "December, 1910," what happened to relations between novelists and readers? Certain familiar debates about the impact of novel-reading on the general public continued, involving familiar conflicts over specific novels: the charges of obscenity aimed at Joyce's *Ulysses* and Lawrence's *Lady Chatterley's Lover*, for instance, and even the charge that Wells's much less explicitly "indecent" *Ann Veronica* was nonetheless "poisonous."[3] Moreover, when Woolf was contemplating Mrs. Brown, and noting the failures of Messrs. Bennett, Galsworthy, and Wells to "see" her, though seeing the upholstery in the railway carriage clearly enough, the cinema, with its own quite distinctive mode of seeing, was just coming into its own. Cultural critics of various ideological persuasions lined up to prophesy that this new technology of entertainment (most of the early critics were not prepared to call it a new form of art) would mean the death of reading, of literacy, and of the wholesome book-culture of the past.[4] The activity of novel-reading, which to many diagnosticians of cultural disease had seemed so dangerous to the mental health of the reading public from the 1700s down to "December, 1910" (and sometimes beyond), now seemed benign and even healthful to those who looked upon the movies as toxic. Exactly the same arguments would be repeated, of course, about television.

Like the novel before them, both the cinema and television have been charged with causing the decline and fall of literacy, of reading, even of civilization. In contrast to the new, visual mass media, however, the novel cannot exist without readers. Claims that novel-reading diminishes reading or somehow undermines literacy are fundamentally contradictory. Yet such claims, internalized within the novel-form itself, have also been basic to its history from Defoe and Fielding at least until "December, 1910." Despite cinema and television, moreover, the writing, publishing, and reading of novels of all sorts and degrees of literary quality have continued apace, not diminished.[5]

In her pioneering study *Fiction and the Reading Public* (1939), Q. D. Leavis documents the rise of mass literacy, but nevertheless equates both it and the mass media with cultural decay instead of progress. She acknowledges the symbiosis between film and printed fiction, but nevertheless argues that "Dr. Johnson's common reader," knowledgeable about literature and the other arts, has given way to a "general public" that "has now not even a glimpse of the living interests of modern literature, is ignorant of its growth and so prevented from developing with it. . . ." Moreover, "the critical minority to whose sole charge modern literature has now fallen is isolated, disowned by the general public and threatened with extinction" (35). Nevertheless, this "general public" indulges indiscriminately in novel-reading.

At times, Leavis insists that—at least in Dr. Johnson's age—novels of real literary merit were once published. At other times, she expresses the anti-novel view that runs back to Hannah More, Dr. Johnson, and beyond: novel-reading "is now often a form of the drug habit" (7; see also 152). The rise of mass literacy is, for Leavis as also for her husband, simultaneously the "disintegration of the reading public" (151). Educating the masses has, she thinks, produced a situation that threatens the very existence of intelligence and literature. Underscoring the modernist division between mass and high culture, she declares that popular fiction, as opposed to genuine literature, impinges "directly on the world of the [sensitive] minority, menacing the standards by which they live" (67), and thus also menacing civilization.

At least Leavis does not confuse literacy with illiteracy. Charges that literacy is declining—in the United States, at least, that half or more of the general public is "functionally illiterate"—depend partly on one's definition of literacy (or anyway of *functional* literacy), and partly on such causes as poverty, racism, and bad schools. But there has never been any clear evidence that supposedly low or debased cultural forms undermine supposedly superior forms, or that engaging in cultural activities that do not require reading undermines reading. The latest versions of the decline or death of literature, of book-culture, and of Western civilization, moreover, relate on the one hand to computers rather than to cinema and television, and on the other to highly academic varieties of literary and cultural theory, and both computers and literary theory involve high degrees of literacy rather than the reverse. Perhaps cinema and television really do undermine literacy (though this argument has never been proven); in contrast, computers demand a new sort of technical literacy, the acquisition of which itself depends upon reading and, ordinarily, upon some amount of higher education. If at some future date, libraries and books printed on paper disappear, this will likely occur because books of all sorts, including the vast heritages of past cultures, are being electronically preserved and are almost instantly available to anyone who can use a computer.

Similarly, pessimistic claims that a new sort of barbarism has invaded higher education itself—the standard list of the new barbarian tribes includes structuralists, deconstructionists (or poststructuralists), psychoanalytic critics, feminists, Marxists, postcolonialists, multiculturalists, and postmodernists—and that these new barbarians have caused or are trying to cause the "death of the author," of the literary canon, of book culture, and even of Western civilization sound suspiciously similar to the cultural pessimisms of Gissing, Matthew Arnold, Thomas Carlyle, Hannah More, and Edmund Burke, except now the charges are directed against some of the best-educated, most literate individuals in contemporary America and Britain—that is, against professors of literature. Once again, in academic jeremiads such as Allan Bloom's *The Closing of the American Mind*, Alvin Kernan's *The Death of Literature*, and Dinesh D'Souza's *Illiberal Education*, literacy is treated as its own worst enemy.

Such pessimistic arguments, however, always leave the main issues untouched. As has often been noted, censorship usually winds up promoting that which it condemns. Whether attacking novels as poisonous and novel-reading as a pernicious waste of time, or the cinema and television in almost identical terms, or high literary and cultural theory within the academy as the subversion rather than product of Western civilization, the cultural pessimists more often than not also just add fuel to the fires they seek to douse. And while such pessimists believe that they are defending both the only correct cultural standards and the masses who, whether literate, semi-literate, or illiterate, sorely need their guidance, all they usually express is outright contempt and fear of the masses—that is, of all of us, including themselves. Indeed, what Raymond Williams so eloquently said about "the masses" in *Culture and Society* can be applied equally to novel-readers and consumers of other forms of so-called popular and mass culture: "To other people, we also are masses. Masses are other people. . . . There are in fact no masses; there are only ways of seeing people as masses" (300).

From the eighteenth century on, it has been the fate of the novel, for better or worse, to develop into the most popular form of reading in the modern era of democratic education and mass literacy. That novels, like all other art forms, come in many forms, styles, and qualities, both intellectual and aesthetic, seems almost self-evident. That novel-readers also come in many forms, with various degrees of sophistication and various tastes, is also self-evident. Throughout its history, however, the novel has been deeply influenced by the anti-novel attitudes and prejudices that have been the main focus of this study. As a result, the novel is the one literary genre that, when it does not explicitly condemn novels and novel-reading, nevertheless acknowledges its status as *pharmakon*, suggesting to the reader that she or he might be reading something more significant, uplifting, or edifying—something less misleading, less addictive, less seductive, less toxic or, well, less fictional than a novel.

NOTES

1. Introduction

1. See Taylor, *Early Opposition to the English Novel*; Joseph Heidler, *The History...* *of English Criticism of Prose Fiction*; Michael McKeon, *Origins of the English Novel*; Archibald Shepperson, *The Novel in Motley*; J. M. S. Tompkins, *The Popular Novel in England*; Devendra Varma, *The Evergreen Tree of Diabolical Knowledge*; Ioan Williams, *The Idea of the Novel in Europe, 1600–1800*; W. F. Gallaway, "The Conservative Attitude toward Fiction"; and Gary Kelly, "'This Pestiferous Reading,'" among others.

2. In *Novels of the Eighteen-Forties*, Kathleen Tillotson takes that decade as pivotal in the growing acceptance of prose fiction. Surveying anti-novel attitudes prior to the 1840s, Tillotson notes that, except for Hannah More's evangelical fictions, "Queen Victoria . . . was allowed to read no novels in her youth." Tillotson also cites Anthony Trollope's statement that, when he was growing up in the 1820s, "the families in which an unrestricted permission was given for the reading of novels were very few, and from many they were altogether banished" (Tillotson 15).

3. For Scott's impact on the respectability of the novel, see Ina Ferris, *The Achievement of Literary Authority*; for Austen, see, among others, the studies by Nancy Armstrong, Marilyn Butler, and Mary Poovey. Novels in the standard, multi-volume format were expensive commodities that, apart from their entertainment value, offered the consumer little or no status value (cf. Lovell 50). Publication in journals or monthly parts lowered the price, but the publishers of novels in bound volumes were dependent for sales on circulating libraries, which, from its establishment in 1842 through most of the Victorian period, meant especially Mudie's Select Library. As much as any other factor, the dominance of Mudie's over the novel-publishing industry helped to tame the more transgressive sexual and political themes and aspects of earlier fiction (Griest; Hiley; Sutherland 24–30). By 1885, mainstream fiction had perhaps become too respectable. In that year, George Moore's *A Mummer's Wife* was published but banned by Mudie's, which led Moore to pen his attack on Mudie's prudish hegemony over Victorian fiction, "Literature at Nurse." Yet until the turn of the century, the novel continued to be seen as an inferior genre, often categorized as "light literature" or mere commercialized entertainment.

4. The actual size of the readership for individual novels remained relatively small through the 1830s. John Sutherland notes that, in the 1830s, "the accessible reading public . . . amounted to some 50,000" (12). Sutherland is speaking, however, about the number of potential readers for relatively expensive novels aimed at a middle-class audience. He also cites Walter Besant's claim that, from 1830 to 1890, "the reading public for books . . . grew from 50,000 to 120,000,000," with the latter figure taking into account the markets opened by imperial expansion (64). But the readership for certain periodicals—Cobbett's *Political Register*, Knight's *Penny Magazine*—and for the cheap fiction of Edward Lloyd, G. W. M. Reynolds, and others was larger before 1830 or 1840 than these figures suggest. In 1816, Cobbett's journal may have had a circulation as high as 70,000; in 1832, the *Penny Magazine* may have reached 200,000 readers. See the figures in Altick, *English*

Common Reader, 392. In "English Publishing and the Mass Audience in 1852," however, Altick claims that there was no genuinely "mass" readership before mid-century. I use "mass" not to suggest universal literacy but rather to indicate large numbers of anonymous readers, of all social classes, whose responses to what they read could neither be controlled nor even accurately predicted. For literacy statistics from the eighteenth century forward, see Altick, *English Common Reader*, 167–172; Graff 313–340; Mitch.

5. So, too, in George Moore's *Esther Waters*, is the illiteracy of the heroine contrasted to "the anemic surface of conventional sentimental fiction" (Stewart 293). The middle-class Miss Rice, who employs Esther as a servant, is a novelist who, however, recognizes the "pale" inadequacy of her fiction in comparison to "the full-blooded crises of Esther's worldly trials" (Stewart 293). And as I point out in the final chapter, utopian innocence is equated with the disappearance of bourgeois fiction, but more generally with the decline of books and reading, in William Morris's *News from Nowhere*. For an important study of literacy and its opposite in Dickens's last novel, see Altick, "Education, Print, and Paper in *Our Mutual Friend*."

6. Between the 1790s and 1820s, besides More's and West's, there were a number of attempts to improve or purify the novel by writing better, morally or religiously edifying novels. These include Mary Wollstonecraft's feminist fictions and Maria Edgeworth's didactic tales. According to Marilyn Butler, both Wollstonecraft and Edgeworth belong to "the group of rational women writers of this period [late eighteenth century] whose first novels were so to speak anti-novels" (*Maria Edgeworth* 307). Similarly, More's *Coelebs in Search of a Wife* was, like her shorter tracts, written "to counteract the poison of novels by something which assumes the form of a novel" (qtd. in Ferris 53).

7. In "Plato's Pharmacy," Jacques Derrida points out that Socrates uses *pharmakon* as a metaphor for writing in general (65–94). Like the English word *drug*, in ancient Greek *pharmakon* carries a double meaning: medicine or remedy on the one hand, poison on the other. Derrida continues: "Socrates compares the written texts Phaedrus has brought along to a drug" (70). This *pharmakon*, this "medicine . . . which acts as both remedy and poison," "with all its ambivalence" (70), becomes central to the dialogue named for Phaedrus and also to Socrates' conception of writing. Socrates recounts an Egyptian myth about the origin of writing, according to which the clever god Theuth, who in addition to writing also "invented numbers and calculation, geometry and astronomy," presented each of these inventions to Ammon, the king of Thebes (75). When he got to writing, Theuth offered it as a "recipe"—a "pharmakon," Socrates says—that "will make the Egyptians wiser and will improve their memories" (75). But, says King Ammon, writing can't preserve memory; instead, it will deaden it by taking its place. Writing can't enter the realm of true presence (for Plato, the realm of ideal forms), but is forever mere secondhand representation. Writing for Plato, Derrida shows, signals the death of speech and of presence, just as Theuth the clever god and inventor of writing turns out also to be the god of death. So while Socrates thinks that writing may be in some sense medicinal (perhaps useful as a reminder, though no substitute for memory), it is also simultaneously a poison. Hence, whether wise or foolish, beautiful or ugly, all books are inherently poisonous. Derrida has only to add that all forms of communication are forms of writing—that there is "nothing outside the text"—to suggest how culture as such, in its entirety, may be toxic, or anyway simultaneously poisonous and medicinal, enervating as much as life-enhancing. Carla Peterson both makes the connection between "Plato's Pharmacy" and early-nineteenth-century novels, French as well as English, and stresses the paradox that "the debate over book reading and, most particularly, novel reading . . . took place in large part within the novel itself" (19). See also Nicholas Hudson, *Writing and European Thought*.

8. An early, familiar example of a text that identifies itself as poison is Jonathan Swift's "The Battle of the Books." In one famous passage, Swift describes an argument between a spider and a bee. Aesop interprets their argument by identifying the spider with Modern authors and the bee with the Ancients. "For anything else of genuine [worth] that the Moderns may pretend to," Swift's Aesop says, "I cannot recollect, unless it be a large vein of wrangling and satire, much [like] the spider's poison. . . ." But the bee, on the other hand, by producing honey and wax, "furnish[es] mankind with the two noblest of things, which are sweetness and light" (368). In this example, Swift implicates himself— he of course is a Modern author and also a "wrangling" satirist: he cannot help but be one of the poisonous spiders, and hence the very satiric essay he has written must contain more dirt and venom, as he puts it, than honey and wax. Swift does not follow Socrates by suggesting that all writing may be in some sense toxic; but he too offers a sweeping generalization—all *modern* writing is poisonous—that ironically applies to himself, just as Plato's privileging of speech over writing is preserved down to the present in the suspect form of the *pharmakon* of writing. In *Culture and Anarchy*, Matthew Arnold famously appropriated Swift's metaphor of "sweetness and light" for one of his key definitions of culture.

9. On Quixotism in fiction, see Walter Reed, *An Exemplary History of the Novel*, and Alexander Welsh, *Reflections on the Hero as Quixote*, among others.

10. Typical of the Emma Bovary or female Quixote pattern is the story of the reformed prostitute Mary Smith in Henry Gladwyn Jebb's *Out of the Depths: The Story of a Woman's Life* (London: Macmillan, 1859), for whose fall novels are at least partly to blame: "It was during this period [aet. 15] that I first read a novel . . . and I soon procured others for myself, which I carefully concealed from my mother's eyes; for I had an instinct that she would disapprove of such books, though I had never so much as heard of a novel till then. . . . I can see now that there was no character more certain to derive injury from novel-reading than mine as it was at that time; and the trash I devoured did its baneful work indeed" (11).

11. On "penny dreadfuls," see Neuberg, *Popular Literature*, 144–217; Dunae, "Penny Dreadfuls"; and Springhall, "'A Life Story for the People'?" Compare the passage from Wilde to Mortimer Collins, *Marquis and Merchant*, 2:174–175: "These quasi-human animals I see around me—have those in trousers anything beyond an instinct for intoxicating liquid?—those in petticoats (more or less gaudy) anything beyond an instinct for the opposite sex? I doubt it. They are mere animals, and, for the most part, very inferior animals. . . . What is the use of educating such people? The result is that they read *Paul Clifford*, *Jack Sheppard*, *Eugene Aram*, and the *Police Gazette*. They see how some vile blackguard has murdered a whole family, including a young girl just about to marry, and they grow emulous of the murderer. . . . The best fate that can happen to nine hundred and ninety-nine men out of a thousand is to know but little, and to do what they are told."

12. For an account of the motif of the "fatal book" in fin-de-siècle literature, see Linda Dowling, *Language and Decadence*, 104–174. The era of the "yellow book" (and also of the decadent journal of that name) was the era of "yellow journalism" as well, which unlike Huysmans's or Wilde's decadent elitism, catered to the mass reading public. See the examples of Trevelyan and Hobson later in this chapter.

13. On metaphors of eating and consumption in general in relation to popular literature, see Janice Radway, "Reading Is Not Eating."

14. For the sociological idea of the "literary field," see Pierre Bourdieu, *The Field of Cultural Production*, especially 29–73 and 161–175. Bourdieu offers his analysis partly as a way to avoid both the ahistoricity of formalist literary analysis (e.g., the New Criti-

cism) and the external "economism" of other versions of the sociology of literature, including Marxist ones such as that offered by Norman Feltes in *Modes of Production of Victorian Fiction*. Bourdieu's model may itself seem too mechanistic, but it allows for individual agency within a matrix of institutional and social class power relations. See also Jon Klancher's comment about Bourdieu's *Distinction* in relation to Kantian aesthetics and the emergence of the high versus mass culture dichotomy (Klancher 13).

15. In her study of Mudie's Circulating Library, Guinevere Griest writes: "The prestige of the the three-volume novel, in part attributable to Scott, was nurtured and strengthened by Mudie's, catering as it did to the middle and upper-middle classes. It is difficult for twentieth-century readers to evaluate the status which [Mudie's] Select Library's complex organization helped to confer on the three-volume form. It was customary, certainly, for successful three-deckers to be re-issued in single volumes, but there hovered over a first edition in three stately tomes an aura of dignity and worth which tended to obscure those works unfortunate enough to be issued originally in a meagre one volume" (Griest 46). See also John Sutherland, 24–30; Nicholas Hiley.

16. For plagiarism as a practice in the "cheap literature" trade, see Louis James, *Fiction for the Working Man*, 45–71.

17. On Thackeray's rhetoric of direct address to his readers see Stewart, 49–52, 277–282; Kate Flint, "Women, Men and the Reading of *Vanity Fair*"; and Wolfgang Iser, *The Implied Reader*, 101–120.

18. For a major statement about intellectuals' alienation in the first half of the nineteenth century, see Raymond Williams's chapter, "The Romantic Artist," in *Culture and Society*, 30–48.

The meanings of *popular* and *mass* as adjectives qualifying *culture* are notoriously overlapping, vexed, and contradictory. I prefer *mass*, because suggesting cultural forms that have been mass-produced for mass consumption, without suggesting that those forms have been directly, democratically selected by the populace, the general public, or popular consensus from a clear range of alternatives. Mass culture, in short, is modern, industrialized culture produced in both capitalist and socialist economies, but in neither case is it clearly, necessarily, or inherently democratic. For some of the problems and contradictions involved in the concepts of "mass" and "popular" culture (and, of course, in the concept of "culture" itself) see Williams, *Keywords* and *Culture and Society*, and also my *Bread and Circuses*.

19. Some of the best accounts of how actual readers responded to novels are studies of Victorian publishers and publishing houses. See, among others, John Sutherland, *Victorian Novelists and Publishers*; Robert Patten, *Dickens and His Publishers*; and Peter Shillingsburg, *Pegasus in Harness: Victorian Publishing and W. M. Thackeray*.

20. Coleridge elaborates the idea of "the clerisy" in *On the Constitution of Church and State* (1829). See Ben Knights, *The Idea of the Clerisy in the Nineteenth Century*.

21. Did the supposedly apolitical working-class readership targeted by the Society for the Diffusion of Useful Knowledge even exist, or was it just wishful thinking on the part of Knight, Henry Brougham, and their middle-class allies? And if it did exist, to what extent did it lead a double life by also reading such radical fare as Cobbett's *Political Register*? This question is not answerable within the mainly rhetorical terms of Klancher's taxonomy, useful though that taxonomy may be.

22. In her Foucauldian study of fiction, Nancy Armstrong at least does not automatically assume that novels always exercise a panoptical or policing function. She agrees with Lennard Davis that the novel's origins "were in some sense criminal" and involved in "violence and social unrest from the lower classes" (266 n. 9). She also points out that

until the latter half of the eighteenth century "the reading of fiction was considered tantamount to seduction" (18). But in the hands of Jane Austen, Sir Walter Scott, Fanny Burney, and others, "certain novels" began to seem morally respectable enough "to occupy the idle hours of women, children, and servants" (18), though Armstrong does not add that they began to seem respectable only to certain readers.

23. Arnold thought of novels in general as a kind of "intellectual food" that, if not always toxic, was intoxicating in the wrong way. Occupying no higher place in the value-hierarchy of cultural forms than that of newspapers, and in contrast to classical poetry and drama, the modern novel for Arnold seemed incapable of exercising the humanizing or disciplinary function of guiding (*interpellating* is the Althusserian term) its readers, by way of "sweetness and light," to "perfection," to be the best they could be. Arnold thus agreed with the many earlier literary critics—Coleridge, for example—who granted to poetry a nearly religious function, but who viewed novel-reading as not just a "pass-time," but a "kill-time," deadening alike to the heart and the mind (Coleridge, *Seven Lectures*, 3). On one of the few occasions when he mentions novels, Arnold agrees with Joubert that most fiction "'has no business to exist'" because it simply mirrors ugly reality without transcending it: most of the novels that pass through booksellers' hands and circulating libraries are just "'monstrosities'" (202). Elsewhere Arnold quotes the French critic Maurice de Guerin on writers of popular fiction, "'whose books, unwelcome to all serious people, welcome to the rest of the world, to novelty-hunters and novel-readers, fill with vanity these vain souls, and then, falling from hands heavy with the languor of satiety, drop for ever into the gulf of oblivion'" (21). The only novelists Arnold has much good to say about are George Sand and Tolstoy, though in his 1881 essay "The Incompatibles," he briefly praises *David Copperfield*. See George Ford, *Dickens and His Readers*, 96–99.

24. On the public library movement in relation to "the fiction question," see Peter Keating, *The Haunted Study*, 412–420, and also Richard Altick, *English Common Reader*, 231–235.

25. The novel may aid and abet the police, as D. A. Miller contends, if only because it is often about crime and punishment (and crime, in the precincts of fiction, rarely goes unpunished). The novel may be a non-material, internalized "panopticon," but what the warden—that is, the reader—sees from this panopticon is fundamentally different from what the warden might have seen from Jeremy Bentham's carceral "dream building" (if it had ever been built). Miller's assertion of "a radical *entanglement* between the nature of the novel and the practice of the police" (2) is certainly true in the very general sense that, in common with all literature, the novel—even at its most criminal, transgressive, or pornographic—upholds the Law because it is rooted in, is a product of, the Symbolic Order. But understanding why and how the novel is *not* the police is surely just as important as understanding how it also instantiates certain ideological and disciplinary effects—ones that of course do entail a sort of internalization of policing. But if the novel were merely an extension of the "long arm of the law," there would have been no reason for anyone to have ever considered it dangerous, even criminal. No one would ever have dreamed, for instance, of bringing criminal proceedings against Flaubert for publishing *Madame Bovary*, or Henry Vizetelly for publishing English translations of Zola, or James Joyce for publishing *Ulysses*.

26. On the female readership and authorship of novels in the late 1700s and early 1800s, see Nancy Armstrong, *Desire and Domestic Fiction*; Ina Ferris, *The Achievement of Literary Authority*; Mary Poovey, *The Proper Lady and the Woman Writer*; and Dale Spender, *Mothers of the Novel*, among others.

27. By "explicit politics," I mean ideological debates about radicalism, revolution, the franchise, and so on. Of course "the personal is political," and so therefore is sexuality. It is also the case that, in representations of the French Revolutionary experience, political and sexual liberation are often equated (on the erotic dimensions of the French Revolution see, for instance, Lynn Hunt, *Family Romance*). But within most novels published between 1760 and 1830, there is no perceived relationship between politics and sexuality.

28. When in 1888 the National Vigilance Association sued Henry Vizetelly, translator and publisher of Zola in English, for the dissemination of "pernicious literature," the issue was taken up in Parliament. One M.P. asked: "Were they to stand still while the country was wholly corrupted by literature of this kind? Were they to wait until the moral fibre of the English race was eaten out, as that of the French was almost? Look what such literature had done for France. It had overspread that country like a torrent, and its poison was destroying the whole national life. France, to-day, was rapidly approaching the condition of Rome at the time of the Caesars" (National Vigilance Association 355). But English literature itself was not far behind the French; the M.P. also condemned the literary "garbage on which the children of London fed . . . the penny dreadful and the penny novelette." Whether French or English in origin, the literature of the masses (or, in Zola's case, to be more accurate, the literature *about* the masses) threatened the nation with ruin; it constituted a "terrible pestilence . . . spreading throughout the country" (356). Though both penny dreadfuls and Zola's novels provoked extreme reactions, it is also the case that, throughout the nineteenth century, many social and cultural observers, including many novelists, worried about the possibly debilitating influence of novels and novel-reading in general on the moral and intellectual fibre of the nation. For the National Vigilance Association and its predecessor, the Society for the Suppression of Vice, see Edward Bristow, *Vice and Vigilance*, especially pp. 32–50 and 201–216, and Donald Thomas, *A Long Time Burning*, 179–213 and 258–272. Both societies were keen to suppress "indecent" literature of various sorts.

2. Gothic Toxins

1. According to Ina Ferris, between the 1790s and 1820s, reviewers "consistently situate the contemporary novel in a context of generic decline from the great and male tradition of the eighteenth century as represented mainly by four novelists: Henry Fielding, Samuel Richardson, Tobias Smollett, and Laurence Sterne" (71). Among the various essays that make such an argument is William Hazlitt's 1815 "Standard Novels and Romances," which Ferris summarizes (73). In *Mothers of the Novel*, Dale Spender notes that, while canonizing the male novelists of the eighteenth century, including Defoe, Watt ignored hundreds of female novelists.

2. In his reception study of Gothic, David Richter hypothesizes a shift in readerly sensibility from what might most simply be called realistic to romantic, but this is tautological: "the Gothic novel came in simultaneously with a new wave in reader response. In answer to the inevitable question—what caused what?—I would reply that the vogue of the Gothic probably functioned as both cause and effect. That is, the Gothic was able to develop as a genre owing to the ready-made presence of an audience segment already partially prepared, by Richardson, Prévost and the sentimental novelists, to read for imaginative play and escape" (Richter 127). But this suggests the opposite of a major shift in readerly sensibility: the readers of Gothic were responding to the same pleasure that they had already experienced in Richardson, etc.

3. Francisco de Goya's etching "The Dream of Reason Produces Monsters" appeared in his *Los Capricios* series, 1810–1815.

4. For a speculative analysis of the novel-reading public in Johnson's time, see J. Paul Hunter, "'The Young, the Ignorant, and the Idle.'"

5. The view that all novels are essentially pornographic is similar to Fredric Jameson's assertion, in the first sentence of *Signatures of the Visible*, that "the visual is *essentially* pornographic" (1)—an apparently essentialist generalization that means, in part, that there is no innocent seeing. Just so, for many early critics of the novel and of mass literacy, there is no innocent reading.

6. As Richardson, writing to Lady Echlin, put it: "Instruction, Madam, is the Pill; Amusement is the Gilding. Writings that do not touch the Passions of the Light and Airy, will hardly ever reach the heart" (qtd. in Warner 5).

7. According to Frye, "Romance is the structural core of all fiction: being directly descended from folktale, it brings us closer than any other aspect of literature to the sense of fiction, considered as a whole, as the epic of the creature, man's [*sic*] vision of his own life as a quest" (15).

8. For an important analysis of Freud's essay on the uncanny as itself a sort of Gothic novel, see Hélène Cixous, "Fiction and Its Phantoms."

9. In *The Schoolmaster* (1570), Roger Ascham declaims against "books of chivalry" whose only purpose is "pastime and pleasure, which, as some say, were made in monasteries by idle monks or wanton canons . . ." (68).

10. Tompkins could have cited even earlier precedents, of course, particularly from Elizabethan and Jacobean drama, as in Shakespeare's *Measure for Measure*. On the nationalistic implications of Gothic fiction, see Cannon Schmitt, *Alien Nation*.

11. On women as novel-readers, see, among others, Alan Richardson, *Literature, Education, and Romanticism*, 167–212. Between Charlotte Lennox's *Female Quixote* and the 1830s, there are many parodies or satires that depict young women as victims of novel-reading. Besides *Northanger Abbey*, among the most notable of these satiric works is Eaton Stannard Barrett's *The Heroine*, first published in 1813, which starts with Cherubina's decision, based on novels, that she is not the daughter of her father, who is merely an untitled farmer, but of a mysterious aristocrat, and also with her father's burning of most of her novels, "by way of purification," as he tells her: "They talk so much of flames, that I suppose they will like to feel them" (32). The conflagration does no good, however; Cherubina has already decided that she, the "victim of thrilling sensibility" (31), will live the life of a "heroine" of romance. For *The Heroine* and many other parody novels and romances, see Archibald Shepperson, *The Novel in Motley*.

12. As noted earlier, the titles Catherine and Isabella read reflect partly on the Gothic productions of the Minerva Press. See Blakey.

13. For a Foucauldian "genealogy" of Gothic writing, see Miles.

14. Though Walpole seeks a certain cultural legitimacy for his fantasy by insisting upon its theatrical properties and precedents, of course it is not a tragedy, much less a Shakespearean one. Walpole echoes *Hamlet* and *Macbeth* and their various ghosts, witches, and preternatural occurrences, but even more clearly he echoes the "mummery" that Ariel, following Prospero's bidding, stages to frighten the courtiers in *The Tempest*. Anne Williams suggests that "Gothic romance is family romance" (32).

15. On Poe, mass culture, and literary hoaxes, see Jonathan Elmer, *Reading at the Social Limit*.

16. Studies that stress this motif include R. F. Brissenden, *Virtue in Distress*, which connects Richardson to the Gothic and to Sadean pornography via the "sentimental novel";

Anna Clark, "The Politics of Seduction in English Popular Culture, 1748–1848"; and Kate Ferguson Ellis, *The Contested Castle*, who begins her study this way: "The strand of popular culture we call the Gothic novel can be distinguished by the presence of homes in which people are locked in and locked out. They are concerned with violence done to familial bonds that is frequently directed against women" (3).

17. "By 'paranoid Gothic' I mean Romantic novels in which a male hero is in a close, usually murderous relation to another male figure, in some respects his 'double,' to whom he seems to be mentally transparent. Examples of the paranoid Gothic include, besides *Frankenstein*, Ann Radcliffe's *The Italian*, William Godwin's *Caleb Williams*, and James Hogg's *Confessions of a Justified Sinner*" (Sedgwick, *Epistemology* 186 n. 10).

18. Though he was not charged with blasphemy, Matthew Arnold makes a similar suggestion in *Culture and Anarchy*, when he opines that the Bible is a bad guide for modern morals and laws relating to marriage. How could it be a good one, asks Arnold, when the wisest of men in the Old Testament had five hundred wives and nine hundred concubines?

19. Ambrosio is the ancestor both of Hawthorne's repressed Puritans and of George Steiner's Nazis, who read Goethe and listen to Beethoven. See Steiner, *In Bluebeard's Castle*, 29–33.

20. For a thorough study of blasphemy in relation to nineteenth-century fiction and culture after Lewis, see Joss Lutz Marsh, *Word Crimes*.

21. In *The Literature of Terror*, David Punter points out that *Caleb Williams* is "usually—and, I believe, reasonably—included in discussions of the Gothic, although this is often only because of the extreme difficulty of relating [it] to anything else" (133). See his full discussion of Godwin's novel, 132–141.

3. The Reading Monster

1. Compare Paulson 216, and also see George Rudé, *The Crowd in the French Revolution*.

2. For the term *hauntology*, Derrida's pun on *ontology*, and for numerous other Gothic metaphors that he elaborates in relation to Marx and the alleged death of Marxism, see his *Specters of Marx*.

3. Lee Sterrenburg notes that Barruel locates the origin of the Illuminati conspiracy in Ingolstadt, where Victor Frankenstein attends university (Sterrenburg 156).

4. These and other examples appear in Roland Bartel, "Shelley and Burke's Swinish Multitude." See also E. P. Thompson's *Making of the English Working Class*, 90.

5. De Maistre continues, with examples that foreshadow *Frankenstein*: "Man, by his own powers, is at most a Vaucanson; to be a Prometheus, he must climb to heaven, for *the legislator cannot gain obedience either by force or by reasoning*" (57; his italics). Vaucanson was famed as the creator of an especially magical-seeming automaton.

6. As Raymond Williams and other historians of the idea of ideology have noted, the term itself first emerged during the French Revolution. Coined by Destutt de Tracy, ideology was to be a science of ideas or consciousness, aimed at the education of citizens of the new republic. First Napoleon, and then Marx and Engels, redefined it as "false consciousness," and, hence, as the modern form of *superstition*. See Williams, *Keywords*, 153–157.

7. Coleridge's negative remarks about "the reading public" are one target of Thomas Love Peacock's satiric rendering of him as Mr. Flosky in *Nightmare Abbey*. Mr. Flosky says: "How can we be cheerful when we are surrounded by a *reading public*, that is grow-

ing too wise for its betters?" (Peacock 71). For the Learned Pig, see Altick, *Shows of London*, 40–41.

8. An entry in Mary Shelley's *Journal* for October 1838 reads: "since I had lost Shelley I have no wish to ally myself to the Radicals—they are full of repulsion to me— violent without any sense of Justice—selfish in the extreme—talking without knowledge— rude, envious, and insolent—I wish to have nothing to do with them" (qtd. in Sterrenburg 168).

9. Autobiographical readings of *Frankenstein* have tended to interpret its nightmarish family romance by identifying Frankenstein as William Godwin and the Monster as his daughter, Mary Shelley. Following Ellen Moers's "Female Gothic" (reproduced in Levine, *The Endurance of Frankenstein*, 77–87), it has also become standard to interpret Victor's creation of the Monster as a nightmarish birth trauma, expressing Mary Shelley's horror over the births and tragic early deaths of her children. And the horror is magnified by recalling that Mary Wollstonecraft died in giving birth to the author of *Frankenstein*. These autobiographical interpretations sometimes also point to the male double-goers in Mary Shelley's life, her husband and Lord Byron, who, however radical their political intentions, marginalized and victimized her no matter what she did or wrote (see, for instance, Knoepflmacher 96–97). How else to explain the fact that *both* Victor and his Monster are gendered male? Whatever the full range of meanings of its gender troubles, *Frankenstein* obviously belongs among the works of paranoid Gothic that George Haggerty and Eve Sedgwick identify with the difficulties and traumas of representing male homosexuality.

10. Compare Peter Brooks's comment that in *Frankenstein* "there is no transcendent signified because the fact of monsterism is never either justified or overcome, but it is simply passed along the [signifying] chain, finally come to inhabit the reader himself who, as animator of the text, is left with the contamination of monsterism. . . . the text remains as indelible record of the monstrous, emblem of language's murderous lack of transcendent reference" ("'Godlike Science'" 220).

11. For an interpretation of *Frankenstein* in relation especially to theories of women's education, see Alan Richardson, *Literature, Education, and Romanticism*: "In describing the education of a monster, Shelley challenges . . . the tradition of writing on female education and conduct associated especially (after Wollstonecraft) with [Rousseau's] *Emile*, in which women are at once sentimentalized and viewed, anxiously, as deformed or monstrous in comparison with an explicitly male norm" (206).

12. The first reviewers of *Frankenstein* often dismiss it in similar terms—"a tissue of horrible and disgusting absurdity," John Wilson Croker calls it (189)—while worrying about its possible nefarious effects on its readers. Croker believes that *Frankenstein* is too "insane" to do much damage, although he writes that "it inculcates no lesson of conduct, manners, or morality; it cannot mend, and will not even amuse its readers, unless their taste have been [already] deplorably vitiated" (190).

13. For various versions of the French Revolution as "family romance," see Lynn Hunt.

14. For Lacan, the mirror-stage is the moment when an infant begins to move from the Imaginary into the Symbolic, into language, and thus into the self-alienation that language entails. Compare Peter Brooks in Levine (207–208).

15. For a related analysis of *Frankenstein* in terms of the epistolary novel and letters not sent, mis-sent, and "correspondence" more generally, see Mary Favret, *Romantic Correspondence*, 176–196. On orality versus writing during the Romantic era, see also Nicholas Hudson, *Writing and European Thought*, 143–160.

16. Slavoj Žižek, *The Sublime Object of Ideology*. In *Enjoy Your Symptom!* Žižek contends that "the monster is the subject of the Enlightenment" (134).

17. George Lillie Craik's two-volume *The Pursuit of Knowledge under Difficulties* was published by the Society for the Diffusion of Useful Knowledge in 1830. It is hardly a publication expressing a working-class radical perspective; instead it is, as Richard Altick makes clear, a forerunner of Samuel Smiles's relentlessly bourgeois, individualist best-seller of 1859, *Self-Help*. Nevertheless, the thought that workers had to pursue knowledge or education "under difficulties" is standard in working-class autobiographies and other publications from well before 1830. On Craik's "machine age" version of "what collections of saints' legends had been to the Middle Ages," see Altick, *The English Common Reader*, 242, and also Charles Knight, *Passages*, 2:133–135.

18. Compare the "Iron Man" or self-acting mule from Andrew Ure's *Philosophy of Manufactures*, cited by Engels (253), and also the ballad by Joseph Mather, quoted in Martha Vicinus, *The Industrial Muse*, 23: "That monster oppression behold how he stalks/ Keeps picking the bones of the poor as he walks . . ." and so forth.

19. The guillotine replaced the gallows in March 1792. Invented by Dr. Joseph-Ignace Guillotin, but named "La Guillotine," this feminized contraption was one of the first machines, during the Industrial Revolution, to be commonly designated as monstrous. Carlyle notes that this "cunningly devised Beheading Machine, which shall become famous and world-famous," was immediately christened through "popular gratitude or levity by a feminine derivative name, as if it were [Dr. Guillotin's] daughter," and treats the "worthy" doctor himself as a sort of mad scientist in a Gothic romance: "Unfortunate Doctor! For two-and-twenty years he, unguillotined, shall hear nothing but guillotine, see nothing but guillotine; then dying, shall through long centuries wander, as it were, a disconsolate ghost, on the wrong side of Styx and Lethe; his name like to outlive Caesar's" (*French Revolution* 114–115).

4. How Oliver Twist Learned to Read, and What He Read

1. For "police gazettes," both legal and illegal, during the early 1830s, see Joel Wiener, *The War of the Unstamped*, 175–177. To avoid the stamp duty on newspapers, many of the police gazettes published fictional crime stories. They were, in part, the new urban substitute for older forms of "street literature," chapbooks and broadsides, that had included such subgenres as hanged men's last words, as reflected in Hannah More's "Mr. Fantom" and also in Godwin's *Caleb Williams*. For the *Hue and Cry*, see R. K. Webb, *British Working-Class Reader*, 75.

2. In *Prince of Fences: The Life and Times of Ikey Solomons*, J. J. Tobias contends that, mainly because Solomon's physical description doesn't match Fagin's, Dickens must not have had him in mind as a model. But Solomons was notorious; Dickens undoubtedly knew about him; and something of his career and character must have rubbed off on Fagin.

3. On criminal elements in penny fiction, see Louis James, 154–170; Richard Maxwell; and Victor Neuberg, 144–174.

4. "The immanent logic of a society based upon the pursuit of private interest," writes Peter Dews, "leads to the totalitarian extinction of that very individuality which originally set this logic in motion" (Dews 154–155). The death of the subject is not something dreamed up by Foucault or poststructuralism; it is instead one result of the dialectic of Enlightenment, a process begun during the eighteenth-century spawning of "disciplines" that match and ultimately overmatch the "liberties" (Foucault, *Discipline*, 222).

5. Has it mattered in the long discourse of modern history that Lombroso considered some insects and even plants to be naturally or congenitally criminal? Perhaps not, but as Stephen Jay Gould notes in *The Mismeasure of Man* (122–145), there is no break in the chain from Lombroso and Galton's eugenicist arguments to the pseudo-scientific speculations of recent sociobiologists about the inherent criminality of the XYY chromosome. If a plant can be criminal, why not a chromosome? On the connections between Benthamism, associationism, and penology, see Forsythe 11–13.

6. See Hollis; Wickwar; and Joel Wiener.

7. Policing discourse always involves criminalizing certain types of culture and, because they cannot be silenced, fencing them off from other types and then patrolling the fences more or less coercively. Literary criticism is a mild form of such policing; legal censorship is obviously more coercive. As Richard Ohmann says in *English in America*, "Better the MLA than the FBI" (252 n. 11).

8. See Philip Collins, "Dickens and the Ragged Schools," and also his *Dickens and Education*, 86–93.

9. At the Lambeth Ragged School, the motto prominently displayed on the wall read, "Thou Shalt Not Steal." See the picture in *The Illustrated London News* for 11 April 1846.

10. For Mary Carpenter, see the biographies by Jo Manton and J. Estlin Carpenter.

11. Kucich cites Humphry House's well-known remark about the contrast between the murder of Nancy and "'the earnest moralities of the Preface! To understand the conjunction of such different moods and qualities in a single man is the beginning of serious criticism of Dickens'" (qtd. in *Repression* 201).

12. For the text of "Sikes and Nancy," see Philip Collins, ed., *Charles Dickens: The Public Readings*. For a suggestive account of Dickens's public readings in relation to issues of social class, mass audience, and the politics of the Second Reform Bill of 1867, see Helen Small, "A Pulse of 124."

13. For an example of environmental determinism emphasizing "slums" and unsanitary housing, see Hollingshead.

14. Although *London Labour and the London Poor* was first published in its now-familiar four-volume format in 1861–1862, the data and interviews were gathered in the preceding decade; the beginnings of the entire project were Mayhew's "letters" on "Labour and the Poor" commissioned by the *Morning Chronicle* and published in that paper between 19 October 1849 and 12 December 1850. It is possible that Mayhew had read Darwin or read about Darwin by 1861–1862, but the economic and statistical ideas in *London Labour* reflect older social science and "natural history" paradigms.

15. For both G. W. M. Reynolds and Edward Lloyd, see Louis James, 25–26, 40–43. John Sutherland notes that Reynolds's *Mysteries of London* sold 40,000 copies per weekly issue (41).

16. For Bakhtin's conception of the "novelistic" properties of modern fiction, see *The Dialogic Imagination*, especially pp. 3–83.

17. "Increasingly in the nineteenth and twentieth century, penal practice and then penal theory will tend to make of the dangerous individual the principal target of punitive intervention" (Foucault, "The Dangerous Individual," 139–140).

18. The sort of argument offered by F. B. Smith in "Mayhew's Convict," *Victorian Studies* 22:4 (Summer 1979), pp. 431–448, seeking to show that the testimony of Mayhew's informants is unreliable and therefore that *London Labour* cannot be naively used as a source of evidence by social historians, is both technically correct and also more proof of my contention that "nomadology" rather than "science" is the genre to which it really

belongs. Otherwise Smith's painstaking demonstration of the lies told by one of Mayhew's subjects is, from my perspective, irrelevant. Of course thieves, prostitutes, beggars, and even seemingly law-abiding street people can't be relied upon to tell the literal truth about their lives. But then who can? Perhaps it's the case that "nomads" are generally more skillfull about telling the truth—in the sense of what's typical or representative about their individual experiences—through the of course treacherous mirrors of fiction than are "straight," bourgeois types, including social historians. From the "sedentary" perspective of "state history," as Deleuze and Guattari put it, the truths of fiction must necessarily seem to be another case of overproduction, or of the wrong sort of production.

19. Anne Humpherys sees Mayhew as unable to reconcile his impulses toward "rebellion and respectability," resulting in "a seemingly self-induced failure" to do anything at all substantial with his life (11), though she also rightly treats *London Labour* as a major achievement.

5. Poor Jack, Poor Jane

1. For the radical, working-class press and "the war of the unstamped" against "the taxes on knowledge," see Patricia Hollis, *The Pauper Press*; William Wickwar, *Struggle for Freedom of the Press*; Joel Wiener, *War of the Unstamped*; David Vincent, *Literacy and Popular Culture*, 241–258; Paul Murphy, *Toward a Working-Class Canon*, 7–31. For Chartist fiction, see Martha Vicinus, *The Industrial Muse*, 113–135.

2. For the Society for the Diffusion of Useful Knowledge and the "cheap literature" movement in the 1820s and 30s, see Bulwer-Lytton, *England and the English*, 291–296; Charles Knight, *Passages*, 2:169–194; Alan Richardson, *Literature, Education, and Romanticism*, 217–232; Harold Smith, *The Society for the Diffusion of Useful Knowledge*; and R. K. Webb, *The British Working-Class Reader*.

3. The ineffectiveness of the SDUK in reaching a working-class readership seemed evident even to some of its promoters. In 1852, Henry Brougham told Matthew Hill that he was afraid "the Useful Knowledge Society," in having "made science entertaining," had won new readers over to fiction rather than fact, "for nothing else is now-a-day [*sic*] read but novels" (qtd. in Altick, *English Common Reader*, 272; 271 n. 29).

4. Industrial novels written to support the Ten Hours Movement include Frances Trollope's *Michael Armstrong, The Factory Boy* (1839) and Charlotte Elizabeth Tonna's *Helen Fleetwood* (1841).

5. In his *Household Words* essay "Railway Strikes," Dickens writes that trade union leaders "are not always, perhaps, the best workmen. They are, sometimes, not workmen at all, but designing persons, who have, for their own base purposes, immeshed the workmen in a system of tyranny and oppression. Through these, on the one hand, and through an imperfect or misguided view of the details of a case on the other, a strike . . . may be easily set a-going" (312).

6. Rosemarie Bodenheimer notes that in the idealized Lancashire of Elizabeth Stone's *William Langshawe, the Cotton Lord* (1842), there are no causes for working-class unrest. Hence, trade unionism is wholly irrational; the strike in the novel is entirely "got up by 'political demagogues'" (Bodenheimer 81).

7. For an important reading of Felix Holt as a man of culture, and of Eliot's novel as an anticipation of Arnold's *Culture and Anarchy*, see Gallagher, *Industrial Reformation*, 217–267. Besides Esther, there are other female Quixotes in industrial novels. Mary Barton, for instance, indulges in daydreams and in "simple, foolish, unworldly ideas she had picked

up from the romances which Miss Simmonds' young ladies were in the habit of recommending to each other" (74). It is partly her novel-reading that encourages Mary to respond romantically to Harry Carson's attempt to seduce her.

8. As Bodenheimer remarks, *Felix Holt* "rejects politics altogether" and is "radical" only by "resisting the way power flows within the middle class and in refusing to fantasize about virtuous arrangements of power within conventional structures of social order" (106, 108).

9. That Luddism in *Shirley* reflects its author's anxieties about Chartism has been often noted, for instance by Terry Eagleton in *Myths of Power* (45–46).

10. As Elizabeth Gaskell points out, Brontë based the character of Robert Moore on William Cartwright of Rawfolds, who was given a reward of £3000 by his fellow manufacturers for defending his mill against the Luddites, and who was rumored to have "some foreign blood in him" (Gaskell, *Life*, 85).

11. "*Shirley* is built on the intertwined stories of unemployed rebellious workers and idle, suppressed middle-class women," Bodenheimer notes; but she adds that it would be "misleading to read the novel in a way that foregrounds its power of social protest" (37). *Shirley* instead reasserts the necessity both of male domination over women and of middle-class "paternalism" over the working class (Bodenheimer 36–53).

12. "But this is not to be a regular autobiography: I am only bound to invoke memory where I know her responses will possess some degree of interest . . ." (98).

13. As Mark Hennelly suggests, the characters in *Jane Eyre* who come closest to being female Quixotes are Georgiana Reed and Blanche Ingram (Hennelly 696).

14. For Terry Eagleton, Bertha "is a projection of Jane's sexually tormented consciousness" (32). For Gayatri Spivak, she is a projection of imperialist guilt and racism. For Gilbert and Gubar, she is the expression of whatever womanly self-assertion and independence that cannot be tamed by Mr. Rochester's patriarchal values. And so forth.

15. It isn't necessary to follow Terry Eagleton in identifying the characters in *Wuthering Heights* with precise social classes or class fractions (Heathcliff first as proletarian, then as a vindictive exaggeration of the violence of capitalism, for instance) to read it as a *general* allegory of class conflict, with gaining and losing literacy as the obvious key to gaining or losing class status and property.

6. Cashing in on the Real in Thackeray and Trollope

1. In "Half a Crown's Worth of Cheap Knowledge" (1838), Thackeray takes the "gentleman" reader of *Fraser's* on a slumming expedition to explore "the literary tastes of the lower class" (132). Thackeray reviews fifteen examples of publications aimed at the working-class reader and identifies these as the results of "the March of Intellect." He simultaneously condemns working-class radicalism as mere "hatred" of the rich and claims that he does not aim to produce a "political dissertation" but "to examine the case merely in a literary point of view" (132). This disclaimer does not of course prevent him from condemning those publications that he considers radical, frivolous, or immoral, which is most of them. There is no similarly explicit expression of anxiety about working-class literacy in Trollope, though the pathetic *illiteracy* of most of the old men in *The Warden*, who sign their Xs to the petition (a mock version of the last Chartist petition of 1848?), comes close.

2. Thackeray's portrayal of "literary men" in *Pendennis* as mostly mercenary "humbugs" precipitated the debate about the dignity of literature between himself, John Forster,

Dickens, and others. See Craig Howes, "*Pendennis* and the Controversy on the 'Dignity of Literature,'" and also Peter Schillingsburg, *Pegasus in Harness*, 17–21.

3. On the narrative instabilities of *Vanity Fair* in relation to its modes of addressing readers, see, among others, Wolfgang Iser, 106–120; Jack Rawlins, 1–35; and Robyn Warhol, 83–100.

4. See Becky's long letter to Amelia: "Sir Pitt is not what we silly girls when we used to read Cecilia at Chiswick, imagined a baronet must have been" (76); "And oh my dear the great hall I am sure is as big and as glum as the great hall in the dear Castle of Udolpho" (78).

5. Amanda Anderson is one recent critic who stresses the analogy between Becky as storyteller, liar, but also active maker of her own life story, and Thackeray as author (Anderson 10–11). Compare the similar parallel between Lizzie Eustace and Trollope that I analyze later in this chapter.

6. Cf. Andrew Miller, *Novels behind Glass*, 163–167. My interpretation of *The Eustace Diamonds* agrees with Miller's, though I see Trollope as more pessimistic than Miller apparently does. While acknowledging the slipperiness of all forms of property and possession (as represented by the disappearing diamonds), including self-possession, Miller nevertheless emphasizes the solidity of Trollope's valorization of property (even when it goes missing) and of Trollope's insistence upon his own "honesty." I am stressing, rather, the paradox involved in the "failure of mimesis": the more the realistic novelist insists upon the truthfulness or honesty of his or her novel, the more she or he has to acknowledge its untruthfulness, its fictionality: remember, dear reader, that the novel you are reading is *merely a novel*, no different in kind from the other sorts of fictional or counterfeit writing that circulate through the text as well as through the body politic.

7. As John Kucich notes, "many of Trollope's assertions about his own honesty, literary or otherwise, are notoriously unreliable" (*Power* 63). Kucich's astute analysis of the productive power of lies in Victorian culture and fiction parallels my argument about realism, though Kucich does not quite arrive at the conclusion that one highly productive form of "lying" was the realistic novel.

8. On the origins of the term and concept *best-seller*, see Peter Keating, *The Haunted Study*, 439–445.

9. In his study of Trollope, Michael Sadleir makes the same judgment: Trollope put his own reputation in the shade for two generations by honestly insisting upon the commodity status of his own novels, or the equation between money and realistic fiction (Sadleir 348–350).

7. Novel Sensations of the 1860s

1. In *Consuming Fictions*, Terry Lovell writes of the period between 1770 and 1820, when "the literary credentials of the novel were at their lowest point," that opposition to fiction amounted to a "moral panic," and goes on to say that such panics occur "whenever a new cultural commodity" appears. In the twentieth century, both cinema and television have aroused such "moral panics" (Lovell 8).

2. Sensation fiction influenced, among others, George Eliot, George Meredith, Thomas Hardy, Ouida, Marie Corelli, Arthur Conan Doyle, and modern mystery-detective fiction. Without drawing hard-and-fast lines between it and earlier Gothic romances or later detective fiction, the sensation novel emerged in the context of the powerful influence of Dickens, of both Gothic and domestic realism in fiction, of stage melodrama, and of "sensational" journalism, bigamy trials, and divorce-law reform. As Alexander Welsh

notes in *George Eliot and Blackmail*, the sensation novel of the 1860s also reflects new developments in communications and transportation: the telegraph, cheap daily newspapers, commuter railway service, tourism, the beginnings of consumerism and advertising on a modern scale. In her 1862 *Blackwood's* review "Sensation Novels," Margaret Oliphant points as well to the shock of major wars—the Crimean War and Indian Mutiny of the 1850s, but also the American Civil War. In the 1850s, she writes, the "distant roar" of warfare came "to form a thrilling accompaniment to the safe life we lead at home." In the 1860s, the Americans, "a race *blasée* and lost in universal *ennui* has bethought itself of the grandest expedient for procuring a new sensation; and albeit we follow at a humble distance, we too begin to feel the need of a supply of new shocks and wonders" (564). Compare her argument to de Sade's about Gothic romances in relation to the French Revolution.

3. For the connections between melodrama and sensation fiction, see, e.g., Winifred Hughes, *Maniac in the Cellar*, 9–15, and Joseph Litvak, *Caught in the Act*, 128–145. Most of the writers of sensation novels also wrote melodramas, and best-sellers such as *East Lynne* and *Lady Audley's Secret* were quickly dramatized. With his enthusiasm for all things theatrical, Dickens set the pattern. "Every writer of fiction," he declared, ". . . writes, in effect, for the stage" (qtd. by Ley 87). In the preface to his early novel *Basil* (1852), Collins asserted that "the Novel and the Play are twin-sisters in the family of Fiction" and invoked the poetic license for "extraordinary accidents and events" that he associated with the theater. And Charles Reade thought of himself as a "philosophical melodramatist" first, a novelist second: fiction was just "a lesser form of the drama" (qtd. in Burns 113). Any piece of fiction—his own, Smollett's *Peregrine Pickle*, Trollope's *Ralph the Heir*, Zola's *L'Assommoir*—was grist for Reade's melodramatic mill. In more than one instance he even converted a play into a novel, rewriting his melodrama *Masks and Faces* (1852), for example, as *Peg Woffington* (1853).

4. Elaine Showalter presents the case for sensation novels as at least proto-feminist in chapter 6 of *A Literature of Their Own*, "Subverting the Feminine Novel: Sensationalism and Feminine Protest," 153–181. This approach is, of course, very different from the Foucauldian one offered by D. A. Miller in *The Novel and the Police*, which treats the sensation novel as exercising surveillance and social control over the specters of transgression that it conjures up.

5. Of course the emergence of the detective in fiction reflects the history of policing. Anthea Trodd shows how sensation novels deal with the development of the Detective Department of the Metropolitan Police from 1842 forward (Trodd 12–44). Inspector Bucket and Sergeant Cuff represent a penetration of criminal low life and of "the mysteries of London" that their creators both envied and identified as part of their own novelistic equipment. But mystery and detection in fiction are also correlatives of the more general growth of professional and technical specialization, and hence express versions of Foucauldian discipline and surveillance, as D. A. Miller claims. As the disintegration of narrative authority in sensation fiction suggests, however, surveillance, despite the totalizing aspirations both of science and of policing, is never total and is always belated: the detective arrives only after the crime has occurred; the novel, narrated in past tense, is always a simulacrum of memory or, in the absence of an omniscient narrator, of memories that are necessarily fragmentary, partial, faulty.

6. According to Fredric Jameson, "a new kind of flatness or depthlessness, a new kind of superficiality in the most literal sense, [is] perhaps the supreme formal feature of all . . . postmodernisms . . ." (*Postmodernism* 9).

7. Of *It Is Never Too Late to Mend*, he says, "a noble passage in the *Times* of Sep-

tember 7 or 8, 1853, touched my heart [and] inflamed my imagination." Of *Hard Cash*, he says that "an able and eloquent leader on private asylums" gave him the main theme for his exposé novel. And *Put Yourself in His Place* grew out of Reade's perusal of *Times* articles "upon trades unions and trade outrages" (Reade 377–378).

8. In *War of the Unstamped*, Joel Wiener writes: "In June 1855 the final remaining penny of the British newspaper duty was removed, and in the following September the *Daily Telegraph* appeared at the price of 1*d*. The era of democratic journalism had formally arrived . . ." (xi). The final tax, on paper, was removed in 1861. For an analysis of sensation fiction in relation to newspaper "sensationalism," see Thomas Boyle, *Black Swine in the Sewers of Hampstead*.

9. Donald Read lists the estimated circulation of the *Daily Telegraph*, which sold for a penny an issue, at 190,000 in 1870, whereas the estimated circulation of the *Times* for that year, which sold for threepence, was 63,000. See also the figures in A. J. Lee, *Origins of the Popular Press*.

10. In 1835, Benjamin Day's New York paper the *Sun* had offered a sensationally false elaboration of British astronomer John Herschel's observations of the moon, describing the strange life-forms it claimed Herschel had seen. Also in 1835, James Gordon Bennett founded the *New York Herald*, and Bennett was not an editor who liked to wait for the news to come to him. His best-known creation of news came in 1871, when he sent Henry Morton Stanley to Africa to discover Livingstone—as if Livingstone had needed discovering or didn't know where he was.

11. *The Monk*, for example, straddles the fence between a gruesome, sadomasochistic thriller and a religious fantasy with horrific but just religious penalties visited upon Ambrosio at the end. The mysteries in *East Lynne*, *Lady Audley's Secret*, and *The Moonstone*, however, have no such even pseudo-religious content.

12. W. R. Greg, "French Fiction: The Lowest Deep," reproduced in Page, *Wilkie Collins: The Critical Heritage*. See also Kate Flint, *The Woman Reader*, 287–288, and Kathleen Tillotson, *Novels of the Eighteen-Forties*, 7–9.

13. In *The Novel and the Police*, D. A. Miller speaks of "the novelistic Panopticon" (32). His argument suggests that, if the narrator as warden has gone missing, the reader takes his place, or in other words incorporates the necessary lessons of policing and surveillance to do the job himself (or herself). But this Foucauldian perspective does not allow him adequately to account for the "nervousness" in readers that he also emphasizes, nor for the dialogical and "novelistic" elements that Bakhtin identifies with the novel in general. Even when they have omniscient narrators, from Bakhtin's perspective novels are never as "monological"—therefore, never as panoptical—as Miller believes them to be.

14. In *Domestic Crime in Victorian Fiction*, Anthea Trodd documents the disreputable social status of the first professional detectives.

15. Several of Collins's other novels—*No Name* and *Man and Wife*, with their treatments of the injustice of the marriage laws, for example—take up social reform themes in the Dickens manner. And no matter how sensational, Reade's novels explicitly advocate various social reforms.

16. According to Thomas, sensation plots "offered up the disturbing possibility that the secret terms in which personal identities and intimate relations had been established within the culture and within the family were themselves fictions, acts of commerce, forms of trade, commodities to be bought and sold. While such novels may have reinforced superficially the conventional values of their readers by promising that every sin would come to light and that overweening class ambition would eventually end in disaster, the

plots were on a more fundamental level deeply subversive of those same values. The secret they ultimately exposed was the essential commercialization of the family and of the individual subjects involved in its most intimate transactions" (482).

17. As Sally Mitchell notes, aspects of sexuality in sensation novels are often not hidden or merely implicit, but explicitly rendered. Though sexual acts are not usually described, "there was a run on scenes of women nursing their infants. Birth became a physical process and not merely a spiritual one; morning sickness and postpartum weakness were used as plot devices; new fathers emerged shaken and restored to moral rectitude by realizing what their wives had gone through in the birth chamber," and so on (Mitchell 87).

18. Certainly bigamy, adultery, and the problem of divorce law were much on the minds of Victorians in the 1860s. Jeanne Fahnestock has shown the influence of—among other "sensational" events—the 1861 Yelverton bigamy-divorce trial on the fiction of Braddon, Reade, and others. "After the Yelverton revelations, the public was painfully aware of the disgraceful accumulation of laws governing marriage . . . which made bigamy legally possible" (50–52); Captain Yelverton himself escaped without serious legal penalty.

19. "Detective fiction involves the transformation of a fragmented and incomplete set of events into a more ordered and complete understanding. As such it seems to bridge a private psychological experience, like dreaming, and literary experience in general. And like a psychoanalysis, the detective story reorders our perception of the past through language" (Hutter 191). On sensation fiction and psychoanalysis, see also Welsh, *George Eliot and Blackmail*, 25–26.

20. Sensation novels, Winifred Hughes points out, "reveal a recurrent preoccupation with the loss or duplication of identity. . . . Everywhere in the lesser sensation novels the unwitting protagonists experience their strange encounters with the empty form of the *doppelgänger*." Hughes goes on to point out that "incident as well as character is subject to the principle of duality." The plots of sensation novels "are typically structured around a recurrence of similar or identical situations, not infrequently in the shape of dreams or omens and their ultimate fulfillment." A structuralist explanation for this doubling of incidents can be found in Tzvetan Todorov's essay on detective novels in *The Poetics of Prose*, in which Todorov shows that they are always double narratives. The first narrative concerns the past and the crime that has been committed; it is wound up and unraveled in the second narrative, which concerns the present and recounts the detection of the cause of the crime. Todorov relates this pattern of double narration to the Formalist distinction between "fable," which corresponds to "what happened in life," and "subject" or plot, which corresponds to "the way the author presents it to us." But in the detective novel "what happens in life" is virtually reduced to a variant of "the way the author presents it to us." Whereas serious literature imitates life partly by reducing and simplifying its scale and complexity, the mystery novel imitates serious literature by carrying its reductive and simplifying tendencies to extremes. Like the sensation novel from which it evolved, the mystery novel shrinks "fable" to a single event or a few related ones (a crime or crimes, murder or theft often combined in sensation novels with bigamy and the assumption of false identities), just as it also shrinks mystery to a soluble level and diverts the problem of identity into a pattern of exorcism or of the projection of guilt onto another. "Plot" then follows the path of detection through conveniently placed clues to the final explanation of this simplified version of "fable," correctly identifying the culprit—the personified cause of the "fable"—and dishing out punishment and rewards. Like the fatal "hand" that keeps pointing Robert Audley down the path of detection, or like the pattern of improbable

coincidences in most melodramas and sensation novels, the unraveling of the plot seems to represent dimly the working out of destiny: everything is put back in order at the end, and all questions have been answered.

21. For analyses of Braddon's attitude toward novel-reading as reflected in *The Doctor's Wife*, see Robert Paul Wolff, *Sensational Victorian*, 126–131, and Kate Flint, *The Woman Reader*, 288–291.

8. The Educations of Edward Hyde and Edwin Reardon

1. Honoré Fregier may have been the first to use the phrase *dangerous classes*; his *Des classes dangereuses de la population dans les grandes villes* appeared in 1840. The phrase was current in English by the 1850s, along with *criminal classes*, *predatory classes*, and some others. See Gertrude Himmelfarb, *The Idea of Poverty*, 371–400.

2. For the impact of Fenianism on late-Victorian fiction, see Barbara Melchiori, *Terrorism in the Late Victorian Novel*.

3. On handwriting and the difficulties of maintaining secrecy in an age of rapidly developing mass communications, see Alexander Welsh, *George Eliot and Blackmail*, 55–56.

4. In the parliamentary debates leading up to passage of the Education Act of 1870, Lowe said in his speech of 15 July 1867, "I believe it will be absolutely necessary that you should prevail on our future masters to learn their letters" (qtd. in John Hurt, *Elementary Schooling and the Working Class*, 21). I have rendered his language as it has been frequently, and dramatically, misquoted: "We must educate our masters."

5. For a general account of how late-Victorian intellectuals responded to "the masses" and mass culture, see John Carey, *The Intellectuals and the Masses*. Jerrold Hogle's interpretation of *Jekyll and Hyde* in terms of Julia Kristeva's concept of "abjection" makes perfect sense in psychoanalytic terms; I am suggesting that, as it is usually figured, "the masses" is a sociopolitically "abject" category. See Hogle, "Struggle for a Dichotomy," in Veeder and Hirsch, eds., *Dr Jekyll and Mr Hyde after One Hundred Years*. For that matter, all of the psychoanalytic interpretations of Stevenson's tale in Veeder and Hirsch's anthology make sense, but do not preclude the more historical interpretation I am presenting here. Besides Hogle's essay, see also the essays by Veeder, Peter Garrett, and Ronald Thomas.

6. For accounts of the publishing situation in late-Victorian Britain, see Nigel Cross, *The Common Writer*; Norman Feltes, *Literary Capital*; John Gross, *Rise and Fall of the Man of Letters*; and Peter Keating, *The Haunted Study*.

7. For Tillotson's, see Nigel Cross, *Common Writer*, 208; Peter Keating, *Haunted Study*, 44–45. Fiction had appeared in newspapers or, at least, cheap periodicals purporting to carry news well before the 1870s, but not usually by middle-class, "respectable" authors. In the 1830s and 1840s, as Kathleen Tillotson notes, "the new popular weekly papers were providing serial fiction for the masses." She mentions the *Family Herald*, *Lloyd's Penny Weekly Miscellany*, and *Reynolds' Miscellany*, and notes that such penny periodicals paved "the way for Dickens's twopenny weekly *Household Words*" (31–32). For fiction in the cheap papers of the 1830s, see Louis James, *Fiction for the Working Man*, 12–27, and Joel Wiener, *War of the Unstamped*, 173–178. For fiction in the Chartist newspaper, the *Northern Star*, and in other working-class periodicals during the 1840s, see Louis James and also Paul Murphy, *Toward a Working-Class Canon*, 91–96.

8. On the emergence of literary agents like Whelpdale in the 1880s and after, see Peter Keating, *The Haunted Study*, 64–71.

9. "The mirror in the roadway" is Stendhal's often-quoted metaphor for realism from *Le Rouge et le Noir*, chap. 69.

9. Overbooked versus Bookless Futures in Late-Victorian Fiction

1. Morris's model for *The Earthly Paradise* is Chaucer, but Chaucer's realism gives way to an explicit escapism. In *Sigurd the Volsung*, Morris tries to recapture the Icelandic skald's rugged sense of heroism and of conflict with nature; but here, too, the poet is lost in the past, not grappling with the problems of "six counties overhung with smoke." Instead of proclaiming himself to be a romantic visionary or seer, in all of his major poems Morris implies or declares, "Of heaven or hell I have no power to sing." In *Chants for Socialists*, Morris addresses the social problems of late Victorian Britain, but his stance is again self-effacing, that of socialist hymn-writer, using familiar language from the Bible and from political oratory for the good of the cause.

2. From his liberal perspective, Matthew Arnold had made a similar argument in his preface to the 1853 volume of his poetry. Explaining why he had withdrawn his own greatest poem, "Empedocles on Etna," from republication, Arnold argued that it was no longer possible to write great poetry in the modern era when "the dialogue of the mind with itself" had begun. By this logic, however, he condemned all of his poetry, not just "Empedocles."

3. See Patrick Parrinder, ed., *H. G. Wells: The Critical Heritage*, 169–174.

4. See, for instance, Rosalind Williams, *Dream Worlds*, 80–83, quoting Louis Haugmard in 1913: "'the masses' are like a grown-up child who demands a picture album to leaf through in order to forget his miseries. . . . Through [the cinema] the charmed masses will learn not to think anymore, to resist all desire to reason and to construct, to open their large and empty eyes, only to look, look, look. . . ."

5. There is some evidence that the new mass media—the movies, at least—stimulate rather than retard the reading of books, especially novels. "The cinema and the wireless were most important in promoting reading," according to Joseph McAleer (64). For the mass media in relation to "cultivated elites" and "the aesthetic tradition," see also LeMaheiu, *A Culture for Democracy*.

WORKS CITED

Ackland, Joseph. "Elementary Education and the Decay of Literature." *The Nineteenth Century* 35 (March 1894): 412–423.

Aday, David P. *Social Control at the Margins: Toward a General Understanding of Deviance*. Belmont, Calif.: Wadsworth, 1990.

Alison, Archibald. "Progress of Social Disorganization, Part 1: The Schoolmaster." *Blackwood's Magazine* 35 (Feb. 1834): 228–248.

Allott, Miriam, ed. *Novelists on the Novel*. New York: Columbia UP, 1966.

Altick, Richard D. "Education, Print, and Paper in *Our Mutual Friend*." In *Writers, Readers and Occasions*: 52–68.

———. *The English Common Reader: A Social History of the Mass Reading Public 1800–1900*. Chicago: U of Chicago, 1963.

———. "English Publishing and the Mass Audience in 1852." In *Writers, Readers and Occasions*: 141–158.

———. *The Shows of London*. Cambridge, MA: Harvard UP, 1978.

———. *Victorian Studies in Scarlet*. New York: Norton, 1970.

———. *Writers, Readers and Occasions: Selected Essays on Victorian Literature and Life*. Columbus: Ohio State UP, 1989.

Anderson, Amanda. *Tainted Souls and Painted Faces: The Rhetoric of Fallenness in Victorian Culture*. Ithaca: Cornell UP, 1993.

Anderson, Benedict. *Imagined Communities: Reflections on the Origin and Spread of Nationalism*. London: Verso, 1991.

Armstrong, Nancy. *Desire and Domestic Fiction: A Political History of the Novel*. Oxford: Oxford UP, 1987.

Arnold, Matthew. *Culture and Anarchy*. Cambridge: Cambridge UP, 1963.

Arnold, Matthew. "Copyright." In *English Literature and Irish Politics*. Ann Arbor: U of Michigan P, 1973: 114–135.

———. *Lectures and Essays in Criticism*. Ann Arbor: U of Michigan P, 1962.

———. "Up to Easter." In *Essays, Letters, and Reviews by Matthew Arnold*. Ed. Fraser Neiman. Cambridge, Mass.: Harvard UP, 1960: 338–354.

Ascham, Roger. *The Schoolmaster*. Ed. Lawrence V. Ryan. Ithaca: Cornell UP, 1967.

Auden, W. H. *The Dyer's Hand and Other Essays*. New York: Vintage, 1968.

Austen, Jane. *Northanger Abbey*. London: Penguin, 1985.

Bakhtin, Mikhail. *The Dialogic Imagination*. Austin: U of Texas P, 1981.

Baldick, Chris. *In Frankenstein's Shadow: Myth, Monstrosity, and Nineteenth-Century Writing*. Oxford: Clarendon, 1987.

Barish, Jonas. *The Antitheatrical Prejudice*. Berkeley: U of California P, 1981.

Barrett, Eaton Stannard. *The Heroine; or, Adventures of Cherubina*. 1815. London: Elkin Mathews and Marrot, 1927.

Bartel, Roland. "Shelley and Burke's Swinish Multitude." *Keats-Shelley Journal* 18 (1969): 4–9.

Bartley, George C. T. *The Schools for the People*. London: Bell and Daldy, 1871.

Becker, George J., ed. *Documents of Modern Literary Realism*. Princeton: Princeton UP, 1963.

Benjamin, Walter. "The Work of Art in the Age of Mechanical Reproduction." In *Illuminations*. Ed. Hannah Arendt. New York: Schocken, 1969: 217–251.

Bennett, Arnold. *The Author's Craft and Other Critical Writings of Arnold Bennett*. Ed. Samuel Hynes. Lincoln: U of Nebraska P, 1968.

Besant, Walter. "Literature as a Career." In *Essays and Historiettes*. Port Washington, N.Y.: Kennikat, 1970: 308–336.

Blake, William. *Selected Poetry and Prose*. Ed. Northrop Frye. New York: Random, 1953.

Blakey, Dorothy. *The Minerva Press, 1790–1820*. London: Oxford UP, 1959.

Block, Ed, Jr. "James Sully, Evolutionist Psychology, and Late Victorian Gothic Fiction." *Victorian Studies* 25 (1982): 443–467.

Bodenheimer, Rosemarie. *The Politics of Story in Victorian Social Fiction*. Ithaca: Cornell UP, 1988.

Botting, Fred. *Making Monstrous: Frankenstein, Criticism, Theory*. Manchester UP, 1991.

Boumelha, Penny. *Charlotte Brontë*. Bloomington: Indiana UP, 1990.

Bourdieu, Pierre. *The Field of Cultural Production*. New York: Columbia UP, 1993.

Bowlby, Rachel. *Just Looking: Consumer Culture in Dreiser, Gissing and Zola*. London and New York: Methuen, 1985.

Boyle, Thomas. *Black Swine in the Sewers of Hampstead: Beneath the Surface of Victorian Sensationalism*. New York: Penguin, 1990.

Braddon, Mary Elizabeth. *Lady Audley's Secret*. New York: Dover, 1974.

Brantlinger, Patrick. *Bread and Circuses: Theories of Mass Culture as Social Decay*. Ithaca: Cornell UP, 1983.

Brissenden, R. F. *Virtue in Distress: Studies in the Novel of Sentiment from Richardson to Sade*. New York: Harper, 1974.

Bristow, Edward. *Vice and Vigilance: Purity Movements in Britain since 1700*. London: Gill and Macmillan, 1977.

Brontë, Charlotte. *Jane Eyre*. Oxford: Oxford UP, 1969.

———. *Shirley*. Oxford: Oxford UP, 1979.

Brontë, Emily. *Wuthering Heights*. Oxford: Oxford UP, 1976.

Brooks, Peter. "'Godlike Science/Unhallowed Arts': Language, Nature, and Monstrosity." George Levine, ed. *The Endurance of Frankenstein*. 205–220.

———. *The Melodramatic Imagination: Balzac, Henry James, Melodrama, and the Mode of Excess*. New York: Columbia UP, 1985.

Bulwer-Lytton, Edward. *England and the English*. Chicago: U of Chicago P, 1870.

Burke, Edmund. *Reflections on the Revolution in France*. Ed. Connor Cruise O'Brien. Harmondsworth: Penguin, 1976.

———. *Letters on a Regicide Peace*. In *Works*, vol. 5. Boston: Little, Brown, 1881.

Burns, Wayne. *Charles Reade: A Study in Victorian Authorship*. New York: Bookman, 1961.

Butler, Marilyn. *Jane Austen and the War of Ideas*. Oxford: Clarendon, 1975.

———. *Maria Edgeworth*. Oxford: Clarendon, 1972.

Calder, Jenni. *Robert Louis Stevenson: A Life Study*. New York: Oxford UP, 1980.

Carey, John. *The Intellectuals and the Masses: Pride and Prejudice among the Literary Intelligentsia, 1880–1939*. London: Faber, 1992.

Carlyle, Thomas. *Chartism*. In *English and Other Critical Essays*. London: Dent, Everyman's Library, 1964.

————. *The French Revolution*. New York: Modern Library, n.d.

Carpenter, J. Estlin. *The Life and Work of Mary Carpenter*. London: Macmillan, 1881.

Carpenter, Mary. *Juvenile Delinquents*. 1853; Montclair, N.J.: Patterson Smith, 1970.

————. *Reformatory Schools for the Children of the Perishing and Dangerous Classes and for Juvenile Offenders*. 1853; London: Woburn, 1968.

Certeau, Michel de. *The Practice of Everyday Life*. Berkeley: U of California P, 1988.

Chadwick, Edwin. "Preventive Police." *London Review* 1 (Feb. 1829): 252–308.

Chambers, William. *Memoir of Robert Chambers, with Autobiographic Reminiscences of William Chambers*. New York: Scribner's, 1872.

Cixous, Hélène. "Fiction and Its Phantoms: A Reading of Freud's *Das Unheimliche* (The 'uncanny')." *New Literary History* 7:3 (Spring 1976): 525–548.

Clark, Anna. "The Politics of Seduction in English Popular Culture, 1748–1848." In *The Progress of Romance: The Politics of Popular Fiction*. Ed. Jean Radford. London and New York: Routledge, 1986: 47–70.

Cohen, Stanley, and Andrew Scull. *Social Control and the State: Historical and Comparative Essays*. Oxford: M. Robertson, 1983.

Coleridge, Samuel Taylor. *Coleridge's Miscellaneous Criticism*. Ed. Thomas Raysor. Cambridge, MA: Harvard UP, 1936.

————. *Lay Sermons*. Ed. R. J. White. *Collected Works*, vol. 6. Princeton: Princeton UP, 1972.

————. *Seven Lectures on Shakespeare and Milton*. London: Chapman and Hall, 1856.

Collins, Mortimer. *Marquis and Merchant*. 3 vols. London: Hurst and Blackett, 1870.

Collins, Philip, ed. *Charles Dickens: The Public Readings*. Oxford: Clarendon, 1975.

————. *Dickens and Crime*. Bloomington: Indiana UP, 1968.

————. *Dickens and Education*. London: Macmillan, 1964.

————. "Dickens and the Ragged Schools." *Dickensian* 55:328 (May 1959): 94–109.

Collins, Wilkie. *Armadale*. New York: Dover, 1977.

————. *The Moonstone*. Harmondsworth: Penguin, 1979.

————. "Petition to the Novel-Writers." *My Miscellanies*: 107–118.

————. "Reminiscences of a Story-teller." *Universal Review* 1 (May–August 1888): 182–192.

————. "The Unknown Public." *My Miscellanies*. London: Chatto and Windus, 1875.

Cottom, Daniel. "*Frankenstein* and the Monster of Representation." *Substance* 28 (1980): 60–71.

Croker, John. "From the *Quarterly Review* (January 1818)." Excerpt of review in Mary Shelley, *Frankenstein*: 187–190.

Cross, Nigel. *The Common Writer: Life in Nineteenth-Century Grub Street*. Cambridge: Cambridge UP, 1985.

Cullen, Michael J. *The Statistical Movement in Early Victorian England: The Foundations of Empirical Social Research*. Hassocks: Harvester, 1975.

Curtis, L. P. *Anglo-Saxons and Celts: A Study of Anti-Irish Prejudice in Victorian England*. Bridgeport, Conn.: Bridgeport UP, 1968.

Cvetkovich, Ann. *Mixed Feelings: Feminism, Mass Culture, and Victorian Sensationalism*. New Brunswick, N.J.: Rutgers UP, 1992.

Dalziel, Margaret. *Popular Fiction 100 Years Ago: An Unexplored Tract of Literary History*. London: Cohen and West, 1957.

Davis, Lennard. *Factual Fictions: The Origins of the English Novel*. New York: Columbia UP, 1983.

Defoe, Daniel. *Roxana, The Fortunate Mistress*. London: Penguin, 1982.

Deleuze, Gilles, and Felix Guattari. *A Thousand Plateaus: Capitalism and Schizophrenia*. Minneapolis: U of Minnesota P, 1987.

Derrida, Jacques. *Disseminations*. Chicago: U of Chicago P, 1981.

———. *Given Time I: Counterfeit Money*. Chicago: U of Chicago P, 1992.

———. *Specters of Marx*. New York and London: Routledge, 1994.

Dews, Peter. *Logics of Disintegration: Post-Structuralist Thought and the Claims of Critical Theory*. London: Verso, 1987.

Dickens, Charles. "Crime and Education." *Miscellaneous Papers*: 1:25–29.

———. "Ignorance and Crime." *Miscellaneous Papers*: 1:107–110.

———. *Miscellaneous Papers*. Ed. P. J. M. Scott. Millwood, N.Y.: Kraus Reprints, 1983. 2 vols.

———. *Oliver Twist*. Harmondsworth: Penguin, 1985.

———. *Our Mutual Friend*. Oxford: Oxford UP, 1989.

———. "Railway Strikes." *Miscellaneous Papers*: 1:310–316.

Dijsktra, Bram. *Defoe and Economics: The Fortunes of Roxana in the History of Interpretation*. New York: St. Martin's, 1987.

Disraeli, Benjamin. *Sybil, or The Two Nations*. Harmondsworth: Penguin, 1980.

Donajgrodzki, A. J., ed. *Social Control in Nineteenth-Century Britain*. London: Croom Helm, 1977.

Dowling, Linda. *Language and Decadence in the Victorian Fin-de-Siècle*. Princeton: Princeton UP, 1986.

Dunae, Patrick A. "Penny Dreadfuls: Late Nineteenth-Century Boys' Literature and Crime." *Victorian Studies* 22 (1979): 133–150.

Eagleton, Terry. *Myths of Power: A Marxist Study of the Brontës*. London: Macmillan, 1988.

Eigner, Edwin. *Robert Louis Stevenson and Romantic Tradition*. Princeton: Princeton UP, 1966.

Eliot, George. *Felix Holt, the Radical*. Oxford: Clarendon, 1980.

Eliot, T. S. "Wilkie Collins and Dickens." In *Selected Essays*. New York: Harcourt, 1960: 409–418.

Ellis, Kate Ferguson. *The Contested Castle: Gothic Novels and the Subversion of Domestic Ideology*. Urbana: U of Illinois P, 1989.

Ellis, S. M. *William Harrison Ainsworth and His Friends*. London: Lane, 1911. 2 vols.

Elmer, Jonathan. *Reading at the Social Limit: Affect, Mass Culture, and Edgar Allan Poe*. Stanford: Stanford UP, 1995.

Emsley, Clive. *Crime and Society in England, 1750–1900*. New York: Longman, 1987.

Engels, Friedrich. *The Condition of the Working Class in England*. Tr. W. O. Henderson and W. H. Chaloner. Stanford: Stanford UP, 1968.

Fahnestock, Jeanne. "Bigamy: The Rise and Fall of a Convention." *Nineteenth Century Fiction*. 36:1 (June 1981): 47–71.

Favret, Mary. *Romantic Correspondence: Women, Politics, and the Fiction of Letters*. Cambridge: Cambridge UP, 1993.

Feltes, Norman. *Literary Capital and the Late Victorian Novel*. Madison: U of Wisconsin P, 1993.

———. *Modes of Production of Victorian Novels*. Chicago: U of Chicago P, 1986.

Ferris, Ina. *The Achievement of Literary Authority: Gender, History, and the Waverley Novels*. Ithaca: Cornell UP, 1991.

Fielding, Henry. *The History of Tom Jones.* 2 vols. Ed. Martin C. Battestin and Fredson Bowers. Middletown, Conn.: Wesleyan UP, 1975. vol. 1.

Flint, Kate. "Women, Men and the Reading of *Vanity Fair.*" In James Raven, Helen Small, and Naomi Tadmor, eds., *The Practice and Representation of Reading in England.* Cambridge: Cambridge UP, 1996: 246–262.

———. *The Woman Reader 1837–1914.* Oxford: Oxford UP, 1993.

Ford, George. *Dickens and His Readers: Aspects of Novel-Criticism since 1836.* New York: Norton, 1965.

Forster, John. *The Life of Charles Dickens.* Boston: Osgood, 1875. 2 vols.

Forsythe, William James. *The Reform of Prisoners 1830–1900.* New York: St. Martin's, 1987.

Foucault, Michel. "The Dangerous Individual." In *Politics, Philosophy, Culture: Interviews and Other Writings 1977–1984.* Ed. Lawrence D. Kritzman. New York: Routledge, 1988: 125–151.

———. *Discipline and Punish.* New York: Vintage, 1979.

———. *The History of Sexuality-I: An Introduction.* Tr. Robert Hurley. New York: Vintage, 1980.

———, ed. *I, Pierre Rivière.* Tr. Frank Jellinek. New York: Pantheon, 1987.

———. *Language, Counter-Memory, Practice.* Ithaca: Cornell UP, 1977.

———. *Madness and Civilization: A History of Insanity in the Age of Reason.* New York: Vintage, 1971.

———. *Power/Knowledge: Selected Interviews and Other Writings 1972–1977.* Ed. Colin Gordon. New York: Pantheon, 1980.

Freud, Sigmund. *Civilization and Its Discontents.* 1930. New York: Norton, 1961.

Frye, Northrop. *The Secular Scripture: A Study of the Structure of Romance.* Cambridge, Mass.: Harvard UP, 1976.

Gagnier, Regenia. *Subjectivities: A History of Self-Representation in Britain, 1832–1920.* New York and Oxford: Oxford UP, 1991.

Gallagher, Catherine. "The Body versus the Social Body in the Works of Thomas Malthus and Henry Mayhew." Catherine Gallagher and Thomas Laqueur, eds. *The Making of the Modern Body: Sexuality and Society in the Nineteenth Century.* Berkeley: U of California P, 1987: 83–106.

———. *The Industrial Reformation of English Fiction, 1832–1867.* Chicago: U of Chicago P, 1985.

Gallaway, W. F. "The Conservative Attitude toward Fiction, 1770–1830." *PMLA* 55 (1940): 1041–1059.

Garrett, Peter K. "Cries and Voices: Reading *Jekyll and Hyde.*" William Veeder and Gordon Hirsch, eds. *Dr Jekyll and Mr Hyde after One Hundred Years*: 59–72.

Gaskell, Elizabeth. *The Life of Charlotte Brontë.* Oxford: World's Classics, 1966.

———. *Mary Barton.* Harmondsworth: Penguin, 1970.

Gattrell, V. A. C. "Crime, Authority and the Policeman-State." F. M. L. Thompson, ed., *The Cambridge Social History of Britain*, vol. 3, *Social Agencies and Institutions.* Cambridge: Cambridge UP, 1990: 243–310.

Gibbs, Jack P., ed. *Social Control: Views from the Social Sciences.* Beverly Hills, Calif.: Sage, 1982.

Gilbert, Sandra, and Susan Gubar. *The Madwoman in the Attic.* New Haven: Yale UP, 1979.

Gilbert, W. S. *A Sensation Novel in Three Volumes.* London: Joseph Williams, 1912.

Gissing, George. *New Grub Street*. London: Penguin, 1985.

———. *The Odd Women*. London: Penguin, 1993.

———. *The Private Papers of Henry Ryecroft*. New York: Signet Classics, 1961.

Godwin, William. *Caleb Williams*. London: Oxford UP, 1970.

———. *Enquiry Concerning Political Justice*. Harmondsworth: Penguin, 1985.

Gosse, Edmund. "The Tyranny of the Novel." *National Review* 19 (April 1892): 163–175.

Gould, Stephen Jay. *The Mismeasure of Man*. New York: Norton, 1981.

Goux, Jean-Joseph. *The Coiners of Language*. Norman: Oklahoma UP, 1994.

Graff, H. J. *The Legacies of Literacy: Continuities and Contradictions in Western Culture and Society*. Bloomington: Indiana UP, 1987.

———. *The Literacy Myth: Literacy and Social Structure in the Nineteenth-Century City*. New York: Academic, 1979.

Graham, Kenneth. *English Criticism of the Novel, 1865–1900*. Oxford: Oxford UP, 1965.

Greenwood, Thomas. *Public Libraries: A History of the Movement. . . .* London: Cassell, 1891.

Greg, W. R. "French Fiction: The Lowest Deep." *National Review* 11 (1860): 400–427.

Gross, John. *The Rise and Fall of the Man of Letters: English Literary Life since 1800*. Harmondsworth: Penguin, 1969.

Grylls, David. *The Paradox of Gissing*. London: Allen and Unwin, 1986.

Habermas, Jürgen. *The Structural Transformation of the Public Sphere*. Cambridge, Mass.: MIT P, 1989.

Haggerty, George. "The Gothic Novel, 1764–1824." In *The Columbia History of the British Novel*. Ed. John Richetti. 220–246.

———. "Literature and Homosexuality in the Late Eighteenth Century: Walpole, Beckford, and Lewis." In *Homosexual Themes in Literary Studies*. Wayne R. Dynes and Stephen Donaldson, eds. New York: Garland, 1992. 8: 167–177.

Hammerton, J. A. *Stevensoniana: An Anecdotal Life and Appreciation of Robert Louis Stevenson*. Edinburgh: John Grant, 1907.

Hammond, J. L., and Barbara Hammond. *The Town Labourer: The New Civilization, 1760–1832*. Garden City, N.Y.: Anchor, 1968.

Heidler, Joseph P. *The History, from 1770 to 1800, of English Criticism of Prose Fiction*. Urbana: U of Illinois P, 1928.

Heller, Tamar. *Dead Secrets: Wilkie Collins and the Female Gothic*. New Haven: Yale UP, 1992.

Henderson, Philip. *William Morris: His Life, Work, and Friends*. New York: McGraw–Hill, 1967.

Hennelly, Mark M., Jr. "*Jane Eyre*'s Reading Lesson." *ELH* 51 (1984): 693–717.

Hiley, Nicholas. "'Can't You Find Me Something Nasty?': Circulating Libraries and Literary Censorship in Britain from the 1890s to the 1910s." In *Censorship and the Control of Print in England and France 1600–1910*. Robin Myers and Michael Harris, eds. Winchester: St. Paul's Bibliographies, 1992: 123–147.

Himmelfarb, Gertrude. *The Idea of Poverty: England in the Early Industrial Age*. New York: Vintage, 1985.

Hirsch, Gordon. "*Frankenstein*, Detective Fiction, and *Jekyll and Hyde*." William Veeder and Gordon Hirsch, eds. *Dr Jekyll and Mr Hyde after One Hundred Years*: 223–246.

Hobbes, Thomas. *Leviathan*. New York: Collier, 1962.

Hobson, J. A. *The Psychology of Jingoism*. London: Grant Richards, 1901.

Hogle, Jerrold E. "The Struggle for a Dichotomy: Abjection in Jekyll and His Interpreters." William Veeder and Gordon Hirsch, eds. *Dr Jekyll and Mr Hyde after One Hundred Years*: 161–207.

Hollingshead, John. *Ragged London in 1861*. London: Everyman's Library, 1986.

Hollingsworth, Keith. *The Newgate Novel, 1830–1847*. Detroit: Wayne State UP, 1963.

Hollis, Patricia. *The Pauper Press: A Study in Working-Class Radicalism of the 1830s*. London: Oxford UP, 1970.

Howes, Craig. "*Pendennis* and the Controversy on the 'Dignity of Literature.'" *Nineteenth Century Literature* 41 (Dec. 1986): 269–298.

Hudson, Nicholas. *Writing and European Thought, 1600–1830*. Cambridge, Mass.: Cambridge UP, 1994.

Hughes, Winifred. *The Maniac in the Cellar: Sensation Novels of the 1860s*. Princeton: Princeton UP, 1980.

Humpherys, Anne. *Travels into the Poor Man's Country: The Work of Henry Mayhew*. Athens: U of Georgia P, 1977.

Hunt, Lynn. *The Family Romance of the French Revolution*. Berkeley: U of California P, 1992.

Hunter, J. Paul. "'The Young, the Ignorant, and the Idle': Some Notes on Readers and the Beginning of the English Novel." In *Anticipations of the Enlightenment in England, France, and Germany*. Alan C. Kors and Paul J. Korshin, eds. Philadelphia: U of Pennsylvania P, 1987: 259–282.

Hurt, J. S. *Elementary Schooling and the Working Classes, 1860–1918*. London: Routledge and Kegan Paul, 1979.

Hutter, Albert. "Dreams, Transformations, and Literature: The Implications of Detective Fiction." *Victorian Studies* 19 (1975): 181–209.

Hutton, Richard Holt. "Sensational Novels." *The Spectator* (August 8, 1868): 931–932.

Huyssen, Andreas. *After the Great Divide: Modernism, Mass Culture, Postmodernism*. Bloomington: Indiana UP, 1986.

Ignatieff, Michael. *A Just Measure of Pain: The Penitentiary in the Industrial Revolution, 1750–1850*. New York: Pantheon, 1978.

Iser, Wolfgang. *The Implied Reader: Patterns of Communication in Prose Fiction from Bunyan to Beckett*. Baltimore and London: Johns Hopkins UP, 1974.

James, Henry. "Miss Braddon." *The Nation* 1 (9 Nov. 1865): 593–594.

James, Louis. *Fiction for the Working Man, 1830–1850*. London: Oxford UP, 1963.

Jameson, Fredric. *The Political Unconscious: Narrative as a Socially Symbolic Act*. Ithaca: Cornell UP, 1982.

———. *Postmodernism: or, The Cultural Logic of Late Capitalism*. Durham: Duke UP, 1991.

———. *Signatures of the Visible*. New York and London: Routledge, 1992.

Jebb, Henry Gladwyn. *Out of the Depths: The Story of a Woman's Life*. London: Macmillan, 1859.

[Johns, B. G.]. "The Literature of the Streets." *Edinburgh Review* 165 (1887): 40–65.

Johnson, Edgar. *Charles Dickens: His Tragedy and Triumph*. 2 vols. New York: Simon and Schuster, 1952.

Johnson, Samuel. *The Rambler*. 3 vols. Ed. W. J. Bate and Albrecht Strauss. New Haven: Yale UP, 1969. 1:19–25.

Jones, M. G. *Hannah More*. Cambridge: Cambridge UP, 1952.

Keating, Peter. *The Haunted Study: A Social History of the English Novel 1875–1914*. London: Secker and Warburg, 1989.

Kelly, Gary. "'This Pestiferous Reading': The Social Basis of Reaction against the Novel in Late Eighteenth- and Early Nineteenth-Century Britain." *Man and Nature: Proceedings of the Canadian Society for Eighteenth-Century Studies* 4 (1985): 183–194.

Kendrick, Walter. *The Secret Museum: Pornography in Modern Culture.* New York: Penguin, 1987.

Kerman, Sandra Lee, ed. *The Newgate Calendar, or Malefactor's Bloody Register.* New York: Capricorn, 1962.

Kingsley, Charles. *Alton Locke, Tailor and Poet.* New York: Macmillan, 1889.

Kintgen, Eugene. *Reading in Tudor England.* Pittsburgh: U of Pittsburgh P, 1996.

Klancher, Jon. *The Making of English Reading Audiences, 1790–1832.* Madison: U of Wisconsin P, 1987.

Knight, Charles. *Passages in a Working Life.* 3 vols. 1864; Shannon: Irish UP, 1971.

Knights, Ben. *The Idea of the Clerisy in the Nineteenth Century.* Cambridge: Cambridge UP, 1978.

Knoepflmacher, U. C. "Thoughts on the Aggression of Daughters." George Levine and U. C. Knoepflmacher, eds. *The Endurance of Frankenstein*: 98–119.

Kucich, John. *The Power of Lies: Transgression in Victorian Fiction.* Ithaca: Cornell UP, 1994.

————. *Repression in Victorian Fiction: Charlotte Brontë, George Eliot, and Charles Dickens.* Berkeley: U of California P, 1987.

Lawler, Donald. "Reframing *Jekyll and Hyde*: Robert Louis Stevenson and the Strange Case of Gothic Science Fiction." William Veeder and Gordon Hirsch, eds. *Dr Jekyll and Mr Hyde after One Hundred Years*: 247–261.

Leavis, Q. D. *Fiction and the Reading Public.* London: Chatto and Windus, 1939.

Lee, Alan J. *The Origins of the Popular Press in England, 1855–1914.* London: Croom Helm, 1976.

LeMahieu, D. L. *A Culture for Democracy: Mass Communication and the Cultivated Mind in Britain Between the Wars.* Oxford: Clarendon, 1988.

Levine, George. *Darwin and the Novelists: Patterns of Science in Victorian Fiction.* Cambridge, MA: Harvard UP, 1988.

Levine, George, and U. C. Knoepflmacher, eds. *The Endurance of Frankenstein: Essays on Mary Shelley's Novel.* Berkeley: U of California P, 1979.

Lewis, Matthew Gregory. *The Monk.* Ed. John Berryman. New York: Grove, 1959.

Ley, J. W. T. *The Dickens Circle: A Narrative of the Novelist's Friendships.* New York: Dutton, 1919.

Litvak, Joseph. *Caught in the Act: Theatricality in the Nineteenth-Century English Novel.* Berkeley: U of California P, 1992.

Lonoff, Sue. *Wilkie Collins and His Victorian Readers: A Study in the Rhetoric of Authorship.* New York: AMS, 1982.

Lovell, Terry. *Consuming Fiction.* London: Verso, 1987.

Maistre, Joseph de. *Considerations on France.* Tr. Richard A. Lebrun. Cambridge, Mass.: Cambridge UP, 1994.

Maixner, Paul, ed. *Robert Louis Stevenson: The Critical Heritage.* London: Routledge and Kegan Paul, 1981.

Malchow, Howard. *Gothic Images of Race in Nineteenth-Century Britain.* Stanford: Stanford UP, 1996.

Mansel, Henry. "Sensation Novels." *Quarterly Review* 113 (1863): 481–514.

Manton, Jo. *Mary Carpenter and the Children of the Streets.* London: Heinemann, 1976.

Marcuse, Herbert. *Eros and Civilization: A Philosophical Inquiry into Freud*. New York: Vintage, 1962.

Marsh, Joss Lutz. *Word Crimes: Blasphemy, Cuture, Literature in Nineteenth-Century England*. Chicago: U of Chicago P, 1998.

Martineau, Harriet. *Autobiography*. 3 vols. London: Smith, Elder, 1877.

———. *Cousin Marshall*. In *Illustrations of Political Economy*, vol. 3.

———. *A History of the Thirty Years' Peace, 1816–1846*. 4 vols. London: George Bell, 1877.

———. *Illustrations of Political Economy*. 9 vols. London: Charles Fox, 1834.

———. *A Manchester Strike*. In *Illustrations of Political Economy*, vol. 3.

———. "Preface." In *Illustrations of Political Economy*. London: Charles Fox, 1834. 1:iii–xviii.

Marx, Karl. *Theories of Surplus Value*. 3 vols. London: Lawrence and Wishart, 1967.

Masson, Rossaline, ed. *I Can Remember Robert Louis Stevenson*. New York: Frederick A. Stokes, 1923.

Mathias, Thomas James. *The Pursuits of Literature: A Satirical Poem in Four Dialogues*. Dublin: J. Milliken, 1799.

Mayhew, Henry. *London Labour and the London Poor*. 1861–1862; New York: Dover, 1968. 4 vols.

Mays, Kelly J. "The Disease of Reading and Victorian Periodicals." In *Literature in the Marketplace: Nineteenth-Century British Publishing and Reading Practices*. John O. Jordan and Robert L. Patten, eds. Cambridge: Cambridge UP, 1995: 165–194.

McAleer, Joseph. *Popular Reading and Publishing in Britain, 1914–1950*. Oxford: Clarendon, 1992.

McKeon, Michael. *The Origins of the English Novel, 1600–1740*. Baltimore: Johns Hopkins UP, 1987.

Melchiori, Barbara. *Terrorism in the Late Victorian Novel*. London: Croom Helm, 1985.

Michaels, Walter Benn. *The Gold Standard and the Logic of Naturalism*. Berkeley: U of California P, 1987.

Miles, Robert. *Gothic Writing 1750–1820*. New York and London: Routledge, 1993.

Miller, Andrew. *Novels behind Glass: Commodity Culture and Victorian Narrative*. Cambridge: Cambridge UP, 1995.

Miller, D. A. *The Novel and the Police*. Berkeley: U of California P, 1987.

Mitch, David F. *The Rise of Popular Literacy in Victorian England: The Influence of Private Choice and Public Policy*. Philadelphia: U of Pennsylvania P, 1992.

Mitchell, Sally. *The Fallen Angel: Chastity, Class and Women's Reading, 1835–1880*. Bowling Green, Ohio: Bowling Green U Popular P, 1981.

Modleski, Tania. *Loving with a Vengeance: Mass-Produced Fantasies for Women*. New York and London: Methuen, 1982.

Moore, George. *Literature at Nurse, or Circulating Morals: A Polemic on Victorian Censorship*. Ed. Pierre Coustillas. Hassocks, Sussex: Harvester, 1976.

More, Hannah. *Works*. New ed., 18 vols. London: T. Cadell and W. Davies, 1818. vol. 4.

Moretti, Franco. *Signs Taken for Wonders*. London: Verso, 1988.

Morris, William. "Art Under Plutocracy." In *Works*. 23:164–191.

———. "How We Live and How We Might Live." In *Works*. 23:3–26.

———. *News from Nowhere and Other Writings*. Ed. Clive Wilmer. London: Penguin, 1993.

———. "The Society of the Future." In *Political Writings*. Ed. A. L. Morton. New York: International, 1973: 188–204.

————. *The Collected Works*. 24 vols. Ed. May Morris. London: Longmans Green, 1912.

Morrison, Arthur. *A Child of the Jago*. Chicago: Herbert Stone, 1896.

Murphy, Paul. *Toward a Working-Class Canon: Literary Criticism in British Working-Class Periodicals, 1816–1858*. Columbus: Ohio State UP, 1994.

National Vigilance Association. "Pernicious Literature." In George Becker, ed., *Documents of Literary Realism*: 350–382.

Neuberg, Victor E. *Popular Literature: A History and Guide*. Harmondsworth: Penguin, 1977.

Nietzsche, Friedrich. "On Truth and Lie in an Extra-Moral Sense." *The Portable Nietzsche*. Ed. Walter Kaufmann. New York: Penguin, 1978: 42–47.

Noble, Andrew, ed. *Robert Louis Stevenson*. London: Vision, 1983.

Nordau, Max. *Degeneration*. New York: Appleton, 1895.

O'Flinn, Paul. "Production and Reproduction: The Case of *Frankenstein*." *Literature and History* 9 (1983): 194–213.

Ohmann, Richard. *English in America: A Radical View of the Profession*. New York: Oxford UP, 1976.

Oliphant, Margaret. "Modern Novelists—Great and Small." Excerpt in Miriam Allott, ed., *Charlotte Brontë: The Critical Heritage*. London: Routledge and Kegan Paul, 1974: 311–314.

————. "Sensation Novels." *Blackwood's* 91 (May 1862): 564–584.

Olmsted, John, ed. *A Victorian Art of Fiction: Essays on the Novel in British Periodicals, 1870–1900*. New York and London: Garland, 1979.

Osbourne, Lloyd. *An Intimate Portrait of R.L.S.* New York: Scribner's, 1924.

"Our Novels: The Sensational School." *Temple Bar* (July 1870): 410–424.

Page, Norman, ed. *Wilkie Collins: The Critical Heritage*. London: Routledge, 1974.

Paine, Thomas. *Rights of Man*. Ed. Philip S. Foner. Secaucus, N.J.: Citadel, 1974.

Parreaux, André. *The Publication of the Monk: A Literary Event 1796–1798*. Paris: Didier, 1960.

Parrinder, Patrick, ed. *H. G. Wells: The Critical Heritage*. London: Routledge and Kegan Paul, 1972.

Patten, Robert. *Dickens and His Publishers*. Oxford: Clarendon, 1978.

Paulson, Ronald. *Representations of Revolution (1789–1820)*. New Haven and London: Yale UP, 1983.

Peacock, Thomas Love. *Nightmare Abbey and Crotchet Castle*. New York: Capricorn, 1964.

Peck, Louis F. *A Life of Matthew Gregory Lewis*. Cambridge, Mass.: Harvard UP, 1961.

Peterson, Carla L. *The Determined Reader: Gender and Culture in the Novel from Napoleon to Victoria*. New Brunswick, N.J.: Rutgers UP, 1986.

Pick, Daniel. *Faces of Degeneration: A European Disorder, c. 1848–c. 1918*. Cambridge, Mass.: Cambridge UP, 1989.

Poole, Adrian. *Gissing in Context*. Totowa, N.J.: Rowman and Littlefield, 1975.

Poovey, Mary. *The Proper Lady and the Woman Writer*. Chicago: U of Chicago P, 1984.

Porter, G. R. *Progress of the Nation*. 4 vols. London: Charles Knight, 1843.

Pritchett, V. S. "Foreword." George Gissing. *The Private Papers of Henry Ryecroft*: vii–xvi.

"Prospectus of a New Journal." *Punch* 44 (9 May 1863): 193.

Punter, David. *The Literature of Terror: A History of Gothic Fictions from 1765 to the Present Day*. London and New York: Longman, 1980.

Radway, Janice. "Reading Is Not Eating: Mass-Produced Literature and the Theoretical,

Methodological, and Political Consequences of a Metaphor." *Book Research Quarterly* 2:2 (Fall 1986): 7–29.

———. *Reading the Romance: Women, Patriarchy, and Popular Literature*. Chapel Hill: U of North Carolina P, 1984.

Rae, W. Fraser. "Sensation Novelists: Miss Braddon." *North British Review* 43 (September 1865): 180–205.

Raven, James, Helen Small, and Naomi Tadmor, eds. *The Practice and Representation of Reading in England*. Cambridge, Mass.: Cambridge UP, 1996.

Rawlins, Jack P. *Thackeray's Novels: A Fiction that Is True*. Berkeley: U of California P, 1974.

Read, Donald. *England 1868–1914: The Age of Urban Democracy*. London: Longman, 1979.

Reade, Charles. "Facts Must Be Faced." *Readiana. Works*. 9 vols. New York: Collier, n.d. 9:377–379.

Reed, Walter L. *An Exemplary History of the Novel: The Quixotic versus the Picturesque*. Chicago: U of Chicago P, 1981.

Repplier, Agnes. "English Railway Fiction." In *Points of View*. Boston: Houghton-Mifflin, 1893: 209–239.

"Review of *Jane Eyre*," *The Christian Remembrancer*. In Miriam Allott, ed., *Charlotte Brontë: The Critical Heritage*: 88–92.

"Review of New Publications." *Gentleman's Magazine* 75:2 (December 1805): 1129–1147.

Richardson, Alan. *Literature, Education, and Romanticism: Reading as Social Practice, 1780–1832*. Cambridge, Mass.: Cambridge UP, 1994.

Richetti, John, et al., eds. *The Columbia History of the British Novel*. New York: Columbia UP, 1994.

Richter, David. "The Reception of the Gothic Novel in the 1790s." In Robert W. Uphaus, ed., *The Idea of the Novel in the Eighteenth-Century*. East Lansing, Mich.: Colleagues, 1988: 117–137.

Romano, John. *Dickens and Reality*. New York: Columbia UP, 1978.

Rose, Jonathan. "Reading the English Common Reader: A Preface to a History of Audiences." *Journal of the History of Ideas* (1992): 47–70.

Rudé, George. *The Crowd in the French Revolution*. Oxford: Oxford UP, 1959.

Ruskin, John. *Fiction, Fair and Foul*. In *The Works of Ruskin*. Ed. E. T. Cook and Alexander Wedderburn. 39 vols. London: George Allen; New York: Longmans, Green, 1908. 34:264–397.

Sabor, Peter, ed. *Horace Walpole: The Critical Heritage*. London and New York: Routledge and Kegan Paul, 1987.

Sade, Marquis de. "Reflections on the Novel." In *The 120 Days of Sodom and Other Writings*. Tr. Austryn Wainhouse and Richard Seaver. New York: Grove, 1966. 97–116.

Sadleir, Michael. *Trollope: A Commentary*. Oxford: Oxford UP, 1961.

Sala, George Augustus. "On the 'Sensational' in Literature and Art." *Belgravia* 4 (February 1868): 449–458.

Sanchez, Nellie Van de Grift. *The Life of Mrs. Robert Louis Stevenson*. New York: Scribner's, 1920.

Schmitt, Cannon. *Alien Nation: Nineteenth-Century Gothic Fictions and English Nationality*. Philadelphia: U of Pennsylvania P, 1997.

Sedgwick, Eve Kosofsky. *Between Men: English Literature and Male Homosocial Desire*. New York: Columbia UP, 1985.

———. *Epistemology of the Closet*. Berkeley: U of California P, 1990.

Seiler, R. M., ed., *Walter Pater: The Critical Heritage*. London: Routledge and Kegan Paul, 1980.

Shelley, Mary. *Frankenstein*. New York: Norton, 1996.

Shepperson, Archibald. *The Novel in Motley: A History of the Burlesque Novel in English*. Cambridge, Mass.: Harvard UP, 1936.

Sheridan, Richard Brinsley. "The Rivals." In *The School for Scandal and Other Plays*. Ed. Eric Rump. London and New York: Penguin, 1988: 41–124.

Shillingsburg, Peter. *Pegasus in Harness: Victorian Publishing and W. M. Thackeray*. Charlottesville: U of Virginia P, 1992.

Showalter, Elaine. *A Literature of Their Own: British Women Novelists from Brontë to Lessing*. Princeton: Princeton UP, 1977.

Small, Helen. "A Pulse of 124: Charles Dickens and a Pathology of the Mid-Victorian Reading Public." In Raven, 263–290.

Smith, Harold. *The Society for the Diffusion of Useful Knowledge, 1826–1846: A Social and Bibliographical Evaluation*. Halifax: Dalhousie U Occasional Papers, no. 8, 1972.

Smith, Paul. *Impressionism: Beneath the Surface*. New York: Abrams, 1995.

Smollett, Tobias. *Roderick Random*. Ed. Paul-Gabriel Boucé. Oxford: Oxford UP, 1979.

Sorensen, Janet. "Writing Historically, Speaking Nostalgically: The Competing Language of Nation in Scott's *Bride of Lammermoor*." In *Narratives of Nostalgia, Gender, and Nationalism*. Ed. Jean Pickering and Suzanne Kehde. New York and London: Macmillan, 1997: 30–51.

Spender, Dale. *Mothers of the Novel*. London: Pandora, 1986.

Spinney, G. H. "Cheap Repository Tracts: Hazard and Marshall Edition." *Library* series 4, no. 20 (1939): 295–340.

Springhall, John. "'A Life Story for the People'? Edwin J. Brett and the London 'Low-Life' Penny Dreadfuls of the 1860s." *Victorian Studies* 33 (1990): 223–246.

Steiner, George. *In Bluebeard's Castle: Some Notes toward the Definition of Culture*. New Haven: Yale UP, 1971.

Sterrenburg, Lee. "Mary Shelley's Monster: Politics and Psyche in *Frankenstein*." In George Levine and U. C. Knoepflmacher, eds., *The Endurance of Frankenstein*: 143–171.

Stevenson, Robert Louis. *The Letters of Robert Louis Stevenson*. Ed. Sidney Colvin. New York: Scribner's, 1911. 4 vols.

———. *The Strange Case of Dr Jekyll and Mr Hyde and Other Stories*. Harmondsworth: Penguin, 1979.

Stewart, Garrett. *Dear Reader: The Conscripted Audience in Nineteenth-Century British Fiction*. Baltimore and London: Johns Hopkins UP, 1996.

Sutherland, John. *Victorian Novelists and Publishers*. London: Athlone, 1976.

Swearingen, Roger. *The Prose Writings of Robert Louis Stevenson*. Hamden, Conn.: Archon, 1980.

Swift, Jonathan. "The Battle of the Books." In *Gulliver's Travels and Other Writings*. Ed. Louis A. Landa. Cambridge, Mass.: Riverside Editions, 1960. 357–380.

Taylor, Jenny Bourne. *In the Secret Theatre of Home: Wilkie Collins, Sensation Narrative, and Nineteenth-Century Psychology*. London: Routledge, 1988.

Taylor, John Tinnon. *Early Opposition to the English Novel: The Popular Reaction from 1760 to 1830*. New York: King's Crown, 1943.

Thackeray, William Makepeace. *Barry Lyndon*. Oxford: World's Classics, 1984.

———. *Catherine, A Shabby Genteel Story . . . and Miscellanies, 1840–1*. Oxford: The Oxford Thackeray, 1912, vol. 3.

———. "The Fashionable Authoress." In *The Yellowplush Papers and Early Miscellanies*: 561–576.

———. "Half a Crown's Worth of Knowledge." In *The Yellowplush Papers and Early Miscellanies*: 131–151.

———. "On a Lazy Idle Boy." In *Roundabout Papers*: 1–9.

———. "On a Peal of Bells." In *Roundabout Papers*: 322–334.

———. *Pendennis*. Harmondsworth: Penguin, 1972.

———. "The Professor." In *The Yellowplush Papers and Early Miscellanies*: 111–129.

———. *The Roundabout Papers*. In *Works*, vol. 22. New York: Scribner's, 1923.

———. *Vanity Fair*. New York: Norton, 1994.

———. *The Yellowplush Papers and Early Miscellanies*. Oxford: The Oxford Thackeray, 1912, vol. 1.

Thomas, Donald. *A Long Time Burning: The History of Literary Censorship in England*. New York: Praeger, 1969.

Thomas, Ronald R. "The Strange Voices in the Strange Case: Dr. Jekyll, Mr. Hyde, and the Voices of Modern Fiction." In William Veeder and Gordon Hirsch, eds., *Dr Jekyll and Mr Hyde after One Hundred Years*: 73–93.

Thompson, E. P. *The Making of the English Working Class*. New York: Vintage, 1963.

———. *William Morris, Romantic to Revolutionary*. New York: Pantheon, 1977.

Tillotson, Kathleen. "The Lighter Reading of the Eighteen-Sixties." Introduction to Wilkie Collins, *The Woman in White*. Boston: Houghton, 1969: ix–xxvi.

———. *Novels of the Eighteen-Forties*. Oxford: Oxford UP, 1954.

Tobias, J. J. *Prince of Fences: The Life and Times of Ikey Solomons*. London: Vallentine, Mitchell, 1974.

Todorov, Tzvetan. *The Poetics of Prose*. Ithaca: Cornell UP, 1977.

Tompkins, J. M. S. *The Popular Novel in England, 1700–1800*. 1932; London: Methuen, 1969.

Trevelyan, G. M. "The White Peril." *Nineteenth Century* 50 (December 1901): 1043–1055.

Trilling, Lionel. "Aggression and Utopia, A Note on William Morris's 'News from Nowhere.'" *Psychoanalytic Quarterly* 42 (1973): 214–225.

Trodd, Anthea. *Domestic Crime in the Victorian Novel*. New York: St. Martin's, 1989.

Trollope, Anthony. *Autobiography*. Oxford: World's Classics, 1953.

———. *The Eustace Diamonds*. Harmondsworth: Penguin, 1973.

———. "Novel Reading." In John Olmsted, ed., *A Victorian Art of Fiction: Essays on the Novel in British Periodicals, 1870–1900*: 111–130.

———. *Thackeray*. London: Macmillan, 1879.

Varma, Devendra P. *The Evergreen Tree of Diabolocal Knowledge*. Washington, D.C.: Consortium P, 1972.

Veeder, William. "Introduction." In *Dr Jekyll and Mr Hyde after One Hundred Years*. Ed. Veeder and Hirsch. ix–xviii.

Veeder, William, and Gordon Hirsch, eds. *Dr Jekyll and Mr Hyde after One Hundred Years*. Chicago: U of Chicago P, 1988.

Vernon, John. *Money and Fiction: Literary Realism in the Nineteenth and Early Twentieth Centuries*. Ithaca: Cornell UP, 1984.

Vincent, David. *Literacy and Popular Culture: England 1750–1914*. Cambridge: Cambridge UP, 1989.

Wall, Charles. "The Schoolmaster's Experience in Newgate." *Fraser's Magazine* 34:6 (Nov. 1832): 460–498.

Walpole, Horace. *The Castle of Otranto: A Gothic Story*. London: Oxford UP, 1964.

Warhol, Robyn R. *Gendered Interventions: Narrative Discourse in the Victorian Novel*. New Brunswick, N.J.: Rutgers UP, 1989.

Warner, William. "Licensing Pleasure: Literary History and the Novel in Early Modern Britain." In John Richetti, et al., eds., *The Columbia History of the British Novel*: 1–22.

Watt, Ian. *The Rise of the Novel*. Berkeley: U of California P, 1959.

Webb, R. K. *The British Working-Class Reader: Literacy and Social Tension*. London: George Allen and Unwin, 1955.

———. *Harriet Martineau, A Radical Victorian*. New York: Columbia UP, 1960.

Welsh, Alexander. *George Eliot and Blackmail*. Cambridge, Mass.: Harvard UP, 1985.

———. *Reflections on the Hero as Quixote*. Princeton: Princeton UP, 1981.

West, E. G. *Education and the Industrial Revolution*. New York: Harper and Row, 1975.

West, Jane. *The Infidel Father: A Novel*. London: 1802.

Wickwar, William. *The Struggle for Freedom of the Press. 1819–1832*. London: Allen and Unwin, 1928.

Wiener, Joel H. *The War of the Unstamped: The Movement to Repeal the British Newspaper Tax, 1830–1836*. Ithaca: Cornell UP, 1969.

Wiener, Martin. *Reconstructing the Criminal: Culture, Law, and Policy in England, 1830–1914*. Cambridge: Cambridge UP, 1990.

Wilde, Oscar. "The Decay of Lying." In *The Soul of Man under Socialism and Other Essays*: 33–72.

———. "Pen, Pencil, and Poison." In *The Soul of Man under Socialism and Other Essays*: 75–99.

———. *The Picture of Dorian Gray*. New York: Norton, 1988.

———. "The Soul of Man under Socialism." In *The Soul of Man under Socialism and Other Essays*: 227–271.

———. *The Soul of Man under Socialism and Other Essays*. Ed. Philip Rieff. New York: Harper, 1970.

Williams, Anne. *Art of Darkness: A Poetics of Gothic*. Chicago: U of Chicago P, 1995.

Williams, Ioan. *The Idea of the Novel in Europe, 1600–1800*. London: Macmillan, 1979.

Williams, Raymond. *Culture and Society: 1780–1950*. New York: Columbia UP, 1983.

———. *Keywords*. New York: Oxford UP, 1983.

Williams, Rosalind. *Dream Worlds: Mass Consumption in Late Nineteenth-Century France*. Berkeley: U of California P, 1982.

Wills, W. H. "Review of a Popular Publication." *Household Words* 1 (1850): 426–431.

———. "The Modern Science of Thief-Taking." *Household Words* 1 (1850): 368–372.

Wilson, Charles. *First with the News: The History of W. H. Smith, 1792–1972*. Garden City, N.Y.: Doubleday, 1986.

Wilt, Judith. *The Ghosts of the Gothic: Austen, Eliot, and Lawrence*. Princeton: Princeton UP, 1980.

[J. R. Wise]. "Belles Lettres." *Westminster Review* 86 (July 1866): 268–280.

Wolff, Robert Lee. *Sensational Victorian: The Life and Fiction of Mary Elizabeth Braddon.* New York: Garland, 1979.

Wollstonecraft, Mary. *An Historical and Moral View of the French Revolution.* In *Works,* vol. 6. London: William Pickering, 1989.

Woolf, Virginia. *The Virginia Woolf Reader.* Ed. Mitchell A. Leaska. New York: Harcourt, 1984.

Wordsworth, William. *Wordsworth's Literary Criticism.* Ed. W. J. B. Owen. London and Boston: Routledge and Kegan Paul, 1974.

Worsley, Henry. *Juvenile Depravity.* London: Gilpin, 1849.

Žižek, Slavoj. *Enjoy Your Symptom! Jacques Lacan in Hollywood and Out.* New York and London: Routledge, 1992.

———. *The Sublime Object of Ideology.* London: Verso, 1989.

Zola, Émile. "Naturalism in the Theatre." In George Becker, ed., *Documents of Literary Realism*: 197–229.

INDEX

Acker, Kathy, 2
Ackland, Joseph, 174–75, 182
Addison, Joseph, 30
Ainsworth, William Harrison, 9, 71–72
Alison, Archibald, 78, 79
Alton Locke (Kingsley), 93–94, 103, 104–107, 111, 114
America, 18. *See also* American Revolution
American Revolution, 5, 26
Animal Farm (Orwell), 54
Ann Veronica (Wells), 209
anti-novels, 2, 196–203
antisemitism. *See* race, racism
A Rebours (Huysmans), 10
Argosy, 149
Aristotle, 37
Armadale (Collins), 145, 152, 154–56, 160
Arnold, Matthew, 11, 19, 22, 23, 24, 89, 96, 107, 108, 109, 116, 118, 120, 170, 174, 180, 181, 185, 190, 193–94, 205, 209, 211
arts-and-crafts movement, 198–99, 203
Auden, W. H., 157
Aurora Floyd (Braddon), 152, 163
Austen, Jane, 2, 3–4, 9, 12, 21, 22, 28, 29, 32–34, 49–50, 154
Austin, Alfred, 22–23
Australia, 149

Bakhtin, Mikhail, 2, 81, 82, 87
Balzac, Honoré de, 76, 86, 87, 122, 154
Barchester Towers (Trollope), 139
Barruel, Abbé, 52
Barry Lyndon (Thackeray), 124, 125
Barthes, Roland, 7
Baudelaire, Charles, 10, 11, 140–41
Beckett, Samuel, 2
Beckford, William, 40–41
Beggar's Opera, 87
Beggs, Thomas, 73
Behn, Aphra, 29
Belgravia, 149, 164
Belinda (Edgeworth), 33, 34
Bell, Dr. Andrew, 58
Bellamy, Edward, 196–97, 199, 203
Benjamin, Walter, 200
Bennett, Arnold, 207–209
Bennett, John, 28
Bentley's Miscellany, 71, 74
Bentham, Jeremy, 67. *See also* utilitarianism
Besant, Walter, 206, 209

Bewick's *History of British Birds,* 116
Binny, John, 79, 83, 89
Bible, 42–46, 80–81, 90, 103, 107, 108, 118
The Black Arrow (Stevenson), 172
Blackwood's Magazine, 78, 115
Blake, William, 14, 43, 76, 91
Blanc, Louis, 107
blasphemy, 27, 29, 38–39, 42–46, 118, 177–80
Bleak House (Dickens), 79, 148, 154, 156, 157
Boer War, 23
Borrow, George, 71
Boucicault, Dion, 145, 160
Bovaryism, 9
Bow Street Runners, 73
Boxer Rebellion, 23
Braddon, Mary Elizabeth, 9, 18, 136, 143, 144, 146, 149–54, 155, 157, 158–59, 163, 164–65, 184
Brady, Matthew, 133
The British Critic, 46
British Museum, 186, 194, 195–96, 202, 204
Brontë, Charlotte, 29, 63, 112–17, 158
Brontë, Emily, 115, 118–20, 158, 195
Brougham, Henry, 97
Broughton, Rhoda, 151
Bulwer-Lytton, Edward, 18, 19, 22, 23, 24, 72, 90, 124, 125, 163
Bunyan, John, 128
Burke, Edward, 5, 16, 22, 50–57, 59, 63, 65, 68, 106, 211
Burney, Fanny, 3, 21–22, 33
Byron, Lord George, 59, 67, 76, 95, 108, 138
Byronism, 124–27

Caleb Williams (Godwin), 7–9, 11, 40, 46–48, 50, 83
Camilla (Burney), 33
Capital (Marx), 122
Carlile, Richard, 79
Carlyle, Thomas, 65–68, 93, 106, 172, 194, 211
Carpenter, Mary, 77, 79, 80, 89
The Castle of Otranto (Walpole), 31, 35–39, 42, 45, 46, 50, 52, 59, 142
Castle Spectre (Lewis), 41
Catherine (Thackeray), 2, 72, 124
Catholicism, Roman, 27, 30, 35, 38, 44
Catnach, James, 148
Cecilia (Burney), 33
Celebrated Trials, 71
censorship, 46, 72, 79–80, 82, 107, 183, 209, 211.

PATRICK BRANTLINGER
is Professor of English and Victorian Studies
at Indiana University. He served for ten years as editor
of *Victorian Studies* and is author of *The Spirit of Reform:
British Literature and Politics, 1832–1867* (1977), *Bread
and Circuses: Theories of Mass Culture as Social Decay*
(1983), *Rule of Darkness: British Literature and
Imperialism* (1988), and *Fictions of State:
Culture and Credit in Britain,
1694–1994* (1997).